FROM SYNTAX TO DISCOURSE

STUDIES IN THEORETICAL PSYCHOLINGUISTICS

VOLUME 29

Managing Editors

Lyn Frazier, *Dept. of Linguistics, University of Massachusetts at Amherst*
Thomas Roeper, *Dept. of Linguistics, University of Massachusetts at Amherst*
Kenneth Wexler, *Dept. of Brain and Cognitive Science, MIT, Cambridge, Mass.*

Editorial Board

Robert Berwick, *Artificial Intelligence Laboratory, MIT, Cambridge, Mass.*
Manfred Bierwisch, *Zentralinstitut für Sprachwissenschaft, Akademie der Wissenschaften, Berlin*
Merrill Garrett, *University of Arizona, Tucson*
Lila Gleitman, *School of Education, University of Pennsylvania*
Mary-Louise Kean, *University of California, Irvine*
Howard Lasnik, *University of Connecticut at Storrs*
John Marshall, *Neuropsychology Unit, Radcliffe Infirmary, Oxford*
Daniel Osherson, *MIT, Cambridge, Mass.*
Yukio Otsu, *Keio University, Tokyo*
Edwin Williams, *Princeton University*

The titles published in this series are listed at the end of this volume.

FROM SYNTAX TO DISCOURSE

Pronominal Clitics,
Null Subjects and Infinitives in Child Language

by

CORNELIA HAMANN
University of Geneva and University of Tübingen

KLUWER ACADEMIC PUBLISHERS
DORDRECHT / BOSTON / LONDON

A C.I.P. Catalogue record for this book is available from the Library of Congress.

ISBN 1-4020-0439-7 (HB)

Published by Kluwer Academic Publishers,
P.O. Box 17, 3300 AA Dordrecht, The Netherlands.

Sold and distributed in North, Central and South America
by Kluwer Academic Publishers,
101 Philip Drive, Norwell, MA 02061, U.S.A.

In all other countries, sold and distributed
by Kluwer Academic Publishers,
P.O. Box 322, 3300 AH Dordrecht, The Netherlands.

Printed on acid-free paper

All Rights Reserved
© 2002 Kluwer Academic Publishers
No part of the material protected by this copyright notice may be reproduced or
utilized in any form or by any means, electronic or mechanical,
including photocopying, recording or by any information storage and
retrieval system, without written permission from the copyright owner.

Printed in the Netherlands.

To the ones who, in the past and the present,
have supported me with their love

Ssane kann ma nich kaufen   Andrea   2;7
Sterne kann man nicht kaufen
'you cannot buy the stars'

TABLE OF CONTENTS

CHAPTER 1
INTRODCUTION TO LANGUAGE ACQUISITION 1

1. The Innateness Hypothesis 1
2. Arguments and Counterarguments from
   Different Points of View 2
3. Generative Approaches to Language Acquisition 5
4. The Principles and Parameters Model 6
5. P&P and the Learnability Question 7
6. Early parameter Settting and 'Late' Phenomena 9
   6.1. The Head-Complement Parameter 9
   6.2. Verb Raising to Inflection 11
   6.3. Verb Raising in Verb-Second Languages 12
7. Aim and Outline of the Present Study 14
8. A Note to the Reader 18

CHAPTER 2
THE ACQUISITION OF THE PRONOMINAL SYSTEM IN FRENCH
- THE PRODUCTION OF SUBJECT AND OBJECT CLITICS 21

1. Introduction 21
2. Subject and Object Clitics 23
   2.1. Background 23
   2.2. The Method 28
   2.3. Verbal Utterances 29
   2.4. Results on Subject and Object Clitics 31
   2.5. The Delay of Object Clitics as a Phenomenon 38
   2.6. Discussion of the Subject/Object Asymmetry 41
3. Distributional Constraints 44
4. The Distribution of Clitics in Tensed and Untensed Clauses 47
   4.1. The data 47

4.2. Implications for the Analysis of Root Infinitives	52
4.3. Implications for the Position of Object Clitics in French	59
5. Summary	61

CHAPTER 3
THE BINDING PRINCIPLES AND ACQUISITION RESEARCH   65

1. Overview of Binding and its Acquisition	65
1.1. Theoretical Background	65
1.2. The Standard Binding Principles	66
1.3. The 'Delay of Principle B' from a Crosslinguistic Perspective	67
2. Modifications of the Binding Theory in Relation to the Acquisition Results	72
2.1. The Standard Principles and the Coreference Rule	72
2.2. Accidental Coreference and Acquisition	78
3. New Views on Binding	81
3.1. Binding Theory and Reflexivity	81
3.2. Reflexivity and Acquisition	85
3.3. Free Variables, Reference Assignment and the Exceptional Coindexing Rule	87

CHAPTER 4
ROMANCE CLITICS AND BINDING   91

1. A Syntactic Analysis of Clitic Pronouns	91
1.1. Review of the Properties of French Clitics	91
1.2. The Syntax of Object Clitics in French	94
2. Clitics and the Chain Condition	96
3. Clitics and Accidental Coreference	98
3.1. Structural Deficiency	98
3.2. Clitics, Indices and Accidental Coreference	101
4. Previous Experiments on the Acquisition of Binding in Romance	108
4.1. Predictions	108
4.2. Experiments on French and Italian	109

CHAPTER 5
TWO EXPERIMENTS ON BINDING EFFECTS WITH
FRENCH CLITIC PRONOUNS   113
1. The First Experiment   113
    1.1. Procedure and Design   113
    1.2. Participants   115
    1.3. Test Conditions   116
    1.4. Control Conditions   119
    1.5. Results   122
    1.6. Discussion   125
2. The Lexical Approach   126
    2.1. The Reflexivity Feature   126
    2.2. Results on Spanish   127
    2.3. Results on Norwegian   128
    2.4. Conclusion   130
3. The Child May Create Two Guises   130
    3.1. Extended Guise Creation   130
    3.2. The 'Mirror Experiment'   133
    3.3. Conclusion   142
4. A Structural Ambiguity and Guise Creation   142
    4.1. Structural Ambiguity and the Reconstruction of the Clitic   142
    4.2. The Lower Subject Guise   143
5. Conclusion and Outlook   145

CHAPTER 6
CHILDREN'S NULL SUBJECTS AND INFINITIVES   149

1. Child Null Subjects   149
2. The Phenomenon of Subject Omission in Child Language   151
3. Theories on Empty Subjects in Adult and Child Language   160
    3.1. Pro-drop, Licensing and Identification   160
    3.2. Morphological Uniformity   164
    3.3. Discourse Oriented Approaches   166
4. The Phenomenon of Optional Infinitives   168
5. Empirical Facts about Null Subjects and Infinitives   174

CHAPTER 7
THEORETICAL APPROACHES TO INFINITIVES AND NULL SUBJECTS   177

1. Introducing the Approaches   177
2. Truncation, Root Infinitives, and Child Null Subjects   178
   2.1. Truncation and Root Infinitives   178
   2.2. Truncation, Topic-drop, Split CP and (Diary) Null Subjects   181
   2.3. Two Problems for Truncation   194
3. Optional Tense and Related Approaches   196
   3.1. Optional Tense   196
   3.2. Optional Tense and Types of Subjects   198
   3.3. Optional Tense and Optional Agreement   202
   3.4. Underspecification of Tense   206
4. Economy of Projection and Non-Merger   209

CHAPTER 8
EMPIRICAL DATA AND THE EVALUATION OF THE APPROACHES   213

1. Areas of Investigation   213
2. Danish and French Grammar   215
   2.1. Inflection   215
   2.2. Verb Placement   216
3. The Finite/Non-finite Asymmetry in Danish and Other Languages   220
4. The Developmental Similarity of Infinitive Use and
   Finite Subject Omission   225
5. The Auxiliary/Main Verb Asymmetry in Danish and
   Other Languages   232
6. Pro-drop and Optional Infinitives   242
7. Finite Null Subjects and Morphological Reanalysis
   in the UCC Account   247

CHAPTER 9
WH-QUESTIONS: INFINITIVES, NULL SUBJECTS AND THE
PROBLEM OF INTERPRETATION   251

1. Overview   251
   1.1. Predictions   251
   1.2. Wh-questions in Early English   253
   1.3. Wh-questions in Early German   254

1.4. Wh-questions in Early Danish	254
1.5. Wh-questions in Early French	259
2. French Consitutent Questions: Fronted Wh and Wh-in-situ	262
2.1. Theoretical Background	262
2.2. The Data from Child French	263
2.3. The Licensing of Null Subjects in Wh-in-situ	273
2.4. The Problem (Again)	275
3. Towards a Solution	277
3.1. The By-passing Mechanism	277
3.2. The Ingredients	277
3.3. Child and Diary Null Subjects	278
3.4. Null Subjects and Wh	279
4. Summary	281

CHAPTER 10
OTHER AREAS OF INVESTIGATION: NEGATION AND
LATE ARGUMENT DROP   285

1. Introduction	285
2. Negation and Infinitives	286
2.1. The NegP and the Neg-Criterion	286
2.2. Truncated Structures	287
2.3. Negation and Non-finite Utterances in French	288
2.4. Negation and Non-finite Utterances in V2-Languages	292
3. Late Argument Drop	296
3.1. More Than One Type of Null Subject	296
3.2. More German Grammar	298
3.3. Ambiguous Input and Null Subjects in German Child Language	300
3.4. Method	301
3.5. Results	302
4. Summary	310

CHAPTER 11
DISCOURSE ANCHORAGE AND THE CP   311

1. Discourse Anchorage and Child Grammar	311
2. Anchoring from a Semantic Point of View	317
2.1. Similarities of Pronouns and Tense	317

2.2. Elaborating the Syntax and Semantics of Tense ... 320
2.3. Implications for Child Language ... 327
3. Conclusions and Outlook ... 330

CHAPTER 12
CHILD LANGUAGE: FROM SYNTAX TO DISCOURSE ... 331

1. Looking Back ... 331
2. Remaining Problems ... 334
3. Conclusion ... 335

NOTES ... 337

REFERENCES ... 345

INDEX ... 361

LIST OF FIGURES

Figure 1:	Number of Subject and Object Clitics as a Function of Age	37
Figure 2:	Placeholders, Subject Clitics and Null Subjects as a Function of Age	54
Figure 3:	Placeholders, Overt and Non-overt Determiners	56
Figure 4a,b:	Anne's and Jens' MLU	154
Figure 5a,b:	Anne's and Jens' Verbal Development	155
Figure 6a,b:	Anne's and Jens' Null Subjects	156, 157
Figure 7a,b:	Augustin's and Philippe's Null Subjects	158, 159
Figure 8a,b:	Anne's and Jens' Percent Infinitives	171, 172
Figure 9a,b:	Anne's and Jens' Finite and Non-finite Verbtokens	173, 174
Figure 10a,b:	Anne's and Jens' Null Subjects on Infinitives	221
Figure 11a,b:	Anne's and Jens' Null Subjects and Infinitives	222, 223
Figure 12a,b:	Finite Null Subjects in Danish	225, 226
Figure 12c,d:	Finite Null Subjects in French	226, 227
Figure 13a,b:	Anne's and Jens' Finite and Non-finite Null Subjects	228
Figure 14a,b:	Anne's and Jens' Infinitives and Finite Null Subjects	230
Figure 15a,b:	Augustin's and Philippe's Infinitives and Finite Null Subjects	231, 232
Figure 16a,b:	Anne's and Jens' Copula and Main Verb Null Subjects	235

LIST OF FIGURES

Figure 17a,b:	Christoph's and Elisa's Null Arguments	303
		304
Figure 18:	Elisa's Null Topics	305
Figure 19a:	Anne's Subjects and Null Subjects with Previous Mention	312
Figure 19b:	Jens' Subjects and Null Subjects with Previous Mention	313
Figure 20a,b:	Anne's and Jens' Previous Mention of 3rd Person Pronouns	314
Figure 21:	Anne's Use of the Past Tense	329

LIST OF TABLES

Table 1:	Distribution of finite and non-finite verbs with respect to negation/French, Pierce	12
Table 2:	Distribution of finite and non-finite verbs with respect to V2/German, Poeppel and Wexler	13
Table 3:	Distribution of finite and non-finite verbs with respect to V2/German (Clahsen et al.)	14
Table 4:	Number of utterances and verbal utterances of all kinds in the Augustin-corpus	30
Table 5:	Occurrences of subject and object clitics in verbal utterances in the Augustin-corpus	32
Table 6:	Breakdown of different subject clitics in the Augustin-corpus	34
Table 7:	Breakdown of different object clitics in the Augustin-corpus	35
Table 8:	The use of object clitics in comparison with lexical objects and object omission	36
Table 9:	Adult and child clitics in the Augustin-corpus	38
Table 10:	Percentages of subject and object clitics in the corpora of Philippe and Gregoire (Friedeman)	39
Table 11:	Cross-sectional spontaneous production, French clitics (Jakubowicz et al. 1996)	40
Table 12:	Cross-sectional spontaneous production, German pronouns (Jakubowicz et al. 1996)	40
Table 13:	Occurrence of *ça* in different verbal environments in the Augustin-corpus	46
Table 14:	Occurrence of object citics, subject clitics and other subjects in finite structures and root infinitives in the Augustin-corpus	50
Table 15:	Percentage of finite structures and root infinitives in clitic constructions	51
Table 16:	Use of subject pronouns (after Pierce 1989, 1992)	52

LIST OF TABLES

Table 17: Use of subject clitics (Hamann et al. 1996, Rasetti 1995)	52
Table 18: Distribution of clitics and weak pronouns in French and Dutch (Haegeman 1996)	59
Table 19: Cross-linguistic results on pronoun interpretation in Principle B environments	70
Table 20: The participants' ages	116
Table 21: Percent "Yes" responses on control conditions eliciting adult "Yes" responses	123
Table 22: Percent "No" responses on control conditions eliciting adult "No" responses	123
Table 23: Percent "No" responses on test conditions eliciting adult "No" responses	124
Table 24: T-test	124
Table 25: Percent "Yes" responses on test conditions eliciting adult "Yes" responses	125
Table 26: participants' ages, Mirror experiment	134
Table 27: Control conditions: percentage of correct responses of the different age groups, Mirror Experiment	140
Table 28: Test conditions: percentage of correct responses of the different age groups, Mirror Experiment	140
Table 29: Distribution of finite and non-finite verbs with respect to negation (French, Pierce 1989,1992)	197
Table 30: Distribution of finite and non-finite verbs with respect to V2 (German, Poeppel and Wexler 1993)	197
Table 31: Distribution of finite and non-finite verbs with respect to V2 (German, Clahsen et al. 1996)	197
Table 32: Case distribution with respect to finiteness in English (Schuetze and Wexler 1995)	201
Table 33: Distribution of null subjects in adults interacting with the child	219
Table 34: Cross-linguistic distribution of null subjects in finite and infinitive/ non-finite structures	224
Table 35: Null subject use on copulas and finite main verbs (Danish, Anne and Jens)	234
Table 36: Cross-linguistic distribution of null subjects with respect to verb form	236
Table 37: Cross-linguistic occurrence of optional root infinitives	242
Table 38: Jens and Anne: null subjects on finite verbs, on past tense forms, and copulas	249

Table 39 : Null subject use overall in finite verbal utterances for Anne and Jens (modified periods and counting method)	255
Table 40: Overview of null subject occurrences in finite fronted Wh-questions for Jens and Anne	258
Table 41: Development of Root Infinitives (RI), Null Subjects (NS), Fronted Wh (Fr-Wh) and Wh-in-situ (Wh-i-s) questions for Philippe, Augustin and Marie	264
Table 42: Finite and non-finite Wh-questions	265
Table 43: Distribution of root infinitives in Philippe's auxiliaries (Phillips 1995)	266
Table 44: Distribution of root infinitives in Philippe's main verbs (Phillips 1995)	266
Table 45: The development of question formation concerning null subjects and root infinitives for Philippe (Crisma 1992)	268
Table 46: Occurrence of Wh, root infinitives and null subjects in the Augustin-corpus	269
Table 47: Occurrence of Wh, root infinitives and null subjects in the Marie-corpus	269
Table 48: Null subject use in fronted Wh and Wh-in-situ for Philippe, Marie and Augustin	270
Table 49: Percentage of null subject utterances by child in Wh-questions, yes-no questions, and declaratives (Levow 1995)	271
Table 50: Occurrence of infinitives and null subjects in specific question types	277
Table 51: Distribution of non-finite structures in verbal utterances (French, Pierce 1989, 1992)	289
Table 52: Distribution of non-finite structures in verbal utterances (French, Verrips and Weissenborn 1989)	290
Table 53a,b: Distribution of non-finite structures and infinitives in verbal utterances (French, Friedeman 1992)	291
Table 54: Distribution of infinitives in verbal utterances (French, Hamann)	291
Table 55: Distribution of infinitives in negated verbal utterances (German, Tracy 1990)	292
Table 56: Distribution of non-finite structures in negated verbal utterances (German, Verrips and Weissenborn 1989)	292
Table 57: Distribution of infinitives in verbal utterances (German, Hamann)	294
Table 58: Distribution of infinitives in verbal utterances	295

(Austrian German, Schaner-Wolles 1994)
Table 59: Distribution of infinitives in verbal utterances 295
(Dutch, Haegeman 1996)
Table 60: Periods and ages (Christoph and Elisa) 302
Table 61: Types of null subjects in percentages of all null-subjects 307

ACKNOWLEDGEMENTS

Many parts of this work grew in steps and have been presented at conferences or even been published in some related form. So I am indebted to the reviewers of this book, but also to the commentators and reviewers of my papers and the participants in many a conference discussion. I particularly thank all those who helped with data, statistics, programming, and linguistic suggestions, namely Adriana Belletti, Gerard Bol, Anna Cardinaletti, Harald Clahsen, Robin Clark, Sebastien Dubé, Nigel Duffield, Uli Frauenfelder, Marc-Ariel Friedemann, Ira Gawlitzek-Maiwald, Theresa Guasti, Liliane Haegeman, Harald Hestvik, Nina Hyams, Christopher Laenzlinger, Paola Merlo, Natascha Müller, Bill Philip, Kim Plunkett, Susan Powers, Lucienne Rasetti, Tom Roeper, Luigi Rizzi, Jeannette Schaeffer, Carson Schütze, Michal Starke, Arnim von Stechow, Rosemarie Tracy, Sten Vikner, Jürgen Weissenborn, and Ken Wexler. What I made of these comments and suggestions, is, of course, entirely my own responsibility.

I also want to thank all those who made the experiments possible, first and foremost the children who left their class rooms to play guessing gaims with us. My thanks include the students who provided the native French input, the directors and teachers of the Ecole Maternelle and the Ecole Primaire Yves de Tonnac in Versonnex, and to Arlette who provided the sort of warm athmosphere at Les Stroumphs, a Genevan crêche, which made work with under four year olds possible.

Special thanks go to my parents, who traveled thousands of miles to take over my household chores, to my daughters, who did not lose their smiles, and last, but by no means least, to the clandestine organization of what I call the "old girl network" - all my friends who were ready to take care of my daughters at all times and at short notice and often for more than just one day.

At various stages of this work I was supported by the Swiss National Fund Grants No. 11- 33542.92 and 1213-42212.94 and by the Interfaculty Project of the University of Geneva.

CHAPTER 1

INTRODUCTION TO LANGUAGE ACQUISITION

1. THE INNATENESS HYPOTHESIS

In the generative tradition, the study of language acquisition is of great importance for linguistic theory. There are two principal reasons for such a role. First, there is the assumption that the language faculty is innate which is central to generative linguistics and which obviously has to reflect in the properties of language development in the child. Second, there is the notion of 'explanatory adequacy' which should oblige any theoretical linguist to show that his or her proposal for an analysis of a particular structure can be learnt. However, the field of language acquisition has long led a life in the shadows of linguistic theory. Fortunately this has changed in the last two decades so that for an introduction to language acquisition I would like to give some background about what was the *status quo* up to the eighties, what caused the change, and what sort of results have been achieved since then.

Almost half a century ago, Chomsky argued that the language faculty is part of the genetic endowment of the human species (Chomsky 1959). His arguments are usually subsumed under the label 'poverty of stimulus' and are actually threefold. The best known argument is that the child is able to produce phrases and sentences which he or she has never heard before and so can make infinite use of finite means right from the beginning. This ability could be due, however, to a general cognitive ability to generalize, i.e. deduce (recursive) rules from given data patterns. So this argument is not convincing. The second argument attacks the possibility of pattern generalization by pointing out that the child is able to produce correct sentences even when the data set is imperfect, faulty, incomprehensive and incomplete, i.e. the prerequisites of successful generalization can never be guaranteed. The third argument pushes this line of reasoning even farther. It points out that there are areas of grammar which are not amenable to generalization processes because the decisive data are not available in the input or are so rare that they will almost never be encountered by a child in its first two or three years of life and hardly ever by an adult who nevertheless has clear grammaticality judgements in such cases.

The idea that language has biological foundations goes back at least to Darwin, who spoke of the human language ability as an "instinctive tendency to acquire an art". In this view, the child's acquisition of language could be compared to a little bird's acquisition of flight in that both follow a biological program. Chomsky formulated this view much more precisely in his book 'Aspects of the Theories of Syntax' which appeared in 1965:

> "In brief, it seems clear that the present situation with regard to the study of language learning is essentially as follows. We have a certain amount of evidence about the character of the generative grammars that must be the "output" of an acquisition model for language. This evidence shows clearly that taxonomic views of linguistic structure are inadequate and that knowledge of grammatical structure cannot arise by application of step-by-step inductive operations (segmentation, classification, substitution procedures, filling of slots in frames, association, etc.) of any sort that have yet been developed within linguistics, psychology, or philosophy. Further empiricist speculations contribute nothing that even faintly suggests a way of overcoming the intrinsic limitations of the methods that have so far been proposed and elaborated." Chomsky (1965:57).

This position is central to the whole generative approach and has, up to this day remained controversial among linguists and psycholinguists. It is important to note that Chomsky talks about 'knowledge of grammatical structure', not about the acquisition of the lexicon, nor about morphological or phonological regularities. So acquisition research in the generative tradition centers on syntax. The controversy about innateness has broadened, however, and tends to include arguments about phonological categorization or morphological rules which we will briefly discuss in section 2 before returning to generative models in section 3.

2. ARGUMENTS AND COUNTERARGUMENTS FROM DIFFERENT POINTS OF VIEW

Arguments against a biologically determined language faculty come specifically from researchers working with connectionist models of language learning, see Elman et al. (1996). This research is mostly centered on the acquisition of morphological rules like plural or past tense formation. The claim is that such morphological processes can be learnt without symbolization and innate knowledge. See Rumelhart and McClelland (1986) for the original model of past tense acquisition, Plunkett and Marchman (1993), Nakisa, Plunkett and Hahn (1996) and Elman et al. (1996) for developments and extensions to other morphological processes, and Marcus et al. (1992) and Pinker and Prince (1988) for criticism.

One line of investigation supporting the view of language as a genetic endowment is closely linked to traditional research on language acquisition and argues as follows: If language is innate there must be phenomena that should be accessible from birth in one form or the other. Thus it is clear that the language of children, especially young children and preferably babies should be investigated. As babies unfortunately don't talk, the abilities that are available from birth must be established in ways different from the usual linguistic analysis.

Psycholinguistic research of the last few years has shown that at the age of 4 and 8 months and even during their first week of life children already have important language skills. From the fourth day, infants distinguish their mother tongue from other languages. From the first months children prefer the sound of speech to 'other noise'. At the age of 4 months, infants prefer pauses at syntactic boundaries to random pauses. From the first months, (French) babies can distinguish syllables from non-syllables, can distinguish different syllables and know that larger linguistic units are made up of syllables. At the age of 4 months, infants are able to categorize sounds into phonemes and can distinguish different phonemes. At this stage, infants have a universal phoneme inventory, which is then fixed to the inventory of distinctive phonemes of their mother tongue between the age of 8 and 12 months.

The most significant research on phoneme perception was the experiment of Eimas et al. (1971), who showed that four months old infants already group the sounds of language into categories which correspond to phonemes. The babies were presented with a sound continuum of /pa/ to /ba/. They did not react as to a continuum, however, but perceived a categorial change from /pa/ to /ba/ which mirrors the adult phoneme categorization. The crucial test was the presentation of two different sound pairs where the members of each pair differed for exactly the same wavelength. In the one case, however, both sounds would be categorized by an adult as /pa/, and in the second case, they would be categorized as starting with two different phonemes, /p/ and /b/. In the first case babies did not show any special interest in the new sound, in the second case they did. This line of inquiry has been pursued till it could be established that neo-nates can distinguish all the possible contrasts which could occur in any natural language in a way exactly similar to adults (cf. Mehler and Dupoux, 1990:235).

It is interesting to compare this result about the early discrimination of phonemic contrasts to the result about the comparative lateness of the exclusive availability of the phoneme system of the native language. In the beginning, infants have a universal phoneme system, after eight or twelve months they only perceive the contrasts which are pertinent to their native language and have thus acquired the phoneme system of their target language (Werker and Tees 1983).

Mehler and Dupoux (1990) concluded that this early capacity of selecting sounds conforming to a specific model (human language) has its foundation in the brain and particularly in what has been called the language organ. In order to reject the position that this organ develops after birth and only with exposure to language (Lenneberg 1967), the fact that adults react faster to contrasts in language sounds if they are presented to the right ear was exploited by the above authors. In contrast to this, musical sounds are distinguished better when presented to the left ear. The explanation is that the right ear is dominantly connected with the left hemisphere, whereas the left ear is dominantly connected with the right hemisphere, the seat of the musical faculty. Since Broca (1865), it is the left hemisphere which is considered to be the seat of the language faculty. Experiments could establish that four-day old babies perceive minimal linguistic contrasts better if they are presented to the right ear whereas musical notes are better distinguished on the other side. For the above authors, this concludes the argument for a biological foundation of the language faculty as it shows that, from birth, language is processed in its appropriate place, the left hemisphere of the brain.

Research on language perception and processing has become very important in the field of early language acquisition as recent studies by Gerken (1994), Gerken et al. (1990), Jusczyk (1997) or Hoehle and Weissenborn (1998) show. Apart from very early language perception, there are other facts, however, that argue against the view that language is solely a social phenomenon, largely determined by the surrounding culture. First, never in the history of discoveries has a mute tribe been found and though we have many descriptions of living stone-age cultures there is nothing like a stone-age or primitive language. All languages use the same tools and principles on the same level of sophistication though in different ways. Second, when the high plains of New-Guinea, the last white spot on the map, were explored in the 1930ties, more than eight hundred new languages were discovered. These languages were all different though the cultural needs and the natural environment of the individual isolated village were not much different from that of the next village. Third, children can actually "reinvent language" as Pinker (1994) puts it reporting on the research on Creolization. Bickerton (1984) found that pidgins can be transformed into a full complex language, a Creole, in one generation. The point here is that a pidgin consists of strings of words borrowed from several languages, but especially the dominant language. These strings contain no or very little grammatical material indicating roles, connections, and dependencies between the lexical items. A Creole, on the other hand, has grammatical devices like inflection, i.e. the grammatical glue between the words, while retaining the mixed vocabulary borrowed from several languages. The creation of Creoles in one generation or by one sole child have recently been documented in pidgin speaking communities. Another case of language creation, proving the same point, is the spontaneous creation of sign languages in deaf communities.

3. GENERATIVE APPROACHES TO LANGUAGE ACQUISITION

Within the generative tradition and in accordance with the above quote from Chomsky, the focus of acquisition research is on grammatical knowledge, i.e. on syntax. In view of the above debate on whether the language faculty is innate, one aim of such research is to establish early knowledge, preferably in areas that are underdetermined in the sense of poverty of stimulus. One such area is the acquisition of the referential properties of pronouns, which has been intensively investigated, and which we will investigate anew from the point of view of pronominal clitics.

However, the role of research in the acquisition of syntax is not only to provide the arguments for the biological foundations of language. It is equally important from an intrinsic point of view. With the notion of 'explanatory adequacy' introduced in Chomsky (1965), language acquisition became as important as linguistic intuition for the formation of linguistic theories. An analysis of a grammatical construction can be called explanatory adequate only if in addition to capturing adult intuitions ('descriptive adequacy') it could explain how the construction could be acquired. This aspect of acquisition could be more or less ignored by theoretical linguists for almost two decades because a sufficiently rich initial system together with an idealized 'instantaneous' acquisition had been conveniently assumed. Only recently, acquisition data and their theoretical impact have received more attention. The data from a given child phase have been compared to the data linguists collect from a newly discovered language or dialect (see Rizzi 1992), and Wexler (1997) exhorts acquisition researchers to "be bold" and to point out the theoretical consequences of their findings. This could concern the Case checking mechanisms (Eisenbeiss and Penke 1996), the analysis of V2-clauses (Gawlitzek-Maiwald, Tracy and Fritzenschaft 1992, Santelman 1996), the analysis of the tense and agreement system (Schütze and Wexler 1996a,b) or scope marking and other interpretative mechanisms (Hamann 1996c, and Weissenborn, Roeper, and de Villiers 1996). It is this aspect of acquisition research which hopefully becomes more and more influential so that linguistic theory and acquisition research can enter into a relationship of mutual give and take, equals in theoretical relevance.

4. THE PRINCIPLES AND PARAMETERS MODEL

The growing interest in acquisition was only possible with the introduction of the Principles and Parameter model (Chomsky 1981). Before that 'instantaneous' acquisition made it uninteresting to investigate phases and steps in child development which were necessarily due to extra-linguistic factors. Moreover, research results, especially acquisition results on other languages than English, were blurred by the fact that languages were distinguished by the complex rule systems describing their grammars. Therefore little was known about the initial state and the process of language acquisition as such. In 1965, Chomsky stated this clearly and at the same time put his finger on a dilemma inherent in the assumption of a rich initial system. He wrote:

> It is, for the present, impossible to formulate an assumption about initial, innate structure rich enough to account for the fact that grammatical knowledge is attained on the basis of the evidence available to the learner. Consequently, the empiricist effort to show how the assumptions about a language acquisition device can be reduced to a conceptual minimum is quite misplaced. The real problem is that of developing a hypothesis about initial structure that is sufficiently rich to account for acquisition of language, yet not so rich as to be inconsistent with the known diversity of language." (Chomsky1965:58).

With the Principles and Parameter (P&P) model a perfect tool was created to solve this problem: It provides a system which is rich enough but not too rich to be rigid. As parametric theory made it possible to formulate cross-linguistic differences in a precise manner, it brought new impetus to comparative linguistics (see Rizzi 1993). This more precise formulation of the possible differences made it easier to focus on the common core, the system of principles which is called Universal Grammar, UG. It was only a small step to assume that it is this common core of principles that is innate and that the acquisition process is a process of parameter setting through exposure to language particular input.

5. P&P AND THE LEARNABILITY QUESTION

Admittedly, a P&P model can offer a theoretical solution to the above sketched dilemma in that it is a finite set of parameters which has to be considered. This means that in the worst case the enumeration of all the logically possible parameter settings can provide the basis for a systematic search for the correct grammar.

This theoretical possibility does not survive the practicality test, however. For 30 parameters, and this is not a high number of parameters to characterize a natural language, the number of possible combinations is 2^{30}. Clark (1992) calculated that it would take about 34 years to arrive at the correct grammar - assuming a machine that could test every member of this set of possible grammars in one second. So the learner obviously does not match every possible parameter combination against the input. If this were the case, the verifaction becomes too costly as was just demonstrated.

The next step is to view UG as a constraining device which delimits hypothesis formation and so offers deductive short-cuts. The learner's task is to set parameters correctly with the help of a certain input and the core principles of UG. The role of UG and input are now clear in as much as the learner, confronted with a suitable sequence of texts from the target language, will choose the parameter setting so that UG will map these values correctly to the target grammar.

But even the idea that the principles of UG constrain the possible choices does not deliminate the space narrowly enough. The problem of a UG constrained deductive system is that parameters interact, so that the learner would have to consider the consequences of any one parameter alone, any two parameters together, any three parameters etc. This means that for 30 parameters, the learner will have to test all combinations of 30 parameters taken k at a time as k ranges from 1 to 30 in order to test the consequences of taking any k interacting parameters together. The number of hypotheses to test is very high: 2^{30} - 1, which, for all practical purposes, is the same as for a purely enumerative search.

In order to solve the problem of how parameters are set, the notion of a trigger was introduced together with the constraint that only one parameter should be set at a time. A trigger, defined naively, is any input string that provides unambiguous evidence for a certain parameter setting (see Lightfoot 1989 for a discussion). One of the first explicit models capturing these ideas is that of Hyams (1986) in its well-known form:

Initial state=UG $\subset G_1 \subset ... G_{i-1} \subset G_i \subset ...G_{i+1} \subset G_n=$ target grammar

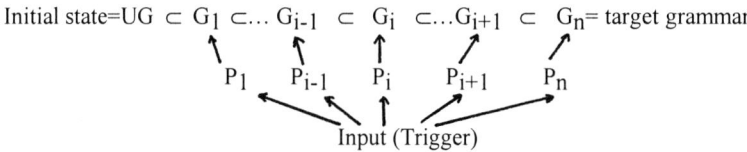

Problems persist, however , as it remains unclear whether parameters are unset in the beginning or whether they are set to a default. A special problem is whether it is possible to recover from wrong parameter settings. With the reasonable assumption that negative evidence is not available to the child, the learner should not be able to recover from a situation where he has set his parameters in such a way as to arrive at a grammar creating a language which is larger than and contains the target language. No input string would provide evidence for the setting to the "smaller" value as each string of the smaller language is also contained in the larger language. Possible solutions to this problem have been suggested by Clark (1992) and by Gibson and Wexler (1994).

It emerges that any theory of language learnability must specify how the learner uses the input data to drive hypothesis formation (Clark 1992). It is equally clear that the learner must be able to recover from a wrong generalization, and it seems inevitable that frequency or some other sort of statistical calculation plays a role. One such statistical measure is the entropy measure introduced by Kapur and Clark (2000). Another one is a frequency measure for triggers as introduced by LeBlanc (1995) in a model that seeks to capture the notions of a P&P model with connectionist tools.

Another possibility to account for sudden progress and different phases in language development is to assume maturational factors. Just as a child does not try to walk from its first day but a certain maturation of muscular strength and co-ordination is necessary for such a development, it is possible that there is maturation of the language faculty itself - always assuming that it is a biological endowment. Another view, originating in the psycholinguistic tradition (see Piaget 1955), is to assume maturation or development in the cognitive abilities of the child which will then lead to a new phase in its language use. The latter view may perhaps not be relevant when considering pure syntactic phenomena. It will be worth considering, however, whenever we are touching on interface phenomena, especially on phenomena which have to do with pragmatic notions like shared 'conversational background' or 'knowledge of the world'. So we will have to carefully evaluate these two possibilities later on when we are discussing concrete phenomena of language development.

This short discussion has shown that learnability is a central issue within generative acquisition research. In the following, however, its more technical aspects will be left aside, and I will concentrate on actual phenomena of language acquisition. The theoretical framework will remain a P&P model which will from time to time be expanded with more recent notions taken from the 'Minimalist program' as developed in Chomsky (1995).

6. EARLY PARAMETER SETTING AND 'LATE' PHENOMENA

The impetus that the P&P model provided for acquisition research can be directly measured in the wealth of recent studies and results. The surprising fact emerging from these studies is that parameters appear to be set very early in the acquisition of syntax. This is true for the so-called head-complement parameter, the verb-raising parameters, the clitic parameters, and even the pro-drop parameter. Let us briefly illustrate this claim with three examples.

6.1. The Head-Complement Parameter

In the X-bar theory of phrase structure, every phrase has a specifier, a head and a complement which can be formally represented as in (1a, b).

(1) a. XP -> {Spec, X'}   b. X' -> {X^0, Comp}

This is considered to be a principle of UG. The order of constituents is parameterized, however. This can be seen in the canonical order of verbs and their complements, especially for verbs in the infinitive as these do not undergo any of the verb raising processes. Thus we find the structures (2a) for German and (2b) for English and French capturing the examples (3a) and (3b,c).

(2) a.   b.

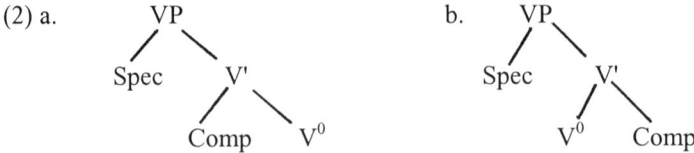

(3) a. Jetzt möchte der Vater [das Baby *sehen*]
  b. Maintenant le père veut [*voir* le bébé]
  c. Now the father wants [*to see* the baby]

According to this parametric difference, German is characterized as Subject-Object-Verb or SOV, whereas English and French are Subject-Verb-Object or SVO. This regularity is mastered from the first two word combinations, i.e. from the beginning of syntax itself. In Radford (1997:22) we find: "children consistently position heads before their complements from their earliest multiword utterances." This is shown in the combinations given in (4) also quoted from Radford (1997).

(4) touch heads, cuddle book, want crayons, open door, want biscuit, bang bottom, see cats

German children do the opposite. They position objects behind verbs as a study of the child Simone by Penner, Schönenberger and Weissenborn (1994) has shown.

(5) Simone Obj. + Inf 545
   2.0-2.2. *Inf + Obj. 9

(6) baby nich nuckel habe(n)
  baby not pacifier have

Example (6) gives a typical utterance of Simone's, and the data in (5) shows that 98% of her objects and infinitives are correctly placed with respect to each other.

6.2. Verb-Raising to Inflection

Another parameter concerns the position of finite verbs. From the contrast in (7a) and (7b) Pollock (1989) deduced that the finite verbs moves to Inflection in French whereas it stays in its base position in English. The tree in (8) and the examples below demonstrate that in French it is only finite verbs, not infinitives or participles which raise. The demonstration hinges on the fact that adverbs like *souvent* 'often' as well as the negation *pas* 'not' have a fixed place in the phrase structure tree, and that verbs show up on either side of these elements according to their being inflected or not.

(7) a. Jean voit souvent Marie
    b. John often sees Mary

(8)

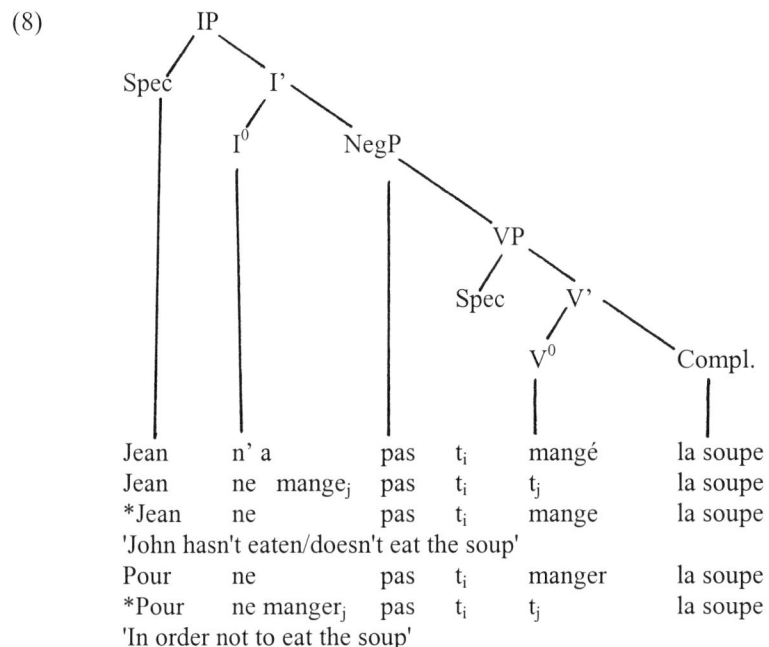

Jean	n' a	pas	t_i	mangé	la soupe
Jean	ne mange$_j$	pas	t_i	t_j	la soupe
*Jean	ne	pas	t_i	mange	la soupe

'John hasn't eaten/doesn't eat the soup'

| Pour | ne | pas | t_i | manger | la soupe |
| *Pour | ne manger$_j$ | pas | t_i | t_j | la soupe |

'In order not to eat the soup'

Pierce (1989, 1992) successfully demonstrated that French children as young as two years are sensitive to the finite/non finite contrast, see (9b), with respect to negation just as French adults are, see (9a). Table 1 shows that the distribution is consistent and that the verb raising parameter is set correctly.

(9) a. je (n') marche pas   vs.   je ne veux pas marcher   adult
        I ne walk   not   I ne   want not to walk
        'I don't walk'   'I do not want to walk'
    b. veux pas lolo   vs.   pas dormir   (Pierce 1992)
        want not water   not sleep (inf)   child

Table 1: Distribution of finite and non-finite verbs with respect to negation
French (Pierce 1989: three children ranging from 1;8 to 2;6)

	+finite	-finite
pas verb	11	77
verb pas	185	2

6.3. Verb-Rraising in Verb-Second Languages

Examples (10a-f) show a similar phenomenon of verb raising in German. Here, however, the finite verb always ends up in the second position of the sentence. This argues for the fact that the verb moves further up in the tree than to the Inflectional Phrase (IP), and the usual hypothesis is that the verb moves as far as the head of the complementizer phrase which provides the highest layer of structure in a phrase. The examples (11b,c,d) show that adverbs and other topicalized constituents can be in the first position of the sentence in German followed by the verb and then the subject. As the complementizer phrase (CP) is the place where topicalized constituents are placed, and the specifier of the IP is the canonical place for subjects, this hypothesis finds support in the data. Subordinate clauses also support the assumption as it turns out that in German subordinate clauses with an overt complementizer the finite verb does not raise to second position but remains sentence final.

(10) a. Hans kauft jetzt immer Blumen für Marie
         John buys now always flowers for Mary
         'John now always buys flowers for Mary'

b. Jetzt kauft Hans immer Blumen für Marie
   now buys John always flowers for Mary
   'Now John always buys flowers for Mary'
c. Blumen kauft Hans jetzt immer für Marie
   flowers buys John now always for Mary
   'John now always buys FLOWERS for Mary'
d. Für Marie kauft Hans jetzt immer Blumen
   for Mary buys Hany now always flowers
   'John now always buys flowers FOR MARY'
e. Er hat immer Blumen gekauft
   he has always flowers bought
   'he has always bought flowers'
f. Er will immer Blumen kaufen
   he wants always flowers buy
   'he always wants to buy flowers'

Tables 2 and 3 show that young German children already know that the finite verb must be moved to second position whereas infinitives must not. Table 2 shows the analysis of the speech of one child during one day. V2/not final means that these are clear cases of second position where another constituent followed the verb, not cases where the verb occurred in final position which also happened to be second.

Table 2: Distribution of finite and non-finite verbs with respect to V2
   German (Poeppel and Wexler 1993: Andreas 2.1)

	+finite	-finite
V2/not final	197	6
Vfinal/not V2	11	37

Table 3 is an analysis of four German children of a young age following the same criteria in that only utterances longer than two words were considered. Both tables show that the Verb-Second (V2) property of German is respected from the beginning.

Table 3: Distribution of finite and non-finite verbs with respect to V2
German (Clahsen, Eisenbeiss and Penke 1996:
Simone 1;10-2;7, Matthias 2;3-3;6, Annelie 2;4-2;9, and Hannah 2;0-2;7)

	Simone	Matthias	Annelie	Hannah
finite/non-finite				
Vfin in V2	93% (511)	87% (69)	88% (117)	80% (4)
Vfin in final pos.	7% (41)	13% (10)	12% (16)	20% (1)
V-fin in V2	2% (4)	2% (1)	1% (1)	X
V-fin in final pos.	98% (189)	98% (52)	99% (80)	X

Because of these and many other such results the general consensus is that parameters are acquired early, see also Wexler (1998) for more details and more examples. It should follow that the principles connected with these parameters are in place even earlier.

7. AIM AND OUTLINE OF THE PRESENT STUDY

The results mentioned in 1.6. make the acquisition process look very easy, and acquisition could be taken as a free ride on UG as in the times before the P&P model. That this is not the case is apparent in those areas where non-adult structures are used systematically over several months or even years. Such areas are in particular the use of null subjects, the use of non-adult infinitives in declaratives, and the comprehension of pronouns.

In (11a-d) we find examples of null subjects in several languages, starting from the familiar English phenomenon first discussed by Hyams (1983, 1986) in her epoch-making investigation of child null subjects. With more research, it emerged that such child null subjects occur almost exclusively in the initial position of root clauses in languages that are not pro-drop languages (Valian 1990, Rizzi 1994). This means, in particular, that child null subjects are rare in constituent questions or in topicalization structures in V2 languages. In pro-drop languages, on the other hand, null subjects occur from the beginning in the positions that are allowed by adult grammar (Guasti, 1993/4, Rizzi 1998, 2000). These facts will be discussed in chapter

6, 8 and in 7 with respect to the explanations proposed for the occurrence of child null subjects.

(11) a. want more apple   Eric   2;1   English
      b. oter tout ça   Augustin   2;1   French
         take off all that
      c. bin wieder lieb   Elisa   2;10   German
         am good again
      d. wordt al donker   Hein   2;6   Dutch
         becomes already dark
         '(it) is getting dark already'
      f. ikke k¢re traktor   Jens   2;0   Danish
         not drive tractor
         'I/you/he don't/doesn't drive the tractor'

The examples (12a-f) show the use of infinitives. Starting from Wexler (1994), who made the point that these infinitives are optional in that they occur side by side with finite constructions (hence the term 'optional infinitive' or OI), several observations have been discussed in the literature about child infinitives. One observation is that such infinitives do not occur in all languages, they are very rare in Italian and practically non-existent in Spanish or Catalan (see Hoekstra and Hyams 1996, Wexler 1998 and others for a comparative discussion). Another observation is that such infinitives seem to be largely restricted to root clauses (hence the term 'root infinitive' or RI) as Rizzi (1994) pointed out. Still another point is that child null subjects and infinitives must be closely related (Kraemer 1993, Rizzi 1994, Schuetze and Wexler 1996a,b, Wexler 1994). I will take up these and other points in chapters 6, 7, and 8.

(12) a. him fall down   Nina   2;3   English
      b. manger ça   Augustin   2;0   French
         eat (inf) that
      c. Thorstn das habn   Andreas   2;1   German
         Thorsten that have
         'Thorsten has that'
      d. zo ikke in doen   Hein   2;4   Dutch
         so I in put
         'so I put (it) in (there)'

      f. hun sove   Jens   1;10   Danish
         she sleep (inf)

The well studied problem of pronoun comprehension concerns sentences as shown in (13a) and (13b).

(13)   a. Mowgli is scratching himself.
          b. Mowgli is scratching him.

Several experiments have established that English children interpret (13a) correctly as Mowgli scratching Mowgli. Children have two possible interpretations for (13b), however: the adult interpretation of Mowgli scratching somebody else and the possibility that Mowgli is scratching Mowgli, see Chien and Wexler (1990), Philip and Coopmans (1996a,b) and others. These results have been very puzzling and the innateness of the binding principles seemed to be at stake - until cross-linguistic research showed that children learning a romance language do not have so much difficulties. We will report on and discuss several experiments and add two experiments of our own on French which will provide more data for the decision as to the theoretical explanation of the observed 'delay of principle B', see chapter 3 to 5. Before we enter into a discussion about the interpretative properties of French pronouns, we will, however, give the data on the surprisingly early and surprisingly correct production of subject pronouns in French complemented by the data on a delay in the production of object clitics, see chapter 2.

    In treating the above topics, one aim of this study is to provide a broad and detailed discussion of the available data. Whatever turns linguistic theory might take, the data will stay the same and will provide a basis for evaluation even under new theoretical aspects. The more ambitious aim, of course, is to examine the possible causes of a delay in the acquisition of the target structures in just the areas described above. I will argue for a common cause for all of these problems which can be subsumed under the broad label of 'difficulty with interface conditions' - though different aspects of such difficulties are responsible for the different phenomena.

    The first hint of such an explanation, oriented towards a problem in the interface of syntax and pragmatics, comes from the investigation of the referential properties of pronouns. The assumption that a certain pragmatic principle is not in place yet and causes children to sometimes assign the wrong referent to pronouns has proved to go a long way towards a solution of the delay-problem in this area of language development. It will also be shown that the use of null subjects and third person pronouns by young children in no way depends on previous mention in the discourse (see also Hamann and Plunkett 1998). So, obviously, an anchoring difficulty is involved in the latter cases. Extending this idea to the use of infinitives is not trivial and requires some semantic apparatus, but the basic idea is again that tenses, especially embedded tenses, have to be anchored not only to the time of utterance but to other times given in the discourse. If such discourse anchorage is not available, default solutions will be sought. These defaults may be language specific.

So the book starts with an example of fast acquisition and then goes on to describe cases of delayed acquisition: chapter 2 treats the acquisition of clitic pronouns in French, which shows the faultless pattern of acquisition of a correctly set parameter for subject clitics. I will then focus on the delay in the acquisition of complement clitics and subsequently in chapters 3-5 investigate the referential properties of complement clitics. A cross-linguistic investigation of the use of infinitives and null subjects in the crucial third year will follow in chapters 6-8. Before deciding on a theory for these phenomena, child infinitives and null subjects will be investigated in the context of constituent questions and negation and the late occurrence of argument drop in German will be reported, chapters 9 and 10. With the introduction of a semantically oriented tense theory and some insights from research on language impaired children, I will conclude the argument about discourse anchorage, see chapter 11.

The appeal to anchoring difficulties and interface problems may remind of a competing factors model to language acquisition. In such a model, processing and pragmatic limitations may be responsible for certain non-adult phenomena in language development. Cognitive development will then help overcome these language problems, a view we also find in the well-known Piagetian paradigm. The results on language development in impaired children point to the fact, however, that it is their delayed development in syntax which is responsible for the observed anchoring difficulties. So it will be argued that the development of adult discourse anchorage is driven by syntax, not any cognitive development. So the ultimate result is that children step from syntax to discourse, not the other way round, and the modular view of language (Fodor 1983) is preserved.

8. A NOTE TO THE READER

Let me point out that this monograph will not provide an introduction to generative grammar. It is a book about problem areas in language development, and I will assume a certain familiarity with the standard notions of the generative framework and refer the reader not so familiar with these notions to the excellent introductions by Haegeman (1993) or Radford (1990 and 1997).

I will thus take it for granted that a phrase contains at least three layers of projections, the verb phrase (VP) with the lexical-thematic information, the inflectional phrase (IP) with the inflectional material like agreement markings on the verb, and the complementizer phrase (CP), which hosts subordinating elements or interrogative pronouns and provides the link to superordinate structures like matrix clauses or discourse. I will also take it for granted that the IP splits into at least an agreement phrase (AgrP), where subject-verb agreement is marked, and a tense phrase (TP), where tense morphology is located (see Pollock 1989). Other theoretical notions like the idea that elements move in order to pick up morphological markers or (as was suggested more recently in Chomsky's Minimalist Program 1995) to have their features checked will not be explained either. Any specific theoretical apparatus necessary for the understanding of an individual chapter will be provided, however, especially if this involves recent developments of the framework or non-standard solutions. I will thus give a fairly detailed introduction into the binding theory and the different versions and developments suggested since Chomsky (1981). I will also give an introduction to the syntax and semantics of negation and questions in the relevant chapters, and I will discuss the approaches to clitic pronouns in detail.

The syntactic apparatus will remain on the conservative side, however, in using the framework of government and binding and the P&P model more than the minimalist program or notions from even more recent models. This is due in some respects to the fact that the work of rewriting the whole book seemed too daunting a prospect to be attacked in earnest. In other respects, however, the P&P model is geared to handle acquisition problems, and the government and binding framework has provided many convincing standard analyses of linguistic phenomena which the acquisition worker can use so to speak ready-made. In the minimalist framework many things are in flux and so research in more applied fields cannot bee too sure of its footing. Another point in favor of the older framework is the fact that more people feel comfortable with it or have at least grown used to its concepts and ideas.

As to the assumptions about acquisition made in the course of the book, I have introduced some of them already and will introduce more specific models for the different phenomena later without assuming any knowledge on the part of the reader. This procedure is aimed at the linguists who want to know more about acquisition. On the whole, the book should be readable and interesting for all researchers in acquisition who have kept up a bit with the developments in linguistics and for all linguists who have not totally turned their back on generative theory.

CHAPTER 2

THE ACQUISITION OF THE PRONOMINAL SYSTEM IN FRENCH – THE PRODUCTION OF SUBJECT AND OBJECT CLITICS

1. INTRODUCTION

The acquisition of the pronominal system of a language in exemplary fashion touches on the two questions of earliness and of relevance for linguistic theory. Though recent publications specifically address the acquisition of pronouns (see Hamann, Rizzi, Frauenfelder 1996 or Powers and Hamann 2000) there remains the simple question of what the data actually are in different languages. With respect to earliness, there are two questions about the acquisition of the French pronominal system. One targets the setting of the clitic-parameters, the other concerns the earliness or delay of the binding principles for clitic pronouns. Research of experimental psycholinguistics has concentrated on this area for a long time, and by now a clear pattern has emerged. The principles concerning anaphors and referential expressions are in place at the age of 3 for English children, whereas the principle regulating the reference of pronouns seems to be significantly delayed for English. In Romance languages, such a delay was not found, so that there is reasonable certainty that the principles are not delayed at all, and the question now is what it is that masks the performance on pronouns for English children, but does not interfere with the performance of a Romance child. The obvious answer is that the properties of English pronouns and Romance clitics, which are different in many respects, also determine their behavior with respect to the binding principles. We will come back to these intriguing questions in chapters 3 to 5 where we report on experimental findings and on the theory.

Turning to the second task of acquisition research, investigating the French pronominal system is very promising because many questions concerning the analysis of Romance or Germanic clitics are still unresolved. We can expect that data on clitic acquisition give indications for which of the competing theoretical analyses for a certain clitic phenomenon is to be preferred. Torrens and Wexler (2000) is an example of this approach in that the authors try to show that the correct use of clitic doubling and other crucial constructions by the Spanish child Maria argues directly for an analysis of object clitics as proposed by Sportiche (1992). The result on the delay of object clitics with respect to subject clitics in the acquisition of French as documented by Hamann, Rizzi and Frauenfelder (1995, 1996) gives support to any analysis which postulates a structural difference between these two clitic types in French. This could be the original analyses of Kayne (1975) or Rizzi (1986b), an approach to the clitic system as outlined by Cardinaletti and Starke (2000) or an approach which crucially relies on different cliticisation sites. It argues strongly against an approach which treats both types of French clitics as heads and analyses French subject clitics as agreement markers.

With respect to the data aspect, i.e. the questions of what children start with in the process of language acquisition, and what they acquire when, why and how, it is clear that especially clitics which occupy designated positions in the clause can serve as evidence par excellence for the existence of functional categories, movement, licensing and locality constraints from early on. The surprising observation across Romance languages is that clitics are used early and once they are used, they are always used correctly. This was reported by Pierce (1989) and Friedemann (1992) for French (though Haverkort and Weissenborn 1991 speak of some errors with object clitics in imperatives), by Guasti (1992, 1993) for Italian and by Torrens and Wexler (2000) for Spanish clitic-doubling. A detailed study with respect to the question of correct placement in French was recently conducted by Hamann, Rizzi and Frauenfelder (1996) and will be reported in what follows.

The outline given above determines the content of chapter 2. Using material from Hamann, Rizzi, Frauenfelder (1996) we will first concentrate on the delay of object clitics and its implications for the analysis of the clitic system of colloquial French. Clearly, the result is important for any theoretical account, so that it may be instructive to say something about the techniques and difficulties of acquisition research in order to evaluate the relevance of such a result. Second, the same study showed the early mastery of clitic placement and thus can be used to argue for the early existence of the IP system as well as for the correct setting of the clitic-parameter. We will then show that the non-occurrence of subject clitics with root-infinitives is a solid result for French child language. These two results together imply that the child certainly has functional projections, but that in root infinitives some structure is missing nonetheless. The discussion of the problems and cross-linguistic differences in the mastery of the binding principles will be deferred until chapter 3, 4, and 5.

2. SUBJECT AND OBJECT CLITICS

2.1. Background

Romance pronominal clitics differ from full nominal and pronominal expressions with respect to a number of properties: they cannot be used in isolation (4a,b), cannot be conjoined (2a,b), cannot be modified (3a,b), cannot receive focal stress as in (4a,b), cannot be separated from the verb (unless by another clitic, or under very special circumstances in some Romance varieties); all in all, their distribution is severely restricted when compared to full nominal and pronominal expressions (see Kayne 1975 for the original discussion of these properties). With the specified properties as a first test for clitic-hood, it is natural to assimilate subject and object unstressed pronouns in French:

(1) a. Qui est venu? * Il
      who is come   He
      'who came'
   b. Qui as-tu vu?   * Le
      who have-you seen   Him
      'who have you seen?'

(2) a. *Il et elle viendront.
      he and she will-come
      'he and she will come'
   b. *Je le et la connais.
      I him and her know
      'I know him and her'

(3) a. *Ils deux viendront.
        they two will-come
        'these two will come – they will come both'
    b. * Je les deux connais.
        I them two know
        'I know these two – I know them both'

(4) a. *IL viendra (pas Marie)
        HE will-come (not Mary)
        'HE will come (not Mary)'
    b. *Je LE connais (pas Marie)
        I HIM know (not Mary)
        'I know HIM (Mary)'

(5) a. *Il probablement viendra.
        he probably will-come
    b. *Pierre le probablement connaît.
        Peter him probably knows

The structural representation of clauses as shown in (6) strongly suggests, however, that an assimilation between the two cases is misleading:

(6)

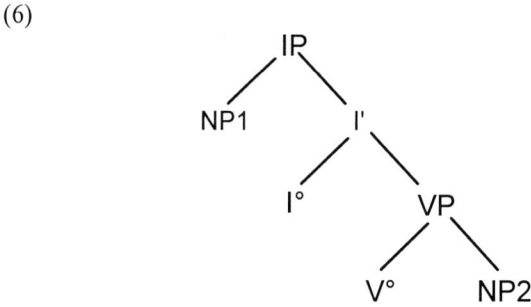

The standard assumption is that the clitic position is associated to I°, the surface position of the inflected verb in French. It follows that a clitic can legitimately bind a trace in object position (possibly through a number of intermediate steps, if the object pronoun first moves to the Spec of some intervening functional projection on its way to the cliticization site), but not in subject position, due to the fact that I° does not c-command NP1. If some version of the VP-Internal Subject Hypothesis were adopted and hence a subject trace lower than I° in (6) were postulated, this would not solve the problem. A sufficiently strong version of the Extended Projection Principle (Chomsky 1981) makes position NP1 obligatory and forces it to be filled by a legitimate element.

A traditional way of tackling this problem is to assume that subject clitics are full NPs in the syntax. Under this hypothesis they occupy position NP1 at SS, so that on this level (and at LF), there is no trace binding to worry about. They undergo a cliticization process only in the phonology, where the proper binding requirement is irrelevant (Kayne 1983, Rizzi 1986b). If phonological cliticization is limited to linearly adjacent positions, this option is not open to object clitics. These must undergo syntactic movement and give rise to representations which satisfy proper binding.

So in this approach the syntactic status of subject and object clitics is very different. Their common properties follow from the fact that they are all clitics in the phonology. More recently a refinement of this approach has been proposed by Cardinaletti & Starke (1995). These authors suggest that French subject and object clitics represent two different kinds of structurally impoverished elements. The former are "weak pronouns", constrained to occur in a strict specifier-head configuration with the licensing head; the latter are genuine clitics, undergoing head movement in order to be associated to their licensing head. In this approach the differences of subject and object clitics will follow because they are 'impoverished' to a different extent, whereas their common properties follow from their being both structurally impoverished.

What these approaches have in common is the fact that subject and object clitics are very different entities on the abstract levels of mental representation SS and LF. This leads Hamann, Rizzi, Frauenfelder (1996) to expect dissociations between the two classes in certain fields. They mention: syntactic behavior, cross-linguistic distribution, selective manifestation and loss in language development and language impairment.

Nevertheless, subject and object clitics are often given the same analysis, and there is a lively debate whether subject clitics are simple agreement markers on the verb and so languages with subject clitics are all pro-drop languages. This analysis is suggested by the paradigm of the Northern Italian dialects and opens the question whether the case of Colloquial and Standard French can be treated in the same manner, as has been proposed by Harris (1985), Jaeggli (1982), Roberge (1990), Kaiser (1992, 1994) and Zribi-Hertz (1994). Kaiser (1994) and Friedemann (1995) offer a full discussion, which I present briefly. If one examines the paradigm of coordination one might arrive at the conclusion that Standard French is an exception but that Colloquial French can be treated on a par with the northern Italian Dialects because it is "unnatural not to repeat the clitic pronoun in the second conjunct" (Friedeman 1995:153, my translation).

(7) a. La canta e la balla   Florentine and Trentino
       she sings and she dances
       'she is singing and dancing'
    b. *La canta e balla
       she sings and dances

(8) a. Elle chante et elle danse   Colloquial French
       she sings and she dances
       'she is singing and dancing'
    b. ??Elle chante et danse
       she sings and dances

(9) a. ?Elle chante et elle danse   Standard French
       she sings and she dances
    b. Elle chante et danse
       she sings and dances

The same conclusion can be drawn if one considers the fact that subject clitics normally occur together with a full NP subject. Kaiser (1994) reports on studies from Canadian and European French which show that between 55% and 80% of all finite sentences containing a subject NP also contain a subject clitic.[1]

However, the facts of free inversion of the subject as exemplified in (10a,b) and the fact that quantifiers cannot occur in clitic doubling structures in neither Standard French nor Colloquial French as shown in (11b,c), dissociates Standard French and Colloquial French from the Northern Italian dialects.

(10) a. E gli parla la maestra   Florentine
        there(expl) him talks the teacher
        'the teacher talks to him'

    b. *Il lui parle la maîtresse   Colloquial and Standard Fr
       there(expl) him talks the teacher
       'the teacher talks to him'
    c. *Il a appelé Marie   Colloquial and Standard Fr
       there has called Marie
       'Marie has called'
    d. Il est arrivé une fille
       there arrrived a girl
       'a girl arrived'

(11) a. Nessuno l'ha detto nulla   Florentine
       nobody he has said nothing
       'nobody has said anything'
    b. *Personne il a rien dit   Colloquial French
       nobody he has said nothing
       'nobody has said anything'
    c. *Personne il n'a rien dit   Standard French
       nobody he has said nothing
       'nobody has said anything'

Confusion may arise because (10d) is possible. However, this is a construction which is peculiar to indefinite subjects and must be explained in a different way, cf. Beletti (1993). Some French dialects also allow a clitic subject after a quantifier and if one takes the quantified NP *tout le monde*, this seems to be possible even in Standard French:

(12) a. tout le monde il est aux fenêtres   Picard
       all the world he is at the windows
       'everybody is at the windows'
    b. tout le monde il est beau, tout le monde il est gentil.   Standard
       all the world he is beautiful, all the world he is nice   French
       'everybody is beautiful, everybody is nice'

Again, this is a very special context and one can argue either that this has become an idiomatic expression (Friedeman 1995), or that the quantifier no longer is a proper quantifier and the expression functions just like any other NP. In any case, free inversion and doubling of the subject after quantifiers is heavily constrained even in Colloquial French and does not apply in the same contexts and as freely as in the Northern Italian dialects. This is important because these two properties go together with the package of pro-drop properties. The two possibilities then are to analyse the subject clitic as an agreement marker as shown in (13a), or to analyse it as a full XP as shown in (13b). Let us examine the two analyses under this aspect.

(13) a. subject clitic as agreement marker   b. subject clitic as XP

The analysis in (13a) clearly assumes *pro*. It commits us to the view that Colloquial French is a pro-drop language, which is very clearly stated in Kaiser (1994) and more recently in Hulk (1997) or Jakubowicz et al. (1998). But if we take the occurrence of free inversion as following from the positive setting of the pro-drop parameter, then an analysis as in (13b) seems more plausible for Standard and Colloquial French given the fact that free inversion does not occur in either variety of French.[2] In the context of our investigation, the choice of variety (13a) makes another clear commitment: given the fact that subject and object clitics are both heads in this analysis and occupy the same surface position no great differences in syntactic behavior, in language development and loss are expected.

2.2. The Method

In the following, I report from the study of Hamann, Rizzi and Frauenfelder (1996) and refer the reader to that study for more detail. What is said here about the child that was studied and the procedures and conventions used for the analysis of the raw data also holds for the rest of this book unless specified differently.[3]

One monolingual child acquiring French, Augustin, was studied longitudinally over a period of approximately 10 months. He was recorded ten times at his home in Neuchâtel in 45 minute sessions. The first 30 minutes of each session were transcribed. The recording sessions occurred roughly every 3 to 4 weeks. However, there was a 2 months break between the 7th and 8th recording sessions and a 2 1/2 month break between the 8th and 9th recording sessions. The subject's age, at the first recording, was 2 years, 0 months and 2 days, and 2 years, 9 months and 30 days at the final recording. Generally, the mother and the experimenter were both present at recordings.

The following conventions were used. If the child utterance was made up of fully comprehensible adult words, an orthographic transcription was given and no interpretation was added as in (14a). If a child utterance did not quite correspond phonetically to the adult utterance but was easily comprehensible, it was rendered in orthographic phonetic transcription, cf. *ça toune* and an interpretation was added in inverted commas *'ça tourne'* (*that turns*) as in (24a). When the phonetic deviance from adult utterances was more marked (and often systematic as in [t] for [s]) a phonetic transcription was given in square brackets [ ]. The phonetic symbols correspond to the computer-coded phonemic notation of SAM-PA as discussed in Wells (1989) for European languages, which is similar to UNIBET used in the Childes database, cf. MacWhinney (1991). When possible, an interpretation was added (14b). Sometimes, when the rest of the utterance was clearly comprehensible as in (14d), a phonetic chunk was left uninterpreted. In some cases a phonetic transcription was completely uninterpretable. Such a case was included in the transcription for further verification, but not included in the counts of utterances.

2.3. Verbal Utterances

Because they require a verbal element as their host, Romance clitics are verbal clitics. A preliminary count therefore must establish the number of verbal utterances, as well as the ratio of verbal utterances to the total of utterances. This is important because we must make sure that there is a sufficient number of potential clitic environments in the transcriptions to warrant further analysis.

Of the total of 2191 utterances in the corpus there are 771 verbal utterances, which is 35.2%. During the period of observation, there was a considerable increase in the use of verbal utterances. In the period from 2;0,2 to 2;4,, Augustin's verbal utterances range from 15.7% to 26.6% of the total, while in the period from 2;6,16 to 2;9,30, the proportion of verbal utterances ranges from 53.2% to 56.6%. Thus Augustin's verbal development corresponds closely to the findings of Valian (1991) for English.

Table 4: Number of utterances and verbal utterances of all kinds in the Augustin-corpus

Sample	Age (y;m,d)	total number of utterances (u)	number of verbal utterances (v)	percentage of verbal utterances
A.01	2;0,2	270	57	21.1
A.02	2;0,23	150	30	20.0
A.03	2;1,15	140	22	15.7
A.04	2;2,13	224	55	24.5
A.05	2;3,10	164	45	27.4
A.06	2;4,1	224	62	27.6
A.07	2;4,22	204	54	26.5
A.08	2;6,16	218	116	53.2
A.09	2;9,2	309	175	56.6
A.10	2;9,30	288	155	53.8
	total	2191	771	35.2

Table 4 shows the numbers and the ratio of all utterances and of utterances containing a verb form. This count and calculation includes all occurrences of finite verbs as in (14a), all infinitives (14b,c,d), even those introduced by prepositions (14d), and all occurrences of past participles (14e). It also includes the occurrences of verb forms ending in [e] together with an auxiliary or modal pro-form as in (14f) where no decision is possible as to the status of this form as infinitive or participle, but the form nevertheless is clearly verbal. An auxiliary-verb complex was counted as one verbal form (14g). The count also includes imperatives (14h).

(14)   a.   on joue   A 2;0,2
               we play
       b.   Exp: Tu veux quoi?   A: [ote tu ta] 'ôter tout ça'   A 2;0;2
                    you want what   take-away all this
       c.   manger, maman, manger
           eat, mummy, eat
           (A. wants to open a box of chocolates)   A 2;0,2

d.	[katschuk]pour faire pan pan	A 2;9,2
	to do *pom pom*	
e.	[kake] 'cassé'	A 2;0,2
	broken	
f.	[e pa deA~Ze sa] '[e] pas derang[e] ça'	A 2;0,2
	'veux/vais pas déranger ça'	
	want/will not disturb this	
	'ai/est pas dérangé ça'	
	have/is not disturbed this	
g.	est pa(r)ti papa	A 2;0,2
	is left Daddy	
h.	attends, attends [KitE]	A 2;0,2
	wait, wait	

2.4. Results on Subject and Object Clitics

Hamann, Rizzi, Frauenfelder (1996) report that there is a clear difference in the appearance of subject and object clitics in the Augustin corpus. Different kinds of subject clitics are present already at the age of 2;0 (see also table 4), whereas the first genuine object clitic occurs at the age of 2;2,13 in the form of an enclitic: *éteinds-le (turn-off it)*. In fact, this is the only occurrence of an object clitic in the first six files (2;0,2 - 2;4,1), and there is only one more object clitic in the next recording at 2;4.22. In the same period, i.e. between 2;0,2 - 2;4,22, 74 occurrences of subject clitics can be identified. It is only when the child's age is 2;9 that a substantive number of object clitics occurs. At the same age, the percentage of subject clitics first doubles and then continues to rise dramatically. This is shown in table 5.

In this count the total set of verbal utterances also includes contexts in which subject clitics would be banned in adult grammars: imperatives, subject questions, subject relatives and infinitives introduced by prepositions. If these contexts are eliminated and the ratio of subject clitics is recalculated to relevant verbal utterances, the resulting proportion raises only slightly as the authors point out. The corrected percentages are given in table 6. A similar procedure was used to make sure that the absence of object clitics is not due to an accidental absence of complement taking verbs or a failure to use complements. The percentage for object clitics presented in table 5 has been recalculated in a more appropriate fashion as a function of the total number of the occurrence of complement-taking verbs with the results shown in table 7. Since object clitics are practically absent until relatively late, this recalculation does not change the picture very much, and the observed differences between subject and object clitics remain very sharp.

Table 5: Occurrences of subject and object clitics in verbal utterances in the Augustin-corpus

Age (y;m,d)	verbal utterances	subject clitics	% of verbal utterances	object clitics	% of verbal utterances
2;0,2	57	17	29.8	0	0
2;0,23	30	4	13.3	0	0
2;1,15	22	4	18.2	0	0
2;2,13	55	16	29.1	1	1.8
2;3,10	45	12	26.6	0	0
2;4,1	62	10	16.1	0	0
2;4,22	54	11	20.4	1	1.9
2;6,16	116	25	21.6	2	1.7
2;9,2	175	80	45.7	10	5.7
2;9,30	115	99	63.4	22	14.2
total	771	278	36.1	36	4.7

The values for clitics in table 5 represent the occurrences of *je, tu, il, elle, on, nous, ils, elles* and *c'* in the subject case. Clearly identifiable pro-forms which did not match the adult forms perfectly, but could be considered phonetic approximations, were equally counted as clitics. Thus Augustin used either *'l* or *i* for *il*, depending on whether the following verbal element started with a consonant or a vowel, as in:

(15) a. [i ku apE] 'il court après'   A 2;0,2
       he runs after
    b. 'l est gros 'il est gros'   A 2;0,2.
       he is fat

From alternations, sometimes in the same recording, as shown in (16a) and (16b), the authors deduce that the form *'l est* is not just a misanalysis of the auxiliary form.

(16) a. est tout tout tout [kake] 'caché' A 2;0,2
         is all all all hidden
     b. 'l est gros A 2;0,2
        he is fat

(16a) is a case of a null subject sentence, whereas (16b) is the variant with an overt pronominal subject. In some dubious cases, the decision whether the sentences contained an overt subject clitic or not was taken on the basis of an analysis of the acoustic wave-form.

An alternation similar to *'l/i* could be observed for *je*. Here, Augustin used [j] as in *[j] ai fini (I have finished)* before vowels and often a schwa or [e] before consonants. In order to remain on the safe side and avoid possible confusion with homophonous proto-syntactic devices (Bottari et al. 1992), only the [j] form was counted as a clitic. Another problem was the occurrence of examples involving the adult *il y a (it there has, 'there is/are')* construction which is phonetically reduced to *y a* even in informal adult speech. These examples were not counted as occurrences of *il*. They were included in the count for the object clitic *y*, however.

The forms *il* and *ils* are phonetically indistinguishable except in *liaison* contexts. So they were counted as the plural form only in two utterances in which the verbal agreement unambiguously required a plural subject:

(17) a. ils sont où les ciseaux A 2;9,2
        they are where the scissors
     b. ils sont là. A 2;9,30
        they are there

Following these guidelines, Hamann, Rizzi, Frauenfelder (1996) obtained table 6 indicating the occurrence of individual subject clitics. They point out that the 3rd person clitics (*il, on, c'*) are attested from the earliest recorded productions, while 1st and 2nd person singular clitics are massively attested only in the latest files, an observation also made by Kaiser (1994) with respect to bilingual children. As this result is surprising in view of Clark (1985)'s findings, the authors mention that the late occurrence of *je* in their count could be due to the restrictive way of distinguishing the occurrence of a clitic and a pro-form as discussed before. Non-third person plural clitics are not attested at all in the Augustin corpus.

Table 6: Breakdown of different subject clitics in the Augustin-corpus

Age	je	tu	il	elle	on	ils	c'	total	%of relevant verbal utterances
2;0,2			4		11		2	17	33.3
2,0,23			3				1	4	16.6
2;1,15					4			4	25.0
2;2,13			4	1	9		2	16	36.3
2;3,10			5		7			12	35.3
2;4,1		1	4		1		4	10	18.2
2;4,22			10				1	11	22.9
2;6,16			10	1	2		12	25	24.7
2;9,2	18	12	13	12	3	1	21	80	55.2
2;9,30	22	11	13	18	7	1	27	99	73.9
total	40	24	66	32	44	2	70	278	42.6

According to the readjustments discussed above, table 7 illustrates the occurrence of object and other complement clitics in the Augustin corpus, calculated for each recording against the total of complement taking verbs occurring in that session. This count includes all occurrences of verbs with an overt direct or indirect object or a complement (locative or partitive). It also includes verbal utterances without an overt complement if the verb obligatorily takes a complement. To facilitate the matching with object clitics, double complement taking verbs were counted twice. Unclear cases, where it could not be decided whether an object clitic, some unidentifiable pro-form, or a null object was present, were excluded. I have corrected the misprint in Hamann, Rizzi, Frauenfelder (1996) concerning the percentage of object clitics in the last recording given there as 23.9 to 33.9.

Table 7 : Breakdown of different object clitics in the Augustin-corpus

Age	me	te	se	le	la	les	en	y	total	% of comp. taking vbs
2;0,2										0
2;0,23										0
2;1,15										0
2;2,13				1					1	3.8
2;3,10										0
2;4,1										0
2;4,22	1									5.0
2;6,16	1						1		2	3.9
2;9,2	1	2	1	2		2	2		10	14.3
2;9,30	1		4			4		13	22	33.9
total	4	2	5	3		2	6	14	36	10.5

In order to give a better view of the development of object use, table 8 is presented here. The counting conventions are (more or less) the same as for table 7. This table gives the number of complement contexts as well as the number and percentages of missing objects, clitic objects, and lexical objects. It can be observed that the use of lexical objects is around 70% of all complement taking contexts up to the last recording where we find a sudden drop. As this recording shows the first substantial rise in object clitics, this finding is not surprising. Missing objects are fairly frequent in the beginning (20-40%), are equal in proportion to clitic use at 2;9,2 and then in a 10% jump in 28 days become less frequent than object clitics. Clearly, the child starts to use object clitics in a more systematic way in the last two recordings and at the same time shows a drop in object omission.

To round off their discussion of the occurrences of object clitics, Hamann, Rizzi, Frauenfelder give an exhaustive list of the object and other complement clitics produced by Augustin for which I refer to the original article. Some of the occurrences were not counted as they were rote-learnt forms from songs or the formula *s'il te plait 'please'*. The form *vas-t-en*, on the other hand was included because Augustin uses *s'en aller* productively as exemplified by his use of *elle s'en va*. There are two enclitic forms in positive imperatives (the one at 2;2,13 is the first genuine occurrence of an object clitic form; the second one is *vas-t-en* at 2;9,2). Cases of erroneous proclitic forms in positive imperatives, which occur in other corpora according to Haverkort and Weissenborn (1991) are not found in the Augustin corpus. Nor is there any 3rd person dative clitic.

Table 8. The use of object clitics in comparison with lexical objects and object omissions

Age	comp. contexts	null objects	%	object clitics	%	lexical objects	%
2;0,2	12	4	33.3	0	0	8	66.6
2;0,23	20	5	25	0	0	15	75
2;1,15	10	4	40	0	0	6	60
2;2,13	19	5	26.3	1	3.8	13	69.9
2;3,10	23	9	39.1	0	0	14	60.9
2;4,1	20	5	25	0	0	15	75
2;4,22	21	4	19.0	1	5.0	16	76
2;6,16	50	10	20	2	3.9	38	76.1
2;9,2	69	10	14.4	10	14.3	49	71.3
2;9,30	65	14	21.5	22	33.9	29	44.7
total	309	70	22.6	36	11.6	203	65.7

The data thus show the existence of a major difference in the acquisition of subject and object clitics and so confirm the prediction made in 2.1. They are also in accordance with recent findings of White (1996) concerning L2-acquisition or with the results presented in Kaiser (1994) and in Crysmann and Müller (2000) on bilingual French-speaking children. The latter authors' observation on the occurrence of reflexives before the occurrence of genuine object clitics is not confirmed by these data. As to language impairment, a substantial delay of object clitics has been observed by Jakubowicz et al. (1998) in the elicited production and by Hamann et al. (in press) in the spontaneous production of French children with SLI.

Hamann, Rizzi, Frauenfelder sum up their results in the following manner: Subject clitics are attested from the earliest recording in the Augustin corpus, they remain stable throughout the period from 2;0 to 2;6, and in the last recordings (2;9) their proportion of occurrence jumps to over half of the relevant verbal utterances. Object clitics are nearly absent in the period 2;0-2;6 and show an increase only in the last two recordings (2;9). This finding emerges very clearly from figure 1.

They conclude that there is a major difference in the acquisition of subject and object clitics: Subject clitics are attested from the earliest recording, remain stable throughout the period from 2;0 to 2;6, and at the age of 2;9 their proportion of occurrences is more than 50%. Object clitics are nearly absent in the period 2;0-2;6 and show an increase only in the last two recordings.

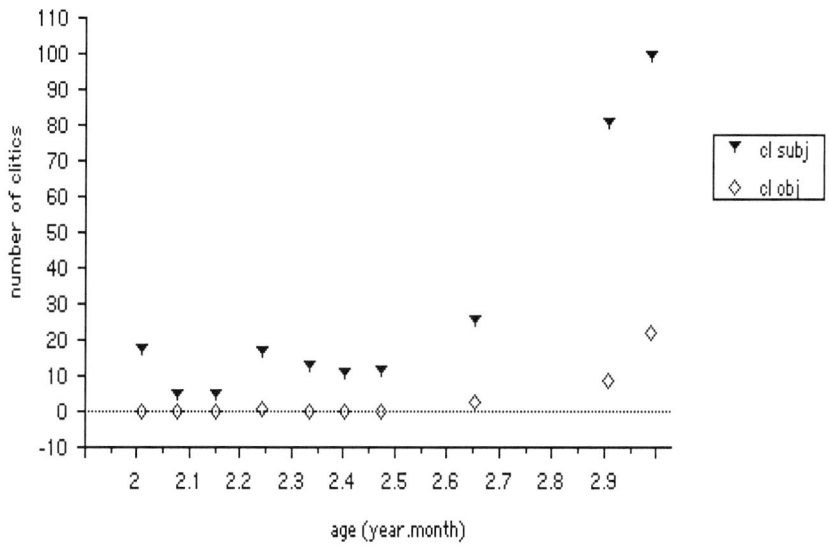

Figure 1: Number of Subject and Object Clitics as a Function of Age

Hamann, Rizzi, Frauenfelder (1996) also raise the question of how far this dissociation of subject and object clitics is restricted to children. In other words, they want to know, whether such a difference in use is also found in adults and how frequent object clitics (and, more generally, complement clitics) are in the adult French production. So they calculated the ratio of all subject and object (and other complement) clitics produced by the adults involved in the recordings (experimenter, mother, father, cousin, aunt, uncle). Table 9 shows the result of their calculation.

Table 9: Adult and child clitics in the Augustin corpus

	adults	child (A)
all clitics	3051	314
subject clitics	2332	278
	76.4%	88.5%
object clitics	719	36
	23.6%	11.5%

They conclude that adults produce fewer complement clitics than subject clitics (as expected, given the Extended Projection Principle and the fact that French is not a Null Subject Language). The ratio is almost 1:3, however, much higher than the 1:9 ratio of the child production. Moreover, even this huge global gap does not do full justice to the developmental effect shown by tables 7 and 8 because complement clitics are clearly mastered by the child in the latest recordings. In the first seven recordings only two complement clitics are produced by the child in comparison to 74 subject clitics, whereas in the last recording the child produces 22 complement clitics and 99 subject clitics. This gives a ratio already close to the adult ratio. Therefore Hamann, Rizzi and Frauenfelder seem to have caught a genuine developmental asymmetry, with subject clitics already productive at 2;0 and complement clitics becoming productive roughly after 2;6, and more precisely at 2;9, in Augustin's development.

2.5. The Delay of Object Clitics as a Phenomenon

The result of Hamann, Rizzi, Frauenfelder (1996) is not an isolated result. In earlier studies on the acquisition of French, it was claimed that object clitics are found relatively late in development, cf. Clark (1985). This was challenged in Weissenborn (1988) where the occurrence of the object clitics *en, le ,te, la, les* is documented in the speech of three French children between the ages of 2;0 and 2;4 (Weissenborn (1988:6,7). This result, though remarkable, is now somewhat isolated and could be due to different standards of transcription and analysis. Pierce (1989, 1992) found evidence of early mastery of the system of subject clitics in French, Friedemann (1992) observed a delay in the mastery of French object clitics, which was also found by White (1996) for L2-French, by Kaiser (1994) for French/German bilingual children, and by Jakubowicz et al. (1998) or Hamann et al. (in press) for French children with Specific Language Impairment. Haegeman (1996b) observes that object clitics are much rarer than subject clitics in early Dutch. On the basis of the new empirical material offered by the Augustin corpus, I would like to examine existing results on monolingual French children and discuss them in connection with the new data.

Friedemann (1992) presents the figures in table 10 for Gregoire and Philippe from the Leveillé corpus on the Childes data base.

Table 10: Percentages of subject and object clitics in the corpora of Philippe and Gregoire

	subject clitics	object clitics
Philippe (2;1-2;3)	18%	6.7%
Gregoire (2;0-2;3)	17%	2.5%

The bare figures are even more impressive: Gregoire produces only 1 object clitic in the whole period compared to 33 subject clitics, Philippe produces 42 object clitics compared to 192 subject clitics, but from the age of 2;6 his production increases to 35% object clitic use in complement contexts

In a recent cross-linguistic study, Jakubowicz et al. (1996, 1997) also show a substantial delay of object clitics in French. They made a cross-sectional study of the natural production of object and subject clitics in children with an MLU < 3.5 and compared this to the production of children with an MLU > 3.5. The basic result is that subject clitics are present to about 41%, whereas object clitics are used under 10% of the time by the children with the smaller MLU. Subject clitics occur 65% of the time, whereas object clitics occur about 30% of the time in the speech of the children with the higher MLU. Interestingly, Jakubowics et al. observed that for subjects the competing construction is omission (38%), whereas the competing construction for object clitics is the use of lexical objects, and omissions occur only 15% of the time. The children under survey were grouped as follows: there were four French children with an MLU < 3.5 and five children with MLU > 3.5. The ages ranged from 2;5. to 2;7. in the first group and from 2;4. to 2;5. in the second group. This is shown in table 11, for which the figures were reconstructed from the bar charts given in Jakubowicz et al. (1996) without taking all their different error types into account.

Table 11: Cross-sectional spontaneous production, French clitics
(Jakubowicz et al. 1996)

MLU<3.5	subject	object	MLU>3.5	subject	object
omission	38%	15%		10%	10%
clitic	41%	9%		65%	30%
lexical	5%	68%		7%	60%

The same study was also made for German with 3 children with an MLU < 3.5 and 3 children with an MLU > 3.5. Here attention has to be drawn to the fact that the count only considers non-adult omissions. This means that initial null subjects or null objects, which are possible in adult German and are analyzed as topic-drop, were not considered. This will distort the picture for the phenomenon of child null subjects in German because it is clear that children 'overuse' the topic-drop option and it has been argued that German child null subjects, even if initial, are not only topic-drop (see Hamann 1996b and chapter 10). Once it is clear that table 12 only considers post-verbal null subjects and in-situ null objects, the results are very interesting, however. It turns out that pronouns in subject position are used 65% of the time by the younger group of children, whereas object pronouns are used only 35% of the time, which, at first glance, seems to mirror the French asymmetry. However, there is a marked quantitative and also developmental difference: Object pronouns are used much more frequently than in French (which is also true for subject pronouns) and they do not seem to be acquired later than subject pronouns. Non-adult argument drop (post-verbal null subjects and in-situ null objects) shows a markedly different picture from French. We find 10% of subject drop compared to 40% object drop for the children in the low MLU group.

Table 12: Cross-sectional spontaneous production, German pronouns
(Jakubowicz et al. 1996)

MLU<3.5	subject	object	MLU>3.5	subject	object
omission	10%	40%		2%	0%
pronoun	65%	35%		80%	30%
lexical	20%	20%		15%	40%

2.6. Discussion of the Subject/Object Asymmetry

The discussion so far has shown that a sharp dissociation exists between the acquisition of subject and complement clitics, the latter being significantly delayed. For Hamann, Rizzi, Frauenfelder (1996), who do not analyze Colloquial French as a pro-drop language, this supports the view that subject and complement clitics are distinct theoretical entities and, in spite of their common properties, should not be fully assimilated. They find that the order of acquisition, subject clitics > object clitics, is consistent with the theory of markedness and acquisition that derives from Cardinaletti & Starke's (1995) typology of pronouns. Subject clitics, as "weak pronouns", (maximal projections constrained to occur in strict Specifier-head configurations with special licensing heads) are less deficient, hence less marked elements than object clitics, which are simple heads incorporated into the verbal host.

Jakubowics et. al (1996 and 1997) arrive at a different conclusion. The cross-linguistic parallel and the assumption that German subject and object pronouns are not scaled by morphological deficiency, leads them to argue against an account which assumes that the marked, i.e. the most structurally deficient form is acquired last. Following Kaiser (1992) and Zribi-Hertz (1994), they classify French subject clitics as agreement markers, not as weak pronouns. Under this analysis, there is no structural difference which could explain the difference in the acquisition scheme. These authors therefore suggest a pragmatic explanation: The high percentage of lexical objects and the low percentage of both object omissions and object clitics is due to the fact that the VP usually introduces new information. Therefore dropping the object or using a pronoun is not possible given pragmatic principles of discourse organization.

First, this explanation will have to find an account for the adult use of object clitics, which has been shown to be not as frequent as the use of subject clitics, but is certainly higher than the early child use. Second, many cases of object drop involve double-complement taking verbs, in fact the unambiguously transitive verbs are really only *mettre* 'put' and *donner* 'give', which require an additional direct object and a locative or dative object. Here, it is often the case that one argument is dropped, but not the other. Therefore an explanation involving the information value of the whole VP does not apply. The same follows from the fact that in German we do find 40% of object drop, so that a pragmatic account would have to explain this in some fashion. Moreover, a recent study on Danish (cf. Hamann and Plunkett 1997, 1998) shows that there is no effect of old or new information on subject drop. For this purpose the presence or absence of the subject or the referent of the subject in previous discourse was put into relation with the omission of subjects. No effect of previous mention of the subject could be established. Last, it is possible that the result on German can be explained in the same way as the result for French, i.e. by appealing to a scale of structural deficiency. It is clear that both German object and subject pronouns are ambiguous between a weak and a strong form as illustrated in (18) and (19).[4]

(18) a. Er, Peter, kommt gleich. strong
him, Peter, comes soon
'him, Peter, will soon come'
b. Er ist weg, der Topf. weak
he is away, the pot
'it is lost, the pot'

(19) a. Ihn, Peter, hab ich schon gesehen strong
him, Peter, have I already seen
'I have already seen him, (I mean) Peter'
b. Ich hab ihn schon gesehen, den Topf. weak
I have seen him already, the pot
'I have already seen it, (I mean) the pot'

Now, the observed higher rate of pronoun use in German may be due to the fact that the child starts off with the strong pronoun form which is not different in structure from any other DP.[5] Therefore pronouns will be used just as lexical DPs and do not introduce any difficulty. French deficient pronouns introduce such a difficulty and therefore are not used to such a high rate as in German. In view of the difference in the rate of subject and object clitic use by French adults, the asymmetry observed for German children is probably not as striking as it appears to be and we would need calculations on adult use. Moreover another scaling effect may be involved.

It is a rather solid result across languages that strong pronouns can only refer to human entities, but that weak pronouns can refer to both human and non-human entities as shown in (20) and (21), see Cardinaletti and Starke (1995, 2000).

			[+human]	[-human]
(20)	a.	Il est beau	ok	ok
		he is beautiful		
	b.	Lui est beau	ok	*
		HE is beautiful		

			[+human]	[-human]
(21)	a.	Sie ist schön	ok	ok
		she is beautiful		
	b.	Sie und die anderen sind schön	ok	*
		she and the others are beautiful		
	c.	Sie und die anderen Pflanzen sind herrlich grün	-	*
		she and the other plants are wonderfully green		

Thus an inanimate entity can only be referred to by a weak pronoun. If by some chance the German objects were mostly inanimate, while the subjects were mostly animate, then the above result would not be surprising and could be explained by exactly the upper half of the same scale of deficiency: strong > weak > clitic. More details on this interesting study would therefore be needed to give the results an unequivocal interpretation.

Kaiser (1994), who observes the same delay of object clitics in two bilingual children, points out that it seems to be a fact across languages that object agreement is aquired later than subject agreement, as Meisel and Ezeizabarrena (1996) show for Basque. He therefore assumes that whatever is responsible for this delay in the acquisition of object agreement, also is responsible for the delay in the acquisition of object clitics. Pursuing the same basic intuition, Jakubowicz et al. (1998) suggest that object clitics appear late because they are non-canonical arguments and have to be inserted in a non-canonical position, whereas subject clitics are part of inflection and the verbal paradigm is unproblematic for children in the Romance languages.

There is another, more recent approach, to the delay of object clitics. This is the so-called Unique-Checking Constraint (UCC) introduced by Wexler (1998), which also relies on a basic structural difference of object and subject clitics. Wexler (in press) assumes a rather classical analysis for subject clitics as suggested in 2.1. together with the analysis of object clitics as heads which have to move in order to check their features. The position to the left of the finite verb becomes the ultimate landing site because Wexler proposes a referentiality projection which is part of the inflectional layer. The object clitic must attain this projection because otherwise the interpretation will not be able to assign a referent to the clitic. Because the child can only check a D-feature once by the UCC, the child is apt to produce null clitics. This approach ties unique checking together with the idea that the occurrence of root infinitives implies that either the Agreement Projection or the Tense Projection are left out. I will therefore come back to this approach in chapter 7 in connection with the hypotheses about child infinitives.

As it stands, we can conclude that there is a developmental difference in object and subject clitics which has to be captured in any theoretical description of the clitic system of Colloquial French. This conclusion will be supported by the findings on the occurrence of clitics in tensed vs. un-tensed environments, which we will present in the last section.

3. DISTRIBUTIONAL CONSTRAINTS

In the literature one often finds statements to the effect that when they are used, clitics are always placed correctly (see Cardinaletti and Starke 2000, Hamann, Rizzi, Frauenfelder 1996). This can be taken for an indication that the respective lexical item is correctly classified as a clitic and that the syntactic consequences of such a classification are known. In other words, the child has correctly recognized his or her language as a language with clitic pronouns and has set the parameter accordingly. The study of Hamann, Rizzi and Frauenfelder (1996) provides detailed data with respect to the question of positions and investigates the contrast of the positions of clitic forms and the positions of one strong pronoun used by Augustin. This contrast then enables the authors to argue that the properties of clitics are acquired early.

In order to address the question, of whether French children respect the designated positions of clitics, Hamann, Rizzi, Frauenfelder (1996) start from an inventory of clitic and non-clitic positions. In adult French, the major clitic position is the immediate preverbal position. This can be adjacent to the verb, or can be separated from the verb by another clitic, as in *Je la lui donne (I it him give)*. There are also two kinds of immediate post-verbal positions occupied by clitics in special constructions: main questions for subject clitics (*est-il parti? (is-he left)*) and non-negative imperatives for object clitics (*prends-le (take-it)*).

In all other positions, clitics are excluded: they cannot occur in non-verbal utterances, i.e., they cannot be used in isolation (22a), nor in post-copular predicate position (22b), in post-verbal object position (22c), as objects of prepositions (22d), as right or left dislocated elements (22e-f):

(22) a. Qu'as-tu vu?   *le   (cf. OK ça)
        Who have you seen? Him
     b. * Jean est le   (cf. Jean est intelligent, Jean l'est)
        John is it   (cf. John is intelligent, he (it) is)

c. * Jean dit toujours le (cf. Jean dit toujours ça)
   John says always it (cf. John says always that)
   'John always says it' (cf. John always says that)
d. * Jean parle de le (cf. Jean parle de ça)
   John speaks of it (cf. John speaks of that)
   John speaks about it (cf. John speaks about that)
e. * Je le connais, le (cf. Je le connais, lui)
   I him know, him (cf. I him know, HIM)
   'I know him' (cf. I know HIM')
f. *Le, je le connais (cf. Lui, je le connais)
   him, I him know (cf. HIM, I him know)
   'him, I know him' 'HIM, I know him'

The authors then ask whether these distributional constraints are respected in the child's utterances and their answer is yes, "apparently without exceptions". In the Augustin corpus there are 281 occurrences of unambiguous subject or object clitic forms *je, tu, il, on, ils, ce, me, te, se, le, les, y, en*. The authors excluded the 32 occurrences of *elle*, a subject clitic which is ambiguous with the oblique form: *elle vient (she comes), pour elle (for her)*; see tables 4 and 5 for individual occurrences. None of the included clitic forms were found in a non-verbal utterance, or in any other non-clitic position of (22).

The next step is the comparison of the restricted distribution of clitic forms with the very wide distribution of the non-clitic demonstrative pronoun *ça*. In the adult grammar, in addition to preverbal subject position, *ça* freely occurs as a post-copular pro-predicate in the expression *c'est ça ('that's it')*, as a post-verbal object, as a prepositional object (the expression *comme ça (like this)* is presumably to be assimilated to this case), in right and left dislocated position (particularly in the expressions *c'est beau, ça (it is nice, this)* and *ça, c'est beau (this, it is nice)*) modified by the universal quantifier *tout*, and in non verbal utterances, for instance as a short answer to a question. This wide distribution is mirrored exactly by the early production. Consider the examples in (23) and the results given in table 13:

(23) a. ça toune   'ça tourne'   A 2;3,10
        that turns
     b. [teta]   'c'est ça'   A 2;0,2
        it.is that
        'that's it'

c. manger ça? A 2;0,2
   eat that
d. oter ça A 2;4,22
   empty that
e. e fais ayec ça   'je fais avec ça' A 2;6,16
   I do with that
f. c'est pour ça A 2;9,2
   it is for that
g. [e kate ta]   'est cassé ça' A 2;4,1
   is broken that
h. c'est quoi, ta   'c'est quoi, ça' A 2;6,16
   it is what that
   'what is it'
i. ça, c'est quoi? A 2;6,16
   that, it is what
l. Qu'est-ce que tu veux enlever? - ça A 2;4,22
   what is it that you want take away - that
m. Qu'est-ce qu' il y a encore dans la boite? - encore ça   A 2;4,1
   what is it that there has still in the box - still that
   'what is there still in the box? that (is still there)'
n. Qu'est-ce que tu veux reparer? - ça A 2;6,16
   what is it that you want to repair - that

Table 13: Occurrences of ça in different verbal environments in the Augustin-corpus

Age	Sub	Pred c'est ça	Obj	prep. Obj	comme ça	right disl.	left disl.	tout ça	utt	total
2;0,2	2	1	4	0	1	1	0	0	0	9
2;0,23	0	0	3	0	1	3	0	0	1	8
2;1,15	1	0	0	0	1	0	0	1	0	3
2;2,13	1	0	0	0	2	0	0	0	0	3
2;3,10	1	0	1	0	5	3	0	0	2	12
2;4,1	0	0	0	0	3	2	0	0	1	6
2;4,22	1	0	4	0	6	6	1	0	2	20
2;6,16	0	1	2	2	2	3	6	0	2	18
2;9,2	2	0	4	1	7	4	2	1	0	21
2;9,30	0	1	2	3	18	2	3	0	0	29
total	8	3	20	6	46	24	12	2	8	129

The authors report that of the 129 occurrences of *ça*, no less than 121 are found in a position from which a clitic would be excluded in the adult grammar, whereas all the 282 unambiguous clitic forms are correctly placed in clitic position. Already in the first two files (ages 2;0,2 and 2;0,23), 15 of the 17 occurrences of *ça* are in positions from which a clitic would be banned in the adult grammar, whereas all the 21 occurrences of clitics (see following tables) are placed in clitic position.

The Augustin corpus thus provides rather robust evidence that, from the earliest syntactically relevant production, the child masters the lexical distinction between clitic and non-clitic forms, as well as the major syntactic consequences of this distinction. So it can be concluded that the clitic parameter is set correctly.

4. THE DISTRIBUTION OF CLITICS IN TENSED AND UNTENSED CLAUSES

4.1. The Data

In section 1 of this chapter, it has been mentioned that the data on the acquisition of clitics may also be indicative for the model that will be best suited to capture the properties of this particular phase of language development. In this regard, the Augustin corpus provides more evidence for the earlier result of Pierce (1989) about the occurrence of subject clitics exclusively in finite contexts. The data analysis will be extended to the distribution of object clitics, however.

In adult French, subject and object clitics mirror the distribution of free subject and object NPs with respect to the tensed/untensed distinction: objects (clitic or not) can occur in both tensed and untensed clauses, while subjects (clitic or not) are restricted to tensed clauses, see (24) and (25) for examples:

(24) a. Que Jean aime Marie, c'est normal.
           that John loves Mary, it is normal
           'that John loves mary is normal'
      b. (*Jean) aimer Marie, c'est normal.
           (John) love Mary, it is normal

(25) a. Qu'il l'aime, c'est normal.
    that he her loves, it is normal
    'that he loves her is normal'
  b. (*Il) l'aimer, c'est normal.
    (he) her love, it is normal

Hamann, Rizzi, Frauenfelder asked what kind of pattern is found in acquisition and point out that root infinitives, contrary to adult embedded infinitives, appear to be able to co-occur with lexical subjects (examples from Pierce 1989).

(26) a. Monsieur conduire
    man drive
  b. Tracteur casser maison
    tractor destroy house

So it makes sense to ask whether subject clitics could occur in root infinitives. Pierce (1989, 1992), based on the French corpus available on Childes (MacWhinney and Snow 1990) and the Lightbown (1977) corpus, showed that subject clitics tend not to occur in this construction, an important property which sheds light on the structural constitution of root infinitives. Hamann, Rizzi, Frauenfelder then asked whether object clitics show the same asymmetric distribution and what this shows about the structural properties of root infinitives.

As Augustin is well within the "root infinitive" period, i.e. he produces non-adult infinitives in declaratives next to inflected structures, some indicative results could be expected. Such infinitives correspond to 10.9% of his verbal utterances on average.

For the count of finite constructions, imperatives and the complex constructions where the auxiliary or modal is a proform like [e] were excluded, cf. (14f). Thus the count includes finite forms like *mange* and clear Aux+Participle and Aux/Mod+Infinitive complexes. The count of root infinitives includes all the clear cases of non-adult infinitives, but also the cases where the pragmatic situation allows an infinitive in adult speech, (14b). Infinitives introduced by prepositions were not counted, (14d). For convenience these examples are repeated here:

(14) b. Exp: Tu veux quoi?   A: [ote tu ta] 'ôter tout ça'   A 2;0,2
          you want what   take-away all this

          d. [katschuk]pour faire pan pan   A 2;9,2
                to do *pom pom*
          f. [e pa deA~Ze sa] '[e] pas derang[e] ça'   A 2;0,2
                veux/vais pas déranger ça'
                want/will not disturb this
                'ai/est pas dérangé ça'
                have/is not disturbed this

Bare participles, though non-finite forms, were not included in the count for table 14.[6] On the other hand, special subject proforms (proto-syntactic devices, in the terminology of Bottari et al. 1992) as in the following cases were included.

(27)   a. [o] jouer [kitEl]   '[o] jouer, Christelle'   A 2;2,13
                                       play, Christelle
       b. [a tikot a bE jakEt]   '[a] tricote la belle jaquette' A 2;2,13
                                       knit the nice cardigan
       c. [e te pa]   '[e]   sais pas'   A 2;2,13
                                         know not
       d. [@] dois [fE]   '[@]   dois faire'   A 2;9,30
                                         must do

The occurrences of post-verbal subjects were not included separately in table 14. Post-verbal lexical subjects were simply counted as lexical subjects. If a right dislocation occurred as in an adult construction (i.e. with a preverbal clitic subject) then this case was counted as involving a subject clitic, not a lexical subject.

(28)   a. est plus beau ça   *lexical subject*   A 2;4,22
          is more nice this
          'this is nicer'
       b. c'est que là, que là il va, mon crayon *subject clitic* A 2;9,2
          it is that there, that there it goes, my pencil
          'it is there, there that my pencil fits'

Table 14: Occurrences of object clitics, subject clitics and other subjects in finite structures and in root infinitives in the Augustin-corpus

Age	verbal utt.		with clitic sub.	with clitic obj.	with 0-subj.	with lex. subj.	with s-proto-synt. device	(il) y-a case
2;0,2	fin	42	17		16	9		
	inf	7			7			
2;0,23	fin	14	4		6	2	2	
	inf	9			8	1		
2;1,15	fin	8	4		2	2		
	inf	7			5	2		
2;2,13	fin	38	16	1	11	9	2	
	inf	6			5		1	
2;3,10	fin	29	9		9	7	4	
	inf	4	3		1			
2;4,1	fin	48	9		25	8	6	
	inf	5	1		4			
2;4,22	fin	38	11	1	14	9	4	
	inf	8			8			
2;6,16	fin	93	25	2	30	22	15	1
	inf	7			7			
2;9,2	fin	133	80	8	28	12	13	
	inf	8		2	7		1	
2;9,30	fin	125	98	20	12	1	1	13
	inf	8	1	2	7			
total	fin 568		273	32	153	81	47	14
	inf	69	5	4	59	3	2	

All in all, the authors observed that, out of 278 subject clitics, 273 occur in a tensed clause and only 5 with an infinitive, i.e. 98.2% of all subject clitics occur in tensed clauses and only 1.8% in infinitives. So the results of Pierce (1989) for L1 - and of White (1996) for L2-acquisition of subject clitics are corroborated. On the other hand, 4 of 36 clitic objects occur with an infinitive and 32 with a tensed verb in the Augustin corpus. Thus 88.9% of all object clitics occur with tensed verbs and 11.1% with an infinitive. The details are given in table 14, the summary in table 15.

Table 15: Percentage of finite structures and root infinitives in clitic constructions

	finite verbs	infinitives
subject clitics	98.2%	1.8%
object cl.	88.9%	11.1%

Even though the overall number of object clitics is small, the asymmetry with subject clitics emerges clearly. Root infinitives are about 10% of the verbal utterances in the whole corpus, so object clitics appear to distribute homogeneously across the tensed/untensed distinction. On the other hand, subject clitics almost exclusively occur in tensed environments. All the five exceptional cases involve the subject clitic *on*; three of them occur in the same file and with the same verb *oter* so that the idiosyncrasy is extremely limited, see the original article for more detail.

Before coming to conclusions, let me show that the incompatibility of root infinitives and subject clitics is rather robust. Meisel (1990) reports that one of the bilingual children he studied never used a subject clitic with a non-finite verb form. This result on bilingual children is confirmed by Kaiser (1994), who found that one of the children uses the object clitic *le* "with different verbs, mostly non-finite ones", thus corroborating our finding about Augustin. In a handout used at the ISAS meeting in Trieste 1993, Pierce gave the figures of subject clitics as shown in table 16.

A count which was made subsequently, using the criteria as specified above, i.e. not counting bare participles, unclear verb forms and proto-syntactic devices, gives the comparison as shown in table 17.

Table 16: Use of subject pronouns
(from Pierce (1993) ISAS, Trieste handout)

	Fin	%	Non-Fin
Daniel (20-23mths)	104	88%	14
Nathalie (21-27mths)	162	96%	7
Philippe (25-30mths)	196	99%	3
Grégoire (21-25mths)	143	98%	3

Table 17: Use of subject clitics
Augustin (Hamann, Rizzi, Frauenfelder 1996), Nathalie and Daniel (Rasetti 1996)

	Fin	%	Inf
Daniel	87	98.9	1
Nathalie	103	100	0
Augustin	273	98.2	5

The evidence from the Augustin corpus shows that the rare object clitics of this corpus distribute homogeneously in tensed clauses and root infinitives, whereas subject clitics are basically limited to tensed environments. Together with the results from tables 15 and 16, it can be concluded that the (near) non-occurrence of subject clitics in root infinitives appears to be stable across individual learners.

4.2. Implications for the Analysis of Root Infinitives

In order to place this result on the acquisition of clitics in the appropriate acquisition theoretical context, let us make a brief excursion into the theories which are involved. This will only be a brief introduction into each of the hypotheses. These will be discussed in more detail later when we have considered data on null subjects and root infinitives. It will be interesting to see how the result on clitics bears on the different approaches, however, so that I risk a repetition later and incompleteness here in the interest of the subject.

In the beginning of the last decade, the debate between researchers in language development was centered very much on the early existence or non-existence of functional categories. On the one hand, there were researchers, notably Radford (1990), who assumed that children start with only lexical and thematic positions, so that the early structure is in effect a small clause. Projections are consecutively built up one on top of the other with the lexical acquisition of functional items and paradigms. On the other hand, Hyams (1986), Pierce (1989, 1992), Weissenborn (1990, 1991) and Poeppel and Wexler (1993) argued for the availability of the full array of functional projections from early on. To explain the obvious lack of similarity of adult and child speech, they assumed that certain parameters are open in the beginning or set to a default value or that certain principles of UG mature (cf. A-chain formation, Borer and Wexler 1987). A proposal which aimed for a compromise of these two approaches is Rizzi (1994) who suggests that children have the full array of categories if necessary, i.e. if material has to be accommodated, but can truncate structure if there is no such material. The proposal says in essence that economy constraints are stronger in child grammar than in adult grammar and that the structure building principles gain in force during language development.

The small clause approach is very convincing at first glance for two reasons. It explains the absence of determiners, inflectional endings (third person -s is indeed acquired very late in English), pronouns and complementizers as observed for English by assuming the absence of the D, the I and the C system. Often quoted in this context are the examples in (29a-c) which are from Radford (1990).

(29) a. Cup tea, want piece bar   Alison 1;10
     b. Wayne in garden, baby drive truck,
        mummy doing dinner, Kathryn no like celery
     c. Where does Daddy go? Child Repetition: Daddy go?

Moreover, the absence of these categories and the limitation to theta-structure implies directly that the case system operates vacuously in this phase and that movement cannot exist. There is no D-system on which case could be marked, which implies that there is no A-movement motivated by case reasons. Moreover, as there are no landing sites, the well-known instances of head-movement (V-to-I (to-C), N-to-D) are not possible, and A'-

movement is excluded for the obvious reason that A'-positions or operators cannot exist in a system where all available positions are lexical or theta-positions. Hence, the approach advocated by Radford predicts that in the earliest phase movement does not exist.

The arguments against such an approach crucially make use of the fact that the child is aware of the syntactic consequences of morphological processes in form-position correlations. This was used by Pierce (1989) to prove the early existence of verb movement and thus the existence of the verbal agreeement system, see section 7 of Chapter 1. A similar argument was presented by Guasti (1992, 1993) with respect to Italian. In Italian, however, negation does not provide a test for verb-movement, but the placement of object clitics does. So here it is the presence and the correct use of clitics by children which prove the early existence of verb-movement and so the existence of the I-system.

(30)   clitic + Vfin   *Vfin +clitic
        Vinf + clitic   *clitic + Vinf

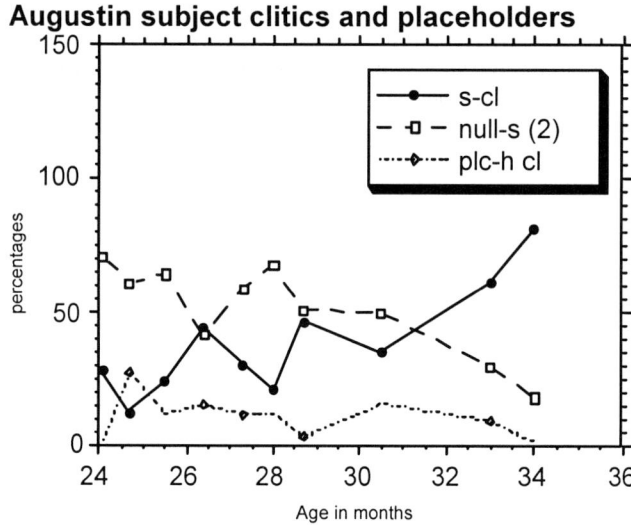

Figure 2: Placeholders, Subject Clitics and Null Subjects as a Function of Age

The early occurrence of subject clitics in French and their exclusive occurrence with finite verbs can also be used to argue for the early existence of an IP as a glance at (6) will make clear. Moreover, recent studies (see Gloor, Lachat and Maini 1996) have shown that Augustin also uses proto-syntactic devices to mark the subject clitic position, see figure 2. These studies do not only consider the first 30 minutes of each of the transcripts, but are based on the full corpus of 45 minutes each.

(31) a. [E mA~]   'ils mangent'   A 2;2,13
                                    they eat
      b. [e] mets dans la poche 'je mets...'   A 2;6,16
                                    I put in my pocket

The use of these placeholders together with the use of correct clitics is quite high in the first recordings and can be considered as clearly indicating that the syntactic position is available to the child even if the correct morpho-phonemic form of the clitics is not fully acquired.

This conclusion is valid only if we follow Bottari et al. (1992) who argue that these vocalic segments in front of lexical items of various types are inserted by the child not merely in order to complete a phonetic string, but because the child has made "some sort of inference about the structural organization of the sentence or of its parts" (Bottari et al. 1992:83). It is therefore crucial to determine that the vocalic segments that are used indeed function as placeholders, i.e. that they do not occur as phonetic approximations, that one segment can occur in different functional positions and that different segments can fill one position. Using these criteria as discussed by Bottari and al. (1992), Gloor, Lachat and Maini (1996) established the inventory of Augustin's placeholder segments and made the count accordingly.

It is interesting to note that Augustin's use of placeholders for determiners shows an important difference to the use of placeholders for subject clitics.

(32) a. [@ lapa]   le lapin
                                 the bunny
      b. [e] moto   le moto
                                 the motorcycle
      c. [a] bonhomme de neige   le bonhomme…
                                 the snowman

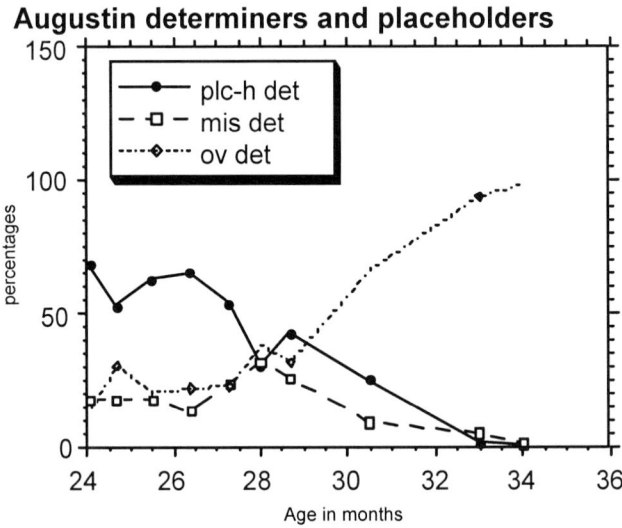

Figure 3: Placeholders, Overt and Non-overt Determiners

Augustin's determiner placeholders (figure 3) show the typical behavior in that the use of the placeholder is the alternative to the use of a correct form while omissions are fairly rare, and with the characteristic crossing of the graphs for placeholders and correct forms (see Bottari et al 1992). Augustin's use of clitic placeholders is quite different (figure 2). The predominant form in the first recordings is the missing subject and this is counterbalanced by correct forms together with placeholders. This behavior of subject placeholders clearly argues for the grammatical nature of the null subject phenomenon in child language, but their use by Augustin also argues for the early existence of a syntactic position.

Hence on the one hand, clitics provide proof for the existence and use of functional categories in child grammar. On the other hand, however, the phenomenon we have described, the non-occurrence of subject clitics together with root infinitives (cf. Pierce 1989, Weissenborn 1988, Friedeman 1992 and Hamann, Rizzi, Frauenfelder 1996) is an argument against any analysis of child root infinitives which assumes the full array of functional projections.

We have already excluded an analysis which assumes a total lack of functional structure. So the straightforward account as given by Radford (1996a) where root infinitives are VPs without any further structure need not be further pursued. The remaining two possibilities to account for these infinitives are a model which assumes optionality or underspecification of tense as originally proposed by Wexler (1994) and Hyams (1996) on one hand, or the possibility of truncating structures as proposed by Rizzi (1992) on the other hand. The general problem with the first sort of approach is the vague theory of tense which is assumed. In Part III, chapter 16 we will investigate what a semantic theory of tense can contribute towards a solution of this problem. Rizzi (1994) outlines his assumption that the CP is the root of any adult clause but that this need not be the case for child grammar. So children can truncate at any projection below CP. If they truncate below TP, the result is a root infinitive.

At first glance, there is not much difference between these two approaches. Both claim that in principle the full array of functional projections is available and both aim to capture the fact that the TP is inactive in a root infinitive. At second glance, there is a principled difference. Though projections can be activated if there is material to be accommodated in Rizzi's system, this system does not allow a projection to be missing if there is higher material. Thus, if the CP is activated as it would certainly be in a question with a fronted Wh-word, the claim is that then all other projections must be equally present and so no root infinitive could occur. So, the prediction is that if the TP is truncated, every higher projection must also be truncated. In the other approach, the TP (or the AgrP) can remain inactive, while the rest of the structure is available. Much the same has been proposed by Roeper and Rohrbacher (2000), so that in this light the truncation approach is more radical and leads to very clear predictions which we will discuss in detail later on.

What is interesting for our present discussion is the fact that the approaches which assume the full array of higher projections even for root infinitives will have to explain why subject clitics cannot occur in this context. The agreement projection would still be available even if tense is not activated, the clitic has a landing site and could cliticize to an empty head. Especially the missing AUX analysis for root infinitives as suggested by Boser et al. (1992), must explain this finding about the restriction of subject clitics to finite contexts. Boser et al (1992) suggest an anlysis as in (33a) for a German child infinitive, which would give something like (33b) for French.

(33) a. [$_{CP}$ der$_j$ [$_C$ e-aux] [$_{IP}$ t$_j$ [$_{VP}$ eine hose anziehen] [$_I$ t-aux]]]
           that   a trousers   on put(inf)
          'that one puts on a pair of trousers'
    b. [$_{IP}$ monsieur$_j$ [$_I$ e-aux] [$_{VP}$ t$_j$ [$_V$ conduire]]]
          gentleman   drive

Phonological clitics can cliticize to empty functional heads as shown by Haegeman (1993) in (34a, b) so that the problem becomes clear.

(34) a. Ik denk dat Marie t Jan wel zal zeggen
       I think that M.   it Jan well will say
    b. zo kan jij t ook doen he
       so can you it also do he

A subject clitic could well be inserted in SpecIP in (33b), an analysis that allows full structure for root infinitives. The same problem surfaces in the recent accounts of underspecified tense or agreement of Hyams (1996), Hoekstra and Hyams (1996), or Schütze and Wexler (1996a,b). The latter authors assume that either tense or agreement is underspecified in a root infinitive, but agreement can be active and must be active if there is a case marked nominative subject. This is clearly the case of a subject clitic. Let us thus assume that the agreement projection, if activated, can receive a subject clitic, but in the given system it would still be possible for the tense phrase to remain inactive. So there is no principled reason to exclude an infinitive from surfacing with a subject clitic - unless specific assumptions are made about the properties of clitics and of the French infinitive morphology. This is indeed what Wexler (1997 and 1998) suggests. He assumes that *parler* only results if both agreement and tense are not specified or missing, whereas the combination [+agr, -tns] will lead to the stem form *parl*, which is then usually analysed as finite, but in Wexler's account would come out as non-finite. If the French infinitive is so specified then it follows that subject clitics cannot occur in infinitives, but it remains to be seen whether this specification of inflectional forms is capturing the facts and how it agrees with the results about verb movement obtained by Pierce. In Rizzi's account it is clear that once the agreement phrase is activated, the tense phrase is active as well and so subject clitics cannot co-occur with root infinitives.

We have now used the evidence we found about French clitic acquisition to argue for a specific approach to language development. In the last section I would like to take up the findings about object clitics and use those together with the assumptions of the truncation approach to argue for a specific cliticization site of French object clitics. In this case, child data together with a certain approach to language development provide evidence for certain theoretical assumptions.

4.3. Implications for the Position of Object Clitics in French

The possible occurrence of object clitics in root infinitives has a clear implication for the analysis of both root infinitives and Romance cliticization, as Haegeman (1996b,e) points out. If root infinitives are truncated structures (Rizzi 1994), then the point of truncation must be at least as high as the functional head that hosts object clitics. Conversely, if the point of truncation is necessarily lower than TP, then the landing site of French complement clitics must be lower than T^0. So acquisition data may bear directly on the much-debated question of the landing site of Romance cliticization, and help to drastically narrow down the range of possible candidates. Let us work out this suggestion in more detail and also use cross-linguistic child data to show what the approach will predict.

Haegeman (1996e) presents a comparison, cf. table 18, of the child use of clitics in French and of weak pronouns in Dutch which shows that Dutch weak pronoun subjects cannot occur with root infinitives, but neither can Dutch weak pronoun objects. So the child data are similar with respect to subject pronouns for French and Dutch, but different with respect to object pronouns.

Table 18: Distribution of clitics and weak pronouns in French and Dutch
From Haegeman (1996e)

	%RI	su-cl/WP	RI	%RI	o-cl/WP	RI	%RI
Aug.	10.8	278	5	1.8%	35	4	11.4
Hein	16.6	472	0	0	53	0	0
Thom.	18.2	643	0	0	25	1	4.0
Niek	12.2	531	0	0	93	0	0

As Haegeman argues elsewhere (Haegeman 1993, 1996b), weak pronoun objects in Dutch raise as high as AgrSP. Therefore it is not astonishing that they do not occur in root infinitives if we adopt the truncation analysis and use the same arguments as above. Let us now exploit our findings for French adult language. It is important to examine infinitive examples because in finite contexts, the verb picks up the clitic and obscures the facts about the cliticization site of the object clitic.

From the example (35a) we can deduce that the specifier of the NegP which hosts *pas* 'not' is higher than the object clitic. (35b) shows that the floating quantifier *toutes*, 'all' which is a subject, must also be lower than the NegP, it must thus be in the specifier of TP. The data from child language and (35c) show that the specifier of the TP is higher than the object clitic, and the facts of (35d), where another floating quantifier object occupies a specifier position lower than Spec TP, identify this positon as SpecAgrOP so that the cliticization site must be $AgrO^0$.

We can thus conclude from these data that the French cliticization site is AgrO. Belletti (1999), however, argues from facts of enclisis and proclisis that Italian object clitics indeed use this cliticization site, but that French object clitics move as DPs to SpecAgrOP and cliticise only later. The evidence from French child language seems to argue, however, that the cliticization site is below TP and that child root infinitives include at least the AgrOP.

(35) a. Ne pas les acheter serait une erreur
ne not them to buy would be an error
'not to buy them would be a mistake'
*ne les pas acheter serait une erreur
ne them not to buy would be an error
b. Les filles ont decidé de ne pas toutes acheter les livres
the girls have decided of ne not all to buy the books
Les filles ont decidé *de toutes ne pas acheter les livres
the girls have decided of all ne not to buy the books
'the girls have decided not to buy all the books'
c. Les filles ont decide de toutes les acheter
the girls have decided of all them to buy
Les filles ont decide *de les toutes acheter
the girls have decided of them all(subject) to buy
'the girls have decided not to buy all of them'

d. Les filles ont decidé de toutes acheter les livres
    the girls have decided of all(subj) to buy the books
    les filles ont decide de toutes tous les acheter
    the girls have decided of all(sub) all(obj) them to buy
    'all the girls have decided to buy all of them'

5. SUMMARY

Let us sum up the data from French child language concerning the acquisition of clitics and rearrange the findings, discussing first their relevance for acquisition theory and then for linguistic theory in general.

With regard to 'earliness' it emerges clearly from the data reported in section 3 that at the age of two, Augustin already masters the major constraints that limit the distribution of clitics and weak pronominal forms. Already in the earliest recordings, he produces a variety of subject clitics, which are always placed in the correct position; the first object and complement clitics also occur correctly placed in a position adjacent to the verb. The observance of such distributional constraints is further supported by the comparison with the free distribution of the non-clitic pronominal form ça, which is produced in a large array of environments from very early on. As often observed before (see the discussion in section 4.2.), the acquisition of the morpho-lexical properties of an item goes hand in hand with the mastery of its syntactic properties. In so far as there is a parameter that marks a language as possessing clitic pronouns or as having special positions for clitics, it can be deduced that this parameter is set early. Moreover, these results clearly argue for the early existence of functional categories and thus give an indication which approaches to language development can be excluded.

Pursuing the latter point, there is, nonetheless, evidence for a certain lack of structure in root infinitives. The difference between subject and complement clitics with respect to the tensed/untensed distinction points to this conclusion. The rare object clitics of the Augustin corpus distribute homogeneously in tensed clauses and root infinitives, whereas subject clitics are basically limited to tensed environments. This emerges as a very stable result after further comparison with data from other children. It indicates that the full array of functional projections, though available in principle, is not activated in child root infinitives. Root infinitives are truncated below TP, but include the AgrOP. Moving away from pure acquisition theory, we can deduce that the cliticization site of French object clitics is narrowed down considerably and is most likely the AgrOP, while Dutch object pronouns move higher up.

The most important finding, reported in section 2, is that the occurrence of object and complement clitics appears to be significantly delayed with respect to subject clitics. Only two genuine examples of object clitics are found in the first 7 files of Augustin's production (2;0,2 - 2;4,22); in the same period he has already produced 74 occurrences of 5 different kinds of subject clitics. That this cannot be attributed to some general, perhaps pragmatically governed, tendency to pronominalize subjects and avoid pronominalization of objects is evident from the distribution of the non-clitic pronominal form *ça* in the same period, which occurs 6 times in subject position and 12 times in object position. Hamann, Rizzi, Frauenfelder's result on the delayed occurrence of object clitics confirms previous findings by Friedemann (1992) on a different French corpus, by White (1996) on the L2-acquisition of French clitics, by Kaiser (1994) on bilingual children, and by Haegeman (1996b) on early Dutch. It has since been confirmed by Jakubowicz et al (1996, and 1997). Hamann, Rizzi, Frauenfelder ague that the order subject clitics > object clitics is consistent with the theory of markedness and acquisition that derives from Cardinaletti & Starke's (2000) typology of pronouns. Subject clitics, as "weak pronouns", (maximal projections constrained to occur in strict Specifier-head configurations with special licensing heads) are less deficient (hence, less marked) elements than object clitics, which are simple heads incorporated into the verbal host. This order of acquisition is also consistent with the assumption that subject and object clitics occupy different positions and thus bring into play different functional categories, as suggested by Sportiche (1992) for French, by Haegeman (1996b) for Dutch and by Crysmann and Müller (2000) or White (1996) for the bilingual or L2 acquisition of French. It seems to be somewhat counterintuitive, however, to assume that the higher position is filled first unless one makes certain assumptions about the case system (Eisenbeiss 1994) and its influence on AgrOP. Another account for the delay of object clitics, avoiding the latter problem, is the Unique-Checking-Constraint introduced by Wexler (1998) which basically makes the same theoretical assumptions as discussed here as the classical account in section 2.1. The result is not compatible, however, with a theoretical analysis where subject and object clitics are treated as the same type of syntactic entity with the same ultimate landing site.

I hope that chapter 2 has provided an insight into the most salient facts of the acquisition of French clitic pronouns. But apart from the data presented here, chapter 2 also hoped to show how generative acquisition research has begun to contribute to theoretical analyses and to the models which can reasonably be assumed for the development of language.

CHAPTER 3

THE BINDING PRINCIPLES AND ACQUISITION RESEARCH

1. OVERVIEW OF BINDING AND ITS ACQUISITION

1.1. Theoretical Background

After the presentation of the results on the early production of French clitics, the referential properties of clitic pronouns and their mastery by French children will be investigated. This investigation is largely comparative and will draw many arguments from cross-linguistic results. It also requires some formal apparatus.

I focus on the acquisition of binding, addressing the so-called 'Delay of Principle B' and the early availability of UG from the point of view of Romance. 'Delay of Principle B' is the somewhat misleading descriptive term for the observation (see Wexler and Chien 1985) that young English children already know the interpretative constraints on anaphors and referring expressions, but have difficulties in constraining the interpretation of pronouns. The adult interpretations are shown in (1a,b,c), where coindexed terms are interpreted as referring to the same individual and contraindexed terms usually refer to different individuals.

(1) a.   John$_i$ saw himself$_i$/*himself$_j$
   b.   John$_i$ saw him$_j$/*him$_i$
   c.   John$_i$ /he$_l$ saw John$_j$/*$_i$

1.2. The Standard Binding Principles

The constraints governing the assignment of reference to these different types of nominal expressions illustrated in (1a,b,c) have been formulated in the **Standard Binding Theory** as given in (2).

(2) a. **Principle A:** An anaphor is bound in its governing domain
 b. **Principle B**: A pronoun is free in its governing domain
 c. **Principle C**: An R-expression is free in its governing domain.

These principles are considered to be part of UG for the following reasons. They seem to be universal, they cannot be deduced from direct evidence (the classical poverty of stimulus argument), and they manifest themselves "early".

Universality of these principles has been shown for language after language with the demonstration that the variable part of the above principles is the specification of what counts as the governing domain in a language and which elements are subject to the principles (for a different view see Zribi-Hertz 1994). These specifications therefore have to be considered as parameterized. The poverty of stimulus argument in its turn has two supports. As emerges from the examples (3a-d), it cannot easily be determined from the available evidence in which cases a pronoun can and in which cases it cannot corefer with a possible antecedent.

(3) a. John$_i$ says that he$_i$ is tired
 b. *He$_i$ says that John$_i$ is tired
 c. When he$_i$ was arrested, John$_i$ was with his wife
 d. The people who know him$_i$ well say that John$_i$ is very intelligent

In fact, a rule in terms of linear sequence suggested by (3a) and (3b), turns out to be false when (3c) and (3d) are examined: the rule governing non-coreference for pronouns can only be stated by using structural information about the sentence, notably Reinhart (1983)'s notion of c-command. Formally, binding is defined in terms of c-command and co-indexation, therefore these principles act as (local) constraints on possible indexations as shown in (1a,b,c). The appeal to structure makes the rule inaccessible to direct evidence.

The second argument comes from acquisition. The binding principles are constraints, so the child needs to encounter unacceptable meaning-utterance pairs, and this is the sort of negative evidence that is not available - even if we admit grammatical corrections and indirect negative evidence as help for the child. McKee (1992:24) gives a summary of this argument: "Mastery of the grammatical constraints on binding demands acquisition of knowledge not apparent in the children's linguistic input".

The argument has recently found even more support in a study by Thornton and Wexler (1999), who consider the binding properties in structures of VP-ellipsis. These are structures like (4a,b), where the second pronoun is not overtly given.

(4) a. Papa Bear licked him and Brother Bear did too.
    b. Papa Bear licked Brother Bear and he did too.

Thornton and Wexler (1999) were able to show that children respect the parallelism constraints involved in VP-ellipsis and respect principle B or Principle C as involved in (4a) and (4b) to the same degree they respect these principles in matrix sentences. They argue (Thornton and Wexler 1999:19): "What is striking about VP ellipsis structures is that the binding principles are applying to linguistic structure that is not phonologically realized. Therefore, showing that children know the range of interpretations that can and cannot be assigned to elided VPs would constitute evidence bearing on the innate specification of the binding principles. Such results could not be explained by learning, since ellipsis does not provide the positive input necessary for acquiring the relevant facts from experience".The Binding Principles thus traditionally provide one of the best arguments for poverty of stimulus and so for UG.

If, following these arguments, we assume that these principles are part of UG, the learning scenario becomes very simple. The child has to assign the features [+pronominal] or [+anaphoric] to certain lexical items and will do so on the positive evidence of sentences like (5a) in a situation where John is pushing somebody else, and (5b) in a situation where John is the agent and the patient of the action of scratching.

(5) a. John is pushing him
    b. John is scratching himself

1.3. The "Delay of Principle B" from a Crosslinguistic Perspective

The above scenario looks perfectly straightforward, and so we expect that young children know the binding principles as soon as they have acquired the lexical items involved. However, experimental research has presented us with a puzzle.

There is consensus that children as young as three years of age (or younger) know Principle A. This holds cross-linguistically and has been shown for English (see Wexler and Chien 1985, Grimshaw and Rosen 1990, Thornton 1990 and others) and Italian (McKee 1992), for French and Danish (Jakubowicz 1989), for Dutch (Sigursjónsdóttir and Coopmans 1996), and other languages with one possible exception, see Solan (1983). For Principle C, recent results (Crain and McKee 1986, Crain and Thornton 1990, Thornton and Wexler 1999) have also shown early mastery, though earlier results were skeptical (Chomsky 1969). However, there is some doubt whether Principle C is a binding principle at all, or whether it follows from pragmatic principles or from the other two principles as suggested by Reinhart and Reuland (1993) or Heim (1993). So far the results support the UG status of the principles by showing early manifestation. The problem only appeared when Principle B was examined. Experiments on English have shown that children can interpret (5a) with anaphoric reference to John and do so about 50% of the time (Wexler and Chien 1985, Coopmans and Philip 1995, and the other references above). This finding has been dubbed the "delay of Principle B".

As all the principles appeal to exactly the same kind of knowledge and mechanisms, an account postulating maturation of B at a time later than A or C can be excluded. The effect of delay has therefore been attributed not to any lack of syntactic competence, but to independent problems children may have. Pragmatic problems have been suggested by Grimshaw and Rosen (1990) and Chien and Wexler (1990). The processing of pronouns has been discussed as a factor adding to the difficulties in pronoun comprehension by Grodzinsky and Reinhart (1993). Grimshaw and Rosen (1990) and more recently Wexler (1996) see the difficulty as arising from children's knowledge that pronouns have to be anchored in context or discourse so that - if an anchor is not immediately obvious - they may look for this anchor in the wrong domain, overriding syntax with pragmatics.

The study of Chien and Wexler (1990) provided solid evidence for early mastery of the syntactic principle and suggested a pragmatic problem restricted to certain cases. Early mastery of Principle B was demonstrated if the potential antecedent is a quantified expression, but poor performance if the potential antecedent is a freely referring expression. This result led these authors to postulate the incomplete acquisition of the pragmatic rule P given in (6).

(6) Contraindexed NPs are noncoreferential unless the context explicitly forces coreference.

This rule does not come into play at all in the case of quantification where interpretation is semantically regulated.

Another pragmatic rule of interpretation or coreference was introduced by Grodzinsky and Reinhart (1993). It says in essence "use an anaphor to express coreference - if you can do this without a change in meaning" and can account for those contexts (see rule P) in which adults can interpret pronouns as coreferring and thus allow what has been called "accidental coreference" (see also Heim 1993). It is argued, that this rule together with a limited processing capacity of young children is ultimately responsible for the imperfect child performance. The evaluation of two possible syntactic structures and interpretations cannot be completed within a limited processing capacity, and the child is left to guess. We will discuss both these pragmatic rules in more detail in sections 2.1 and 3.3 of this chapter.

Cross-linguistic research, notably McKee (1992), has since challenged accounts appealing to a difficulty in pragmatics or processing. The assumption here is, of course, that the same processing limitations should apply to children of all languages at the same ages, and that the pragmatics of pronoun use are the same cross-linguistically. The latter may not hold, however, so that we will have to come back to the pragmatic problems in more detail. The cross-linguistic differences are striking enough, however, and will be presented below.

Using exactly the same experiment for English and Italian, McKee (1992) could show early mastery of Principle A and B for Italian, but a "delay" of Principle B for English. There are results on French pointing to the same early mastery of Romance pronouns (Jakubowicz 1989). Because the latter results were based on act-out tasks or a picture choice, which may only give a preferred, not all the possible interpretations, new experiments were conducted. Using the picture variant of a truth-value judgment task, a recent study on French described briefly in Hamann, Kowalski and Philip (1997) (abbreviated as H,K&P in table 19) fully corroborates the early mastery of pronominals in Romance. The same experimental procedure rendered almost exactly the same results for Spanish as shown by Baauw et al. (1997) and Baauw (2000). The same experimental technique had been employed by Sigurjónsdóttir and Coopmans (1996) (abbreviated as S&C), and Philip and Coopmans (1996a, 1996b) (abbreviated as P&C) had run partly the same experiment for Dutch and English. These authors found exactly the opposite for Dutch, namely a performance far below chance. The cross-linguistic results for children of 4-to-6 six years can be summarized as in table 19, giving children's accuracy of pronoun interpretation in environments subject to Principle B.

Modifying McKee (1992)'s question, it should therefore be asked what it is that masks children's knowledge in the case of Germanic pronouns to different degrees but does not interfere in the case of Romance clitics or the case of quantified potential antecedents. As it turns out, the answer to this question is more complicated than so far assumed.

Table 19: Cross-linguistic results on pronoun interpretation in principle B environments: percentage of adult responses of children between 4 and 6 years of age

language	experiment	lexical antecedent	quantified antecedent
Dutch	S&C	17%	-
	P&C	33%	80%
English	Chien&Wexler	50%	80%
	McKee	50%	-
Italian	McKee	90%	-
French	Jakubowicz	80%	80%
	H,K&P	90%	90%
Spanish	Baauw	90%	90%

In the manner of Coopmans and Philip (1995) and Philip and Coopmans (1996b), Hamann, Kowalski and Philip (1997) ran the classical binding tasks as given in (7) and (8), but extended the experiment to cases resembling Exceptional Case Marking (ECM) - or raise subject-to-object (Postal 1974), or clitic climbing - as given in (9) and found that in those cases performance is below chance level in French.

(7) a. La fille la seche   nearly adult
'the girl is drying her off'
b. La fille se seche   fully adult
'the girl is drying herself off'

(8) Chaque fille la seche   fully adult
'every/each girl is drying her off'

(9) a. La fille la voit danser   40% adult like
'the girl sees her dance'
b. La fille se voit danser   nearly adult
'the girl sees herself dance'

If the better performance in Romance is due to grammatical/lexical properties of clitics, then it is not immediately clear why the performance is worse in the ECM cases. Note that McKee's account concerning different binding domains for English and Italian predicts the same good performance in (7a) and (9a) because the binding domain for the clitic remains the same. If, on the other hand, the performance of English children is due to a pragmatic difficulty interfering with Principle B and clitics are not subject to this pragmatic rule, then it is at least not immediately obvious why this difficulty should be relevant for example (9a). A pragmatic difference of strong pronouns and clitic pronouns is that clitics cannot be focussed as suggested by Avrutin and Wexler (1992) in their discussion of McKee's results. This could not account for a difference in results between (7a) and (9a), however. Deferring a discussion of this point to 5.6. and 5.7, for the time being I will follow Avrutin and Wexler (1992), and assume that clitics are not subject to the coreference rule in simple configurations as (7a), an assumption which will be refined later but is reasonable for run of the mill contexts as (7a).

As to a lexical-grammatical approach to the problem, a comparison with Dutch shows the following. Coopmans and Philip (1995) and Philip and Coopmans (1996b) suggest that in Dutch, certain lexical properties of the pronoun may not be acquired for some time. As these properties may be crucial to the application of the General Condition on A-Chains as formulated by Reinhart and Reuland (1993) problems will ensue. I will argue in chapter 4 that due to positional properties, the Chain-Condition actually helps the Romance child to determine the lexical properties of clitics, so that difficulties due to a misclassification of phi or case features cannot arise (see also Hamann, Kowalski and Philip 1997). The good performance on (7a) also follows straightforwardly from an account of clitics and pronouns in terms of structural deficiency as suggested by Cardinaletti and Starke (1995).

None of the accounts proposed in the literature explains the chance performance in (9a), which is not so much reminiscent of Dutch, but more of the performance of English children in the English equivalent of the simple case of (7a). There are three possible explanations which will be discussed in more depth later. The first possibility is to assume a difficulty with the lexical entries concerning the referentiality of clitics. The second possibility is to investigate the problem with the idea that it is the experimental conditions that create a situational context which qualifies as a core context for accidental coreference. The third idea is that the ECM context involves a structural ambiguity that – for the child - offers a systematic way to allow accidental coreference. It is these latter two possibilities which are attractive for the hypothesis that young children may have a difficulty in tying semantic interpretations of single sentences into the discourse situation and opt for a solution that assigns reference to the pronoun within the sentence.

2. MODIFICATIONS OF THE BINDING THEORY IN RELATION TO THE ACQUISITION RESULTS

2.1. The Standard Principles and the Coreference Rule

However, not only acquisition results point to deeper problems in the standard theory of binding. Notorious theoretical difficulties with examples like (10a,b) have led to the extension of the binding principles with a rule regulating coreference as proposed by Grodzinsky and Reinhart (1993) and discussed in great detail by Heim (1993).

(10) a. If everyone hates Oscar, then Oscar hates him/*himself
 b. I dreamt I was Mel Gibson and kissed me/*myself.

Let us briefly sketch the ingredients of this approach in the LF-oriented variant discussed by Heim (1993). Some formal apparatus is helpful here as only a formalization can clarify the problem of Principle B and the assignment of reference. See Thornton and Wexler (1999) for a less formal introduction. We will adjust to more recent syntactic terminology in replacing Heim's NP by DP, and will sometimes simplify in trying to give the salient facts in a comprehensive way. But though we are using Heim's version, we have to keep in mind that the system we are discussing is the system proposed in Grodzinsky and Reinhart (1993). A discussion of Heim's own extensions will follow once the problems have been clarified.

The first assumption is that we have free, optional indexing of DPs. This means that any DP may, but need not, receive an index, and that different DPs in a sentence may receive the same or different indices. The binding principles are regarded as filters which apply at S-Structure or, in more modern terms, before Spell-out. They are formulated as in (11a) and (11b), and syntactic binding is defined as in (12a) and (12b).

(11) a. **Principle A**: An anaphor is A-bound in its Governing Category.
 b. **Principle B**: A pronominal is not A-bound in its Governing Category.

(12) a. **x binds y** iff x c-commands and is coindexed with y
 b. **x A-binds y** iff x binds y and x is in an A-position.

From the level where indexing has occurred, certain derivations then lead to the syntactic level commonly called Logical Form or LF, which can be interpreted by some variant of model theoretic semantics. The most important of these derivations is Quantifier Raising (QR), which, in this framework, applies optionally and freely to all types of DPs. Heim (1993:3,4) gives the following definition of QR. It replaces an indexed DP α_i by a coindexed trace, adjoins α (without the index) to a dominating node, and prefixes the sister constituent of α with a lambda operator indexed with i as shown in (13).

(13)   [CP .... α_i....]   => [CP α λ_i[CP ......t_i........].

Because QR is optional, a condition on possible LFs has to be added. All indices must qualify as logical variables, and an index is a variable, only if it is a) on a λ or b) on a trace and bound by a λ, or c) on a pronominal or anaphor and A-bound. This eliminates many possible derivations because it requires that, apart from A-bound pronominals and anaphors, all overt DPs, in particular all quantifiers and proper names, must wind up at LF without an index. This makes QR obligatory in many cases. It also implies that indexed pronominals which are not A-bound - and this is the normal case because of Principle B - have to be quantifier raised in order to render a permissible LF. Note also that only indices qualify as variables. This may seem a hairsplitting detail, but it is useful to keep in mind that coindexed NPs actually involve one and the same variable.

So now we have arrived at LF by derivations from the S-structure representations. Let us consider briefly what Heim's assumptions about LF imply. In order to assign referents to the terms in these LF-expressions, we have to interpret them in the usual model theoretic way. This means in particular that all the variables have to be interpreted by an interpretation function assigning an individual from the given universe (set of individuals) to each variable. Quantifiers are then defined in the canonical way over such variable assignments. So assignment of reference is a semantic process independent of the binding principles. The latter only regulate possible indexations. Let us first consider the interplay of indexation and interpretation in the straightforward case of anaphors as shown in (14).

(14)   a. SS:John$_i$ saw himself$_i$
       b. LF: John λ_i [t$_i$ saw himself$_i$]   LF: John λi [ti saw himself$_i$]

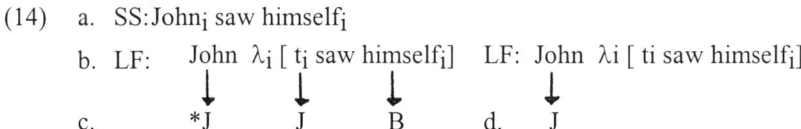

       c.   *J   J   B   d.   J

Here the underlined expressions stand for the values rendered by the interpretation function, i.e. for the actual individuals John and Bill. From Principle A we know that (14a) is wellformed, we have coindexed the c-commanding antecedent with the anaphor, so syntactically the anaphor is A-bound in its governing category as required. We also know that the particular interpretation chosen in (14c) is not possible, because both occurrences of the variable, the one on the trace and the one on the anaphor, are bound by the lambda-operator. The semantics of this operator requires, however, that the variable assignment pick John as the referent of this variable. Therefore in the case of anaphors, the syntactic constraint, Principle A, and the model theoretic semantics of the lambda-operator together rule out any variable assignment that chooses different referents for *John* and *himself$_i$*. The only possible interpretation is given in (14d). Let me point out here that in the given framework the locution 'bound variable anaphora' though accurate in the sense that the variable is lambda-bound, could be highly misleading if we confuse LF and SS and think of the anaphor as the variable bound by the antecedent. The anaphor is syntactically A-bound by the antecedent, semantically the variable on the anaphor is bound by the lambda-operator.

There is another way of interpreting the locution 'bound variable anaphor', however. The above conditions on variables arise from the assumption that natural language does not allow free variables (which implies that "free" pronouns have to quantifier raise as well). If we forgo this assumption for a moment and allow free variables in the manner of Montague (1974), who treated pronouns as variables, then (14a) could be created and interpreted in the following way. We could assume that first a variable *he$_i$* had been merged with the transitive verb, then, in a second step, the variable *he$_i$* had been merged with the VP (already containing this variable as an object). We then need a rule altering the lower *he$_i$* to *himself$_i$* in certain cases. Now we have one variable in two different morphological shapes, which again implies that only the index can count as the variable. Because a variable assignment is a function and the definition of a function requires that there is a unique value for any element in the domain of the function, the two occurrences of the variable can never refer to two different individuals. If we then 'quantify in' *John*, both occurrences of the variable necessarily refer to John. The beauty of Montague's 'quantifying in' was that it could turn any noun phrase into an operator which could 'bind' a variable. It kept semantics parallel to syntax and captured the intuitive import of indexation for assignment of reference. It seems that this idea, the idea of 'quantifying in' the antecedent, is in the back of one's mind when one speaks of the 'bound variable anaphor'. We could also alter the locution and speak of the 'identified anaphor', because the referent of the term *John* in (15b) identifies the variable in so far as the variable assignment must be such that it assigns the same referent to the variable in the lambda-expression.

But let us return to the Logical Form of GB-Theory, where free variables are not allowed, and examine the more complicated case of pronouns.

(15) a. SS: *John_i saw him_i
      b. LF: John λ_i [t_i saw him_i]

If the pronoun has been coindexed with an antecedent as in (15a) we get exactly the same reading or model as shown for (14d). (15b) is an admissible LF because the indexed pronoun is A-bound, so the index qualifies as a legitimate variable, and there is no problem with interpretability. By the above definitions, the pronoun is A-bound, however, and so ruled out by Principle B before Spell-Out. Let us therefore contraindex the pronoun and the name as shown in (15c).

(15) c. SS: John_i saw him_j.
      d. LF: *John λ_i (t_i saw him_j)
      e. LF: John λ_i (him λ_j (t_i saw t_j))   John λ_i (him λ_j (t_i saw t_j))
                 ↓   ↓   ↓   ↓
      f.   J   B   g. J   J

(15c) is an admissible SS. (15d) is an inadmissible LF, however, because the index j is neither on an A-bound pronoun nor on a λ. (15e), on the other hand, is a possible LF, given twice here to show the interpretations. The interpretation in (15f) is natural as it is a convention in mathematics to give different names to variables standing for different things. In normal speech, we find the same convention when different names are given to different persons, and Chien and Wexler (1990)'s principle P seems to be a pragmatic version of this convention applied to pronouns. This does not exclude, however, that the convention can be overridden and two names refer to the same person as Shakespeare knew well, when he wrote: "Glamis has murther'd Sleep, and therefore Cawdor Shall sleep no more, Macbeth shall sleep no more!" So there is nothing to prevent an interpretation which assigns the referent J to the pronoun *him*. This emerges even more clearly, when we realize that in (15e) the variable, i.e. the index, has nothing to do whatsoever with the interpretation, the decisive factor being the semantics of the λ-operator and the interpretation of the expressions *John* and *him*. So pronouns can be contraindexed at the syntactic level and still corefer because the assignment of reference is independent of the syntactic principle, and it is this phenomenon which has been called "accidental coreference" (Lasnik 1989). Interestingly, case (15g) of accidental coreference is not explicitly considered by Heim in her discussion of Grodzinsky and Reinhart (1993). She only considers the case where the pronoun is left without an index. This creates the paradigm case of an LF allowing accidental coreference. But in effect, the case where the pronoun is unindexed at SS and the case where it obeys Principle B at SS are not much different with regard to interpretation when we examine their respective LFs. In both cases, quantifier raised or left in-situ, the pronoun itself is unindexed, and it is the utterance context which has to provide a referent. Because the interpretation of these pronouns only depends on the context of utterance, we can call them deictic. In both the above cases, contraindexed or unindexed, sortal restrictions like gender, number, person feature and case play a decisive role in determining possible reference, but also interacting pragmatic factors including salience and overall plausibility. Crucially, there is the coreference rule (16) that acts as a restriction on possible interpretations and so regulates accidental coreference.

(16) **Coreference rule:**
α cannot corefer with β if an indistinguishable interpretation can be generated by (quantifier raising β and) replacing α with a variable A-bound by the trace of β.

The complicated formulation arises because we cannot say for (13a) that the term *John* A-binds the variable (unless we think of quantifying in). A name is not a quantifier and cannot bind a variable, but we can quantifier raise the name and so λ-bind the variable which gives the familiar (15b), repeated here for convenience.

(15) b. John λ_i (t_i saw him$_i$)

It is to be noted that we do not distinguish between *him* and *himself* on this level. By definition, *him$_i$* qualifies as an A-bound variable in (15b) and the syntactic principles together with the lexicon will then direct the choice of *himself* as the morphologically correct form of A-bound anaphor. Therefore the interpretations of (15b) and (14b) are indistinguishable in the sense that they express the same propositions in a given context: (15b) is true in any world where John saw John and so is (14b). Here the coreference rule applies and rules out (15a) in favor of (14a).

Note also that Chien and Wexler's Rule P, the convention to interpret contraindexed NPs as referring to different individuals, follows from the coreference rule: If coreference were intended, the coreference rule requires the use of an anaphor, i.e. of coindexation. The coreference rule, however, by inference specifies those cases where accidental coreference is possible – and here Rule P speaks only of "contexts" which force coreference.

In order to show this, let us examine (10a). Heim (1993) puts this example in a context where a logic tutor tries to explain the law of Universal Instantiation, so the predicate in the premise and the consequent are meant to denote the same property, that of hating Oscar. So we interpret (17) in the following way:

(17) a. If everyone hates Oscar, then Oscar hates him

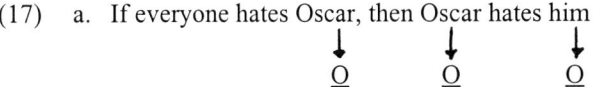

If we now apply the procedure of the coreference rule, we get (17b) as an alternative.

(17) b. If everyone hates Oscar, then Oscar λ_1 (t_1 hates him_1).

Here we have the predicate of hating Oscar in the premise, but the predicate of hating oneself in the consequent and this is not the intended meaning. Heim calls this a case of structured meaning because it matters how the ultimate interpretation is put together structurally. The reasoning for (10b) is analogous. But the decision as to the sameness of meaning is not always so easy, especially in identity statements, where accidental coreference seems to be possible in most cases.

(18) a. Is John the author of these articles?
How can you doubt it, John always quotes him.

In order to make (18a) possible, it is clearly not enough to think about extensional interpretations, all the names and masculine pronouns extensionally refer to the person John. The example is acceptable because the intensions, descriptions, guises are different: we are referring to the person John who the participants of the conversation know well and to the author of some articles whose identity has to be established. So the interpretations of (18a) and of an utterance similar to (18a), but with the pronoun substituted by an anaphor, are different at the intensional level. We need an additional level in our interpretative sketches as shown in (18b) which ultimately necessitates a reformulation of the coreference rule which we will not make precise here, however.

(18) b. LF: John always quotes him

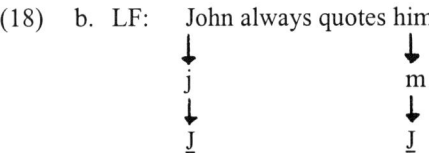

This modification makes it necessary to reconsider the discussion of (15b). It is not enough any more to prove that (15b) and (14b) express the same propositions. We have to establish that only one guise (individual concept, intention) is involved, which we tacitly assumed in discussing an unmarked context with one salient referent.

Summing up, we have two basic environments where the coreference rule will allow a pronoun to corefer with an antecedent. One is a context where structured meaning matters and the other is a context where different guises are introduced. Presumably, these are the contexts mentioned in Rule P that force coreference.

2.2. Accidental Coreference and Acquisition

Wexler and Chien (1985) and Chien and Wexler (1990) provide evidence that difficulties with a pragmatic rule is an important factor for the non-adult interpretation of pronouns by young English children. They found that English children have an anaphoric interpretation for (19a) about 50% of the time, but are 80% correct in (19b).

(19) a. Is Mama Bear touching her?
b. Is every bear touching her?

Philip and Coopmans (1996a,b) found the same: English children give 77% correct interpretations for (20b), and only 32% correct interpretations for (20a). For Dutch they also found that children perform significantly better with the Dutch equivalent of (20b), than with the equivalent of (20a). Hamann, Kowalski and Philip (1997) could establish a likewise good performance in the case corresponding to (20b) in French.

(20) a. The girl is pointing at her
b. Every girl is pointing at her

The reason for the bad performance in the case of (19a) and (20a) has been attributed to the fact that Principle P is not yet acquired, see the discussion in 1.3. of this chapter. Philip and Coopmans (1996) suggest that the trouble is not Principle P directly, but the imperfect mastery of the coreference rule. (See the discussion of the relation of these two rules in 2.1. of this chapter). This rule does not apply in (19b) and (20b) and so the effect of pure Principle B is seen there. In the a-examples, however, both Principle B and the coreference rule apply and the imperfect mastery of the rule masks the performance on Principle

B in so far as a correctly contraindexed pronoun may be interpreted as coreferential with the subject. We conclude that without a convention, which can be formulated as Rule P or as the coreference rule, contraindexation has no influence at all on interpretation in the accepted system of SS and LF. Some revisions are necessary to capture this intuitively correct explanation of the experimental results. But let us first examine the standard assumptions a bit more closely.

Avrutin and Wexler (1992:264) formulate the reason for the non-applicability of the pragmatic rule in the case of the quantified antecedent in the following way: "Quantifiers do not have any definite referents to be accidentally coindexed with (e.g. in the sentence *no bear sleeps*, the NP *no bear* has no reference: it is an operator)." Now this formulation is problematic for the simple reason that it confuses what the authors have very adroitly pulled apart in their foregoing argumentation: rules regulating coindexation and rules regulating the interpretation. It is not the referent that is accidentally co-indexed with an NP, it is two NPs which can be contraindexed, but can accidentally be assigned the same referents. We can save the argumentation by interpreting it as a sortal restriction: the quantified NP is an operator and does not carry a referential index. Thus it cannot be coindexed with the pronoun. So there is no room for ambiguity, and the coreference rule is not needed in these cases. (The operator cannot be contraindexed with the pronoun either, and so Rule P does not apply).

Another version of a pragmatic rule reminiscent of Grimshaw and Rosen (1990)'s original proposal is discussed by Wexler (1996) under the name of Grounding Principle:

(21)   An NP must be grounded

In (21) 'grounding' means that the NP's "reference must be made clear" (Wexler 1996). Wexler then describes the two basic ways of grounding. Either the NP itself points out its reference (proper name, deictic pronoun) or the NP is coindexed with another NP that is itself grounded. The explanation of the 'delay of Principle B' effect now is that the child over-accepts pronouns as grounded because the child cannot always calculate what a listener can know or infer. The child assumes that the pronoun is deictically grounded and that the listener can infer the reference – even if this is not the case.

What we want to keep in mind from this discussion is the fact that there is experimental evidence that Principle B functions flawlessly in those contexts where accidental coreference is either not possible or easy to exclude. It is the coreference rule or its weaker version, Rule P, which is the decisive factor in the "delay of Principle B" effects. Difficulties with the rule will indeed lead to non-adult interpretations. Chien and Wexler (1990) interpret such a breakdown as the lack of a pragmatic rule, Grodzinski and Reinhart (1993) argue that the processing load is too great: the child has to compute two possible interpretations, can't cope, stops and makes a random choice. Though both assumptions lead to different predictions as discussed in Avrutin and Wexler (1992)'s footnote 9, we wish to remain neutral as to the nature of the breakdown of the coreference rule, pragmatic or processing. On the whole, the coreference rule and difficulties with this rule seem well able to explain the adultlike performance on quantified expressions and the poor performance in cases like (19a) or (20a), especially on the assumption that in many cases pronouns are simply left unindexed like other overt DPs. This option would - on the surface of things - explain why Principle B seems to be frequently ignored: it simply does not apply in many cases.

This idea brings us straight to the crux of the matter, however, and leads to the rather heretical question whether the known experimental techniques tell us anything about Principle B at all or can only test the mastery of the coreference rule. This problem becomes evident if we take the time and reconsider our arguments about the irrelevance of contraindexation for the interpretation per se: at LF the pronoun, even if correctly contraindexed at SS, arrives without an index and has to be interpreted straight in context. Therefore, Principle B in its classical form, leading to the classical LFs, does not make any contribution to the ultimate goal of restricting possible referents without the aid of a pragmatic convention. Therefore, testing the possible readings children have of pronouns in played out situations or pictures cannot give any insights about the correct contraindexation of these pronouns at SS.

This conclusion is completely unsatisfactory, however, and calls for certain revisions as outlined in Heim (1993). One obvious step is to readmit free variables into the syntax. In that case the index on a pronoun can survive (so that an LF like (13d) would survive) and will make an important contribution to the interpretation. As it stands, what the child has to know first and foremost is the fact that pronouns have to be interpreted in the given context (discourse or situational) with only the help of phi-features and case restrictions while the lexical entry for the noun will further narrow down the referent of any definite DP. It does not come as a surprise that in such a situation pragmatic difficulties can be shown to exist as all the above experiments prove.

Discontent with the classical binding principles has lead to several reformulations of the binding theory which we turn to in section 3. In 3.1. we discuss the reflexivity framework which tries to reattribute interpretative content to syntactic indexation by a) focussing on the case where indexation is relevant for interpretation, the case of anaphors, and b) introducing a condition on the interpretation of pronoun indices. 3.2. looks at this new version of binding form the point of view of acquisition. In 3.3. we return to the system proposed by

Heim and consider the extensions she proposes in order to eliminate the above problems.

3. NEW VIEWS ON BINDING

3.1. Binding Theory and Reflexivity

The analysis of sentence (22) very early led to the generalization that Principle B only applies to semantic co-arguments (Ross 1982). If we accept this, then it is clear that (23) and other ECM-like cases are not constrained by Principle B.

(22)   James Bond noticed the gun near him/himself

(23)   * Max$_i$ heard him$_i$ criticised.

The fact is that the pronoun and the name are not semantic co-arguments, the arguments of *heard* are *Max* and the embedded clause, so if we restrict it to semantic co-arguments, Principle B does not apply in this case. We have to rule out (23) by other means.

Reinhart and Reuland (1993) make a condition on chains a central ingredient of their account of binding. Though they do not discuss the problems of standard Principle B, they reformulate the binding principles as conditions on Reflexivity, so that nothing is explicitly said about pronouns. This reformulation also requires that the movement properties of binding (Crossover effects) be captured in a different component. The reformulation of the binding principles in terms of reflexivity and reflexive marking as in (25) in turn relies on a typology of anaphoric expressions as in (24).

(24)		SELF (English)	ZICH (Dutch)	Pronoun
reflexivity		+	-	-
referential independence		-	-	+

(25)   **Condition A:**   a reflexive-marked syntactic predicate must be interpreted reflexively.
       Condition B: a reflexively interpreted predicate must be reflexive-marked.

Reflexive marking is either achieved in the lexicon where some predicates are marked as inherently reflexive, by the syntactic operation of adding a -*self* suffix as in the case of English, or by choosing the lexically reflexive marked pronoun as in the case of *se* in French. The definition is given in (26).

(26) a. **A predicate is reflexive**
iff at least two of its arguments are coindexed
b. **A predicate (formed of P) is reflexive marked**
iff either P is lexically reflexive with respect to an indexed argument, or one of P's indexedarguments is a SELF-anaphor.

The conditions talk explicitly only about coindexing, the lexical realization of coindexation and its interpretation. Condition B has much the same effect as the standard Principle B. It works only by exclusion, however, and it does not apply if the semantic argument of a predicate is not the pronoun but a sentence as in (22). This leads to a formal detail: while Condition B applies to semantic predicates, Condition A applies to syntactic predicates. There is another ingredient, the Chain Condition, which is neccessary to rule out (23) and as such may have the odor of ad-hoc rule introduction, but on the other hand can be viewed as an attempt to link syntactic indexing with possible interpretations. Reinhart and Reuland explicitly opt for the broadest possible definition of A-chain as given in (27).

(27) Any sequence of coindexation that is headed by an A-position and satisfies antecedent government is an A-chain (Reinhart and Reuland 1993 : 693,4).

This subsumes the Chomskyan concept which considers only trace-tailed coindexations to be A-chains (only chains originating through genuine movement are A-chains in Chomsky's terms) and chains arising through coindexation for purposes of interpretation. In fact, it integrates both types of chains and treats a sequence of indices arising through a combination of movement and interpretative coindexation as an A-chain. The crucial condition on such general chains is formulated in (28).

(28) **General Condition on A-chains**
A maximal A-chain ($\alpha_1,....,\alpha_n$) contains exactly one link - α_1 - that is both [+referential] ([+R]) and Case-marked.
(Reinhart and Reuland 1993: 696)

For [+R] expressions it holds that they carry a "full specification for phi-features and structural case" (Reinhart and Reuland 1993:697). This is only a necessary condition for referentiality not a sufficient one, however. That this is so can be seen easily by considering that English *himself* and *him* have the same phi- and case features, but the pronoun is [+R] by the above typology, the anaphor is [-R]. It is generally held that [-R] expressions are "referentially defective...which entails that they cannot be used as demonstratives, referring to some entity in the world", (Reinhart and Reuland 1993:658).

We can now illustrate the effect of the Chain Condition with English examples as in (29). We use a trace here because we assume raising to AgrOP, but a control analysis with PRO in the lower clause would lead to a similarly indexed chain.

(29)   Indexation   A-Chain:
   a.   The mom$_2$ sees herself$_2$ dance   (the mom$_2$, herself$_2$, t$_2$)
                                            [+R]   [-R]   [-R]
   b.   *Herself$_2$ sees the mom$_2$ dance   *(herself$_2$, the mom$_2$, t$_2$)
                                            [-R]   [+R]   [-R]
   c.   *The mom$_2$ sees her$_2$ dance   *(the mom$_2$, her$_2$,   t$_2$)
                                            [+R]   [+R]   [-R]

So it is the Chain Condition and not Condition B which rules out (23). The first always applies if we assume that object pronouns have to raise as high as AgrOP to check their case, and examples (30a-c) from the French experiment of Hamann, Kowalski and Philip (1997) show the partial overlap of the effect of the two conditions. (30a,b) are constrained both by the Chain-Condition and Condition B. Condition B does not apply to cases like (30c). These are constrained only by the Chain Condition.

(30) a. *Elle$_2$ la$_2$ montre   point'(j,j) & point$_{NON-REFL}$
          she points at her   ruled out by Condition B
                                            ruled out by Chain Condition

      b. Elle$_2$ se$_2$ montre   Condition B and A satisfied
          she points at herself   Chain Condition satisfied

      c. *Elle$_2$ la$_2$ voit danser   see'(j,P) & P = dance'(j)
          she sees her dance   Condition B does not apply
                                            ruled out by Chain Condition

The examples we have examined so far show that in the reflexivity framework, the Conditions A and B together with the Chain Condition cover the range of cases the standard binding principles cover. It is particularly important to note that in this framework the actual binding conditions rule out a case like (31a) but they license a case like (31b) only if we consider Condition B in its modus tollens form: If a predicate P is not reflexive-marked, then it cannot be interpreted as a reflexive predicate.

(31) a. *John$_i$ saw him$_i$.
      b. John$_i$ saw him$_j$.

The Chain Condition (CC), however, can check this case directly and license or bar it. Let us briefly run through the possible cases in order to see this point more clearly.

(32) a. self-anaphor coindexed (with antecedent) ok by Condition A
                                                    ok by Condition B
                                                    ok by CC

      b. self-anaphor contraindexed   * by Condition A
                                                    * by Condition B
                                                    * by CC

      c. pronoun coindexed   * by Condition B
                                                    * by CC

      d. pronoun contraindexed   (not ruled out by Condition A)
                                                    (not ruled out by Condition B)
                                                    ok by CC

In the case of (32d) we have a pronoun, we know that a pronoun is not reflexive marked, so the predicate cannot be reflexive, i.e. the alternative is to be contraindexed with the antecedent or to be unindexed. So (32d) is one of the cases which is not excluded by Condition B (in its modus tollens form). Alternatively, we could start from the fact of contraindexation, which tells us that we have a non-reflexive predicate. Then it follows from Condition A that we cannot have a reflexive marked predicate, in particular not a self-anaphor, but a pronoun or a referential expression should be alright. Therefore (32d) is one of the cases which is not excluded. We see that (32d) is a case which is not ruled out and so licensed in an indirect way, while the other cases are licensed or ruled out by the conditions in one-step arguments.

The Chain Condition leads to the same conclusion in a straightforward way - because object pronouns have to move to AgrOP to have their case checked. So every object pronoun or anaphor is involved in a short movement chain. Therefore the Chain Condition has something to say in all the above cases, as noted in (32). In the case of (32d) we have a pronoun which we know is [+R] and the condition is satisfied: this pronoun is the top link of the short movement chain and this chain is a maximal chain by its contraindexation with the subject.

3.2. Reflexivity and Acquisition

There are two things to keep in mind that may play a role in acquisition. First, if binding is to be described as in the Reinhart and Reuland (1993) framework, then cases involving anaphors are easier to handle by young children: there is straightforward licensing which depends only on reflexivity and there is a threefold redundancy. In the case of pronouns, redundancy is weaker and the grammatical case is not licensed straightforwardly; it is only not excluded by the binding conditions. This captures some of the intuitions and solves some of the problems we discussed in section 2.1. Second, the Chain Condition plays a key role so that the classification of nominal elements as to their referentiality is just as important as their classification as reflexive marked. This implies that lexical problems with individual items can have wide reaching consequences.

There also is a third aspect of this theory that is very relevant to acquisition, especially when seen in relation with the discussion of the coreference rule. Consider the simple case of pronoun use. To exclude coindexation of the subject and the pronoun as in (31a), we now have several possibilities: Condition B on reflexivity, and the Chain Condition because we would have a chain with two referentially independent expressions as its links. The coreferential interpretation of (31b) is still only excluded by the coreference rule. But this is now made evident, because it is quite clear that pronouns are [+R] just as any other definite DP. So they refer independently. What is not captured in this framework is the fact that pronominal reference is solely determined by context, whereas definite DPs are less context dependent.

We therefore are in the following situation with respect to acquisition: at surface structure, classical Principle B cases are additionally constrained on the one hand by another grammatical principle which crucially relies on lexical features, namely the Chain Condition, and on the other hand by pragmatics, namely the coreference rule. Incomplete mastery of the lexical entry or of the pragmatics or both can lead to different degrees of failure in different specific environments.

This is exactly what Sigurjónsdóttir and Coopmans (1996) and Philip and Coopmans (1996a, 1996b) explored when they investigated the decidedly poor performance of Dutch children. The first authors tested the effects of the Chain Condition in contexts of non-reflexive, inherently reflexive and ambiguous predicates, Philip and Coopmans (1996a, 1996b) tested the effect of the Chain Condition using ECM-like cases as in (33c). They showed that the performance on the Dutch equivalent of (33c) is worse than on the so called simple cases - and worse than the performance of English children, see also section 1.3. The results of their truth value judgement task in those cases where the adult response would be 'no' are given in (33).

Their conclusion is that Dutch children, due to ambiguities in the Dutch case system, have not classified the Dutch pronoun as [+case]. This means that due to a lexical difficulty, the Chain Condition does not rule out coindexation in (33c). In fact, the lexical underspecification will allow an anaphoric interpretation of the pronoun. Once the case system is acquired fully, the problem will resolve itself. This is a slow process, as Philip and Coopmans (1996b) showed: Dutch 8-year-olds are still only 50% adult like on (33a), 65% adult like on (33b) and 38% adult like on (33c).

(33) | | | Dutch 4-6 yrs | English 6 yrs |
|---|---|---|---|
| a. | Is the girl touching her | 36% adult | 32% adult |
| b. | Is every girl touching her | 53% adult | 77% adult |
| c. | Does the girl see her rope jumping | 10% adult | 33% adult |

But as (33a) and (33b) show, there are less problems in cases where Condition B applies and even less difficulties in those cases where accidental coreference is excluded. So there is not only a lexical difficulty. The possibility of assigning accidentally coreferring interpretations to contraindexed nominal expressions is an additional factor and can be attributed to difficulties in the evaluation of context dependent interpretations. Both difficulties together may explain the very bad performance of Dutch children.

Given these results which point to the possibility of specific problems in the lexical/grammatical system of a language and of independent pragmatic problems, the good performance of Romance children should be investigated under these two perspectives: the grammatical and lexical properties of clitic pronominals as compared to free pronominals and their pragmatic potential concerning accidental coreference.

Chapter 4 will examine pronominal clitics from these two perspectives. Therefore we first need to consider the extension of the binding theory and the coreference rule as outlined in Heim (1993).

3.3. *Free Variables, Reference Assignment and the Exceptional Coindexing Rule*

Heim's basic aim is to reinvest the syntactic relations established by indexation with their intuitive semantic import on referentiality. Their separation lead to deep problems, one of which was the question of what possible importance Principle B could have for the interpretation of pronouns. Following Heim's formal definitions and distinctions may be difficult, but in view of the aim of reestablishing the binding principles in their familiar form, it seems worth the effort.

(34)   Every boy said that he called his mother

In order to treat not only cases where co-reference is involved, but also cases which seem to involve something which we can sloppily call co-binding as in (34), Heim (1993) introduces two indices on pronouns. They now have "an inner index that encodes what they are bound by, and an additional outer index to encode what they in turn bind", (Heim 1993:25,26). This notational contrivance can capture what Montague (1974) achieved for (34) by quantifying in at different places in the derivation. As we have pointed out, we can build up a sentence with three occurrences of the same free pronoun: *he$_1$ said that he$_1$ called his$_1$ mother* and as the last step quantify in *every boy (*by the rule $F_{10,1}$ where the second index tells us which variable is to be substitued by *every boy*) so that all the variables simultaneously lose their index. But we can also first generate *he$_2$ called his$_2$ mother*, then quantify in *he$_1$* which yields *he$_1$ called his mother*, then build up further to *he$_1$ said that he$_1$ called his mother* and finally quantify in *every boy* . In this case *his* was bound earlier in the derivation by *he$_1$* while *he$_1$* kept the index to the last step where it was bound itself. The double indexation can also be seen as a formal reflex of what Higginbotham (1983) calls linking and where the above two Montague derivations would lead to two different linking structures. Moreover, it is a conservative extension of attempts to preserve a perfect correspondence between syntactic binding in the sense of Condition A and semantic binding, in so far as the "newly introduced indices serve to express distinctions at SS that otherwise could only be brought out at LF" (Heim 1993:31).

With these modifications, QR now always works like this: the trace retains the outer index of the moved phrase, but the moved phrase itself transfers it to the λ and so loses it. This means that only expressions with an outer index can quantifier raise, though expressions may have only an inner index, or only an outer index, or be doubly indexed. They cannot remain unindexed by the stipulation that all pronouns, proper names and other definites bear an inner index as part of their lexical entry. This implies also that the definiton of variable has to be revised: an index is a variable now if it is a) on a λ, b) on a trace and bound by a λ or c) the **inner** index of a pronominal or anaphor and A-bound.

The two indices now obviously require a new formulation of the binding principles because it is not immediately obvious which index is concerned. Heim defines **linking** so that it captures what formerly was a direct binding relation, whereas **co-linking** expresses that two variables can be bound by the same quantifier, and co-determination is an even broader notion subsuming these two, see (35). Then Principle A and B can be reformulated as (36).

(35)   β is **linked to** α iff α's outer index = β's inner index
         α and β are **co-linked** iff α's inner index = β 's inner index

         α and β are **codetermined** iff
         α= β or either one of α or β is linked to the other or
         α and β are colinked or for some γ, α and γ are codetermined and so are γ and β.

(36)   **Binding Conditions**
         Condition A: An anaphor is linked to a c-commanding A-position in its GC.
         Condition B: A pronominal is not codetermined with any c-commanding A-position in its GC.

Now the coreference rule can be reformulated so that true linking violations of Condition B are never allowed but mere codetermination violations can be allowed under certain discourse conditions. Another significant change is to make the rule not a rule about referents, but about indices. This means coming back to the conventional view about indexation as a representational device for coreference and variable binding in contrast to the view that coreference relations, unlike variable binding, have no syntactic representation. The more conventional view then forces the reintroduction of free variables into syntactic representations. But if we want to avoid the pitfalls discussed in 2.1., we have to go further and disallow any case which does not bear an index and gets interpreted straight off. These cases have to be excluded because they avoid the Binding Conditions and would need a rule on coreference. Therefore it has to be stipulated that all pronouns, proper names and other definites bear an inner index as part of their lexical entry and "thus come automatically indexed when they are inserted in any syntactic structure" (Heim 1993:36). In particular, all referring NPs bear inner indices, and it follows that semantically they are free variables, so we must not exclude these. Heim defines: an index is a variable only if it is a) on a λ, or b) on a trace and bound by a λ or c) the inner index of a pronominal or anaphor and A-bound or d) the inner index of a definite NP and free. The interpretation will now assign a referent per context c and index i, or more precisely, it will assign a guise per context and (inner) index. We obtain rule (37).

(37) **Rule of interpretation**
An LF Φ is interpretable in an utterance context c only if c furnishes a distinct guise $F^c{}_i$ for each index i free in Φ such that it is presupposed in c that $F^c{}_i$ picks out an individual which fits the features and lexical content of any NP indexed i occurring in Φ.

To obtain the referent we have to assign to each α_i the individual $F^c{}_i(w_c)$ which $F^c{}_i$ picks out in the utterance world w_c. This ensures that coindexed free pronouns pick out the same referent under the same guise. But it also ensures that pronouns with different indices will be assigned different guises - these however, may allow that they are assigned ultimately the same referent. So the coreference rule becomes a rule on exceptional coindexing as shown in (38).

(38) **Exceptional Coindexing Rule:**
A pronominal α is (marginally) allowed at SS to be codetermined with a c-commanding A-position β in its GC when the interpretation thus obtained needs to be distinguished from the one that would result if β were given an outer index and moved and α were replaced by a variable A-bound by the trace of β.

(39) John saw him

Let us briefly comment on how a simple case like (39) comes out now. We can exclude a bound variable interpretation as before because this would come out as a linking violation of Condition B. Let us assume a coreferential interpretation. This can arise in two ways. Either we have picked out the common referent under one guise or we have two guises.

The first case would have to be represented with the same inner index on *John* and *him*. This would be a mere codetermination violation. It is excluded by the Exceptional Coindexing Rule, except in special contexts. These are only contexts where structured meaning matters ((8a), (15a,b) above) because the other cases of coreference discussed so far always involved different guises. In (39) we clearly do not have such a context of structured meaning and so we cannot allow the same inner index, the exceptional coindexing rule forces us to choose the anaphor. If we stress the antecedent, we get a context of structured meaning with some effort: we are looking for John and nobody has seen him and there is the notorious wit among us pointing out the obvious in an unhelpful way.

The second case, coreference via distinct guises, would be alright, but requires a context where such distinct guises are readily available, i.e. where the pronoun is stressed or we have an explicit identity debate. This is possible if there is a report that a certain person named John, whom nobody has met so far, has seen the person pointed at, whose name is unknown. In this case we would have the guise of the visual image and the guise of naming and it might turn out that both single out the individual John. The identity debate cases work as before, and this is fine because they seem easier to accept than some of the other cases.

We have discussed this simple example in such depth because it is important to keep in mind that we now have two kinds of 'coreference'. One involves sameness of index and guise and can survive the ECR (37) only in cases where structured meaning matters. The other involves cases where there are different guises, which always require rather special contexts. Note that Thornton and Wexler (1999), who also work with a version of Heim (1993), reduce the cases where structured meaning matters to cases with different guises.

The idea that different guises allow accidental coreference in certain circumstances is important for acquisition from two points of view. If children allow accidental coreference in contexts where adults do not and this is responsible for the 'delay of principle B', we might have the core of an explanation which applies cross-linguistically up to the language specific identification of the possible cases of accidental coreference. If children can get accidental coreference because their interpretations allow for more different guises than adult interpretations, then this almost certainly ties in with children's difficulty with discourse anchorage. Instead of having to look in the wider discourse context for the pronoun's antecedent, the different guise allows the child to interpret the pronoun in the sentence itself.

CHAPTER 4

ROMANCE CLITICS AND BINDING

1. A SYNTACTIC ANALYSIS OF CLITIC PRONOUNS

1.1. Review of the Properties of French Clitics

The French clitic paradigm given in (1) is complemented by a paradigm of strong pronouns (2) which, contrary to clitics, can occur in isolation, in coordination and can be focussed :

(1) **pronominal subject clitics:**

	sg	pl	**object clitics:**	sg	pl
1st	je	nous		me	nous
2nd	tu	vous		te	vous
3rd	il,	ils		le	les
	elle	elles		la	
	on				

clitic anaphors: sg: me, te, se   pl: nous, vous, se

(2) **strong subject pronouns:**   **strong object pronouns:**

	sg	pl		sg	pl
1st	moi	nous		moi	nous
2nd	toi	vous		toi	vous
3rd	lui	eux		lui	eux
	elle	elles		elle	elles

strong anaphoric marker: -même

Notwithstanding some ambiguities (as in the case of *me, te* and *elle*), the existence of syntactic constraints concerning clitics and their contrast with the strong pronoun paradigm provides the Romance child with many clues of a syntactic and lexical nature that are not available to the child learning Dutch or English. These clues will be investigated in 4.2 and 4.3.

The basic problem we have to address in connection with the binding principles is the fact that clitic object pronominals in French and other Romance languages are not arguments at Spell-Out, but heads cliticized to the verb (see sections 2.1. and 2.6 of chapter 2). Therefore it does not seem obvious that, or how, French pronominal object clitics can receive a referential index in their surface position. It has been shown that clitic chains interact with A-chains (Rizzi 1986b) in a way which shows their A-chain-like properties. So the idea which comes to mind for complement clitics is that the whole clitic chain and thus the clitic has its origin in the complement argument position. We will presently take up this idea.

Connected with the problem of how to obtain an index for binding purposes is the general problem of the referentiality of clitics. Clitics cannot be used in isolation which suggests that they cannot refer independently as examples (1) to (5) of section 2.1. in chapter 2 showed, repeated here as (3):

(3)   Question: qui a tu vu   Answer: *le
              who have you seen   him

Also, clitics cannot normally be used with a pointing gesture. The strong form has to be used in these cases. Under very special circumstances this general constraint does not hold, however, as Cardinaletti and Starke (2000) point out. If the referent of the clitic has been previously identified in the discourse, then a pointing gesture is possible as shown in (4).

(4)   Mets-toi ici and regard cette maison.
       put yourself here and look at that house (f).
       Tu (pointing gesture) LA vois maintenant?
       you   HER see   now
       'Do you see IT now?'

Given this general picture, clitics seem to fulfill Reinhart and Reuland's criteria for [-R] expressions and have indeed been analyzed as lacking the structure hosting the referentiality feature (cf. Cardinaletti and Starke 2000) so that they lack an index altogether. In the analysis of these authors this goes together with the argument that clitics don't have a functional case feature, which is reminiscent of the classical definition of variable (an empty category in a case position) and so would imply that clitics never are variables.[1] In the system of Cardinaletti and Starke this holds for all weak pronouns. However, in a simple situation like (5) the clitic receives its reference exactly like a Germanic pronoun, through identification with a contextually salient element fitting the phi- and (morphological) case feature specification. Note that this holds for German strong and for weak pronouns.

(5) Qui a vu Marc/Who has seen Marc/Wer hat Marc gesehen?
     Jean l'a vu   /John has seen him/ John hat ihn gesehen.

     Qui a vu le pot/Who has seen the pot/Wer hat den Topf
                                                           gesehen?
     Jean l'a vu   /John has seen it/   John hat ihn gesehen.

We can conclude that if English *him* or German *ihn* are referential and carry an index, and this is the usual assumption, then so is the clitic. Without a further specification of how the interpretation of these structures is to be achieved in a Cardinaletti and Starke framework, it is not at all clear how binding could work across languages if these pronouns and clitics do not have an index. Note, however, that English *him* or *her* always have natural or semantic gender while a clitic or a German weak pronoun can be [+human], but in the majority of cases encodes grammatical gender. This property will become crucial later.[2]

(6) a. Où est le couteau? Ah, je le vois sur la table.
        where is the (m) knife? ah, I see him on the table
        'where is the knife? Ah, I see it on the table'
    b. Wo ist der Löffel? Ah, ich seh ihn auf dem Tisch.
        where is the (m) spoon. Ah, I see him on the table
        'where is the spoon? Ah, I see it on the table'.

1.2. The Syntax of Object Clitics in French

We will come back to the discussion of referentiality and indexless clitics when we return to the discussion of coreference and will keep in mind for now that the basic duplicity of clitics with respect to argument or head status has led to opposing views. There is the base generation approach which assumes special functional categories for the clitics and thus focuses on their head status (Borer 1984, Sportiche 1992). The duplicity becomes more evident in the movement approach, however, which goes back to Kayne (1975) and Rizzi (1986b), but has recently been discussed by Belletti (1999). We will now follow Belletti's analysis of object clitics in cases like (7) in the familiar syntactic framework without too much thought of the semantics.

(7)   Jean$_i$ le$_j$ voit (adult)
      John him sees
      'John sees him'

Contrary to Cardinaletti and Starke, Belletti assumes that object clitics have a strong case feature, which has to be checked before Spell-Out.[3] Therefore movement is obligatory before LF. This follows because accusative case is checked in AgrOP, so the clitic, which originates as the complement of the verb, has to move at least as far as AgrOP. This also holds for Germanic object pronouns. From (7) and the examples cited in section 2.1 of chapter 2, we can see that the clitic moves higher. Indeed, the clitic clearly is a head and has incorporated to the verbal head in I^0. So a constituent which originates as an argument is a head at its final landing-site. The question we must ask therefore is whether the clitic moves as a head or as a DP. The options exist because in accordance with recent trends in research (Cardinaletti and Starke 2000), third person accusative Romance clitics can be assigned a structure as in (8), with the clitic a D-head in an impoverished DP containing nothing but the clitic:

(8)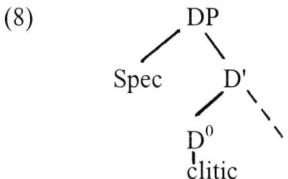

Clearly, the clitic cannot move as a head in one step, because this would violate the Head Movement Constraint. But it cannot move step by step either because then it would have to incorporate to the head in the Participle Agreement Phrase (AgrPartP) which would a) block checking of the agreement features and b) require subsequent excorporation.[4]

Therefore the clitic first moves as a DP. We find open evidence for this in complex tenses, where the number and gender of the clitic agrees with the participle (français elevé). Under the assumption that feature agreement is a manifestation of the Spec-head relation with an agreement head, the clitic in (9) must have moved through SpecAgrPartP as a DP, and the first links of the clitic chain constitute an A-chain.[5] The derivation is shown in (10).

(9) Jean l<u>es</u> a peint<u>es</u>   (plural, feminin)
     John them has painted
     'John has painted them'

(10)

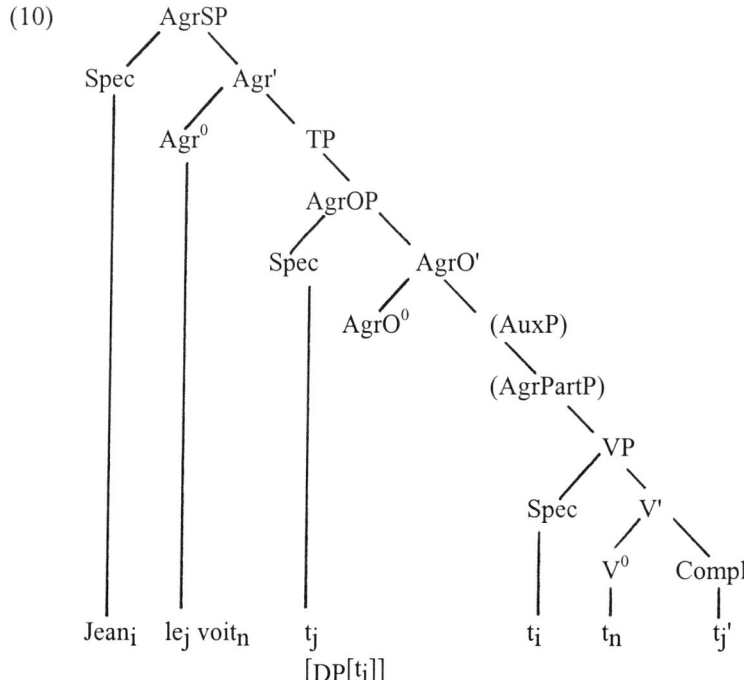

Movement from SpecAgrPartP onwards is then effected as a head to $AgrO^0$ or as a DP to the specifier of AgrOP. Belletti (1999) argues that in Italian the clitic moves as a head at this point, and Haegeman (1996e) assumes the same for French. So both French and Italian object clitics would pass through $AgrO^0$ - which becomes the cliticization site. Let us here assume for reasons of simplicity, that the clitic is still a DP in ArgOP. Furthermore the verb raises to AgrSP in order to check its phi-features, but the clitic also has phi-features which must be checked. Because the impoverished clitic-structure does not allow checking with an N, the clitic D^0 follows the verb to its position in AgrSP, leaving an empty DP-shell in AgrOP as in (10).[6] Let us now examine what the different binding frameworks can do with this structure.

2. CLITICS AND THE CHAIN CONDITION

The Chain Condition obviously applies to the A-chain part of the clitic-chain leading to effects as in (11). We assume that the top link of the DP-chain is the crucial link which as a DP-shell carries the referentiality feature. (This may be shared or not shared with the clitic, hence the parantheses around these elements). The clitic itself carries the same index by movement (which in Heim's terms is an outer index), it is not affected by the constraint and can be reconstructed at LF reuniting the DP-shell with its head. We use the Reinhart and Reuland framework for (11).

(11)   Indexation   A-Chain
   a. La maman$_2$ se$_2$ montre [t'$_2$..[VP..t$_2$]]   (la maman$_2$ (se$_2$)   t'$_2$,   t$_2$)
       the mom points at herself   [+R]   (?R) [-R] [-R]
   b. *La maman$_2$ la$_2$ montre [t'$_2$..[VP..t$_2$]] *(la maman$_2$, (la$_2$) t'$_2$,   t$_2$)
       the mom points at her   [+R]   (?R) [+R] [-R]
   c. La maman$_2$ se$_2$ voit [t'$_2$ [VP [t$_2$ danser]] (la maman$_2$, (se$_2$), t'$_2$,   t$_2$)
       the mom sees herself dance   [+R]   (?R) [-R] [-R]
   d. *La maman$_2$ la$_2$ voit [t'$_2$ [VP [t2 danser]] *(la maman$_2$ (la$_2$), t'$_2$,   t$_2$)
       the mom sees her dance   [+R]   (?R) [+R] [-R]

But there is more overt evidence available to the Romance child. In sentences where coindexation and coreference is excluded for gender reasons as in (12a), the clitic has overtly risen to a higher position and heads its own chain, a chain which is in part an argument chain. Though in recent accounts English or Dutch object pronouns also raise to AgrOP, there is no overt evidence of this movement at Spell-Out, especially not for the child if the case morphology is not fully acquired. In (12a) therefore, the Romance child has unambiguous syntactic evidence for movement and contraindexation with the antecedent and so the existence of a maximal A-chain. Moreover, there is contrastive evidence in sentences like (12b) where the clitic anaphor is used. The anaphor in principle makes the same journey but cannot head its own chain, it must be coindexed with the subject as in (12b)

(12) a. *Marie$_i$ le$_i$ voit (wrong gender)
Mary him sees
'Mary sees him'
b. Jean$_i$ se$_i$ touche
John himself touches
'John touches himself'

One utterance of (12b) in the matching situation where Jean touches himself will tell the child so. Lexical underspecification is thus excluded for syntactic reasons. Indeed, from spontaneous production no mismatches in case or phi features are known. So Romance children show their knowledge of the fact that object clitics (at least in their base position) must have the feature [+referential] as soon as they utter something like (12a) with disjoint reference clearly determinable by the situation. This holds as early as 2.6. as production data show (cf. Hamann, Rizzi, Frauenfelder 1996). So in this framework, the conclusion is that the good performance of children learning a Romance language is due to the early knowledge of the binding principles and the knowledge of the Chain Condition.

Let us repeat the ingredients of the argument: object clitics have a strong case feature, there is obligatory movement, the first links of the clitic-chain constitute an argument chain. The child has overt evidence of movement and knows the Chain Condition. Then the first production of something like (12a) in a disjoint reference context proves that the child has classified the lexical entry of the clitic as containing the feature [+referential]. So the reflexivity/Chain Condition formulation of the binding principles predicts a good performance of Romance children in cases where only the Chain Condition and the Conditions A and B are relevant.

Unfortunately, this conclusion makes it impossible to transfer the analysis proposed for the Dutch findings to the poor performance in French ECM cases (as briefly mentioned in section 3.2 of chapter 3). The Romance child knows all the referentiality, the phi and case features of the clitic, so it cannot mistakenly allow the clitic to be the tail of a chain. In fact, knowledge of the referential properties of clitics predicts a good performance on the ECM cases.

Let us briefly discuss the base generation approach as an alternative to the movement analysis for clitics adopted here. Because of clitic-doubling structures, some authors do not assume movement in order to avoid that two constituents have to share one case-assignment and one theta-role (Borer 1984, Sportiche 1992). Instead, they suggest base insertion of the clitic in a special functional head, the presence of *pro* in argument position and coindexation of both elements for reasons of licensing. These approaches are problematic for several reasons, however, and clitic-doubling can be handled in a movement approach under the assumption that the lexical argument originates as the complement of D' in the clitic-DP of (8) (Belletti 1999). What is important here, is the fact that the argument based on the Chain Condition does not change in its essential form even if we assume base insertion. If the clitic is inserted in its own functional projection, there still is an object *pro* in AgrOP which has to be coindexed with the clitic to be licensed. Again, the pronominal clitic, as a head, will be the top of a mixed chain, with an empty argument heading the argument chain part, both having the same features.[7]

3. CLITICS AND ACCIDENTAL COREFERENCE

3.1. Structural Deficiency

In the introductory discussion of pronouns and accidental coreference, we have already mentioned the general opinion that Romance object clitics do not allow accidental coreference. This is mostly seen as related to the fact that Romance clitics cannot be focused. There is a recent account of pronouns and clitics which makes use of this idea, but treats it as a structural ambiguity problem: free pronominals in English are structurally ambiguous, Romance pronominal clitics are not. Cardinaletti and Starke (1995 and 2000) give a new outlook on accidental coreference and acquisition in trying to resolve the problem not by imposing conditions on the possible antecedents of a pronominal but by formulating a syntactic principle which regulates the choice of weak over strong forms.

Cardinaletti and Starke start with the observation that accidental coreference is possible with English pronouns, but it is not possible in quantifier configurations and it is not possible with Romance clitics. So their question is: Why do English children allow too much accidental coreference? So far, this is very much like Grodzinsky and Reinhart (1993), and a possible answer would be: because the coreference rule breaks down. This, as we have pointed out, does not explain the good performance of Romance children without appealing to special properties of clitics. It is a common move to constrain the applicability of the coreference rule to cases where the pronominal elements can bear contrastive stress and can be used in a demonstrative way with a pointing gesture. But, as Cardinaletti and Starke point out, in special circumstances clitics can be used demonstratively cf. (4) and they can also bear contrastive focus as the following little dialogue shows:

(13) On a dit, que je mangerai ce gateau demain
      we said   that I will eat the cake tomorrow

      Non, que JE mangerai ce gateau demain
      no, that I will eat the cake tomorrow
      Mais non, que JE...
      but no, that I...

So Cardinaletti and Starke (1995) avoid any appeal to focus or the coreference rule and look for the common source of all these properties in the grammatical/lexical structure of clitics and pronouns. They contrast the following examples from Romance and from English:

(14) a. Jean le voit
          John him sees
          'John sees him'
      b. Jean voit (que) lui
          John sees (only) him

(15) a. the snake saw it
      b. the boy saw him

In the examples (14a) and (15a) accidental coreference is not possible, in (14b) and (15b) it is. Cardinaletti and Starke attribute this fact to the clitic or weak status of French *le* and English *it*. The English examples show the problem better than the contrasting Romance (14a,b): the structural configuration is exactly the same in (15a,b), yet one sentence allows accidental coreference, and the other does not.

On the basis of the criteria presented in section 2.1 of chapter 2, but with certain refinements for distinguishing clitics from weak pronouns, Cardinaletti and Starke classify pronominals cross-linguistically in a system of **clitics < weak pronouns < strong pronouns,** in the order of their deficiency. They proceed to show that in English *him* and *her*, among others, are ambiguous in that they can be strong or weak. English *it*, on the other hand, is not ambiguous and must always be deficient and therefore weak. The same is the case for Romance clitics. So the above pattern can be explained by an appeal to deficiency: deficient pronouns do not allow accidental coreference, strong pronouns do.

The next step is to make structural deficiency responsible for the lack of accidental coreference in postulating that it is exactly the position for the referential index which is missing. So weak pronouns and clitics are simply not referential by themselves, but "can be interpreted as referential only if they are associated to a (non-deficient) antecedent" (Cardinaletti and Starke 2000). Cardinaletti and Starke explain this absence of referentiality and thus the absence of an index by the absence of a range restriction which can narrow down the interpretation. This has to do with the old observation that clitics and weak pronouns can be either [+] or [-human], a specification they take over from their discourse antecedent, but which is not lexically inherent in the clitic or weak pronoun. For strong pronouns, the specification [+human] is inherent and serves as range restriction.

We will expand this last idea in our later discussion, and will now present the core principle of this system of structural deficiency. In accordance with other principles of economy, Cardinaletti and Starke introduce the principle of Avoid Structure as in (16).

(16) **Avoid Structure** or 'the deficient form must be chosen whenever this is possible'.

This implies that strong pronouns need a special licensing context to be allowed, as for example after prepositions, in focus structures or in coordination. This also implies that everything else being equal, the English adult will have to interpret *him* in (15b) above as the weak pronoun and will not get an accidental coreference reading. Only if there is focus or another licensing context for a strong pronoun, an accidental coreference reading is possible.

As to child language, it is clear that the Romance clitic is unambiguously weak and therefore Cardinaletti and Starke predict that the child will never allow accidental coreference. In English, however, the child has to discover that there is a lexical-structural ambiguity between a weak and a strong form - and this, Cardinaletti and Starke claim, is one of the worst ambiguities to resolve. As long as this has not happened, the child will treat *him* in (15b) above as a strong pronoun and allow accidental coreference. Cardinaletti and Starke explain the choice of the strong over the weak form by the child in the following way: strong pronouns have the normal structure of noun phrases, while deficient forms correspond to highly marked structures.

The approach, radical and elegant, seems to solve many problems in one go. It does not have much to say about the better performance with quantified antecedents, however. It is impossible to get a co-indexed or contraindexied version in any case because the index on the weak/clitic pronouns is lacking. For the ECM/raising/clitic-climbing structures the approach predicts that in Romance languages the performance is on a par with the performance in simple cases. This is not what we observe. Moreover, let us return to the discussion of the idea that deficient forms do not refer at all and thus cannot do accidental coreference.

3.2. Clitics, Indices and Accidental Coreference

Let us first observe that it is a rather old idea that pronominals do not refer in the same direct way as lexical definite DPs. Instead (if they are not used demonstratively) they must be identified by an antecedent or a salient element in the context (see also the Grounding Priniciple (19) in chapter 3), so that they always present "old information" and therefore cannot be focussed easily. This observation has led to many solutions (see Lakoff 1972, Montague 1974, McCawley 1981, Wexler and Chien 1985, Lasnik 1989, Kaplan 1977, Heim 1993, Wexler 1996), but it does not usually lead to the radical assumption that weak pronouns lack a referential index.

One of the reasons why most authors do not make this radical step is that without any indexation, it will be difficult to distinguish between anaphors and pronouns and the binding principles cannot be formulated at all if not in the rather vague way of (17) where we cannot even define antecedent in any non-circular way, i.e. as the argument which identifies the referent of the pronoun or anaphor.

(17)   A pronoun is referentially identified by an antecedent which must not be in its GC.
An anaphor is referentially identified by an antecedent in its GC.

Moreover, as we have seen in chapter 3, not having an index is the classical situation of receiving reference in the given context - which may be what Cardinaletti and Starke have in mind - but it is unfortunately also the classical case where accidental coreference is not excluded by any principle of syntax or interpretation. Leaving the pronominal without an index thus does not lead to the desired result, but achieves rather the contrary.

We may try to add interpretative rules. We could specify that the index of the pronoun's discourse antecedent is handed on to the pronoun in the step from LF_{n-1} to LF_n, as often proposed before, with the help of discourse boxes or file cards or dynamic semantics (see Kamp 1981, Heim 1982, Cooper 1986, Avrutin 1994, 1999). But even this procedure could allow accidental coreference. Now the discourse antecedent and a DP in the phrase containing the pronoun could corefer, which, by identification of reference, might lead to coreference of the pronoun and this DP in the same phrase. Nothing of this sort is worked out in Cardinaletti and Starke (1995 and 2000), however, and the reader is left with the rather vague impression that the binding principles apply as usual - to entities without an index.

The framework as presented in Heim (1993) has a canonical slot to treat the intuition that strong pronouns are less referential than definite lexical DPs and names, and that weak pronouns and clitics are even less referential than strong pronouns. This slot is the presupposition mentioned in the rule of interpretation given as (37) in the last chapter. Obviously, the less information a term carries inherently, the more has to be brought into the presupposition by the context. This idea has a direct bearing on weak pronouns and clitics and their general resistance to allow accidental coreference. A weak pronoun or a clitic needs more 'context' than a strong pronoun to define its guise and so establish the identification with a salient element in the discourse. In section 3.3 of Chapter 3 we had seen that accidental coreference was mostly allowed in cases where different guises for one referent were imaginable. But introducing different guises for the clitic (weak pronoun) and the potential antecedent is almost impossible: The more specific a context has to be to identify a certain guise, the less it will be able to also allow a second guise. We will return to this idea later.

Let us note here, that accidental coreference for clitics is by no means excluded, it is just more difficult to get - just as was pointed out for contrastive stress or the demonstrative use of clitics by Cardinaletti and Starke (2000).

Cases which require focus on the clitic are excluded because the strong pronoun has to be chosen - following Cardinaletti and Starke in their assumption of Avoid Structure or because only the strong pronoun can be new information. Cases where the antecedent is focussed, i.e. cases where structured meaning matters, can be constructed as in (18) and (19), and so can the usual identity puzzles as in (20).

(18)   Elles sont vraiment bêtes. Ou est-ce que tu connais quelqu'un
       'they are really stupid! Or do you know somebody
       qui aime bien Marie et Jeanne?
       who likes (well) Marie and Jeanne'

       Mais bien sure, Marie et Jeanne les aiment bien.
       'but certainly, Marie and Jeanne like them (well)'

(19)   Tout-le-monde deteste Oscar.
       'all the world hates Oscar'
       Marie le deteste, Jean le deteste, même Oscar le deteste.
       'Marie hates him, Jean hates him, even Oscar hates him.'

(20)   Est-ce que Jean est l'auteur de ces articles?
       'Is John the author of these articles?'
       Mais bien sur, Jean le cite tout le temps.
       'Oh sure, John quotes him all the time'

These examples, though quite acceptable, are excluded from the discussion by Cardinaletti and Starke (p.c.) in that they judge that these cases are not solved satisfactorily in any account and so require some independent treatment. This implies that the authors find all those accounts which culminate in Heim's formalization unsatisfactory. It appears to me, however, that exactly these treatments are on the right track and can well explain all the phenomena - if properly extended to clitics in the manner as suggested by Cardinaletti and Starke.

Let us go back to their idea that clitics and weak pronouns do not have an inherent range restriction. Let us assume that it is this specification which is missing in the structure so that clitics and weak pronouns are indeed deficient structurally and referentially. This structural deficiency is the reason why the extremely deficient forms, the clitics, have to attach to the verb to be licensed and must be heads at this point. We will not commit ourselves whether clitics are referential in this position, but will assume that they have to be reconstructed to render a proper LF. This means that when we talk about clitics, we are talking about clitics in their (last) argument position (see derivation (10) in 1.2 of this chapter) and the referential properties they may have in this position.

Unlike Cardinaletti and Starke, we will not assume, that the lack of a range restriction necessarily leads to total lack of referentiality. I think that the authors' sloppy locution 'having no range' instead of 'having no range restriction' leads them to the conclusion that an expression which does not have a range cannot refer, and so is at the heart of the problem. Having no range restriction does by no means imply that the expression does not have a range. On the contrary it implies that the range is the whole universe of the world and context of interpretation. If it were otherwise, sentences with impersonal pronouns like (21), which are one of Cardinaletti and Starke's examples for 'having no range', and which normally involve an existential quantifier for their interpretation would always be false because there is no individual at all which satisfies the sentence.

(21)   Today they cleaned a cow in Switzerland

Let us therefore assume that clitics and pronouns are deficient with respect to the range restriction without adhering to the view that this entails their having no index. This means that we can use the elegant mechanism of Cardinaletti and Starke's system without losing the possibilities which Heim's theory offers. It means picking the best of both approaches, and we need some such move in order to explain the cases of accidental coreference quoted above.

We now have made the assumption that clitics and weak pronouns are referentially deficient in that they do not have a lexically inherent range restriction. It remains to be explained why this leads to the strong resistance to accidental coreference or exceptional coindexing. The answer, as was indicated before, lies in the interpretation rules. The rule given in (37) of chapter 3 is only a minimal rule specifying the sufficient conditions for the interpretability of a free (inner) index - be it on a weak pronoun, a strong pronoun or a full lexical DP. This makes it necessarily vague with respect to how exactly the context furnishes a guise.

Let us try to make this process of how the context can provide a guise a bit more precise without formalizing it (which would involve writing a discourse semantics). Imagine the snatches of dialogue presented in (22):

(22) a. Nobody smokes in our office. Ask my secretary.
b. Nobody smokes in our office. Ask HER/*her.
c. Nobody smokes in our office.
My secretary can tell you. Ask her.

In (22a) a definite lexical DP is used and it is presupposed in the context c belonging to the utterance that there is an individual in w_c, the world or model relevant in c, which has all the features and obeys the range restrictions. The referent can therefore be identified by the hearer. So the contribution of the context here is just the common ground assumed in every situation. To make (22b) work so that the hearer can identify the referent, we need a pointing gesture, and the individual has to be present in the situation of utterance. This implies that the guise which the context furnishes here for the strong pronoun is just the visual impression and so more or less the individual as such. This means that other guises can be introduced without any difficulties. We could not have used a weak pronoun in (22b), however, just as Cardinaletti and Starke point out. For the weak pronoun (or a clitic) to be used, the context must furnish more, it must provide a salient element in the previous discourse (or immediately following discourse, see (18)), otherwise nothing can be identified. The problem seems to be that with weak pronouns, only phi-features are inherent, but [+/- human] is not inherent. This seems to exclude the pointing gesture because it is not even certain that we have to do with a concrete individual that can be pointed at. So we cannot get away with using only common ground as a context, and the situational context itself cannot provide the identification either. Therefore the previous discourse must provide a salient element which can then identify the referent of the clitic. This means that the interpretations of the LF representations of the surrounding utterances now necessarily must be part of the context. This, in turn, implies that the identification of the referent does not simply proceed via the identification of individuals, but that the 'context furnishes a distinct guise' in the form of the guise (and range restriction) of the salient lexical DP. As we are working with a contextually given guise identifying our individual, we cannot - under normal circumstances - suddenly identify the individual using a different, newly introduced guise. This means that the indices of clitics do not act so much as variables but more like constants - in a restricted discourse environment. It also means that under normal circumstances newly introduced lexical DPs which may introduce a new guise do not refer to the same individual as the clitic, which is already specified under a certain guise. So in normal conversational situations (where we assume that different descriptions are used to identify different individuals) accidental coreference via distinct guises is impossible. An accidental coreference reading in (23a) would have to assume that my sister is the director. But this is as difficult or impossible to get as accidental coreference between the terms *ma soeur* and *la directrice* in the second sentence of (22b). This explains the extreme resistance of clitics and weak pronouns to accidental coreference in all normal contexts.

(22) a. J'aimerais rencontrer la directrice. Ma soeur la connaît deja bien.
'I would like to meet the director (f). My sister knows her well already'
b. J'aimerais rencontrer la directrice. Ma soeur connaît deja bien la directrice.
'I would like to meet the director (f). My sister knows the director well already.'

Of course, if the speaker is being funny, the sister could be the director, but this is explicitly violating conversational assumptions and has to be motivated to be acceptable, as for instance with a smile or a punch line intonation.

The argument about how a clitic and a possible antecedent can be made to corefer via the referent of the salient DP predicts that the same reasoning applies to the indices of definite lexical DPs. This seems to be true as (22b) demonstrates, and under normal conversational circumstances lexical DPs show the same resistance to 'accidental coreference'. It may even be the case that clitics show a stronger resistance because the context for allowing accidental coreference is even more specific than for lexical DPs, it must not only motivate the use of two guises for one individual, but also introduce a salient element. The argument also singles out strong pronouns introduced with a pointing gesture as predestined for accidental coreference readings because these always introduce the referent directly (via the visual impression if we want to be precise), no matter what the description has been before. And the pointing gesture is possible because the inherent marking as [+human] of strong pronouns makes sure that there is a concrete person which can be pointed at.

In contexts where it is structured meaning which makes the difference, not the existence of distinct guises, we can coindex the clitic and the potential antecedent without the ECR blocking this. In the case of (19) the clitic has taken over the guise of the index on Oscar in the first sentence. Then the same guise is introduced in the last sentence, and in this case codetermination is allowed because the use of an anaphor would change the predicate, and the sentence would be about self-loathing not about loathing Oscar. (But see Thronton and Wexler 1999 for an explanation of such cases using different guises).

The other possible case was the case where identity is under debate. In that case it is clear that the context will introduce different guises and the meaning of the sentence depends on the discussion of sameness or distinctness of the referents of these distinct guises. Nothing will prevent that the guise of the index of the salient DP has become the guise of the clitic index. The referent of this guise is under explicit debate, but then another lexical DP is introduced with a guise different from this given guise and it turns out that both guises identify the same individual, as is the case for (20) above. Obviously (20) requires that we know from the context that we are debating the identity of the individual identified by the guise interpreting the clitic index.

In the above, I have proposed that clitics are structurally deficient in the manner Cardinaletti and Starke suggest. In my framework, this deficiency does not lead straight to having no referentiality and no index at all, however. The fact of having no inherent range restriction has been shown to lead to the resistance to 'accidental coreference' in normal conversational circumstances because more precise presuppositions are necessary for interpretation. By the nature of the strong identification of clitics with a discourse antecedent, this resistance is at least as strong as the resistance of lexical DPs to 'accidental coreference'. This is so because the index of a clitic is interpreted as a guise which is already fixed in the previous discourse and because different descriptions are normally chosen to distinguish different individuals - unless the context suspends this convention.

Note that this a certain return to Principle P, here applied to definite descriptions and the guises they introduce. So in this account, Principle P does not follow from the coreference rule, but Principle P together with the peculiarities of clitics and the formulation of the ECR in Heim (1993) can explain the resistance of clitics to accidental coreference. Compared to the account sketched in Wexler (1996), where clitics would not allow deictic grounding and so would not allow the child to make a false assumption, we cannot deduce directly that 'clitics don't allow accidental coreference', This is as it should be, however, as I hope to have shown with the examples (18), (19) and (20). The grounding account and also the account offered by Cardinaletti and Starke, miss (or avoid to discuss) just these details. Clitics, in inheriting their guise from a salient lexical DP, behave just like lexical DPs with respect to accidental coreference resisting it strongly in normal contexts, but do admit it in certain specific conversational situations. This, as we will show in chapter 5, will allow us to give an explanation of the unexpected experimental result on ECM cases like '*la fille la voit danser*'.

4. PREVIOUS EXPERIMENTS ON THE ACQUISITION OF BINDING IN ROMANCE

4.1. Predicitions

Let us briefly sum up what the various binding theoretic frameworks we found in the literature predict for the acquisition of the binding properties of Romance clitics. We argued in section 2.2 of this chapter that overt clitic movement together with the Chain-Condition provides syntactic evidence for the French child to determine the referential features of clitics. So French children should be adult-like in contexts like (24c). For Avrutin and Wexler (1992) and in a Cardinaletti and Starke (1995) approach, clitics do not allow accidental coreference (AC). So there should be no problems with the coreference rule either, and (24a) and (24c) should be fine for both Avrutin and Wexler (1992) and for Cardinaletti and Starke (1995). The framework of Heim (1993), with our extensions for clitics, predicts that only special contexts will allow that different guises identify the same individual and so allow accidental coreference. So clitics 'strongly resist accidental coreference', but may allow it in certain contexts. This predicts a good performance in run of the mill discourse situations as used for (24a) and a good performance for (24b) by the usual reasoning. It apriori predicts a good performance on (24c) – unless contexts like (24c) turn out to be special contexts allowing guise creation. We therefore add a question mark to the prediction of 'no trouble' for these cases.

(24)   **Predictions of previous approaches**

	sentence type	errors	explanation
a.	La fille la sèche	none	no 'A C' trouble,
	the girl is drying her		(+ Condition B applies)
b.	Chaque fille la sèche	none	no 'A C' trouble
	every girl is drying her		(+Condition B applies)
c.	La fille la voit danser	none (?)	no 'A C' trouble (?)
	the girl sees her dance		no Lexical trouble
			(Chain-Cond. applies)

4.2. Experiments on French and Italian

In order to obtain a first view of experimental techniques and results we now present earlier work on Romance clitics and binding in more detail than it was done in the more introductory Chapter 3. Jakubowicz (1989) conducted several experiments with French children of different ages. Her act-out task showed that French 3-year-olds perform 60% adultlike with Principle B sentences, 60% adultlike with a quantified potential antecedent and 90% adultlike with anaphors. These results are indicative but cannot be accepted without some remarks. To provide an anchor, Jakubowicz used complex clauses, which introduce an additional difficulty for very young children. Second, the act-out task is not very significant for problems of binding because in the best case it will mirror the preferred interpretation of the child, but will not give information about all the interpretations admitted in the child's grammar.

Jakubowicz explicitly tested for the delay of Principle B in an elicited production and a picture matching task. We present the results of the picture matching task in the form of the percentage of correct adult responses given by the child in a rather summary fashion.

(25)

	age group	3;0-3;5	3;6-4;0	5;0-6;0
a.	Nounours dit que Kiki se brosse	**96%**	97%	98%
	Teddy bear says that Kiki brushes himself			
b.	Nounours dit que Kiki le peigne	**60%**	80%	94%
	Teddy bear says that Kiki brushes him			

It has to be noted that in the 40% errors for pronoun interpretation in the 3.0 -3.5 age group, there were only 20% binding errors. So we find an 80% adult performance on (25b) in 3;0 to 3;5. year olds and a 90% adult performance in 3;6 to 4;0 old children - a remarkable result when compared to the performance of English children. A picture matching task is, however, not quite satisfactory for the investigation of binding. It will give only the preferred interpretation.

The results, nevertheless, lead Jakubowicz (1989) to reject a pragmatic account of the delay of Principle B. She prefers a lexical account, arguing that the phi and case features of pronouns are not firmly acquired while the properties of the reflexive (which are less specific in these two domains) are determined early. This, though reminiscent of the lexical account of Coopmans and Philip (1995), cannot be the right account for Romance clitics as was argued in section 2 of this chapter. That the results for simple Principle B sentences and quantified antecedent tests are the same follows directly from the fact that accidental coreference is hard to get for clitics.

McKee (1992) conducted an experiment on English and Italian children using a truth-value judgement task which involved the staging of scenes. Such a task is well able to control the context, so that all the possible readings can be tested and judged by the child. McKee reports that Italian 4-year-olds show virtually no 'delay of Principle B' with sentences like (26a) while English 4-year-olds tested in exactly the same way readily accepted a coreference reading of *the horse* and *him* in sentences such as (26b).

(26) a. Il cavallo lo spoglia
 b. the horse is dressing him.

McKee (1992) assumes that the highly adult-like performance follows from the fact of the clitic status of the Italian pronoun. It enables the Italian child to determine the target definition of the proper binding domain for pronominals earlier than his or her English peer.

In Italian, McKee (1992) argues, the minimal maximal category containing the clitic and a governor is the IP, which also contains the subject, so that a conflict cannot arise. In English the first category containing a governor and the pronoun is VP. If the child hypothesizes this as the relevant binding domain, then the pronoun and the sentence subject could be coindexed. There are several obvious problems with this account, not the least of which is how the child could ever escape from this superset language (see Berwick 1982 and Manzini and Wexler 1987). This account would also have to answer the question why Dutch children perform even worse than their English peers. Do they have a greater choice of binding domains? Another problem is why the correct binding domain has obviously been identified for the anaphor by English children, but this knowledge remains isolated and is not transferred to the pronoun. Moreover, if we formulate the problem in another way, i.e. as saying that English children first interpret off the deep structure, then there is no reason why the Italian child should not have the same option, the object clitic most certainly is not interpreted off IP. This problem becomes even more acute when we consider the recent analyses of phrase structure where object clitics and object pronouns alike will have to pass through AgrOP to have their case checked. Therefore the English child should find no reason to consider the VP as a possible binding domain.

(27) a. Italian: b. English:

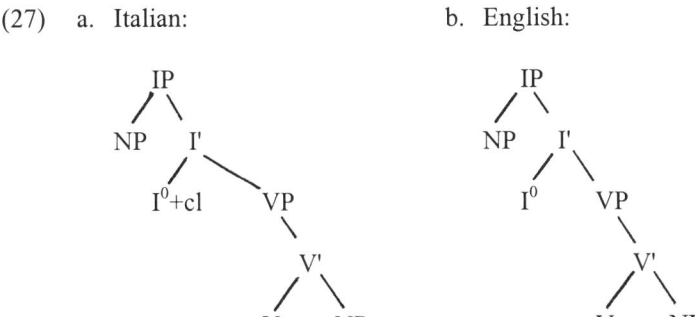

More arguments against the account can be found in Avrutin and Wexler (1992), but what is of interest here is the clear result and the clear prediction that there should be no difference in performance in the cases (28a) and (28b). The clitic in (28b) is in exactly the same surface position as in (28a), incorporated to the verb in $AgrS^0$.

(28) a. La fille la voit
         the girl her sees
      b. La fille la voit danser
         the girl her sees dance

In the next chapter we present our experiment in more detail, especially its techniques and results. We will then return to a discussion of the fact that the prediction about good performance in the ECM-like cases in French as in (28b) - which follows from all the previous accounts - is not born out by the data.

CHAPTER 5

TWO EXPERIMENTS ON BINDING EFFECTS WITH FRENCH CLITIC PRONOUNS

1. THE FIRST EXPERIMENT

1.1. Procedure and Design[1]

The experiment was presented to the child as a game with pictures. One player, who could not see the picture, would try to guess what was happening in each one, while the other players, who could see the picture, gave hints and judged whether or not the guesses were correct. One experimenter played the role of "guesser" throughout the experiment; another experimenter was the "helper" who gave hints; and the child's task was to listen to the guesses, look at the pictures, and judge whether or not the guesses were correct. The material was counterbalanced in such a way that roughly half the time the guesser made incorrect guesses. (For more information about the procedure see Hamann, Kowalski and Philip 1997).

Each experimental item had the following components. The VISUAL INPUT was a single picture showing two people of the same sex but different ages, one of whom was performing some action, or showing three people of the same age each performing some action and another person of a different age but the same sex doing nothing. Most of these pictures were identical to those used by Philip and Coopmans (1996a,b). The CONTEXT-SETTING INPUT was a verbally presented list of all the animate objects depicted in the picture, plus mention of the kind of action one or more of them were performing (without identifying agents or patients). The list of the discourse referents was first presented by the helper, as "hints" for the guesser, and then mentioned once again by the guesser, in a predetermined order, just before the guess was made. This predetermined order made sure that it was the last mentioned full DP that was pronominalized in the guess. The TARGET INPUT was the guesser's guess. This was delivered as a yes/no question so that it would always be felicitous as a simple request for information, if not as a guess. Both the helper and the guesser used normal prosody at all times. Finally, the PRIMARY DATA consisted in the child's "yes" or "no" responses. (For information about the coding of responses see Hamann, Kowalski and Philip 1997).

The experiment consisted of 5 test conditions and 11 control conditions. For each of these experimental conditions there were 3 different trials with syntactically identical target inputs but with different types of objects and actions depicted in the visual input and referred to by the target inputs. For all experimental conditions except LUI1, LUI2, VLAN (VoirLaNo), VSEN (VoirSENo), VLAY (VoirLaYes) and VSEY (VoirSeYes) (see below), the three predicates used for the three different trials of each experimental condition were: *sècher* 'dry off', *toucher* 'touch' and *montrer* 'point at'. Trials of the LUI1 and LUI2 conditions differed only with respect to the kinds of objects depicted in the visual inputs and referred to in the target inputs; the same predicate *mettre* 'put' was used in all cases. For the three different trials of the VLAN, VLAY, VSEN and VSEY conditions, the matrix predicate was always *voir* 'see' and the embedded predicates were *faire des bulles* 'blow bubbles', *sauter à la corde* 'jump rope' and *danser* 'dance'.

The overall design was that of Chien and Wexler's (1990) 4th experiment. Every experimental item whose target input contained a pronominal clitic was counterbalanced by an analogous experimental item whose target input used the same predicate but contained a reflexive clitic. Every experimental item which elicited an adult affirmative response (correct guess) was counterbalanced by an analogous item eliciting an adult negative response (incorrect guess). For all experimental conditions, except LUI1 and LUI2, the pronominal and reflexive clitics tested were *la* 'her' and *se* 'herself/himself', respectively. (Note that *se* is highly underspecified and can also be interpreted as 'itself', 'themselves' or 'each other'). For LUI1 and LUI2 the strong pronoun *lui* 'him' was used. The 48 experimental items were arranged in a single pseudo-random order, intermingled with 6 screening items and 9 filler items, and distributed over 3 test sessions. (For more information about design, and a complete list of the experimental items, see Hamann, Kowalski and Philip 1997).

1.2. Participants

Interspersed with the experimental material were 3 different trials each of two screening conditions (NEG1, NEG2). These were similar to the conditions (LUI1 and LUI2 except that they used full DPs instead of pronouns for the second referent.

(1)   a. **NEG1** (cf. LUI1)
(*Est-ce que le grandpère a mis le ballon de foot derrière le grandpère?*)

'Hm, a soccer ball, a boy, and a grandfather.'
'Has the grandfather put the soccer ball behind the grandfather?'

These always elicited adult negative responses and functioned as basic controls for attention and mastery of the experimental task. Children who ever gave a "yes" response on any of the 6 trials of these screening conditions were excluded from the study. This procedure excluded seven children. The age statistics of the children who always responded "no" under these screening conditions are shown in table 20. Subsequent analysis showed no significant main effect of age, nor a significant age x condition interactive effect, between the six- and seven-year-olds. So these subjects have been pooled into a single age group. In addition, 6 adults (mean age 32 years) participated as a control group. The adults were simply asked the target input questions about the pictures.

116 CHAPTER 5

b. **NEG2** (cf. LUI2) *Est-ce que le père a mis la boite derrière le garçon?*

'Hm..a box, a father and a boy.'
'Has the father put the box behind the boy?'

Table 20: The participants' ages

age group	n	mean age	age range
4 yr	9	4;3	3;5 to 4;8
5 yr	8	5;7	5;3 to 5;11
6-7 yrs	16	6;9	6;0 to 7;3
all	33	5;9	3;5 to 7;3

1.3. Test Conditions

The three test conditions LAN (LaNo), QLAN (QuantifierLaNo) and VLAN (VoirLaNo), which elicited adult "no" responses, are exemplified in English in (2). The input of the guesser is indicated at the bottom of each picture in English; the actual French target input is shown in parentheses at the top.

(2) a. **LAN** (*Est-ce que la fille la touche?*)

Hmmm...a girl and a grandma (context-setting input)
Is the girl touching her? (target input)

b. **QLAN** (*Est-ce que chaque maman la sèche?*)

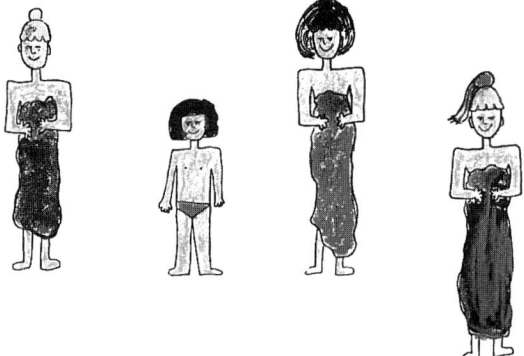

Hmm...three moms with towels and a girl
(context-setting input)
Is every mom drying her off? (target input)

c. **VLAN**(*Est-ce que la fille la voit faire des bulles?*)

Hm...a big mirror, a girl, and a grandma
(context-setting input)
Does the girl see her blow bubbles? (target input)

The LUI1 and LUI2 test conditions, for which an adult could either respond "yes" or "no", are exemplified in (3).

(3) a. **LUI1**
(*Est-ce que le garçon a mis le ballon de foot derrière lui?*)

Hmm...a football, a boy, and a grandpa (context-setting input)
Has the boy put the football behind him? (target input)

b. **LUI2**   (*Est-ce que le garçon a mis la boite derrière lui?*)

Hmm...a box, a boy, and a dad (context-setting input)
Has the boy put the box behind him? (target input)

1.4. Control Conditions

There were three control conditions LAY, QLAY and VLAY which had the same types of context-setting and target inputs as the LAN, QLAN and VLAN test conditions, respectively, but which were paired with pictures similar to those in (4), so that they elicited adult affirmative responses. In addition, there were the three control conditions SEN, QSEN and VSEN exemplified in (4), which tested reflexive rather than pronominal clitics and which elicited adult negative responses. These control conditions were counterbalanced by three other control conditions SEY, QSEY and VSEY, which used the same type of context-setting and target inputs as the SEN, QSEN and VSEN conditions, respectively, but were paired with pictures similar to those in (2) above, so that they elicited adult affirmative responses.

(4) a. **SEN** (*Est-ce que la fille se touche?*)

Hmmm...a grandma and a girl (context-setting input)
Is the girl touching herself? (target input)

b. **QSEN** (*Est-ce que chaque maman se montre?*)

Hmm...a girl and three moms (context-setting input)
Is every mom pointing at herself? (target input)

c. **VSEN** (*Est-ce que la fille se voit faire des bulles?*)

Hmm...a big mirror, a grandma, and a girl (context-setting input)
Does the girl see herself blow bubbles? (target input)

Finally, there were two control conditions QY and QN, exemplified in (5), which independently assessed performance with the distributive universal

(5) a. **QN** (*Est-ce que chaque garçon tient un parapluie?*)

Hmm...some boys and some umbrellas (context-setting input)
Is every boy holding an umbrella? (target input)

b. **QY** (*Est-ce que chaque éléphant tient un ballon?*)

Hmm...3 elephants, 4 balloons, and a boy (context-setting input)
Is every elephant holding a balloon? (target input)

quantifier *chaque* 'every/each'. The context-setting input for the QN condition was always an incomplete description of the contents of the picture. The predicate for the QY and QN conditions was always *tenir* 'have/hold'.

1.5. Results

1.5.1 Individual Trial and Age Effects

In general, there were no significant effects of individual trials for any experimental condition (except for the VLAY condition; see Hamann, Kowalski and Philip 1997). There were also no significant age effects among the five-, six- and seven-year-olds (except, again, for the VLAY condition). There was, however, one major age effect: the four-year-olds showed significantly lower levels of adult-like performance than the older children on several experimental conditions.

1.5.2 Control Conditions

The 6 adults in the control group gave expected "yes" and "no" responses 100% of the time for all control conditions. For the five-, six- and seven-year-olds performance on the control conditions was highly adult-like across-the-board, as shown in tables 21 and 22. The only minor exception to this was the performance of the five-year-olds on the VLAY condition. As for the four-year-olds, as seen in table 22, these children showed a slight tendency to respond "yes" with conditions that elicited an adult "no" response. This suggests that despite their highly adult-like performance on the screening conditions their performance on the experimental conditions was partially confounded by a general strategy of responding affirmatively.

Table 21: Percent "Yes" responses on control conditions eliciting adult "Yes" responses

age group	LAY	QLAY	VLAY	SEY	QSEY	VSEY
4 yrs	82%	89%	70%	96%	85%	93%
5 yrs	100%	100%	63%	100%	96%	96%
6-7 yrs	100%	98%	94%	96%	96%	100%

Table 22: Percent "No" responses on control conditions eliciting adult "No" responses

age group	SEN	QSEN	VSEN
4 yrs	74%	74%	70%
5 yrs	96%	92%	92%
6-7 yrs	100%	85%	96%

1.5.3 Test Conditions

The 6 adults in the control group gave the expected "no" response 100% of the time for the LAN, QLAN and VLAN test conditions. With the exception of the four-year-olds, all the children in the study showed highly adult-like performance on the LAN and QLAN test conditions, as shown in table 23. The four-year-olds' performance was also considerably adult-like for these conditions, although the same slight tendency to give nonadult-like "yes" responses is again observed with the LAN and QLAN conditions. In stark contrast to performance under the LAN and QLAN test conditions, all the children in the study showed extremely low levels of adult-like performance under the VLAN test condition. As seen by the table of p-values from two-tailed t-tests in table 24, the contrast between the LAN and VLAN conditions is highly significant for virtually all age groups, while there is no significant contrast between SEN and VSEN for any age group. Collapsing the age groups into a single sample (n = 33), sign tests also show a highly significant contrast between LAN and VLAN (p ≤ 0.0000) but no significant contrast between SEN and VSEN (p ≤ 0.5488).

Table 23: Percent "No" responses on test conditions eliciting adult "No" responses

age group	LAN	QLAN	VLAN
4 yrs	78%	70%	48%
5 yrs	100%	88%	54%
6-7 yrs	100%	94%	62%
all ages	94%	86%	56%

Table 24: T-Tests

age group	LAN vs. VLAN	SEN vs. VSEN
4 yrs	p ≤ 0.0517	p ≤ 0.7545
5 yrs	p ≤ 0.0135	p ≤ 0.5983
6-7 yrs	p ≤ 0.0014	p ≤ 0.1639
all ages	p ≤ 0.000	p ≤ 0.2895

As for the last two test conditions, the 6 adults in the control group gave the expected "yes" response 100% of the time for the LUI1 condition and 83% of the time for the LUI2 condition. (Most of the adults indicated that a "no" response was also possible for the LUI1 and LUI2 conditions.) Turning to the children, the first general observation is that each age group gave both "yes" and "no" responses fairly often for each of these two test conditions, as seen in table 25. Collapsing age groups (n = 33), a two-tailed t-test comparing the children's performance on LUI1 and LUI2 showed the contrast not to be significant (p ≤ 0.1720). This suggests that the "average French child" between five and seven years of age randomly responds "yes" or "no" under the LUI1 and LUI2 conditions. The second general observation, which may be gleaned from the table of individual performance in Appendix I, is that generally an individual child consistently responded "yes" under one of these two test conditions, and consistently responded "no" under the other.

Table 25: Percent "Yes" responses on test conditions eliciting adult "Yes" responses

age group	LUI1	LUI2
4 yrs	22% (10)	59% (13)
5 yrs	75% (14)	29% (16)
6-7 yrs	73% (10)	35% (10)
all ages	60% (8)	40% (7)

1.6. Discussion

The summary of our results as stated in (6) and as briefly mentioned in chapter 3, table 19, shows that two of our predictions as stated in (24) of chapter 4 section 4.1. were born out in accordance with the results of McKee (1992) and Jakubowicz (1989), whereas the third, contrary to expectation, was not.

(6)   Percent Errors (with 5-7 yrs)

	sentence type	predicted	observed	explanation
a.	la fille la touche the girl is touching her	0%	0%	no 'A C' trouble (Condition B ok)
b.	Chaque fille la touche every girl is touching her	0%	8%	no 'A C' trouble (Condition B ok)
c.	La fille la voit danser the girl sees her dance	0%	**40%**	Chain-cond. applies Condition B does not apply (R&R)

The question we can ask now is whether the result for (6c) is due to some lexical trouble not discussed and foreseen so far. This approach would look for a solution in the reflexivity framework and the Chain Condition, and we will discuss it in section 2. Alternatively we can use Heim's framework and ask whether in the (6c) cases we may find a reason why the rule of exceptional coindexation (ECR) should apply. Due to the difficulties with this rule French children might then perform as randomly as their English peers in contexts like (6a). Pursuing this latter alternative we have two possibilities.

We can assume that the child must have created two guises in this particular experimental set up, investigate why this should be so and explore it in a second experiment. We could also start from the observation that (6c) is a rather special construction where the clitic pronoun has a sort of double-function as object of the matrix clause and subject of the embedded clause. This structural double function may bring into play the ECR and, independently from the experimental set up, two guises. We will pursue these possibilities in sections 3 and 4 of this chapter.

2. THE LEXICAL APPROACH

2.1. The Reflexivity Feature

In Chapter 4, we have shown that the interplay of the movement properties of clitics and the different elements of the Reflexivity framework, the Chain Condition in particular, make it quite improbable that the child has not fully specified the features of the clitic. Nevertheless, it has been suggested that there may be a problem with the lexical acquisition of the referentiality feature connected with the 3rd person pronoun. Such a problem could arise due to the ambiguity of the first and second person object pronouns and due to the basic ambiguity of strong pronouns with respect to pronominal or anaphoric status. In these cases both the pronoun and the anaphor have the same form: *lui* (strong) or *me* and *te* (clitic). This, it could be argued, leads the child to speculate that the clitic *le* or *la* could also be ambiguous. Therefore, the French child, though having overt evidence for the fact that the clitic functions like a +referential expression, may conclude that this does not always have to be so and that the clitic can be marked as [-referential]. This predicts a poor performance in the cases where the Chain Condition is the only condition to apply and so gives the desired result.

However, it also predicts a much worse than only 8% error rate in the simple case (6a) because the pronoun, being ambiguous, will be able to function as an anaphor. Remember that according to (24) of Chapter 3, anaphors and pronouns have opposite values with respect to referentiality, so that if a lexical item of the pronominal class does not have the referentiality feature, the obvious assumption would be that it is an anaphor. The approach, if turned on its head, may even predict that due to phonological similarity to *me*, *te* and also *le*, the clitic anaphor *se* may sometimes be analyzed as a pronoun [+referential] so that we expect errors even in the Principle A case of '*la fille se touche*'.

One may also wonder whether the misclassification of a pronoun as [–referential] may not qualify it as appearing as the tail (or as part) of a chain starting with a quantified antecedent. This would lead us to expect errors in the case of (6b) which is contrary to known cross-linguistic results.

2.2. Results on Spanish

An approach assuming difficulties with the referentially feature as outlined above is suggested by Baauw, Escobar and Philip (1997) for the results on pronominal reference they obtain for Spanish in essentially the same experiment as the one described in the previous sections of this chapter. This means in particular that for the (6c) cases there was a mirror in the picture. These authors find 90% adult performance in the simple condition (6a), 90% adult performance in the quantified antecedent case, but only 64% adult performance in the case corresponding to (6c) for 4 year old children. These results correspond exactly to our results as summed up in (6). Baauw, Escobar and Philip (1997) argue that clitics never allow accidental coreference because they are underspecified for the feature [human] and so must be bound either in syntax or through D-linking in order to provide a feature for this specification. This is in essence the idea of Cardinaletti and Starke (2000) which I develop along similar lines in Chapter 4, section 3.3. However, whereas Baauw, Escobar and Philip totally disallow it, accidental coreference is possible in very special cases in my treatment. It is possible that it is their stretching of the term 'bound' to D-linking which leads these authors to the conclusion that clitics do not allow accidental coreference at all, even though the cases of accidental coreference I discuss for French clitics are also acceptable for their Spanish counterparts,[2] This assumption excludes any explanation of the result on (6c) that might appeal to the coreference rule. Therefore these authors propose the lexical approach based on the ambiguity of the first and second person lexemes which is the same in French and Spanish.

2.3. Results on Norwegian

In an experiment on Norwegian Hestvik and Philip (1997) tested Principle B effects and effects of the Chain Condition. Due to the properties of the Norwegian pronoun system, the mirror condition was not needed in this experiment.

Norwegian pronouns have the so called anti-subject orientation which has been analyzed as an effect of clitic-like head-movement at LF (see Hestvik 1990). The Chain Condition according to Hestvik and Philip (1997) applies to the subject of the clause and the pronoun in its raised LF position and excludes coindexation because the pronoun is seen as the tail of the chain. Such a chain is excluded by their formulation of the chain-condition because the tail of the chain, i.e. the pronoun, is fully specified and anti-subject orientation is the result.

Following Philip and Coopmans (1996a,b) reasoning for Dutch in the reflexivity framework, Hestvik and Philip (1997) assume a lexical problem in that the child does not yet have the full specification for the pronoun. They predict the following error pattern. For quantificational antecedents that are co-arguments of the pronoun, no errors are predicted because the coreference rule cannot apply. For quantificational antecedents that are not co-arguments of the pronoun, they predict some errors because the underspecification will sometimes allow co-indexation under the chain-condition (see 2.1). Non-quantificational antecedents that are coarguments of the pronouns should also show some errors under contraindexation and coreference rule failure. But most errors are predicted for non-quantificational antecedents that are not coarguments of the pronouns because both coindexation and contraindexation may lead to errors, one under the chain-condition together with underspecification, the other under the failure of the coreference rule.

This pattern is indeed found in the results, where the non-coargument tests were partly identical to the LUI-conditions described above, i.e. they involved locative prepositional phrases. There was a 1% error for quantificational antecedents in coargument configurations, and about 10% such errors with non-quantificational coarguments. There were about 32% errors with quantificational locatives (non-coarguments), but 65% errors with non-quantificational non-coarguments.

At first glance these results seem to support the predictions made by Hestvik and Philip (1977)'s assumption of underspecification of the pronoun. Mirrors need not be invoked to test the chain-condition in Norwegian, and the effect of the coreference rule and of the chain-condition can be teased apart. There are empirical and theoretical arguments against this treatment, however.

First, it is surprising that co-argument non-quantificational contexts only showed a 10% error due to the failure of the coreference rule, whereas in English the same situation leads to about 50% errors (likewise due to the coreference rule). Hestvik and Philip (1997) explain this behaviour with the assumption that these pronouns are clitics at LF and the fact that clitics resist accidental coreference. This assumption cannot be upheld without further research into the interpretative conditions of Norwegian pronouns, which do not seem to resemble the properties we discussed for clitics. It also seems to run into problems with the idea that the restrictions for clitics have to do with the [+/-human] specification. Additionally, the Norwegian surface pronoun does allow deictic use and so clearly is ambiguous and can be a strong pronoun. Moreover, the establishment of a chain to explain anti-subject orientation, and its particular treatment leads to certain problems, again theoretical and empirical.

Hestvik and Philip (1997) speak about head-movement so that the problems of what constitutes the argument chain-part of such a chain should be the same as the problems we have discussed in chapter 4. They do not discuss the trace of the pronoun at all - though this is certainly part of the chain. They do not see any problem in integrating the head itself into the argument chain and treat it as the foot of the chain. Actually, if the argument is followed through and we extend the chain to its real foot, the trace of the pronoun, we cannot derive anti-subject orientation, because this foot is certainly underspecified. So Hestvik and Philip (1997) have to assume tacitly that the chain-condition only applies to the part of the chain which is derived by indexation, not to the movement part. This clearly contradicts Reinhart and Reuland (1993)'s definition and intentions, and it also applies the A-chain condition to a chain whose first link is an argument but whose second link is a head. As we do not have any results from natural production as to the correct use of anti-subject oriented pronouns by young children and the help they can get from the gender situation (see example (12) of chapter 4), it is hard to judge what is really going on. If my reasoning of chapter 4 is correct and the head-movement analysis of anti-subject orientation is also correct, then the Norwegian child should be in almost as good a position as the Romance child: the situation and the chain-condition should tell the child that the pronoun is fully specified. Of course, there is one big difference: the Romance child has overt evidence because of overt clitic movement, whereas the Norwegian child has no such evidence. On the whole, I see many problems with the assumption of underspecification. Not the least of these is the doubt that nothing will prevent the child to sometimes analyze the pronoun as an anaphor if the pronoun is really underspecified with respect to referentiality.[3]

2.4. Conclusion

For the reasons I have given in chapter 4 and in the previous sections, I do not think that an approach based on the homophony of pronouns and anaphors and a subsequent underspecification of the referentiality feature is on the right track for the Romance languages. In addition, the investigation of spontaneous speech discussed in Chapter 2 shows a firm mastery of the lexical properties of clitic pronouns from early on. Moreover, the deictic component of *me* or *te* provides an additional feature which forces the interpretation function to choose the 'speaker' or 'hearer' as a guise. Therefore these pronouns are lexically special and it is unlikely that their special features are generalized to other pronouns.

3. THE CHILD MAY CREATE TWO GUISES

3.1. Extended Guise Creation

We had argued with Cardinaletti and Starke (2000) that the structural deficiency of the clitic and its lack of an inherent range restriction go hand in hand. We had concluded that the general resistance of clitics and weak pronouns to accidental coreference follows from the lack of an inherent range restriction and their interpretation via a salient discourse element. We had also argued that special contexts that allow or require different guises to refer to the same individual will allow accidental coreference even for clitics. As a move to an accidental coreference reading makes it unnecessary for the child to scan the wider discourse for a possible antecedent, it can be seen as an attempt at 'grounding' in the smallest domain as described by Wexler (1996) or by Grimshaw and Rosen (1990). If the acceptance of guises and accidental coreference is indeed an attempt at grounding or anchorage, it is only one facet of a general difficulty with discourse anchorage.

An examination of the experimental conditions now shows that the simple case indeed always provides an unmarked "run of the mill" context and the unambiguously deficient clitic can thus not be interpreted as coreferring with the subject of the clause by the child. The question we ask now is whether (6c) may not be a context that systematically introduces two guises.

The assumption that children create two different guises whenever this is remotely possible is totally in accordance with the suggestions of Thornton and Wexler (1999). These authors claim that children create different guises even in contexts where adults cannot do so. This 'Extended Guise Creation' (Thronton and Wexler 1999:102) is responsible for the accidental coreference readings English children assign to simple cases like (6a). Thornton and Wexler (1999) suggest two possible guises for the simple contexts: the 'deictic' or 'pointing' guise and the 'role reversal guise', which can be paraphrased as "the individual who Vs somebody" were V is the transitive verb relevant in the conidtion. Both are not available for clitics in these simple cases because clitics, as we had argued in chapter 4, need to be identified through the guise of the salient DPs they are linked to. So guise creation is severely limited for clitics.

Exploring the idea of 'Extended Guise Creation' the obvious assumption is that the experimental condition for (6c), the mirror situation, introduces what could be interpreted as two guises: the direct visual image and the mirror image of a person. Adults obviously collapse these to just one guise 'visual image', but the presentation of a picture showing both the person and its mirror image could arguably lead the child to use two distinct guises.

So 'Extended Guise Creation' finds an almost ideal context in condition (6c) even for clitics: another guise, the mirror image, is always available and can be used to give a positive answer. As children generally prefer to give positive answers, guise extension might be the consequence - even if the child had well passed the warm up test and identified the mirror image as an image of the relevant person, or even if the child had used the anaphor in spontaneous speech in sentences like *elle se voit dans le miroir* 'she sees herself in the mirror'. Later we will consider another way of guise creation in the situation of (6c), but for the time being we will concentrate on the 'mirror problem' introduced by the experimental implementation of condition (6c).

The potential problem with the mirror context is an involuntary side effect of trying to keep the context concrete, conceptually easy, and such that it can be represented in a simple drawing. The latter is certainly not possible with the notorious (7), but is a necessity of the experimental design.

(7)   Bill considers him an idiot.

This situation is unfortunate when regarded from the perspective of the Chain Condition, which was to be tested with (6c). The Chain Condition can be mastered perfectly, but the experimental context may systematically introduce accidental coreference. On the other hand, the result might confirm that accidental coreference is indeed possible with clitics. In that case we could conclude that the influence of accidental coreference and the rule of exceptional coindexation is decisive for the performance of young children even in Romance languages.

Let us recapitulate. Romance children perform well in the simple case (6a) because clitics resist accidental coreference and require very special contexts to provide distinct guises. English and Dutch children perform at chance level in the simple case because the pronouns are ambiguous between a strong and a weak reading and children prefer to use the normal DP structure, i.e. the strong form. This form allows accidental coreference, and therefore the overacceptance of simple cases by English children can well be due to 'Extended Guise Creation' as Thornton and Wexler (1999) suggest. Children perform well cross-linguistically when the antecedent is a quantified DP (6b) because accidental coreference cannot arise in these cases. Romance children perform at about chance level in the case of (6c) because the context can be regarded as allowing accidental coreference either through an experimental artifact or through a structural ambiguity which will be explored later. English and Dutch children perform worse because there are two factors pushing them towards accidental coreference readings: the choice of the strong pronoun and the context. There may even be lexical complications in the case of Dutch, which will add to the difficulties.

There are certain predictions following from this account, however. First we expect that French or Italian children perform at chance level with strong pronouns. As French strong pronouns are systematically ambiguous between a coreferential and a free reading, while the anaphoric marking mostly (but not always) provides focus, these chance level interpretations are not target deviant, but may be indicative, see (8a,b,c).

(8) a. Jean$_i$ est content de lui$_{i/j}$
Jean$_i$ is proud of him$_{i/j}$
b. ?Jean est content de lui-même
Jean is proud of himself
c. Jean n'est content que de lui-même
Jean (ne)is proud only of himself

Our preliminary tests on *lui* have indeed shown chance performance with perhaps personal preferences for one or the other coindexation.[4]

More important is the following prediction. Whenever a mirror and a mirror image of the person in question is present in the experimental condition and the test condition is a simple sentence involving the verb *'see'* as in (9) we expect the same result as for (6c). This is so because it is the mirror in the picture which introduces the second guise not anything in the complexity of the sentence.

(9) Est-ce que la fille la voit
     'does the girl see her'

The alternative explanation, where guise creation does not depend on the presence of a mirror is equally simple as we will see. In view of the Norwegian experiment reported in 2.3., which did not use mirrors but showed errors in a complex structure involving prepositions, such an explanation may be preferable in the end. However, the possibility of using the 'mirror guise' is so persuasive that an experiment was conducted in the framework of the Interfaculty Project in Geneva in order to exclude the 'mirror guise' as an explanation. The experiment tested especially the above prediction about (9) (see Leyat and Micalizzi 1998) and will be presented in section 3. 2 of this chapter.

3.2. The 'Mirror Experiment'

3.2.1. Procedure and Design

In general the procedure was the same as in the previous experiment. Pictures were used to play a guessing game which amounted to a truth-value judgement task. Moreover, the pictures, conditions and verbs (*voir, secher, montrer du doigt, toucher*) were partially the same. Some slight alterations in the pictures aimed for greater clarity. So a hair dryer was used for the conditions which involved the verb *secher* 'dry' where formerly a towel gave the lexical hint. For the conditions involving *montrer du doigt* 'point at' the drawing was altered so as to always involve a pointing index finger, and for *toucher* 'touch' it was always made clear that one person's hand is making contact with some part of the other person's body – often the head. For all conditions with *voir,* in simple or embedded contexts, a mirror was used in the picture.

As there was no question of trying to establish anew the contrast in the comprehension of simple sentences with a quantified antecedent as compared to a simple DP antecedent, the conditions with quantifiers were left out. As these also involved controls of quantifier interpretation, this removed a heavy load of conditions which could be replaced by conditions probing for the comprehension of field of vision of others (theory of mind), and the creation of guises in the mirror contexts. In order to avoid boredom with the female antagonists, this time boys and fathers were part of the pictures but occurred mostly in the conditions involving the mirror.

The experiment aimed to test for the possibility to create guises in mirror contexts but also for the possibility of a lexical underspecification of pronouns. Because of the latter aim and the discussion in section 2 of Chapter 5, it was not judged appropriate to use all of the conditions with the reflexive pronoun *se* as controls. As in the previous experiment, however, the conditions eliciting an adult 'yes' answer were considered to act as controls.

3.2.2. Participants

For the experiment 5 adults participated as controls, and there was a pilot experiment with a child of 6 years of age, who did well in all of the tests. The participants of the test were 10 monolingual French speaking children recruited from two different Genevan kindergartens. Their ages ranged from 3.2 to 4.3, and they were grouped as the 3 year olds (3.2-3.9) and the 4 year olds (4.0-4.3). There were 5 children in each of these groups.

Table 26: Participants of the 'Mirror Experiment'

	N	age range
3 year olds	5	3.2. – 3.9.
4 year olds	5	4.0. – 4.3
adults	5	18-50

3.2.3. Test Conditions

The conditions LUI1 and LUI2 were the same as before. LAN and SEN (a former control condition) also remained the same, involving the verbs *secher* 'dry', *toucher* 'touch', and *montrer du doigt* 'point at'. The same holds for the conditions VLAN and VSEN, the conditions with the mirror and the embedding. The conditions MLAN (MirrorLaNon) and MSEN (MirrorSeNon) were added. These tested the comprehension of the pronoun or anaphor with the verb *voir* in the mirror context in a simple sentence. In (10a) there is the mirror image of the girl in the mirror visible to her. So if the mirror image is interpreted as a different guise of the girl, this should facilitate a coreference reading.

(10) a. **MLAN** (Est-ce que la fille la voit)

Hmmm… a girl and a mom (context-setting input)
Does the girl see her? (target input).

b. **MSEN** (Est-ce que la grand-mère se voit?)

Hmmm… a girl and a grandmother. (Context-setting input)
Does the grandmother see herself? (target input)

The conditions MON (MirrorOtherNon) and MSN (MirrorSelfNon) did not involve pronouns or anaphors in order to give indications of how the field of vision of other persons is interpreted. For this a new type of picture was created: One person always was with their back to the mirror and out of the field of direct vision of the other person who was looking towards the mirror.

(11) a. **MON** (Est-ce que la fille voit le père)

Hmmm… a girl and a father. (context setting input)
Does the girl see the father? (target input)

TWO EXPERIMENTS ON BINDING IN FRENCH   137

The MSN condition used exactly the same type of picture as the MON condition in (11a), but had a different target input as given in (11b).

    b. **MSN** (Est-ce que le père voit le père)

    Hmmm… a girl and a father. (context setting input)
    Does the father see the father? (target input)

3.2.3. Control Conditions

The conditions NEG1 and NEG2 still acted as a control for the participant's willingness to say 'no'. They were changed, however, so as to involve the verbs *secher* 'dry', *toucher* 'touch', and *montrer du doigt* 'point at'.

(12)   a. **NEG1**(toucher) (Est-ce que la fille touche la grand-mère?)

Hmmm… a boy, a girl and a grandmother. (Context-setting input)
Is the girl touching the grandmother? (target input)

b. **NEG2** (secher) (Est-ce que la mère seche la mère?)

Hmmm… a girl and a mom. (Context setting input)
Is the mother drying the mother? (target input)

The conditions LAY and SEY as well as VLAY and VSEY remain the same as in experiment 1. We add MLAY /MLEY (MirrorLa/LeYes) and MSEY (MirrorSeYes), which both contain a person not reflected in the mirror, but well able to see either the other person (MLEY as shown in (13a)) or their own reflection in the mirror (MSEY as shown in (13b)).

(13) a. MLEY (Est-ce que le garçon le voit?)

Hmmm… a boy and a father (context-setting input)
Does the boy see him? (target input).

b. MSEY (Est-ce que la mère se voit?)

Hmmm… a mom and a girl. (Context setting input)
Does the mom see herself? (target input)

We also add MOY (MirrorOtherYes) and MSY (MirrorSelfYes), where two persons are in front of the mirror with visible reflections, and both are looking at each other's mirror reflection. (14a) exemplifies the MOY condition. MSY uses the same type of picture but has the target input as given in (14b).

(14) a. MOY   (Est-ce que la grand-mère voit la fille?)

Hmmm… a grandmother and a girl. (context setting input)
Does the grandmother see the girl? (target input)

b. MSY   (Est-ce que la fille voit la fille?)

Hmmm… a girl and a grand-ma. (context setting input)
Does the girl see the girl? (target input)

3.2.4. Results and Discussion

Because of the small number of children and the relatively small number of test items for each condition, statistics were not performed on the results. What I present in the following are the percentages of adult responses for each condition.

The adults performed always to expectation, and so for all conditions there was a 100% success. The conditions LUI1 and LUI2 showed chance performance in all age groups and will not be further discussed. Table 26 and table 27 show the results for the different age groups for the control and for the test conditions respectively.

Table 27   Control Conditions:
Percentage of correct responses of the different age groups

age	MLAY	LAY	VLAY	MSEY	SEY	VSEY	MOY	MSY
3 years	93.2	93.2	72.8	100	93.2	93.2	70	40
4 years	93.2	86.4	79.6	100	93.2	100	80	80
adults	100	100	100	100	100	100	100	100

Table 28   Test Conditions:
Percentage of correct responses of the different age groups

age	MLAN	LAN	VLAN	MSEN	SEN	VSEN	MON	MSN
3 years	90	79.8	53	79.8	72.8	86.4	100	80
4	90	86.4	66.2	80	79.6	79.8	100	100

years								
adults	100	100	100	100	100	100	100	100

The children, even the 3 year-olds, performed close to adults in most of the control conditions. The most difficult conditions seem to be VLAY and MOY where 3-year-olds are close to 70% and, quite unexpectedly, MSY, where 3 year-olds are only 40% correct. Note that not all mirror conditions are problematic: the simple pronoun condition with *voir* and the mirror was mastered to 90%. The 4 year-olds are 80% correct in VLAY, MOY and MSEY and better in the rest of the conditions. We note a generally good performance in the conditions with the anaphors (except MSY).

As to the test conditions, we find the same result as in the previous experiment with respect to the bad performance with the pronoun in the embedded context, VLAN, where 3 year-olds are 53% correct and 4 year-olds are still only 66% correct. The performance concerning the field of vision conditions MON and MSN is better than for the corresponding control conditions. The conditions with the anaphor are again mastered quite well.

The good results in the LAN, LAY, SEN and SEY conditions argue against a simple lexical confusion with regard to referentiality. As to our main concern, however, it turns out that the simple pronoun sentence with the mirror and the verb *voir*, MLAN, is mastered even better than the same conditions with other verbs. Just as in the previous experiment, the problematic condition is the one involving 'montrer du doigt' inspite of the systematic amelioration of the drawings. So this slight drop in performance in LAN compared to MLAN is due to difficulties with one verb. We can conclude that the MLAN and the LAN conditions are mastered equally well. This provides counterevidence for the assumption that the mirror context allows to create a different guise, no matter what the sentence is.

On the other hand, apart from the VLAY result, the other marked difficulty, the MSY condition, seems to be connected to what I would like to call 'theory of mind'. Flavel et al. (1981) and Flavel (1992) showed that at the age of three children know that the experimenter sees the dog which is on his side of a vertically held card whereas the child itself sees the cat on his or her side of the card. These authors also showed that at that age difficulties persist with the orientation of the depicted objects with respect to different observers. As such an orientation concerns the guise of an object, this difficulty could give the explanation for the bad performance on the MSY control condition. In fact, in this condition, it is clear that the antagonists see only their reflection, never themselves directly. In the MLAY and MOY conditions, the turn of the head and thus the direction of the eyes allows that the antagonist sees the other person both directly and as a mirror image. In the MLAN and MON conditions the other person is clearly out of the field of vision and without a reflection. So in the MSY condition, we probably have to deal with an interpretation of the reflection as a different guise which, in this case, allows the child to say 'no'.

3.3. Conclusion

Experiment 2 has confirmed the difficulty with the VLAN conditions, i.e. with conditions where the pronoun is embedded in a lower clause and, in the case of the clitic, has overtly moved out of this lower clause. A lexical problem with the classification of the pronoun as both [+] and [–referential] can be excluded by the persistently good results on *se*, *le* and *la* in non-embedded contexts.

A problem with guises remains a possibility in so far as the results on condition MSY may be interpreted as indicating that children do not completely identify the reflection and the person. However, the equally good performance on MLAN and LAN clearly demonstrates, that guise creation is not systematically driven by the mirror context, i.e. the presence of the reflection and the person.

In order to explain the main result of experiments 1 and 2, namely the bad performance on VLAN, we still have to answer the question of what the coreference rule or more precisely the rule of exceptional coindexing (ECR) can contribute - if it is not the fact that we are dealing with two different guises introduced by the mirror. We will now explore a structural ambiguity of (6c) for systematic guise creation.

4. STRUCTURAL AMBIGUITY AND GUISE CREATION

4.1. Structural Ambiguity and the Reconstruction of the Clitic

Experiment 2 has excluded the 'mirror'guise as an explanation of children's performance on (6c). Let us therefore look for another reason why the rule of exceptional coindexing (ECR) and different guises may play a role in (6c).

Obviously, children have problems when real movement is involved and the moved element crosses a clause boundary. This observation was made by Bottari et al. (1996) with respect to Italian Specific Language Impaired (SLI) children. Though these children were able to use pronominal clitics in simple contexts, they never used clitics in so-called clitic climbing structures where a clause boundary has to be crossed as in (15). Bottari et al. attribute this phenomenon to a basic difficulty in Chain Formation.

(15)   lo vuole vedere
         him I want to see

If we follow this idea, we can propose that children are reconstructing the clitic in the lower clause so that coindexation with the subject of the higher clause becomes a licit possibility. The better performance of French children is explained by the fact that the French child, again, has overt evidence that the clitic is in the higher clause, while English and Dutch children do not have this evidence. So reconstruction may be the option which is chosen less often in French. This does not explain the fact that Dutch children do worse than English children and a lexical effect seems to complicate the matter here. It does not explain either how French children can learn not to reconstruct, given that the Chain Condition, the binding principles and the input will not change in the course of development. Moreover, one expects a better than chance performance given the fact that two consecutive choices may be made and only one of the possible combinations will lead to a non-adult response. For these reasons the possibility of reconstruction does not explain the facts in a straightforward way. Fortunately there is another way to relate the embedding context to a structural ambiguity which allows guise creation and accidental coreference.

4.2. The Lower Subject Guise

We develop the argument in the following steps: The coreference rule is a specific instance of one of Grice's conversational maxim's which says: be explicit. The same holds for the exceptional coindexing rule. Clearly, this maxim only applies if there is a possible ambiguity. In the ECM/raising/clitic-climbing cases we find another sort of ambiguity, the structural ambiguity arising because the clitic is the object of the matrix verb but the subject of the verb in the embedded clause.

Let us consider (6c) again, repeated as (16) here. (16) lends itself quite naturally to the idea that children overextend guise creation.

(16) La fille la voit danser
The girl sees her dance

The context is that of a picture with a mirror, the mother and the girl in front of the mirror, the mother standing there and the girl dancing. The context setting input is: Mmh, a mother and a girl. So there are two possibile antecedents for the pronoun in the guises specified by the picture: the mother and the girl. As the condition MLAN of experiment 2 showed, children have no problem of applying Principle B to these guises, which identify different persons, and come up with the adult answer. In (16), there is another guise available for one of the possible antecedents, however.

(17) a. The girl sees her who dances
b. The girl sees her in the action of dancing

We see this, when we paraphrase (16) as (17a) or (17b). As subject of the lower clause, the pronoun refers to the person who dances. Therefore the structural ambiguity systematically introduces the guise 'the dancer'. More generally, in the VLAN contexts like (16) we always have the structure (18).

(18) X sees Y Ving   where V is the verb of the lower clause

So the child can systematically overextend guise creation and can always assume the guise 'the Y which is Ving', which we can call the 'Lower Subject Guise'. This guise is clearly different from the guise of the possible antecedent 'the girl'. So the exceptional coindexing rule applies and allows the child to interpret the pronoun as coreferring with 'la fille', who is indeed the 'dancer', or the person who is Ving. For the child, such an interpretation has two advantages: the child can say yes to the experimenter and the child need not look beyond the given sentence for an antecedent of the pronoun. The latter factor can be considered to be decisive and points to the general difficulty with discourse anchorage young children have.

Again, it would follow straightforwardly that we find chance performance just as in the other cases of 'guise overextension' discussed by Thornton and Wexler (1999). It would also follow that English children perform a bit worse on this condition. They have a choice of different guises and so tend towards an accidental coreference reading more systematically. In the Dutch case, as before, lexical complications would lead to further deterioration of performance.

5. CONCLUSION AND OUTLOOK

In our investigation of the referential properties of pronominal clitics in French we have adopted a framework which assumes that clitics are structurally impoverished (see Cardinaletti and Starke 2000) and therefore have to adopt the guise and referent of their antecedent DP (with certain exceptions). This close relationship to their DP antecedent explains the resistance of clitic pronouns to accidental coreference. However, it was demonstrated that in very special circumstances accidental coreference is possible so that Heim's Rule of Exceptional Coindexing (ECR) is operative for clitics – in certain, sharply constrained contexts.

An experiment was introduced that showed in effect that in normal contexts young French children have no difficulties in correctly assigning reference to pronominal clitics. This goes well with the assumption that there is a strong resistance to allow accidental coreference for pronominal clitics. The surprising result of the experiment is the fact that in so called ECM cases, the interpretation is adultlike only at chance level. This is unexpected in so far as the existing hypotheses about the acquisition of pronominal reference predict a good performance in these cases as well. This is true for the hypotheses which assume a difficulty with the so called 'Coreference Rule' as well as for the hypotheses working in the Reflexivity framework, which have both been strongly advocated in recent work on the acquisition of pronouns.

A certain formal (syntactic) apparatus and the elaboration of the movement properties of clitics was necessary to show that the Reflexivity framework indeed predicts a good performance (Chapter 4) and that the assumption of a lexical problem can be excluded (section 2 of this chapter). More formal (semantic) theory was needed in order to introduce the crucial idea of 'guise' and its influence on the Standard Binding Theory and the Coreference Rule, which becomes the ECR. This was done by introducing the Binding Theory proposed by Heim (1993) in Chapter 3. With such a theory it was then possible to seek an explanation of this surprising result in parallel to recent suggestions made for English (see Thronton and Wexler 1999), namely the overextension of guises and the application of the ECR.

The obvious explanation, the creation of a guise through the mirror context, could be excluded by a second experiment. This experiment showed that simple sentences (without embedding) with '*see*' and a mirror in the picture did not lead to guise creation and non-adult interpretations. The systematic difficulty was thus supposed to arise in another way, and was finally identified with the syntactic properties of the embedding. This, especially the fact that the pronoun acts as an object and a subject at the same time (see Postal 1974 and the transformation 'Raise Subject to Object'), allows systematic guise creation in the form of 'the y who is Ving' where V is the verb in the embedded clause. Whenever two guises are available, however, the child can allow accidental coreference, which is excluded for adults by a Gricean Relevance Maxim in the form of the ECR.

The idea that 'extended guise creation' is possible for clitics only in very special circumstances, can also be tested with Germanic weak pronouns which according to Cardinaletti and Starke (2000) have the same referential properties as pronominal clitics. We predict that the interpretation of German weak and strong pronouns will show notable differences. As it happens, the paradigm of the experiment discussed above provides a unique opportunity to test these. German pronouns are potentially ambiguous like English pronouns, but most of them also exist in a phonetically reduced unambiguously weak form. So one could simply test the phonetically reduced forms in their colloquial uses. There is a better way, however, to make the difference explicit and this is in the possible positions. Only the weak pronoun can appear in the Wackernagel position and only the strong pronoun can appear in argument position as shown in (19a-b).

(19)   a.   Sieht'n der Junge?
               sees'm the boy
               'does the boy see him?'
        b.   *Sieht IHN der Junge?
               sees HIM the boy
               'does the boy see him'
        c.   Sieht der Junge ihn
               sees the boy him
               'does the boy see him'
        d.   *Sieht der Junge'n
               sees the boy 'm
               'does the boy see'm'

The above approach predicts that German children perform better in cases were the pronoun is unambiguously in a weak pronoun position and worse when the pronoun is in a position which admits strong pronouns. In a simple context like (20a) we expect adult performance as in the French case (6a). (21a), however should be exactly like (6c) in French as it would introduce the 'lower subject guise'. (21b) should be worse as it allows the accidental coreference interpretations we always have for strong pronouns and the 'lower subject guise' so it should be like the performance of English or Dutch children.

(20) a. Sieht 'n der Junge?   like French
        sees 'm the boy
        (does the boy see'm)
     b. Sieht der Junge ihn?   like English/Dutch
        sees the boy him

(21) a. Sieht 'n der Junge tanzen   like French
        sees'm the boy dance
        'does the boy see'm dance'
     b. Sieht der Junge ihn tanzen like English/(Dutch)
        sees the boy him dance
        'does the boy see him dance'

If these predictions are born out in a future experiment, we have further support for the claim that the results of experiment 1 (and other cross-linguistic results) are best explained in a framework that allows structural deficiency (forcing the choice of the weaker over the stronger form as suggested in Cardinaletti and Starke 1995 and 2000), but can also account for exceptional cases of accidental coreference in the manner of Heim (1993). Such a synthesis can account for the special referential properties of clitics and, at the same time, allows their integration into a cross-linguistic hypothesis about children's performance on Principle B that appeals to extended guise creation as one instance of children's difficulties with discourse anchorage.

In the following chapters, we will return to the early syntactic system evidenced in children's productions. The focus will be on the use of infinitives and null subjects which will be presented in cross-linguistic detail in order to understand that the cause of a these non-adult uses of syntax may be sought once again in an insufficient mastery of the syntactic-pragmatic interface.

CHAPTER 6

CHILDREN'S NULL SUBJECTS AND INFINITIVES

1. CHILD NULL SUBJECTS

The following section concentrates on one of the best studied phenomena in acquisition literature, the omission of subjects in early child speech. This has attained the status of a classic in so far as Hyams (1983) used this phenomenon in the speech of young English children to outline her model of parameter setting and acquisition. Based on Rizzi (1982), she suggested that parameters are set from a default value to the target value, once a suitable trigger is encountered in the input. With her UG oriented data analysis, she thus was able to set new standards for the field and to open a fruitful debate on triggering, learnability and maturation.

At the time when Hyams and others started to investigate the phenomenon of child subject omission, the theoretical debate centered on how adult pro-drop languages should be characterized. The focus was on the relevant features and on the factors which are responsible for subject omission in various typologically quite distinct languages. Acquisition research and theoretical linguistics had much to contribute to each others' investigations at the time, especially when it came to the formulation of parameters which should be able to characterize the null subject property of a language and, at the same time, should be susceptible to some simple trigger in the child's input. This period can be called the classical period of null subject research in acquisition.

In the early nineties, however, another dimension was added to the research. The well known empirical observation that the child uses non-adult infinitives in declaratives at approximately the same time s/he omits subjects became the center of investigation, and the ultimate goal was to give a theoretical explanation of this temporal coincidence. Many researchers suggested that the use of infinitives is the cause for subject drop, or at least a common cause was stipulated for both phenomena. So null subjects were no longer studied in their own right but as one of the characteristics of the so-called optional infinitive (Wexler 1992, 1994) or root infinitive (Rizzi 1992, 1994) stage.

The new questions and the knowledge gained from the more classical investigations led to the conclusion that the child knows very early whether her/his language is a pro-drop language or not and has set the parameter correctly. The phenomenon of child subject omission is thus no longer treated as a setting of the pro-drop parameter to a default value, but as an option arising straight from certain properties of the child grammar, a grammar which at the same time allows the child to use non-adult infinitives. There is another empirical observation, which ties the child and the adult phenomenon together once again: true pro-drop languages like Italian or Spanish do not show a marked stage of root infinitives in their acquisition. Ultimately, a theory should provide a natural and satisfying explanation of these different observations.

Significant steps have been made recently towards such a theory, and in the following we will examine some of the more promising approaches. One of the possible ways to locate the cause of root infinitive use and of subject omission is to look for problems with the interface of syntax and interpretation. This approach has proved fruitful in binding theory and can be transferred to the area of root infinitives when one considers the anchoring properties of tense. This idea was suggested already in Hamann (1992) and also lies at the bottom of the approach Hyams (1996) or Hoekstra and Hyams (1996) propose, and has also been discussed by Wexler (1996). But any such approach cannot just point to a general "interface" problem. Such a move would only install the well-known "pragmatic waste-basket", formerly found under the generative semanticist's desk, in a rather murky corner of the acquisitionist's office. I will therefore propose a possible implementation of the idea where the problem is treated as essentially syntactic but leads to the observed anchoring difficulty.

The material will be structured in the following way. After a brief introduction to the phenomenon in section 2, I will look at the classical approaches and discuss their impact on acquisition theory in section 3. Subsequently, I will introduce the phenomenon of root infinitives in section 4 and discuss striking empirical facts in section 5. The theories which connect root infinitives and null subjects will be introduced in chapter 7. These will be evaluated in chapter 8 with respect to three fundamental empirical findings, the predominant occurrence of null subjects with infinitives, the occurrence of null subjects in finite constructions and the rare occurrence of null subjects with auxiliaries. The fundamental test of the theories will be new cross-linguistic results (especially from French and Danish) on the development of root infinitives and subject omission. Then more detailed empirical results will be presented in chapter 9 and 10, particularly on the occurrence of infinitives and null subjects in wh-questions and negation and the occurrence of late postverbal null subjects as first discussed by Hamann (1992). Chapter 11 will then outline a theory of tense which locates the interface problem more closely and relates it to the results on binding.

2. THE PHENOMENON OF SUBJECT OMISSION IN CHILD LANGUAGE

The cross-linguistic existence of an empty-subject state in early child language has been well documented for typologically distinct languages. Examples (1) - (5) show subject omission and are taken from Danish, Dutch, English, French and German corpora. None of these languages allows pro-drop, but they are different from each other in many ways: Danish, Dutch, English and German are Germanic languages, French is a Romance language. Danish, Dutch and German are V2 languages, English and French are not. Dutch and German are traditionally considered to be SOV languages, Danish, though V2, is SVO like English and French. Dutch, German and French have V-to-I raising, whereas Danish and English do not. Dutch, German and French have a reasonably rich agreement system, English has only one agreement marker, the 3rd person singular -s, and Danish does not have any agreement marking at all.

The English examples are from Bloom (1970) as quoted by Hyams (1986) and from Radford (1990). The German examples are from the Elisa corpus first introduced in Hamann (1992) and subsequently discussed in Hamann (1994, 1996b), from the Miller corpus (see Miller 1979) as quoted by Weissenborn (1990) and from the Wagner corpus as quoted by Poeppel and Wexler (1993). The Dutch examples are from the Wijnen corpus as quoted by Haegeman (1996c). The French examples come from the Lightbown corpus and a corpus recently collected in Geneva first discussed in Hamann, Rizzi and Frauenfelder (1995, 1996). The Danish examples go back to the so called Danish corpus first introduced in Plunkett and Strömqvist (1990) and recently discussed in Hamann and Plunkett (1997, 1998). The Wagner and Wijnen corpus, and part of the Danish corpus are available on Childes (see MacWhinney and Snow 1990, MacWhinney 1991, and Wagner 1985, Wijnen 1994, Plunkett and Strömqvist 1990).

(1) Danish
    a. se, blomster har   Jens   2;2   (P&S)
       look, flowers have/s
       'look, (I,you, he,she we, etc) have flowers
    b. ikke køre traktor   Jens   2;0   (P&S)
       not drive tractor
       (I, you, he etc) don't drive the tractor

(2) Dutch
    a. heb 't zo koud   Hein   2;9   (Wij)
       have it so cold
       '(I) am so cold'
    b. zit op   Niek   3;0   (Wij)
       sit on
       '(I) sit on (it)'
    c. wordt al donker   Hein   2;6   (Wij)
       becomes already dark
       '(it) is already getting dark'

(3) English
    a. want more apple   Eric   2;1   (B)
    b. see window   Eric   1;10   (B)
    c. read bear book   Kathryn   1;9   (B)
    d. go school   Daniel   1;11   (R)

(4) French
    a. veut pas lolo   Nathalie   2;0   (L)
       want not water
       '(I) don't want water'
    b. a tout tout tout mangé   Augustin   2;0   (H et al.)
       has all all all   eaten
       '(he) has eaten all'
    c. oter tout ça   Augustin   2;0   (H. et al)
       take off all that

(5) German
    a. backe Kuchen   Simone 1;10   (M)
       bake cake
       '(I) bake a cake'
    b. Hubsauber putzen   Andreas 2;1   (W)
       helicopter clean
       '(I) clean the helicopter'
    c. bin wieder lieb   Elisa   2;10   (H)
       am again good
       '(I) am good again'

Though many different fields have contributed to the understanding of this phenomenon, we will stay in the generative framework without a detailed discussion of other approaches, but see Hamann and Plunkett (1998). There is a fruitful diversity of assumptions, arguments and aims, however, so some brief hints are in order. Performance oriented approaches argue with restrictions on memory load, phonological approaches assume the omission of metrically weak elements, and competence oriented accounts aim to capture the parallels of child and adult subject omission. Most competence oriented approaches assume a principles and parameters (P&P) framework and construct their account of the child phenomenon either according to the Italian or according to the Chinese parameter setting and as a legitimate construction of the child's grammar at that particular developmental moment. The first assumption leads to agreement oriented, the latter to discourse oriented models for subject drop.

All these accounts have to acknowledge that there is a well defined phase of subject omission. In order to illustrate how sharply defined the phase of subject omission is, I present here the graphs of two Danish children's subject drop. These are particularly instructive because the children's speech was documented also before and after the null subject phase, so that onset and end of this phase are clearly observable.

For this investigation it is necessary to clarify at which point in the development (null) subjects can first be expected. There are two necessary conditions. The first condition is that the children use verbal utterances, because only predicates have subjects and most predications involve verbs. So we need a sufficient number of verbal utterances in order to be able to determine whether subjects are predominantly overt or omitted. The second condition may seem obvious, but is important nevertheless: only if the child is in the two-word stage, the combination of subject and verb can be observed. If the child is still in the one-word stage, there could be many bare verb forms, but this would not count as evidence that the child's grammar allows null subjects at that time.

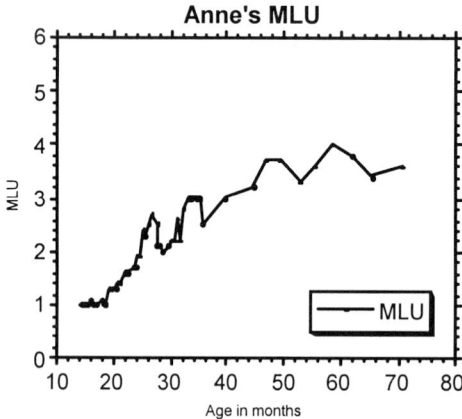

Figure 4a: Anne's MLU

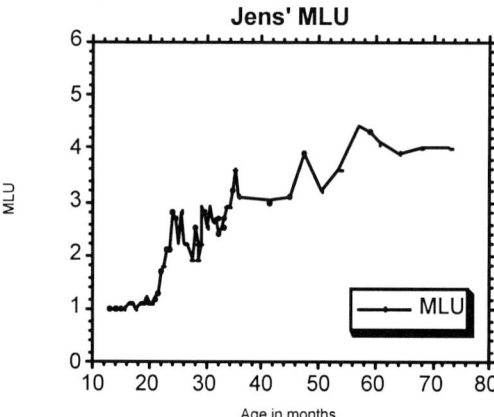

Figure 4b: Jens' MLU

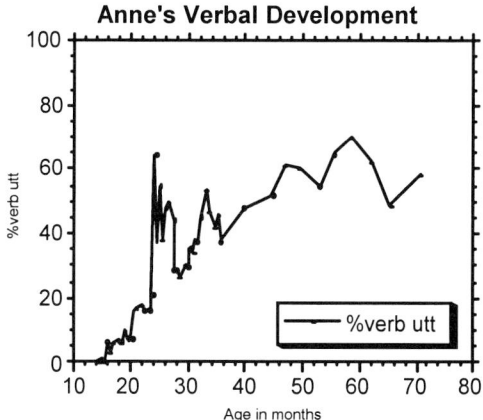

Figure 5a: Anne's Verbal Development

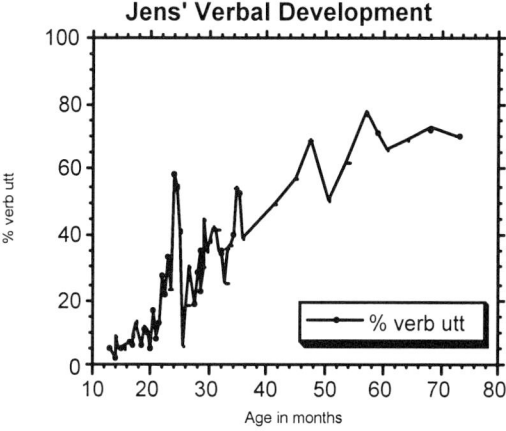

Figure 5b: Jens' Verbal Development

Figures 4a and 4b show the MLU (mean length of utterance) of the children, and figures 5a and 5b show their verbal development. At the age of 1;10 both children are well into the two word stage as their MLU equals or is greater than 1.5 at that time. We also find enough verbal utterances from this time onwards (about 20% of all utterances are verbal at age 1;10) to expect the occurrence of subjects or null subjects.

For the graphs on subject omission the ratio of all verbal utterances and those utterances where the subject is missing was calculated. This method was chosen because a comparison only to pronominal subjects cannot capture the phenomenon in full: the original pro-drop analysis has been shown to be inadequate (see section 3), and so the possibility of topic- or diary-drop has to be included.

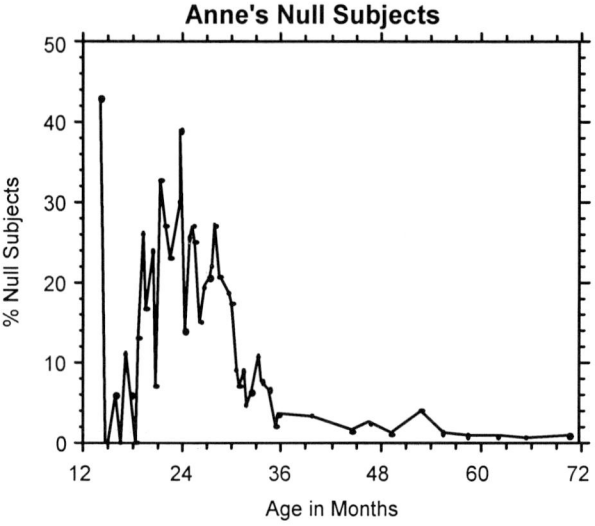

Figure 6a: Anne's Null subjects

The graphs of figures 6a and 6b show clearly that a distinctive rise in subject omission can be observed at the age of 1;7 for Anne, and at about 1;10 for Jens. For a period of a year, Anne drops subjects to about 25%, with a peak of 40% at 2;0. Jens has over 30% null subjects for about a year with a peak of 65% at 2;3. At the age of 2;4 and 2;7 respectively, the omission of subjects decreases rapidly, has dropped under 10% at the age of 3;0 and then vanishes completely.

This particularly clear profile of subject omission seems to indicate that there is indeed a child phenomenon concerning the omission of subjects. This receives corroboration when we compare these profiles with profiles from French (figures 7a and 7b), which is a Romance language and different from Danish in many respects, as the discussion above and chapter 8 show. We take Philippe's first 12 recordings as known from the Leveillé corpus available on Childes (MacWhinney and Snow 1990) and Augustin's 10 recordings.[1] Because of the limited period of observation, the French graphs do not show the development of the null subject phase in such clarity as the Danish data. But it emerges that both French children already drop subjects to almost 40% when recording started, soon after their second birthday, and that subject omission decreases during the second half of their third year.

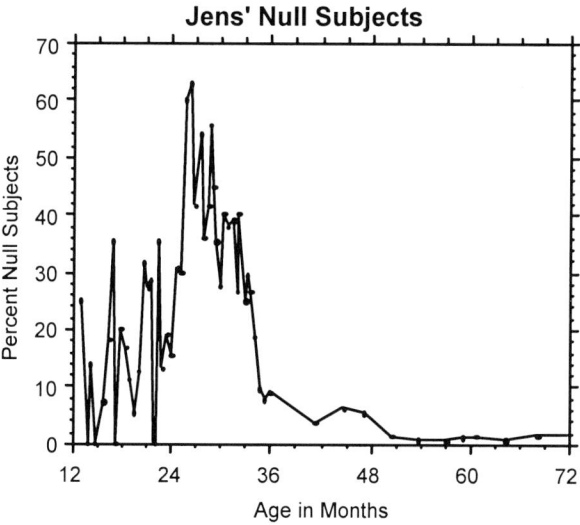

Figure 6b: Jens' Null Subjects

Though these cross-linguistic results show the existence of a phase of subject omission in child speech, it has emerged that there is language specific behavior from early on. This seems to be true in many areas, especially the correct placement of heads and complements in English and German, and also holds with regard to null subject use.

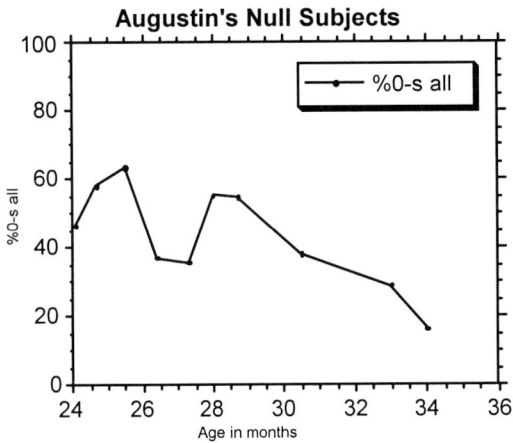

Figure 7a: Augustin's Null Subjects

In English, French and Danish the empty subject phenomenon occurs massively (with peaks of 60%) between the ages of 2;0 to 3;0 and then drops rapidly to under 5%. Anticipating some of the discussion, child null subjects do only rarely occur in fronted (finite) Wh-questions in these languages and not in embedded clauses, which are rare in the null subject phase in any case. In Italian, on the other hand, null subjects do occur in exactly these environments, which are also environments for target null subjects. Rizzi (1992) reports from the Martina corpus[2] that in 13 recordings made rougly each month from 1;7 to 2;7 there were 35 preposed non-subject Wh-questions, 20 of which had a null subject. In German, again, the picture is not the same as for English, French or Danish. The use of empty subjects does not drop from 50% to 5% in a very short space of time, but drops slowly from about 50% to 10-20% and the phenomenon lingers well into the fourth year. In the same phase, objects may also remain empty in Dutch and German. So child null subjects have been analyzed as discourse identified null topics, which also occur in the adult language and thus can be regarded as language specific as de Haan and Tuijnman (1988), Weverink (1989), Weissenborn (1990), Meisel (1990), Sano and Hyams (1994) have suggested. This idea, though explaining part of the German child phenomenon, cannot do justice to all of it. This becomes immediately clear if one considers the fact that an adult topic-drop analysis of child null subjects would predict only finite null subjects - a prediction which is easily proved wrong (see section 5 and chapter 8).

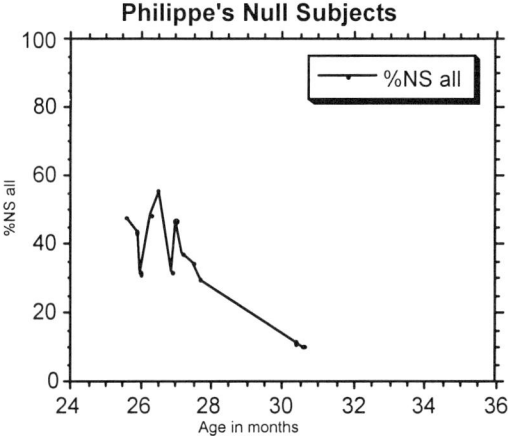

Figure 7b: Philippe's Null Subjects

What comes to mind therefore is that there may be different kinds of null subjects in child speech, due to the child's grammar and dependent on language specific properties. This is exactly what many researchers propose today and though some of the approaches are not totally convincing, the intuition behind the assumption seems to be quite sound. But before I enter into a theoretical and empirical discussion of this assumption, a certain familiarization with the current theories on different kinds of target and child null subjects is necessary.

3. THEORIES ON EMPTY SUBJECTS IN ADULT AND CHILD LANGUAGE

3.1. Pro-drop, Licensing and Identification

3.1.1. Pro-drop in the Target Grammars

Unless specified otherwise, we assume a phrase structure as in (6).

(6)
```
        CP
       /  \
     Spec   C'
           / \
         C⁰   AgrSP
              /   \
            Spec   Agr'
                  /   \
                Agr⁰   TP
                      /  \
                    Spec  T'
                         /  \
                       T⁰    AgrOP
                            /    \
                          Spec    AgrO'
                                 /    \
                               AgrO⁰   VP
                                      /  \
                                   Spec   V'
                                         /  \
                                        V⁰   Compl
```

The Extended Projection Principle (EPP) requires that all sentences have a subject. So there must be an empty category in a subjectless sentence[3]. For finite phrases this empty category, which is pronominal but not anaphoric in character, has been called *pro*. To capture the difference between Spanish (7a) and English (7b), it is natural to appeal to richness of inflection. The difference in the agreement systems of these two languages regulates the occurrence of *pro* (see Taraldsen 1987).

(7) a. Juan/ pro vio ese film
     b. John/*pro saw that film.

This cannot be the whole story, however. Because of cases like German and Icelandic which also have a fairly rich inflectional system, but allow only expletive *pro*, Rizzi (1982, 1986a) suggests that formal licensing and the conditions on interpretation of *pro* have to be kept apart. *Pro* is **licensed** if it is case-marked by a head. It can be **identified** by feature transfer, so that *pro* has the grammatical specification of the features on its licensing head. These two conditions affect several parametric choices. Languages will allow different heads to act as case assigners. In Italian, Agr^0 will license subject-*pro*, and V^0 may license object-*pro*, while in English the class of licensing heads is empty. Content recovery may also be parameterized. Latin, Italian, Spanish use recovery in full and therefore license referential *pro*. German and Icelandic do not allow feature transfer and therefore only license expletive *pro*. The possibilities of nominative case assignment in a language will allow the licensing of *pro* via spec-head agreement and/or via government (see Koopman and Sportiche 1991). The conditions for **licensing and identification** of *pro* can therefore be formulated as in (8).

(8) a. *pro* must be formally licensed by an X^0
       either via i) Spec-head agreement   or ii) Government
    b. (referential) *pro* has the grammatical specification of the features on X^0.

The problem for this approach is the Chinese case where there is no inflection, but empty subjects are used freely. So Rizzi (1986a) claims that Chinese does not use features and the content recovery parameter applies vacuously. This makes licensing of the full range of empty subjects possible. Speas (1994) gives a different account using the parameterization of AgrP, but the basic assumptions remain the same.

3.1.2. Pro-drop and Child Null Subjects

It was essentially this approach to the adult empty subject phenomenon that was applied to the early child phenomenon in Hyams (1983; 1986). Hyams (1983) claimed in essence that English children initially speak Italian, i.e. can license and recover the content of *pro* - or PRO as she argues - as described above. Only when they discover the expletive subjects *it* and *there* in the target, they conclude that in English the subject position has to be lexically filled, and reset the pro-drop parameter (see also Hyams 1987). The original setting of the parameter to the Italian value must therefore be the default case.

There are certain problems connected with this idea. One is the question of how the child could ever reset a parameter which, when reset, would result in the grammar of a language which is a subset of the language created by the grammar with the default parameter. This is the subset problem as described by Berwick (1982). It could only be circumvented if a grammar with a default parameter always were a subset of the grammar with the target parameter setting. In the case of child null subjects one can point out that we are not dealing with a real subset relation because pro-drop languages do not allow expletive subjects, while English does. So in the concrete case under discussion, the problem is perhaps irrelevant, but the subset principle is a very tight constraint on any model of acquisition which involves successive parameter setting.

Apart from this problem, Hyams work led to detailed discussions of parameter resetting and triggering in general which for some researchers culminated in a ban on parameter resetting (see Penner 1992, Müller 1994) and the idea that some parameters remain unset for a certain time. The so-called 'triggering problem', as first discussed by Borer and Wexler (1987), calls in doubt even this possibility. This classic puzzle quite simply asks why it should be the case that the child ignores the input, here the occurrences of expletive subjects in English, for quite some time and then suddenly decides to use this evidence as a trigger for setting the (null subject) parameter. So Hyams work led to rather fundamental questions of learnability and was evaluated critically from theoretical points of view. But also the empirical data soon argued against this model.

The approach predicts that null subjects in English child speech should occur in the same environments in which they occur in the pro-drop languages like Italian, notably in finite embedded clauses and finite root questions.

(9) a. So che ha telefonato
        know that has telephoned
        'I know that he has telephoned'

b. A chi ha telephonato?
   to whom has telephoned
   'who has he telephoned'

So English children should omit subjects in finite embedded-clauses and finite root questions. This, however, is not confirmed by the data, which show rather consistently that early child null subjects are (more or less) confined to sentence initial position. Valian (1990, 1991) first discussed the rarity of null subjects in English root questions, a finding which was confirmed by Weissenborn (1990, 1991) for German, and by Crisma (1992) and Hamann (1996, 2000a) for French. Roeper and Rohrbacher (2000) or Bromberg and Wexler (1995), though finding a considerable number of null subjects in English root questions, do not document many finite cases either. The same holds for embedded clauses, where child null subjects are rare for English, German and Dutch.

Therefore, the next step in acquisition research was to attribute the child null subject not to a default setting of the pro-drop parameter but to locate another property of the child grammar which allowed null subjects. One such property is the often cited "lack" of functional categories as suggested in Radford (1990) for English. For the early null subject stage in German, Clahsen (1991) is another example of such an approach. He gives essentially a classical pro-drop analysis in a framework that assumes only one functional projection above VP, thus using specific assumptions about acquisition. Clahsen (1991:28) suggests the structure in (10) for a phase in which German children do not yet use the full inflectional paradigm, i.e. for the age of 2;0 to 2;6 or to 3;0:

(10)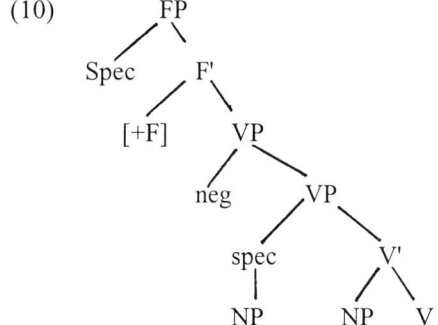

Adopting the procedures of Rizzi (1986a), null subjects in (10) are licensed by [+F(inite)] under spec-head agreement. The recovery parameter, however, is said to be still open because there is no subject-agreement yet, i.e. the child has not discovered the Agr-projection and its properties. No knowledge of agreement implies that "the requirements on the interpretation of *pro* are vacuous at this stage" (see Clahsen 1991:32), and referential subjects can be licensed. Only when the full inflectional paradigm is acquired, the child discovers that German Agr is not rich enough to identify referential *pro*. This analysis does not assume that German just chooses by accident not to make use of recovery by feature transfer but implies a more direct relationship of the richness of Agr and recovery.

3.2. Morphological Uniformity

Richness of inflection is not only determined by the number of inflectional endings on the verb as Jaeggli and Safir (1989) have pointed out. Jaeggli and Safir (1989:30) introduce the notion of Morphological Uniformity, which becomes the necessary condition for licensing given in (11).

(11) a. An inflectional paradigm P in a language L is **morphologically uniform** iff P has either only underived inflectional forms or only derived inflectional forms.
b. Null subjects are permitted in all and only languages with morphologically uniform inflectional patterns.

The paradigms of French and English are not morphologically uniform and do not license null subjects, while Spanish, Italian, Icelandic, and German (!), but also Chinese, Korean, and Japanese are classified as morphologically uniform and license empty subjects (see Jaeggli and Safir 1989). Mainland Scandinavian languages are problematic for this approach because they do not have subject-agreement (all persons are marked *-ar* in Swedish and *-er* in Danish), but nevertheless null subjects are not allowed. Jaeggli and Hyams (1988) avoid the problem by classifying these languages as morphologically mixed on the evidence of the stem form for the imperative. German poses a problem of a different kind, and much the same mechanism as in Rizzi (1986a) is needed to account for the fact that referential null subjects are not licensed in German, while expletive *pro* is possible (see also chapter 10 for a discussion of this property). Jaeggli and Hyams (1988: 244f) assume (12a and b).

(12) a. A thematic null subject must be identified
 b. Agr can identify an empty category as (referential) *pro* iff the category containing Agr case-governs the empty category.

Jaeggli and Hyams (1988) further assume that Tense is the case-governing category in German and is located in Comp (which explains the V2-effect) while Agr is located in Infl. Thus the distribution of Tense and Agr in separate nodes does not allow for identification of referential null subjects. Whether this explanation, especially the assumption about Tense in C^0, can be accepted in this form depends on the adopted framework and would have to be modified in a split CP approach. It is reasonable to assume, however, that a tense feature is found in one of the projections of the Comp system and so the argument can be adapted also to minimalist frameworks (see Chomsky 1995). For the acquisition of German, Clahsen (1982, 1986) reports that an increase in V2-constructions is accompanied by a decrease of subject-drop. According to Jaeggli and Hyams (1988), this shows that Agr and Tense are located in Infl in early German child language; but with the acquisition of Comp and the realization that Tense is located in Comp, identification of thematic null subjects is blocked. This analysis is problematic for several reasons, especially the assumption that the Comp system is not available in a first phase.[5] We will come back to this later and try to make precise what the nature of the problem with Comp and tense really is.

In Chinese and similar languages yet another identification mechanism is at work, that of feature transfer under c-command and of identification through a discourse element. Identification via a discourse element is needed not only for Chinese. It is also operative for 0-topic constructions in Dutch and German where topics can be dropped because they can be recovered through a salient element given by previous context (see Ross 1982).

For the English child phenomenon, Jaeggli and Hyams (1988) and Hyams (1989) propose that the initial hypothesis is that of morphological uniformity, so inflectional paradigms will be uniformized and null subjects will be licensed in early child language. Then positive evidence, the occurrence of a stem form in the paradigm, will tell the child that her/his language is not morphologically uniform and so does not license null subjects. Identification of null subjects in children's French or English is assumed to be achieved along the Chinese pattern through a discourse element. This amounts to saying that the English child initially speaks Chinese. It remains a puzzle, however, why the identification mechanism should be different for Early English and Early German. This is especially surprising since German children unlike their English peers will encounter evidence of discourse licensing in topic-drop structures.

3.3. Discourse Oriented Approaches

3.3.1 Target Topic-drop

There are languages which can topicalize subjects and objects, as for instance most V2 languages, but also Portuguese (Raposo 1986), where such topicalized subjects or objects can be dropped in certain informal registers of language, see (13). Ross (1982) investigated this phenomenon under the term 'pronoun zap' for German, see (14a,b).

    (13)   Portuguese object drop
              A Joana viu ec na televisao ontem é noite
              Joana saw on television last night

    (14)a.   German subject drop
              ec Hab' Hans schon angerufen
              (I) have John already called
              I have called John already

       b.   German object drop
              ec Hab' ich gestern gekauft
              (that) have I bought yesterday
              I bought it yesterday

In the classical analysis of Huang (1984), which we present without comment for the moment, subject topic-drop is analyzed as in (15a) and object-drop as (15b). The empty operators are discourse licensed.

    (15)   a. [$_{CP}$OP hab' [$_{IP}$vbl Hans schon angerufen]]
                     have   Hans already called
              '(I) have called Hans already'

b. [CPOP hab' [IPich gestern vbl gekauft]]
       have   I yesterday   bought
   'I bought (it) yesterday'

3.3.2 Topic-drop and Child Null-Subjects

Because in Dutch child language subjects **and** objects are omitted but both only from sentence initial position, de Haan and Tuijnman (1988) and Weverink (1989) conclude that the Dutch child phenomenon is topic-drop, not *pro*-drop. Weissenborn (1990, 1991) claims that the same is true for German. The occurrence of object- and subject drop and the observation that subject-drop does not vanish abruptly with the acquisition of agreement (see Clahsen and Penke 1992, Hamann 1992, 1996b, and chapter 10 here) seem to suggest that subject omission could be topic-drop, as in adult German.

It is claimed for Dutch and German that the pragmatic conditions for discourse licensing are not acquired and are learned slowly, resulting in a gradual decrease in empty subject use - until the 5%-10% of adult topic-drop are reached.[6] As was briefly mentioned before, such a pure topic-drop analysis needs many refinements, especially as it would predict that early Dutch and German empty subjects are empty operators in SpecCP and occur only with finite verbs - which cannot be maintained. Poeppel and Wexler (1993) found that at the age of 2;1 the German child Andreas (see MacWhinney and Snow 1990, Wagner 1985) has empty subjects predominantly in non-finite constructions, and Krämer (1993) showed the same for Dutch children. This important fact of child subject omission will be evaluated cross-linguistically in chapter 8.

Nevertheless, Dutch and German child null subjects are even now often analysed across the board as topic-drop null subjects. It has recently been claimed (Bromberg and Wexler 1995) that early finite null subjects in languages like French or English, which do not have adult topic-drop, have to be analysed as topic-drop whereas null subjects in infinitivals are a different phenomenon. The attractiveness of the topic-drop analysis lies in the fact that it explains the findings about the non-occurrence of finite child null subjects in Wh-questions or embedded clauses in a straightforward way. These are exactly the environments where adult topic-drop is not allowed, and so the facts of topic-drop in languages like Dutch or German have served as the model for the analysis of child null subjects, notably in Rizzi (1992, 1994)'s approach. We will discuss this in more detail in chapter 7 and follow Haegeman (1996a,b,c) in arguing for an analysis of child null subjects modeled not on adult topic- but on adult diary-drop. For now, we will turn to the investigation of the relationship of child null subjects and child infinitives.

4. THE PHENOMENON OF OPTIONAL INFINITIVES

The frequency of null subjects in infinitives and the fact that the use of infinitives temporally coincides with the omission of subjects in child speech lead to approaches which primarily attempt to isolate that property of child grammar that allows root infinitives and also allows subject omission.

The infinitive phenomenon is remarkable in so far as most children use infinitives only as an option and at the same time can also use inflected verbs. This has been documented in detail by Wexler (1992, 1994), and I will give only some relevant and, if possible, new examples, focussing on German, French and Danish. These three languages mark the infinitive morphologically, so that one can confidently identify the use of infinitives and does not have to consider the possibility of omitted inflections, as it is the case in English. The markings are *-e* for Danish, *-en* for German, which is the same ending as for 1st and 3rd person plural in German, and *-er*, *-ir* and *-re* for French, which leads to the problem of separating the *-er* infinitive from the *-é* past participle.

The examples (16,17,18) document some of the earliest occurrences of infinitives from the Danish corpus and juxtapose them with occurrences of finite forms of the same recording session. For French and German some of the earliest occurrences which are on record in the respective corpora have been chosen and juxtaposed with finite utterances at the same age (German) or in the same session (French). Note that the children use finite auxiliaries but also inflect main verbs at this early time.

		+finite		-finite	
(16)		German			
	a.	da guckt er raus		a'.	Thorstn das habn
		there looks he out			T. that have
		'there he peeps out'			'T. has that' Andreas 2;1
	b.	malt eier		b'.	nich aua mache(n)
		paints eggs			not ouch make (inf)
					'doesn't hurt' Simone 1;10

+finite   **-finite**

(17)   Danish
   a. kører bil   a'. køre bil
      drive (fin) car   drive (inf) car
      '(I/he) etc. drive the car'   drive the car'   Jens 1;10,14
   b. sover   b'. sidde der på
      sleep(s)   sit there on
                                 'sit there'   Jens 1;10,14
   c. det gider ikke   c'. nej, ikke have
      that likes not   no, not have
      'it doesn't like'   no, have not   Jens 1;10,14
   d. det kigger   d'. e kigge
      it looks   e look   Jens 1;10,14
   e. græder   e'. hun sove
      cries   she sleep   Jens 1;10,28
      'she cries'
   f. det er bil
      that is car
      'that is a car'   Jens 1;10,28

   g. det lukker   g'. du tegne
      it closes   you draw (inf)   Anne 1;7,18
   h. der er det   h'. gribe bold
      there is it   catch (Inf) ball
      'there it is'   'catch the ball'   Anne 1;7,18
   i. her er koppen   i'. køre bil
      here is the cup   drive car   Anne 1;8,22
   j. det er ikke Annette
      that is not Annette   Anne 1;8,22
   k. sover   k'. sove
      s/he sleeps   sleep   Anne 1;9,09
   l. er færdig   l'. læse
      is finished   read   Anne 1;9,09
   m. jeg falder   m'. jeg tegne
      I fall (fin)   I draw (inf)   Anne 1;9,09
   n. har appelsin   n'. så tegne stol
      have (fin) orange   so draw (inf) chair Anne 1;9,09

	+finite	**−finite**

(18) French

a. on joue ballon
one plays ball
'we play ball'

a'. oter tout ta
take off all that   Aug 2;0,02

b. est pour maman
is for maman

b'. manger maman
eat maman   Aug 2;0;02

c. veux jouer dinettes
want play cooking
'(I) want to play cooking'

c'. donner n'ta [kitE] Aug 2;0,23
give (inf) that Christelle
give that to Christelle'

d. est beau
is nice

d'. oter la coquille
peel the shell   Aug 2;0,23

e. i' mange [a kup]
'he eats ???'

e'. manger ça
eat (inf) that   Aug 2;0,23

f'. aller [patE] là   Aug 2;0,23
go on the floor there

The examples show beyond doubt that there is a phase were infinitives are used side by side with inflected verbs. A further interest of the above and other data involving the position of the verb lies in the fact that inflected verbs are raised to their canonical position in the phrase, whereas infinitives stay in their base position. Pierce (1989) showed that in French child speech inflected verbs only occur to the left of negation while infinitives occur to its right, which is also true for Danish (see Plunkett and Strömqvist 1990 and examples (17c,c') and (17j)). Clahsen and Penke (1992) and Poeppel and Wexler (1993) showed for German that inflected verbs occur in V2-position whereas infinitives rarely do. These data show that even if the use of an infinitive is possible in the child grammar, this grammar already has a position for inflectional material and contains a verb raising rule in those cases where the target language has one.

It has often been claimed that children go through an early phase where they exclusively use infinitives (see Radford 1990, Aldridge et al 1995) and that the so called optionality is an artifact of the limited empirical basis available to our research. This can be put more directly by saying that we start taping the children too late, so that they have simply passed out of the relevant phase. This may be true for the data from Andreas (2;1), where we have only the recordings of one day in the child's life, or for Augustin, where data taking only started at his second birthday, but fortunately it is not true for all the available corpora.

Actually, there are very few really extensive corpora which can contradict the assertion, but there is the Simone corpus for German (which is not available to a larger public) or the Danish corpus of Plunkett and Strömqvist (1990) which documents the speech of Anne and Jens from their first to their sixth birthday. The results presented in Weissenborn (1990) show a juxtaposition of finite utterances and infinitives for Simone from early on, and the two Danish corpora clearly show that infinitives are not used in a first phase, but start to be used only when finite forms are also used productively. Figures 8a and 8b as well as 9a and 9b provide unequivocal evidence for this claim.

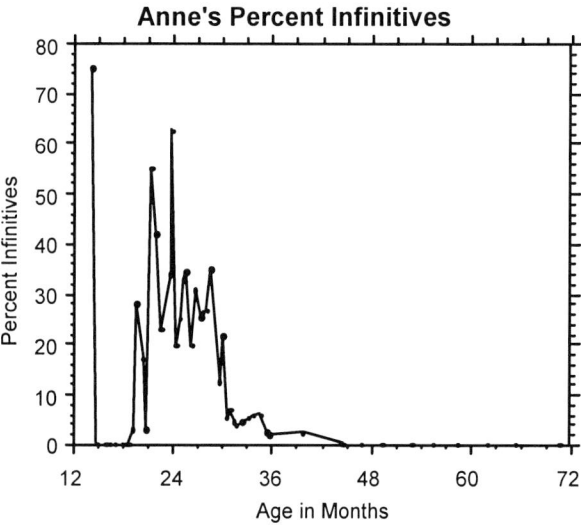

Figure 8a: Anne's Percent Infinitives

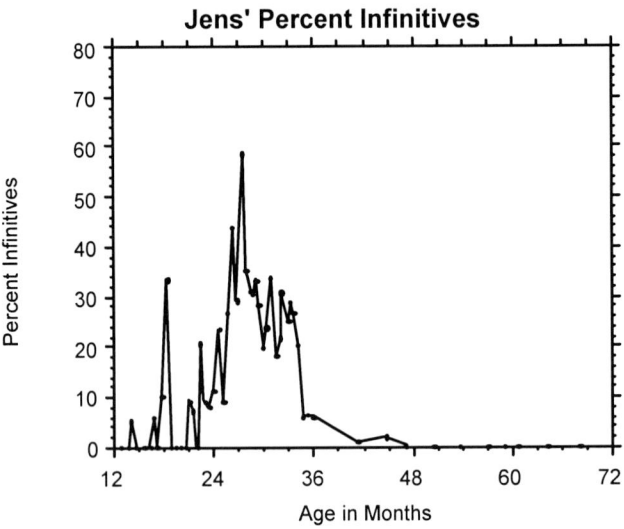

Figure 8b: Jens' Percent Infinitives

The first data point in figure 8a may be taken to show a time when only infinitives are used, but this cannot be maintained because in this session we have only four verb forms, three of which concern the verb *a-e* which means 'to stroke, be gentle with' but can also be a noun and mean 'a cuddle'. So this data point can be neglected for numerical and linguistic reasons. Both children start with the use of formulaic phrases, which are not included in these counts and graphs. When the non-formulaic use of verbs begins but is still rare, we find predominantly finite phrases for both children. Then verbal development starts to accelerate at around 1;6 for Anne and at 1;10 for Jens (compare figures 5a and 5b), and at the same time, the first infinitives are used. However, at no point of the development infinitives constitute the majority of verbal utterances. This becomes clear when the tokens of finite verb forms and infinitives are analyzed as was done in figures 9a and b, where the very early sessions have been excluded because the numbers of occurring verb forms were too small.

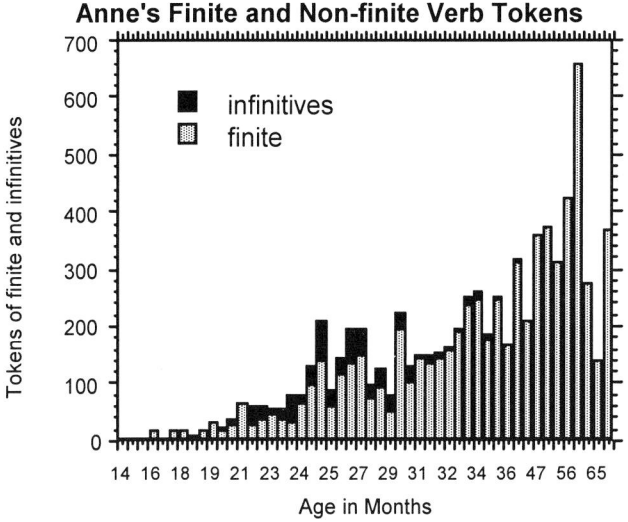

Figure 9a: Anne's Finite and Non-finite Verb Tokens

For these two Danish children, it can therefore be established that there is no phase of infinitive use where the child grammar excludes finite forms. On the contrary, these data show that the use of infinitives is indeed optional, and at no time it is the only possibility of using a verb form. When verbal development gets off the ground, both forms are used side by side. Though it may not be correct to infer that this is true for all children and across all languages, it is at least a strong indication that finite forms are used from early on and that there is no early lack of functional projections. Nevertheless, for certain languages we can safely assume the existence of a phase where children optionally use non-adult infinitives in root clauses.

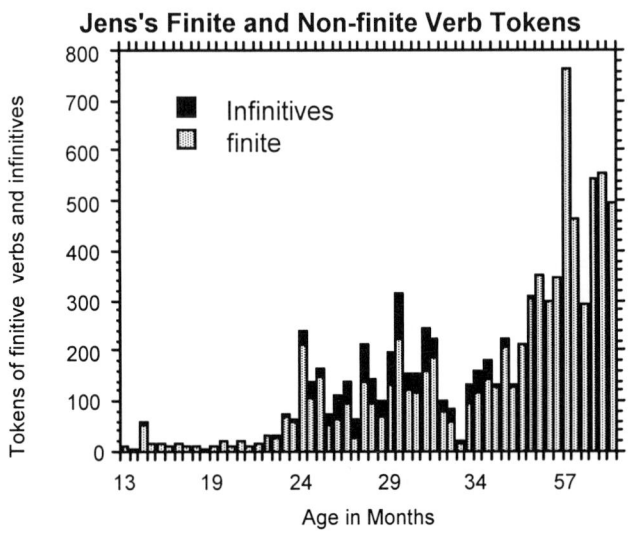

Figure 9b: Jens' Finite and Non-finite Verb Tokens

5. EMPIRICAL FACTS ABOUT NULL SUBJECTS AND INFINITIVES

It is useful at this point to give a brief overview over the empirical observations concerning child null subjects and root infinitives that have emerged over the years. Though some of these empirical findings will be discussed in more detail later on, it is necessary to list these facts in order to understand that the current hypotheses are focusing on different groups of facts.

The first observation was that null subjects and infinitives tend to be produced at the same time. This is not true for pro-drop languages, however, where null subjects have adult properties from the beginning and infinitives occur only rarely or not at all. Another observation tying null subjects and infinitives together concerns the finding that in many languages the rate of subject omission is much higher in infinitivals than in finite constructions. However, null subjects do occur in finite clauses to a rather high percentage in languages like French, German or Danish. This clearly leaves the options of assuming one kind of child null subject appearing in both environments or of postulating two such empty categories, depending on context. At the same time, there is a choice of seeing the null subject in the infinitive as the important one, or to build the theory on the assumption that the finite null subjects provide the crucial evidence.

Another focus of investigation is the position in which a child null subject can appear. There is the observation made early on by Valian (1990) that neither infinitives nor null subjects appear in fronted Wh-questions or in topicalization contexts in V2-languages. This lead to detailed research on Wh-questions turning up much controversial evidence (see the discussion in chapter 9). Nevertheless, this research crystallized the generalization that infinitives and null subjects are restricted to root clauses, in fact that null subjects are restricted to initial position.

Another direction of research taking up the question of optionality of infinitives, concentrated on the type of verbs which allowed infinitives and showed that in some languages, but not in English, only eventive verbs show up in child infinitives and that these infinitives mostly have a modal meaning. The starting point for this branch of research was the observation that auxiliaries do not normally appear in the infinitive and do not allow subject drop to the same rate as main verbs.

With the evolving empirical knowledge the theories evolved, which I will try to trace in the following chapters. The data on Danish which I will present in chapter 8 were particularly relevant in this respect as they provided straightforward evidence for truncation type theories, and forced other approaches to additional assumptions. Before any further data is discussed, a presentation of the different theories will be given in chapter 7.

CHAPTER 7

THEORETICAL APPROACHES TO INFINITIVES AND NULL SUBJECTS

1. INTRODUCING THE APPROACHES

The following approaches to child infinitives and child null subjects have been widely discussed and make the most interesting predictions. First, within a full continuity framework that assumes the presence of all the functional projections from early on, it is a possibility that a null auxiliary is responsible for the occurrence of infinitives in child speech (Boser et al. 1992). Second, there is the assumption that Tense is lacking in a certain sense which will allow certain syntactic derivations which otherwise would crash for lack of interpretability (Wexler 1992, 1994). This idea has led to some interesting variants, notably the idea that the IP is underspecified in the sense that a tense index is missing or has a wrong value and a pragmatic rule regulating its interpretation is not acquired yet, as Sano and Hyams (1994) and Hyams (1996) have proposed. Third, we find the idea that the agreement projection is underspecified or lacking as Clahsen (1991), but also Roeper and Rohrbacher (2000) have suggested. There is also an interesting idea that the number feature plays a crucial role in the specification of the agreement projection as discussed in Hoekstra and Hyams (1996). More recently, the approach to optional infinitives originally suggested by Wexler (1994) has been refined (see Wexler 1998) so as to involve not only the Tense but also the Agreement projection and to include a principle operative in the child grammar called the Unique Checking Constraint. Finally, there is the idea of truncation as introduced by Rizzi (1994), which has also undergone some modifications (Rizzi 2000).

The latter was meant as a compromise between approaches that assume the slow build-up of functional projections (Radford 1990, 1996a,b) and those approaches which assume the presence of the full array of these projections from early on. At the same time it was designed to capture the intuition that the use of infinitives is due to a lack of tense and that null subjects and root infinitives are underlyingly related in a principled way. It is also the simplest approach and in its simplicity perhaps the most elegant one. Nevertheless, it makes far reaching predictions and because of these properties we will discuss it first.

2. TRUNCATION, ROOT INFINITIVES AND CHILD NULL SUBJECTS

2.1. Truncation and Root Infinitives

Rizzi (1992) starts with the observation that the topmost functional layer of every adult root clause is a CP. This is in contradiction to suggestions made by Reis and Rosengren (1991) or Stechow and Sternefeld (1988) for German, where it is proposed that subject initial German main clauses are in fact IPs, not CPs. On the other hand, with the new elaboration of the CP layer into different functional projections (see Müller and Sternefeld 1993, Rizzi 1997), subject initial German main clauses can receive a different analysis from questions or topicalizations within the CP system. This idea has been developed for Dutch by Haegeman (1996c) and carries over to German.

The functional structure of the split CP as proposed by Rizzi (1997) also provides a conceptual argument for why it should be a universal property of root clauses to start with a 'CP'. The topmost layer in the C-system now is the ForceP, which codes the illocutionary force of the sentence. This is necessarily selected by discourse or the embedding verb, whereas other components of the C-layer (like the TopicP or the FocusP) are present only when required by the material of the sentence. Therefore this assumption about CP is only a natural extension of the observation that adults normally make statements or ask questions which are anchored to and motivated by the discourse context. But even without the elaboration of the C-layer, the universal presence of the CP for every root clause can be derived from the intuition that the CP has a connector function which is obvious in subordination and can be extended to main clauses by viewing the CP as relating the discourse and the phrase.

In the more recent formulation of the approach (see Rizzi 2000) the assumption that root declaratives involve a CP is derived from the principle of Categorial Uniformity (1).

(1)   Categorial Uniformity
        Assume a unique canonical structural realization for a given semantic type.

This can be read as a sort of economy constraint on the inventory of elements that enter a syntactic computation. Comparing the root clause *John came home* with the same structure in an embedded environment *I think that John came home* will lead to the conclusion that under Categorial Uniformity both clauses must be of the same type, i.e. have CP status. So we assume (2).

(2)   Root = CP.

Rizzi (1992, 1994) suggested that (2) itself be considered as an axiom of adult grammar, but that it is not mandatory for child grammar - perhaps because children do not anchor to discourse but to speech situation. This means that the CP can be truncated by the child, but it need not be and must not be if there is material which has to be accommodated (for example the Wh-word for forming a root question). But if there is no need to have a well-defined topmost projection in the clause, the structure can be truncated at any place, always according to the material which has to be accommodated. This offers a compromise between a full competence framework and a structure building model, in so far as the child in principle has all the functional projections at his/her disposal and uses them if necessary, but needs to project only as far as the material of the phrase requires. This assumption immediately explains the optionality of root infinitives.

In the newer framework, (1) is in competition with a principle of *Structural Economy* given in (3).

(3)   Structural economy
        Use the minimum of structure consistent with well-formedness constraints.

In adult grammar, Categorial Uniformity wins out over Structural Economy as a declarative root clause, which could well be an IP, necessarily is a CP. In child grammar, the principle of Categorial Uniformity is not yet operative. This is so because for lack of embedded clauses, root declaratives can be analyzed and interpreted as IPs satisfying the principle of Structural Economy. Note that the occurrence of fronted Wh-questions does not presuppose that Categorial Uniformity is operative. Root questions need more than the IP for two reasons. They require a position outside of the IP to place morphological material. They are also not of the same semantic type as root declaratives and they cannot be interpreted by a default setting, there must be a position for the question operator at LF at the latest. Therefore root questions and root declaratives are sufficiently different not to activate the principle.

If we now assume a hierarchy of functional categories as in (4), it follows that a root infinitive occurs if the CP, the AgrSP and crucially the TP have been truncated. It was originally claimed that root infinitives are structures truncated above VP, but Haegeman (1995b, 1996e) and the facts of clitic placement as discussed in chapter 2 argue for the inclusion of ArgOP in the structure of a root infinitive.

(4)   CP > AgrSP > NegP TP > AgrOP > VP

Rizzi (1994) further assumes that whenever a projection has been truncated, the higher projections must also be missing. This also holds in the other direction: whenever a projection is activated, the lower projections must be activated. It implies that we cannot assume a missing or inactive projection in the middle of a structural tree. If truncation takes place at a certain projection, only the lower part of the tree survives.

In this respect, Rizzi's proposal is more radical than any proposal which assumes a missing or underspecified AgrSP or a missing or underspecified TP for the analysis of root infinitives or null subjects. It also makes very precise predictions about the material which can occur in a child's root infinitive. In particular, it follows that fronted Wh-questions should never occur in the infinitive, and that material pertaining to the AgrSP, like inflectional endings but also subject clitics, cannot occur with an infinitive.

Concerning the latter predictions, the absence of inflectional agreement endings seems to be a defining criterion of the infinitive. This is not quite as trivial as it appears because English, the language which has been studied the most, does not mark the infinitive morphologically. So we could get caught in a circle about what to define as a root infinitive and what to expect as a consequence of our theory of root infinitives following from our definition.

Languages that mark the infinitive morphologically are therefore much better suited to the study of this interesting phenomenon. More interesting than the question about inflectional endings is the position of clitics, and we have already discussed the fact that subject clitics never seem to occur with infinitives in French or Dutch child language. The clear conclusion seems to be that the AgrSP is indeed absent from the structure of root infinitives. The incompatibility of infinitives and Wh in child speech was one of the motivations for the formulation of the truncation theory and it holds empirically for languages like German, Dutch, French, which all mark the infinitive morphologically. We will come back to this in chapter 9.

There is one other prediction which will need a separate section for discussion. This is the fact that given truncation and the above sequence of projections, negation is not expected to occur in root infinitives. There is some controversy about the empirical facts concerning this prediction and there is also a lively theoretical debate about the position of the NegP in different languages. We will come back to these problems in chapter 10.

2.2. Truncation, Topic-drop, Split CP and (Diary) Null Subjects

2.2.1. Truncation and Child Null Subjects

Concerning child null subjects, Rizzi (1992) used the German topic-drop construction and the register phenomenon of diary-drop described by Haegeman (1990) as a model for his account. Following Cardinaletti (1990) and Lasnik and Stowell (1991), Rizzi (1994) assumed that the child null subject has the properties of a null definite description or a 'null constant' (nc). More recently the properties of this child null subject have been assimilated to that of traces in a minimalist perspective, where traces as copies fully reproduce the structure of their antecedents (Rizzi 2000).

In order to dispense with an operator analysis for null subjects, which is the only option if one adheres to the ECP in the acknowledged form, Rizzi reformulates the identification clause of the ECP:

(5) An empty category [-p] must be chain connected to an antecedent **if it can.**

It follows that an empty category, especially an empty category which is not licensed by some clause-internal mechanism and can be identified only through an antecedent in the discourse, can occur in the topmost position of a structure and nowhere else. This is true for adult topic-drop in German, but also for diary-drop as described in Haegeman (1990), and it is designed to capture child empty subjects.

In a framework where truncation is allowed, the empty subject phenomenon is now easily explained. If only the CP has been truncated, then an empty category in SpecIP cannot be licensed by a higher position and therefore does not have to be licensed, i.e. recovery of content through context should always be possible. Only when axiom (2) becomes obligatory, this option is restricted to an empty category in the specifier of the topmost Comp projection, and we may call this SpecCP as long as the different Comp projections of a split CP analysis do not play a role for the analysis. If CP and IP are truncated, the same will hold with respect to empty subjects in SpecVP or SpecAgrOP so that empty subjects will surface with infinitives.

Very similar predictions can be obtained in a structure building model. Such a model, however, predicts a strict sequencing of occurrences: if IP is not yet acquired, there will only be infinitives, which may occur with null subjects. Subsequently, with IP acquired, but CP not available, there will be finite clauses which may have missing subjects. Finally, with CP acquired only true topic-drop will survive.

Differentiating between these two approaches obviously requires fine-grained observations of co-occurrence and sequencing of constructions. The data on Danish as presented in the previous chapters already cast doubt on the structure building approach and seem to require an explanation where the co-occurrence of infinitives and finite verbs, or of finite null subjects and non-finite null subjects, or even of root questions and root infinitives in one and the same phase follows directly. Truncation allows such an optionality, structure building does not.

The analysis, which is modeled on the diary-drop or topic-drop paradigm, predicts that child null subjects have the same properties as diary null subjects or dropped topic subjects. It predicts in particular a root/non-root asymmetry. This is roughly confirmed by the fact that empty subjects in Wh-questions and in subordinates are rare in German.[1]

In the following sections, we will show that early child null subjects though resembling topic-drop subjects, are a different phenomenon. This may be a more or less terminological problem, but let us be exact and point out that Rizzi's proposal, though inspired by some facts of German topic-drop, does not treat finite child null subjects as dropped topics: they are analysed as an empty categroy in SpecIP, not in SpecCP. A resemblance is only found in the licensing and identification mechanism: both, finite child null subjects, and subject null topics are licensed and identified because they are in the topmost position of the phrase. In this sense, Rizzi's analysis can be grouped with the discourse oriented approaches.

2.2.2 German Topic-drop and Child Null Subjects

I start with a discussion of German topic-drop, adopting the standard analysis for the V2 effect in German main clauses and assuming that the verb raises to C^0. Without further discussing recent suggestions to the contrary[2], I also assume that German is head final in its IP and VP system, seen in the word order of subordinate clauses. Collapsing AgrSP and TP to IP and using the label CP for the several layers which are involved in the C- system for brevity, I assume (6a) for a main and (6b) for a subordinate clause, an analysis which will be modified later.

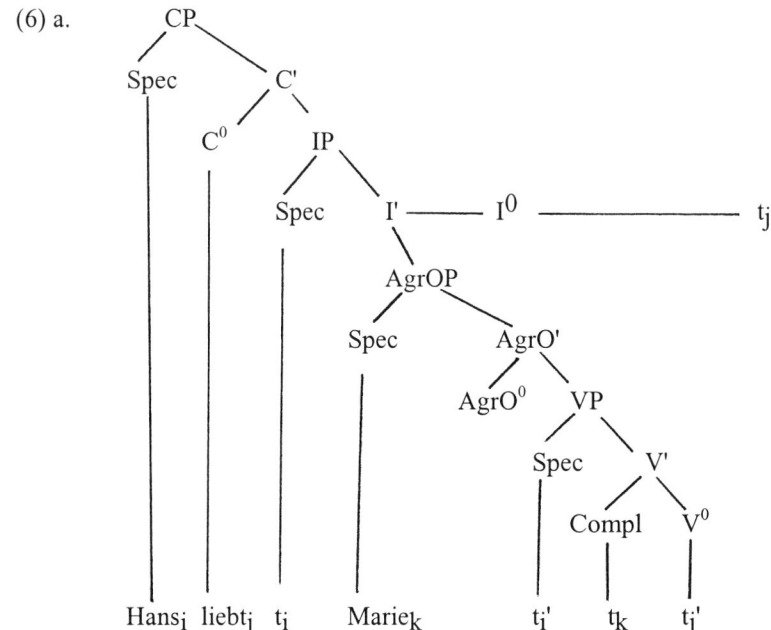

b.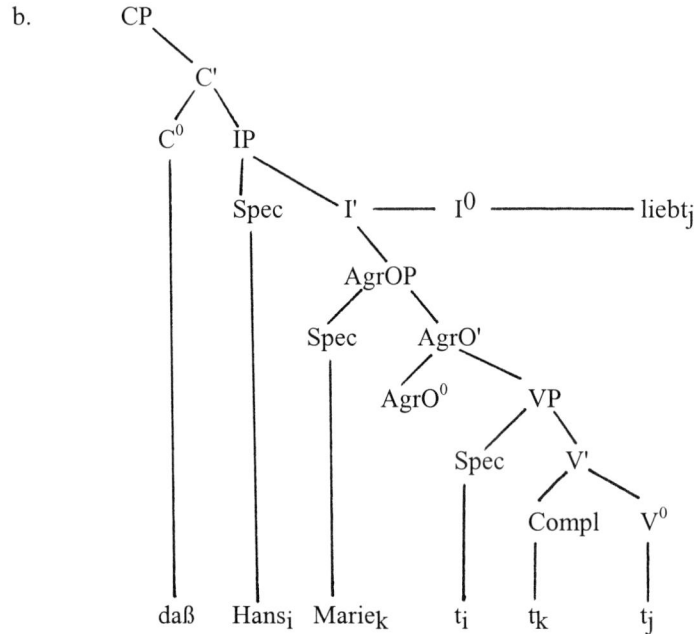

The phenomenon of topic drop (see also chapter 6 section 3) can be illustrated in more detail with (7) and (8) from adult German.

    (7) a.   Ist/sind nich gekommen
              is/are   not   come
              '(he/they) did not come'
        b.   Hatte/hatten   keine Zeit
              had(1st,sg)/(1st,pl) no   time
              '(I,we) had no time'
        c.   Hast/?habt   wieder nich d'ran gedacht
              have (2nd,sg/pl) again not of it thought
              '(you) have forgotten it again'

    (8) a.   Hab ich schon   gesehen
              have I   already   seen
              'I have seen (it/that) already'

b.   Hat er vergessen
     has he forgotten
     'he has forgotten (it)'

Huang (1984)'s analysis as given in (15a,b) of chapter 6 section 3.3.1. has been modified by Cardinaletti (1990), who shows that there is a difference in the person features in omitted subjects and objects. (7a,b,c) and (9) show that subjects in first, second and third person can be dropped, while only third person objects may be omitted.

(9) a.   Siehst du mich?   -   *nein, (2) seh ich nich
         see   you me   no,   see I not
         'can you see me?"   'no, I can't see (you)'

    b.   Siehst du Anna?   -   nein, (3) seh ich nich
         see   you A.   no,   see I not
         'do you see A?'   'no, I don't see (her)'

Thus an operator is involved for objects, but for subjects the empty category is probably *pro* (see Cardinaletti 1990) or a null constant (see Rizzi 1992). If we adopt the null constant, we get the analysis (10a) for the subject case and (10b) for the object case for German topic-drop. Here the nc is referential because its content is contextually recoverable, and it is exempt from formal licensing because of its occurrence in SpecCP or in the specifier of the highest Comp projection. An analysis with a trace, a copy of the DP involved, does not change the essentials here.

(10) a. nc hab t wieder nicht d'ran gedacht
              have   again not   of it thought
          '(I) have forgotten it again'
      b. OP habe ich gestern nc gekauft
              have I   yesterday   bought
          'I have bought that yesterday'

This approach to topic-drop relies heavily on the assumption that only an ec in the highest position can occur unlicensed. But it is this assumption which immediately explains the root/non-root asymmetry manifest in the null-topic construction illustrated in (11), at least in the old framework where only one CP position is available for either the topic or fronted Wh.

(11) a. *Was hab ec gekauft ?
       what have(1)   bought
       'what have (I) bought"
    b. *Hat ec das gekauft ?
       has   that bought
       'has (he) bought that?'
    c. *Ich weiß, daß ec das gekauft hat.
       I   know that that bought has
       'I know that (he) has bought that'
    d. *Gestern hab ec das gekauft.
       yesterday have that bought
       'Yesterday, (I) have bought that'

A topic-drop approach to child null subjects essentially predicts the same root/non-root asymmetry. This is exactly what Weissenborn (1990, 1991) finds for German children: in post-verbal position, in Wh-questions and in embedded clauses null subjects are rare. We could thus assume that for German, child null subjects are indeed topic-drop and are thus language specific from early on. The drawback is that this approach has nothing to say about null subjects in infinitives or about the acquisition of expletive null subjects and that the root/non-root asymmetry is not as clear-cut as suggested above. Moreover the properties of object omission from initial position which clearly is topic-drop in German, are rather different from those of initial subject drop in child language. We will come back to these problems in chapter 10.

Moreover, the analysis has to be modified if we assume an articulated CP. This, with its multiple positions, cannot directly explain the exclusion of null subjects in structures that require the filling of the topic-position or the position for the Wh-operator: mutual exclusiveness is no longer guaranteed.

2.2.3. Split CP, V2 and Null Subjects

Considerations about the multiple functions of the CP, especially the embedded CP which encodes the illocutionary force of the embedded clause but also its finite or non-finite nature, have led to the postulation of at least two different projections in the C-system, a ForceP and a FinP, reflecting illocutionary force and finiteness respectively. In addition to these projections, the C-system may contain projections hosting one or more topicalized constituents (TopP) and one focalized constituent (FocP). Based on preposing data from English and Italian, Rizzi (1997) arrives at the articulated CP structure in (12). Here the TopP is the projection whose specifier hosts the topicalized projection, whereas the specifier of the FocP can host focalized constituents but also preposed Wh-constituents.

(12)   ForceP

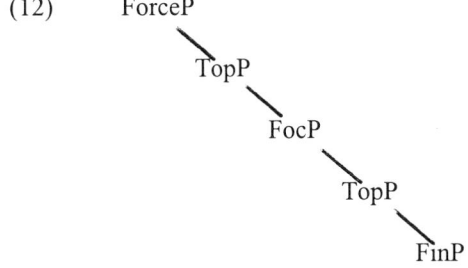

Given this structure, a new analysis for V2 and topicalization in V2 languages has to be given. I present the suggestions of Haegeman (1996c) who proposes that the V2 effect is a function of two elements: (i) the nature of Fin^0, the lowest head in the C system, which encodes finiteness features, and (ii) a generalized null operator strategy for topicalization. If we assume in minimalist terms that Fin^0 has a strong V-feature, it follows that this head will attract the finite verb. Haegeman also assumes that the Fin-head requires a specifier, i.e. that the FinP is subject to the EPP. So in root clauses, the finite verb moves to Fin^0 and one maximal projection, a subject, a topicalized constituent or a Wh-constituent, will move to and sometimes through the specifier. We get the three types of structures in (13), (14), and (15), which Haegeman introduces for Dutch and I adopt for German.

If the subject does not have the feature [+Top] or [+Wh], the clause has the structure (13). If the subject is a Wh-constituent, it occupies the specifier of the FocP. Haegeman (1996c) suggests that the Wh-operator satisfies the Wh-Criterion by passing through the specifier of the FinP thus establishing a chain as in (14).

(13)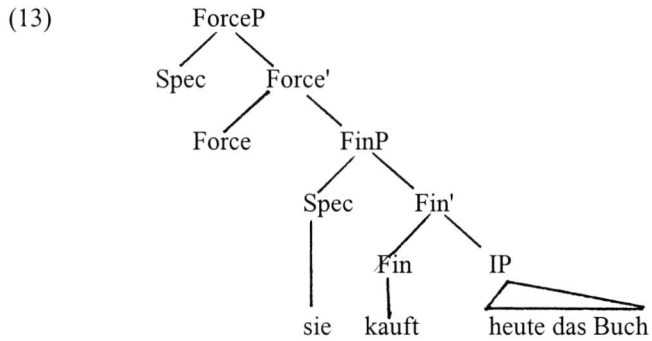

(14)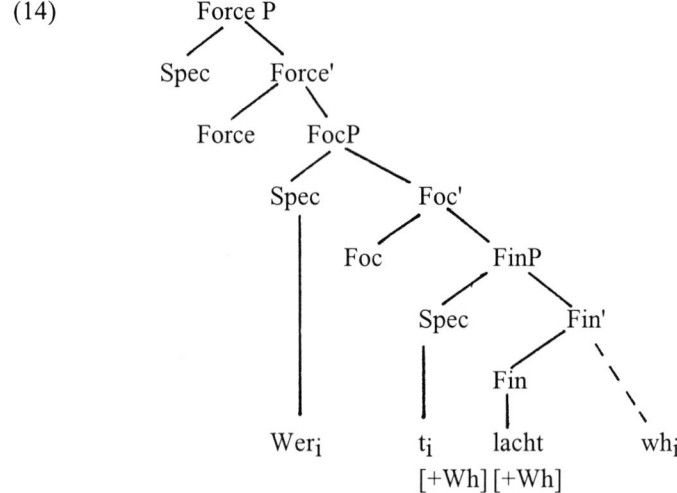

If such a chain cannot be established (because the intervening positions are activated by some sort of material), the finite verb cannot enter into a spec-head relationship and ungrammaticality is the result, as in (15b and c).

(15) a. Wer kauft morgen ein Buch?
 who buys tomorrow a book
 'who will buy a book tomorrow?'
 b. *Wer morgen kauft ein Buch?
 who tomorrow buys a book

c. *Wer ein Buch kauft morgen?
   who a book buys tomorrow

These data could also indicate, however, that the verb has indeed moved as high as Foc^0 in order to satisfy the Wh-Criterion. Haegeman sees the establishment of a chain as the more economical solution and thus as preferable. This is a possible argument for subject-questions because the operators involved often contain agreement, as in the *que/qui* alternation. But there may be doubts whether the Wh-operator can in general move through SpecFinP which is an A-position in V2 languages because, as a verbal position, it carries the verbal agreement. For an object question, such movement is clearly excluded because the overt subject would block movement. If the verb has to move up to FocP in order to satisfy the Wh-Criterion, we get the analysis in (16).

(16)
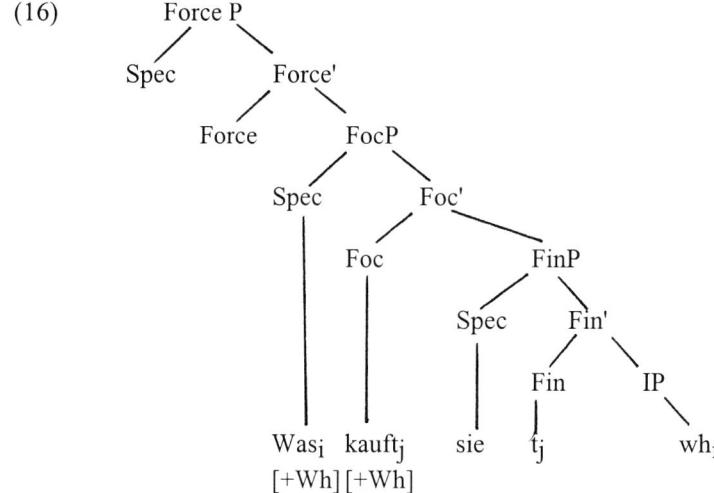

Regarding topicalization, Haegeman (1996c) follows Lasnik and Stowell (1991) and Koster (1978) in assuming that the empty category associated with a preposed topic is connected to this topic by a null operator. It is further assumed that this operator can be spelled out by so called d-words, as in (17). Therefore Haegeman proposes (18) as an analysis of topicalization.

(17) a. Das Buch (das) krieg ich morgen
 the book that get I tomorrow
 'I'll get the book tomorrow'
 b. Gestern (da) haben wir viel gelacht.
 yesterday there have we much laughed
 'yesterday we laughed a lot'

(18)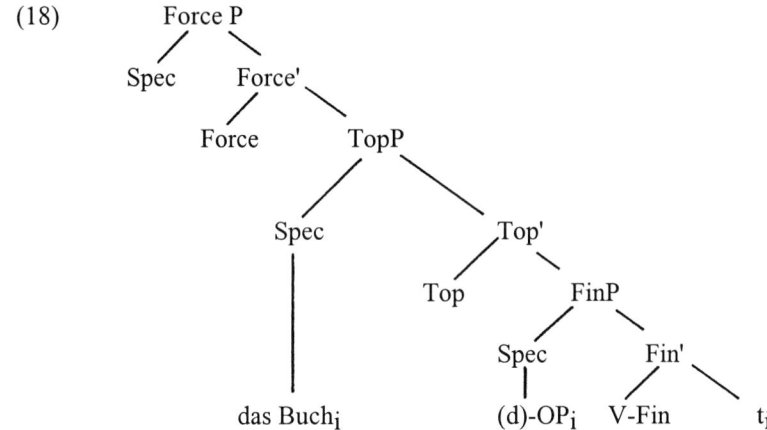

Topicalized constituents are submitted to the Topic Criterion, i.e. the topicalized XP and the head bearing the topic feature must be in a spec-head relationship. This topic-feature is not V-related and does not trigger V-to-Top movement. The EPP is satisfied by the operator (overt or null) in Spec FinP. Multiple topics are ungrammatical because Fin^0 licenses only one such null operator. Given this analysis for topics, Haegeman (1996c:147) writes: "null discourse topics in Dutch and German are null operators of the familiar kind which have attained the specifier of the root, i.e. the specifier of the ForceP....this is related to the option that Force may carry topic features."[3]

The problem which now arises is that the above root/non-root asymmetry can be explained only partly by pointing out that the Wh-operator or the complementizer targets the same position as the null operator. In fact, though an overt complementizer in $Force^0$ does not fit together with the null topic operator in [Spec,Force] due to their feature specification and so null topics are excluded in embedded clauses, the Wh-operator does not occupy the same position at all. But it can be argued that structures as (19)

(19)   OP$_i$ where will t$_i$ go

are excluded because the subject trace is not properly governed in non-pro drop languages (see Rizzi 1997). Therefore, even if we lose a straightforward explanation, the root/non-root asymmetry still follows in a Split CP analysis.

But there is another question now, which concerns the articulated CP. What can be truncated? Can the child truncate inside the C-system? This is in fact what Haegeman assumes: As long as ForceP can be truncated, child null subjects of different kinds can surface.

2.2.4. Diary-drop and Child Null Subjects

Let us now concentrate on the type of null subjects which could be captured by a topic-drop analysis, namely the finite ones, and suggest a different, but related model for their analysis. There is a register in most languages, whether they allow topic-drop or not, which also licenses the dropping of subjects in finite contexts. This is the register of diary-drop as discussed by Haegeman (1990). I quote some of the examples from Haegeman (1996c:136).

(20)   Origo rather contorted: says Italy is blind red hot devoted patriotic; has thrown her wedding ring into the cauldron too. Anticipates a long war.
            (Diary of Virginia Woolf, p.6, 10 January 1936)

(21)   me dit que'l architecte Perret est désireux de passer un moment avec moi
            me   tells that the architect Perret wants to pass a moment with   me
            'he tells me that the architect Perret wants to spend some time with me'
            (Paul Léautaud, Journal particulier, p.44:6.2.133)

Diary-drop resembles topic-drop in that it is incompatible with Wh-preposing and embedding, but it differs from topic-drop in that it concerns only subjects, not any other arguments:

(22) a. *When will ec invite me again
b. *I think that ec will invite me again
c. *she has thrown ec into the cauldron
d. * ec , she has thrown into the cauldron.

This same asymmetry, concerning subject and object drop, has been found by Bloom (1990) for English child argument-drop: while there is about 50% subject drop, there is only about 8% object drop. Moreover, there is a type of null subject which is allowed in diary-drop, but not in topic-drop. Because expletives and quasi-arguments occupy A-positions and cannot be topicalized as Cardinaletti (1990) points out, one does not expect that such subjects can be dropped. In a normal colloquial register in German, this is indeed true.

(23) ??Regnet schon wieder
rains already again
'it's already raining again'

Though (23) is not a totally impossible sentence - it might occur in a diary, or the speaker may be among those who can say *Das regnet* - it is very odd. The same holds for Dutch:

(24) a. *Regende de hele dag
rained the whole day
'it rained the whole day'
b. *Waren veel mensen
were many people
'there were many people'

But true expletives and quasi-arguments can be dropped in the diary register and also in the literary register of interior monologue, which is a sort of diary-style in the third person. I quote some examples from Haegeman (1996c:137) which are interior monologue examples, not true diary style:

(25) He plumped the pillows up behind him and groped in the pocket of his tunic for a cigarette. Weren't any.

(26) Rained in the night, wind, rain and hail.

If finite child null subjects are topic-drop, we do not expect any expletive null subjects nor any quasi-argument null subjects. But both are documented in the literature.

(27) a. yes, is toys in there   Hyams 1983
      b. gaat weer regenen   Niek 3;7, Haegeman 1996c
         'it is going to rain'
      c. taut schon?   Elisa 3;1, Hamann 1992
         thaws already
         'it is thawing already'
      d. is Sonne da   Elisa 3.1, Hamann 1992
         (it) is sun there
         'there is the sun'
      e. is immer noch hell   Christoph 3;4, Hamann 1992
         is always still light
         'it is still light'
      e. is gar nich dunkel   Christoph 3;4, Hamann 1992
         is not at all dark
         'it isn't dark at all'

Haegeman (1996c) gives the following figures from the Wijnen corpus: of 8 initial quasi arguments, 6 are non-overt for Thomas; of 7 initial quasi arguments, 3 are non-overt for Hein, and of 4 initial quasi-arguments, 3 are non-overt for Niek. Though the figures are small, they definitely point to the possibility of dropping quasi-argument subjects in child language. In the German corpus of Elisa, there are 16 quasi-argument subject environments and 6 have non-overt subjects, which are not initial however, and Christoph has 17 quasi-argument subject constructions of which 5 are non-overt. Of these, 7 are initial quasi-argument subjects, 2 of which are non-overt.[4]

These data point to the fact that finite child null subjects and diary null subjects should be given the same analysis. This is indeed what Haegeman (1996c) proposes in suggesting that both are empty elements in SpecIP for French (or English) and that both are empty elements in SpecFinP in V2 languages like Dutch or German - and are made possible by truncation. The difference of the child grammar and the adult register grammar is only that adults can at most truncate the ForceP, but have to project a TP in order to achieve a proposition, whereas children can truncate lower down and so are able to use infinitives.

In a truncation framework one could claim that differentiating topic-drop and diary-drop null subjects is a terminological nicety: in both cases we have an empty element in the topmost position which can survive precisely because it is in the topmost position and which is interpreted via discourse. This would entitle us to speak of child topic-drop even in non-finite contexts, however, and so might lead to some confusion. Moreover, with respect to adult language, topic-drop and diary-drop are different phenomena with different properties and have to be kept apart.

This discussion shows one point quite clearly. If the adopted framework does not allow truncation, it follows that inside such a framework one cannot use the term topic-drop for the finite child null subject, because this would imply the full adult topic-drop analysis with an empty category in SpecCP whose existence would be especially surprising in languages which do not have adult topic-drop. One could claim, however, that the diary register available in most languages is over-used by the child. This may even seem a natural claim, given the fact that the child universe has often been called egocentric and in this resembles the universe of the diary writer, who does not care about what knowledge s/he shares with the hearer.

2. 3. Two Problems for Truncation

There are two questions which the truncation approach, especially in its older formulation, has to answer. One concerns the type of material that can activate a projection, and the other concerns the question of why the child will stop truncating.

Concerning the first problem, Rizzi (1994) mentions 'morphological material' which will activate a projection, and he probably has in mind the inflectional ending of a verb which will activate IP, or the Wh-word which will activate CP. This assumption is clearly uncontroversial. The question must be raised, however, in languages which allow Wh-in-situ as French does. Does the child who leaves the Wh-word in-situ activate the CP because the phrase has to be interpreted as a question and so the Wh-word has to raise to CP at LF at the latest - or does s/he truncate the CP because there is no morphological material to accommodate? The question therefore is whether interpretative material or requirements of LF can activate a projection. On the face of it there seems to be evidence that French children truncate when they use Wh-in-situ because they can use null subjects in this construction. On the other hand, it seems highly unlikely that a child does not mark a question as a question at LF. In chapter 9 I will discuss the occurrence of null subjects in

French Wh-in-situ questions and give it an interpretation which makes use of the split CP so that it can be assumed that part of the CP is activated for interpretative reasons, but part of it is still truncated, allowing the use of the null subject.

In the newer version of truncation, the case of activation of a projection by morphological material clearly follows from the fact that 'Structural Economy' cannot cut off such material. The case of activation through the requirements of interpretation should also be covered by this principle: Structural well-formedness cannot stop at the spell-out level but must be extended to LF – if a derivation does not arrive at an interpretable LF, it crashes. So a position needed for interpretation cannot be cut off by 'Structural Economy'.

The second question is interesting as it involves the subset principle in a very acute form. Truncation is optional, so the grammar allowed by truncation will always be a superset of the target grammar which does not allow infinitives in root declaratives and restricts null subjects to the diary register (if it is neither a pro-drop nor a topic-drop grammar). So, if negative evidence is not allowed as a learning mechanism, there is no possibility to ever arrive at the target grammar. Rizzi (1994) simply suggested that the axiom (2) matures. This is an acceptable solution in the framework of innate grammar because the language ability is regarded as a biological system which matures just as vision or walking matures. Wexler (1996) provides more arguments for maturation and gives a maturational account of optional infinitives. He suggests that it is the interface of syntax and interpretation which matures, and one might speculate that a mature interface requires a full CP for each clause. A mature interface may for instance require that the discourse select a ForceP, as has also been suggested by Roeper (1996). Hyams (1996) gives another approach where the breakdown of an interface rule is responsible for the use of root infinitives and this interface rule may mature. But as long as we do not know more about the interface rules, we can just as well claim that it is the axiom (2) which matures. I will return to this problem and examine in chapter 11 how 'CP trouble' can be responsible for what looks like interface problems.

In the more recent framework, where it is 'Categorial Uniformity' which is responsible for the analysis of every root clause as a CP, this is clearly tied to the uniformity of embedded clauses and root clauses as to categorial status. As was dicussed in this chapter in 2.1., as long as the child does not systematically produce embedded clauses, this principle is probably not operative. Only when subordinate clauses are used frequently, Categorial

Uniformity begins to play a role, and indeed we generally observe that the rise in the use of embedded clauses tends to coincide with the decrease in infinitives and null subjects. One problem with this view is the 'triggering problem' discussed in chapter 6. The contrast of root declaratives and embedded declaratives has been in the input all along.

So we might return to an intermediate proposal, formulated as "Avoid Structure" (see Rizzi 1995a and Haegeman 1996a in a diary-drop approach). The idea is that there is a hierarchy of structure building principles (among them presumably Categorial Uniformity) and that Avoid Structure is stronger in the child than in the adult grammar and can overrule some of these structure building principles. Interestingly, Rizzi (1995a) proposes that the weakest structure building principle concerns selection by discourse, which is obligatory in adult grammar but is overruled in child grammar. This is another way to tie truncation and the CP to the interface without making the interface responsible for the child grammar and it allows maturation in so far as the right weighting of principles may mature.

3. OPTIONAL TENSE AND RELATED APPROACHES

3.1. Optional Tense

Cross-linguistic examples similar to those presented in chapter 6 were extensively discussed in Wexler (1992, 1994), which proved seminal to the discussion of optional (root) infinitives.[5] These papers especially focussed on the observation that the child places finite and non-finite verbs correctly, a fact which was shown to hold across languages. The best known results about verb-placement were given in chapter 1 in tables 1,2,3 and are repeated here in tables 29, 30, and 31. Similar results are obtained with respect to negation for Danish, Swedish and German (Plunkett and Strömqvist 1990, Platzack 1990, Santelmann 1995a, Clahsen 1988, Verrips and Weissenborn 1989) and with respect to V2 for German or Bernese Swiss German, for Dutch, and for Swedish (Clahsen and Penke 1992, Penner 1992, Weissenborn 1990, Weverink 1989, and Santelman 1995a).

Table 29: Distribution of finite and non-finite verbs with respect to negation
French (Pierce 1989: three children ranging from 1;8 to 2;6)

	+finite	-finite
pas verb	11	77
verb pas	185	2

Table 30: Distribution of finite and non-finite verbs with respect to V2
German (Poeppel and Wexler 1993: Andreas 2.1)

	+finite	-finite
V2/not final	197	6
Vfinal/not V2	11	37

Table 31: Distribution of finite and non-finite verbs with respect to V2
German (Clahsen, Eisenbeiss and Penke 1996:
Simone 1;10-2;7, Matthias 2;3-3;6, Annelie 2;4-2;9, and Hannah 2;0-2;7)

	Simone	Matthias	Annelie	Hannah
finite/non-finite				
Vfin in V2	93% (511)	87% (69)	88% (117)	80% (4)
Vfin in final pos.	7% (41)	13% (10)	12% (16)	20% (1)
V-fin in V2	2% (4)	2% (1)	1% (1)	X
V-fin in final pos.	98% (189)	98% (52)	99% (80)	X

Wexler concluded that children know head movement and place finite verbs correctly in AgrSP, but that "they do not yet know that non-finite verbs cannot be used as main verbs in declaratives" (Schoenenberger et al. 1996:50). To account for this observation, Wexler (1994) suggests that Tense is optional in the child grammar during this phase.

If this is the case and the tense feature does not have to be interpreted at LF, then true optionality follows because the child has two equally costly options: the child can either lower I-to-V without subsequent LF-raising because the T feature does not have to be interpreted in the child grammar. This will result in a non-agreeing form, namely the infinitive. Or s/he may raise V-to-I, which will result in the finite form. Wexler (1994) indeed hypothesized that the child does not distinguish values of T so that there is no semantic role for T to play at LF.

It is clear that the child still has to interpret a sentence with respect to time, and Wexler proposes that this is done by a direct interpretation in discourse so that no functional category is needed for coding the time information in an optional infinitive. Though this is intuitively correct, it will emerge in the discussion that the idea needs refinement and that especially the term 'discourse' is too vague. Wexler points out a consequence of the absence of TP which is often overlooked. As the event time is normally assumed to be located in the TP as suggested by the analysis of Enç (1987), the absence of the TP will allow that the event does not have to be placed on the real time line, it could well be an irrealis event. This implies that optional infinitives may have a modal interpretation - an impression which can be very strong for the child use of infinitives and may lead to the missing Aux hypothesis. Though I will argue in chapter 11 that the event time is not located in the TP, but in the Aspect Phrase, and that it is reference time which is located in TP instead, the argument carries over. Reference time is needed to place an event on the time line - event time is then located relative to this other time. So it is reference time which provides the anchor to the actual time line, and if this is missing, the event may be interpreted as ongoing or irrealis.

3.2. Optional Tense and Types of Subjects

3.2.1. Infinitives and Null Subjects

In order to account for the child null subject, it is proposed that this null subject is PRO, which is licensed because it is not (properly) governed by the TP. This analysis is taken straight from adult grammar where infinitives usually have PRO subjects and (28a) serves as gloss for (28b and c):

(28) a. I prefer PRO to leave
b. Ich ziehe es vor PRO zu gehen
c. Je prefère PRO partir

One problem with this account is the fact that it is not quite obvious how this PRO can be identified in child language. Like the adult PRO it is **licensed** by the absence of tense, but adult PRO is **identified** through control, i.e. the subject or object of the embedding clause identifies the interpretation of PRO. This embedding clause is characteristically missing in the optional infinitive stage. To circumvent this problem, Schütze and Wexler (1996b) have argued that there are many cases where adult PRO is neither controlled nor arbitrary, but is identified directly in context or situation, so that this form of identification is what is used in the child grammar.

(29)   It would be stupid PRO to leave now

This assumption about the interpretation of PRO is not quite satisfactory for several reasons. It may be the case that discourse restricts the range of arbitrary PRO in the above example, but there are still grammatical constraints on the interpretation that cannot be overruled by discourse, see (30). And even if PRO in (31) includes John, it is not only about John.

(30)   a. Why do that
        b. It is pouring outside. Really pouring. *Oh, why rain like that.

(31)   As for John, it would be stupid to leave now.

The PRO-analysis of child null subjects makes one strong assumption: it treats only the null subject occurring in infinitives as 'the child null subject' or, put differently, as the null subject pertaining to the optional infinitive phase. There are two immediate problems with this suggestion.

First, in a theory as proposed by Chomsky (1993,1995), overt noun phrases must receive case, and subject case, i.e. nominative, is assigned by Tense. It follows that the missing tense hypothesis strictly predicts that overt subjects should not occur at all in child infinitives. This is clearly wrong as (17e', g', m) of chapter 6 show for Danish and many examples from the literature show for other languages.

(32)   a. Michel dormir   French   Pierce 1989
            Michel sleep
        b. Thorstn das habn   German   Poeppel and Wexler 1993
            Thorsten that have
            'Thorsten has that'
        c. ik ook lezen   Dutch   Weverink 1989, Powers 1995
            I too read
            'I read too'

Numerical analyses showed that at least in some languages (Dutch, German, Danish, English and also French) such overt subjects in infinitives are not just errors but occur quite often. This led to a refinement of the missing tense hypothesis as outlined in Schütze and Wexler (1996a,b), where either Agr or Tns or both can be missing in a child infinitive.

Second, as only missing tense licenses PRO, and PRO is the child null subject, finite null subjects should not occur. Again, this prediction is clearly wrong as (1a), (2a,c), (4a,b) and (5a,c) of chapter 6 already indicate, and as we will show in detail in chapter 8. In the framework of the missing tense hypothesis, finite null subjects can only be due to some other property of the child grammar and need a different analysis. This is indeed what Bromberg and Wexler (1995), Schütze and Wexler (1996a), and Sano and Hyams (1994) propose. They suggest that finite null subjects are topic-drop, a hypothesis which had to be revised later in view of new data French and led to the morphological reanalysis of French and Danish outlined in section 3.3. of this chapter.

3.2.2. Infinitives and Overt Subjects

Let me first take up the problem of overt subjects in infinitives. It has to be acknowledged that these do not only occur, but also show an interesting behavior with respect to case. Schütze and Wexler (1996a) observe that in English, an overt subject in an infinitive can take either the nominative or the accusative case.

(33)   a. she drink apple juice   Nina, file 19
        b. him fall down   Nina 2;3,14, file 17

For Russian, Dutch, German, Faroese, on the other hand, it is consistently reported that the rate of non-nominative subjects in infinitives is essentially zero, whereas in these languages it may happen that a child uses a nominative object as illustrated in (34), quoting from Eisenbeiss (1994).

(34)   ne ich möchte der Caesar   Andreas, 2;1
           no I want(fin) the (nom) caesar

Using the figures from Schütze and Wexler (1996a), we can establish the following. The German child Andreas (2;1) used 189 nominative subjects in 190 obligatory contexts (Schütze 1995), two Russian children (1;6-2;0 and 2;1-2;7) used 210 nominative subjects in 210 obligatory contexts (Babyonyshev 1993), 5 Dutch children (1;9-3;10) used 2697 correct nominative first person subject pronouns out of 2700 first person subject pronouns (Powers 1995), and Jonas (1995) reports no errors for Faroes.

In order to account for these facts, it has been suggested as early as Gruber (1967) that the occurrence of so many non-nominative forms in English children's speech is due to the fact that children use the default case in infinitive constructions, and this happens to be the accusative in English, whereas it is the nominative in Russian, Dutch, German and Faroese. An extreme position was taken by Radford (1990) who claimed that in the optional infinitive stage, children have not acquired the morpho-syntax of the nominative and do not have a case system at all. This assumption cannot cover the facts, however, because children at this stage quite consistently use nominative overt subjects in finite constructions, as table 32 shows.

Table 32 : Case distribution with respect to finiteness: English
(Schütze and Wexler 1996a)

% of non-nominative forms (Acc, Gen)	3rd pers. sing.		1st pers. sing.	
	Finite	Nonfinite	Finite	Nonfinite
Loeb & Leonard 8 children	5%	38%		
Schütze and Wexler				
Nina	5%	46%	5%	22%
Sarah	13%	37%		
Peter			1.2%	22%

Clahsen, Eisenbeiss and Penke (1996) approach the problem from a checking perspective and report that whenever a fully specified DP subject (number and gender present and case marked as subject) was used by the four German children from table 31, subject-verb agreement was correct, thus essentially confirming the finding that finite verbs occur with correctly specified subjects. These authors also report that the German children they analyzed continued to use infinitives after the point they define as the point of the acquisition of the AgrSP. Furthermore, they found no fully specified DP subjects in these optional infinitives, but either subjects were dropped or the children used subjects which do not show number and gender specification. Clahsen, Eisenbeiss and Penke (1996:149, 150, table 4) show that proper names or first and second person pronouns were used.

The figures clearly show that finite constructions almost exclusively display nominative subjects, so one can exclude the assumption that the case module is not in place in the infinitive phase. The truncation hypothesis could approach the observations presented so far in the following way: for the finite constructions, tense and agreement are activated, so the correct case will be assigned. What has to be accounted for, however, is the fact that both nominative and non-nominative subjects occur with infinitives in English. Indeed, table 32 shows that averaged over the children, nominative subjects occur to about 60% with 3rd person pronouns and to 78% for 1st person pronouns. The difficulty is that the data about finite case assignment show the children's knowledge that the nominative is not the default case in English. Therefore the assumption that in an infinitive the default case surfaces, though it cannot be proved wrong by German, Dutch or Russian data, is not quite convincing and does not seem to cover all the facts.

3.3. Optional Tense and Optional Agreement

The model Schütze and Wexler (1996a,b) propose, tries to take account of just this problem by assuming that agreement or tense (or both) can be missing in optional infinitives. This has become known as ATOM, the 'Agreement or Tense Omission Model' (Wexler 1998). It explains the results on subject case in infinitives: if agreement is present, the nominative will be assigned. If it is not present, the case feature is not present in the syntax and so the default will surface.

To motivate their departure from Chomsky (1993, 1995) where it is Tns which assigns nominative case, Schütze and Wexler (1996a) give the following supportive arguments for the function of Agr as the assigner of nominative case. There are two arguments from acquisition. First, overt subjects do occur in optional infinitives. Second, Schütze and Wexler show in a detailed analysis of verb form and case that most of the non-nominative subjects in finite constructions occur with past tense (*-ed*) verbs, whereas they are practically absent in constructions which are marked for 3rd person singular (*-s*). Moreover, there are certain constructions in adult grammars which support the assumption. Portuguese has infinitives which lack tense marking, but show agreement and assign nominative. In many languages, subjunctive has the same property. One can add that Latin infinitives are tense marked, but lack agreement and assign the accusative.

It is essential for the system that a theory like Distributed Morphology (Halle and Marantz 1993) be assumed, where a form without a syntactically marked feature will be spelled out as the least specified member of the paradigm, the default. This may look as in (35) for English and German case, and as in (36) for English tense and agreement.

(35) a. [3] [sing] [masc] [Nom]   he   English
        [3] [sing[[masc]   him

     b. [3] [sing] [masc] [Acc]   ihn   German
        [3] [sing] [masc] [DAT]   ihm
        [3] [sing] [masc]   er

(36)   [+tns=present] [+agr=3rd]   -s   English
        [+tns =past]   -ed
        [tns] [agr]   0   (unspecified)

The paradigm in (36) shows that the absence of agreement and tense just leads to a zero morpheme, which is convincing for English but may be problematic for other languages. Since agreement *-s* can only surface if there is a [+present] specification, it follows from Schütze and Wexler's approach that if tense is unspecified, but agreement is specified, it cannot be spelled out as an *-s* and so surfaces as what looks like an infinitive.

The idea that infinitives are due to either the lack of tense or agreement or both, was inspired by the facts of case assignment in optional infinitives, but now leads to an explanation of null subjects. If only unspecified tense licenses a null subject, we get (37).

(37) [+tns,+agr] NOM assigned   he cries
                   null subject impossible
      [+tns,-agr] NOM unassignable,
                   default ACC   him cry, him cried
                   null subject impossible
      [-tns,+agr] NOM assigned,
                   agreement invisible   he cry
                   null subject possible   cry
      [-tns,-agr] null subject possible   cry
                   default Acc possible   him cry

In brief, [-agr] leads to an optional infinitive by definition of what agreement does, namely adding an -s. So only [-tns] leads to null subjects, whereas [-agr] leads to the spelling out of default case. That Agr and Tns both play a role in the determination of finiteness has long been discussed. It is, however, not so obvious why the absence of agreement should naturally lead to the choice of the infinitive in languages which do not have the coincidence of stem form and infinitive. In English, this may be straightforward, but in languages which mark the infinitive morphologically, a further step is required. The child has to choose the infinitive from among other non-agreeing forms (participles) and it is not trivial why the infinitive should surface as a sort of least marked form in this case.

For Mainland Scandinavian and following the traditional analysis, we expect that the *-er* ending is [+tense=present, -agr], and *-de/t* is [+tense=past, -agr]. So the infinitive can only be differentiated from these forms by the [-tns] feature and it is not obvious how the presence or absence of agreement can play a role in the surfacing of a Danish infinitive.[6] In order to overcome this difficulty and to account for the many finite null subjects occurring in Danish, which cannot be topic drop as discussed in chapter 8, Wexler (2000) suggests the following analysis of the Danish morphology. The *–er* form is analyzed as occurring in the context of an (abstract) specific Agr feature, *-de* is marked [+past] and the infinitive *–e* is the pure default, not marked for anything. In adult language, infinitives only appear when there are no Agr or Tns features. Given ATOM, the child could have included Agr but omitted Tns form the representation, however. According to this approach, the morpheme *–er* would surface. So, what is usually taken as the present tense finite form, is really a manifestation of a 'root infinitive' in the sense that the [agr, -tns] specification allowed by ATOM will be spelled out by an infinitive in English but by the *–er* form in Danish. For French, Wexler (1997, 1998) suggested a similar analysis. [+agr,-tns] leads to the stem form which coincides with the 3 singular finite forms and therefore has always been considered and counted as finite, but, from this perspective, should be counted as a non-finite form. So the *-er* ending in French can only surface if both tense and agreement are missing, [-agr, -tns], and this also explains the non-occurrence of subject clitics in French *-er* marked infinitives. This account, even if it predicts Danish and French "finite 0-subjects" as 0-subjects which are really licensed by the absence of tense, strikes me as rather counterintuitive. For the account to work, it is necessary to assume that verb forms - whether French or Danish - which lack an overt agreement marker are analyzed nonetheless as [+agr]. Assuming an abstract agreement marker in all those cases where the theory requires it, thus seems rather ad hoc, and needs more independent motivation. The approach also runs into problems with the widely quoted distribution of negation or V2 and so called finite verbs, see tables 29, 30, 31. If these verb forms cannot be considered to be truly finite, these distributions prove nothing anymore about the child's ability to respect the syntactic consequences of finiteness. The approach is thus not fully convincing as a cross-linguistic analysis.

More recently, Wexler (1998, 2000) has suggested a principle that will derive ATOM and at the same time predicts that pro-drop languages do not have a root infinitive phase. This principle is called the *Unique Checking Constraint* (UCC) and is defined as in (38):

(38)   Unique Checking Constraint
        The D-feature of DP can only check against one functional category.

As subjects must check against the D-feature on Agr and on Tns and the child under the UCC cannot do this, there are three possible paths to take. The child can violate the UCC and come up with an adult structure. The child can also omit Agr and check against the feature on Tns, or the child can omit Tns and check against the feature on Agr. We have thus derived ATOM. All three violations are equivalent and lead to the optionality observed for the use of infinitives.

As to the fact that pro-drop languages do not show an infinitive stage in development, this is due to the fact that the D-feature of AgrS in these languages is [+interpretable] and therefore should not be checked by the subject as it has to survive to LF. Therefore subjects, in these languages, move only as far as TNS and do not have to check against Agr. UCC is never violated, and neither Tns nor Agr have to be omitted by the child. So infinitives will not surface. This is not to say that the UCC does not have its effects on Romance children: Wexler (in press) derives the frequent omission of object clitics in French child language from the UCC.

3.4. Underspecification of Tense

Like the approaches discussed so far, Hyams (1996) assumes that early null subjects are related to the root infinitive phenomenon, and analyses both as an effect of the underspecification of the inflectional system, especially the tense component. In her account, as in Wexler's, the child null subject is PRO, i.e. the null subject which is licensed in infinitives in adult grammar. Chomsky and Lasnik (1993) suggest that PRO bears 0-case, where 0-case is assigned, if I^0 lacks tense and agreement, and it is this definition of the licensing of PRO which Hyams has in mind.

This account makes some obvious predictions, specifically that such a PRO 0-subject should not occur with finite verbs and in particular not with inflected forms of the auxiliary or copula *be*. Null subjects will be predicted, on the other hand, if the copula or auxiliary is missing - under the assumption that an auxiliary has no semantic content and only functions as a spell-out of agreement features so that underspecification of agreement leads to omission. Sano and Hyams (1994) indeed show that for Eve, neither *am*, *are* or *is* ever occurs with a null subject, Nina has no null subjects with *am* or *are*, but 4% with *is,* whereas Adam has no null subjects with *am* and *are*, but about 11% with *is*. Schütze (p.c. October 1996) analyses Nina's auxiliaries with a different method and finds that the percentage of null subjects compared to all overt subjects with auxiliary verbs is 3% if the auxiliary is finite and 50% when the auxiliary is omitted, i.e. non-finite under the above assumptions. Valian (1991) provides data on the rarity of null subjects in modal constructions, where the obligatory presence of agreement in English also predicts their absence under Hyams account. It comes as a surprise therefore that Hyams found 10% null subjects with finite verbs marked *-s* for Eve and 26% for Adam, and that null subjects occur even more often with finite verbs marked in *-ed* (22.5% for Eve, 56.5% for Adam and 19% for Nina). Sano and Hyams suggest that the occurrence of such null subjects is due to an analysis of the *-s* and *-ed* forms as participles which are located in a lower Aspect Phrase. As an argument for this analysis, Hymas suggests that in embedded clauses a finite verb cannot be misanalysed as a participle and indeed, Valian

(1991) reports that for 23 children ranging from 1;10 to 2;8 in age there were no occurrences of null subjects in 123 finite subordinate clauses.

Hyams sees the advantage of a PRO analysis primarily in the fact that the I-projection is assumed to be always present and that no additional empty category needs to be introduced - but does not discuss the fact that this empty category is needed for independent reasons, see Lasnik and Stowell (1991). The underlying intuition is that infinitives are used in infelicitous contexts, and so the problem must be located on the pragmatic side. The interest of the analysis is the way in which Hyams spells out the pragmatic difficulty and relates the use of infinitives to the use of articleless DPs.[7] The parallel is that I marks finiteness and thus temporal specificity whereas D marks nominal specificity.

The problem must therefore be located in the area of temporal reference and thus requires a syntactic and semantic analysis of tense. Hyams first points out the parallels of tense and pronouns as observed by Partee (1973). Tense can be anchored anaphorically like a third person pronoun, where the anchor need not even be explicit in the linguistic context but can be just a salient element of the conversational background (common knowledge). Or it can be anchored deictically to the utterance situation like a first person pronoun.

Following Enç (1987), Stowell (1993) and Guéron and Hoekstra (1992, 1995), Hyams adopts a framework where these intuitions are turned on their heads but a sort of algorithm results for tense computation. Tense is still treated in parallel to pronouns, but present tense, the deictic tense par excellence, comes out as a bound tense, as anaphoric. Tense can be bound by an indexed operator so that a tense chain can be established which makes the predicate referential by "hooking the V+I complex up" (Hyams 1996: 106) to a temporal operator and hence to the discourse world. This operator has the utterance time as the default value. In order to establish a tense chain, I^0 carries a temporal index, and it can now be either anaphoric or pronominal in the following sense: it is anaphoric if it is bound by the tense operator, i.e. coindexed, or I^0 is pronominal and free, i.e. it is counterindexed. We get the present tense in the first case because the tense operator by default identifies speech time, and the past tense in the second case, see (39).

(39) a. (TO_i) John [I_i] knows the answer   present
     b. (TO_i) John [I_j] drove his car   past

If we now take the temporal index to be the specification of I^0, then speaking of underspefication in child grammar simply means that I^0 is without an index or that it is randomly co- or counterindexed. If it is unindexed, the result is a root infinitive which does not get a syntactic temporal interpretation, but receives the temporal reference in discourse: according to Hyams this will be the "here and now" because of the default interpretation of the tense operator. The same holds for random indexation: the temporal index will have the "now" reading. Let I^0 be co-indexed with the operator, the interpretation will arrive at a present reading, as in the adult grammar. If I^0 is counterindexed, the picture is more complicated. But the child will still allow the "here and now" interpretation because the child will allow a coreferential interpretation of the indices which is disallowed in the adult grammar, given the availability of the anaphor for this reading. What is responsible for the infelicitous use of the child root infinitive is therefore the same problem which underlies the poor performance of English children in Principle B contexts: the non-mastery of the coreference rule.

Hyams approach is striking in that it captures the intuition that children are bound to the "here and now", by using a current theory of tense in conjunction with a well-discussed pragmatic difficulty with pronouns: the coreference rule. It is thus the first approach which explicitly links the nominal and the temporal domains and which locates the difficulty in the mapping between syntax and pragmatics, i.e. in the interface.[8] Moreover, Hyams drew attention to the empirical observation (though this was first discussed by Plunkett and Stroemqvist 1991) that auxiliaries seldom occur with null subjects and that finite null subjects are restricted in occurrence.

There are some obvious problems, however. The first thing which comes to mind is the problem that root infinitives disappear from children's speech at the age of three or soon after, whereas the misinterpretation of pronouns lasts well up to 5 or 6 years of age. Hyams tries to explain this by postulating a temporal and a nominal rule, but this is not very convincing because on the formal level indices are indices and the coreference rule should not be able to distinguish different kinds of indices. Also the theory of tense is not quite satisfactory as we will discuss in depths later. First, as mentioned above, it treats the present in a rather counterintuitive way. Second, speech time should not come out as the default of the tense operator, because it is always given. Consider the case where the tense operator is not interpreted by speech time, but by a salient time of discourse, a reference time. Now the operator is interpreted as some other time different from speech time. For the tense interpretation we need to be able to say that this other time is in a certain relation to speech time. But there is no way to refer to speech time any more: the operator which normally picks it out as a default has another value already and speech time cannot be introduced into the system any more - unless by embedding tenses, which is not an obvious solution for simple tenses. Clearly, we need more than one temporal argument for the accomodation of temporal reference and relations. We will suggest another account of tense later where reference time is incorporated into the syntax as the specifier (i.e. as an argument) of the tense phrase, so that speech time remains available for interpretation. Another problem is the account of the finite null subjects with the assumption of a participle interpretation. Though this may not be counterintuitive in the case of *-ed*, it seems rather far fetched for *-s*, especially in view of the case facts discussed above and the very frequent use of *-ing* forms by English children.

4. ECONOMY OF PROJECTION AND NON-MERGER

Let us briefly take stock. We have extensively discussed the truncation and the missing tense approach to optional infinitives and null subjects. We have already dismissed the null auxiliary hypothesis as proposed by Boser et al. (1992) because of the facts of clitic placement (see Haegeman 1996b:285 and Chapter 2). What remains to be discussed are the non-merger account of Phillips (1995) and the more influential approach of Economy of Projection as proposed in Roeper and Rohrbacher (2000). We will deal with these two approaches in a rather introductory manner and come back to details of the analyses if it is necessary for our own discussion.

Recent accounts of Germanic expletive *pro* and the child phenomenon return to the idea of a direct relationship of the agreement system and subject-drop, working with Economy of Projection. In the Economy accounts (see Speas 1994, Brandner 1993, Roeper and Rohrbacher 2000) a specifier position can remain radically empty only if the head contains phonetic or semantic material. If English has weak agreement which is not inserted in the base but directly marked on the verb, it follows that English does not allow empty subjects. As Roeper and Rohrbacher (2000) observe that empty subjects in the Adam corpus occur predominantly in non-finite contexts, their explanation for the English child phenomenon assumes that no AgrP is projected before the child has acquired the morphological reflex of tense. This leaves a bare VP, and so null subjects satisfy Economy of Projection since all projections are independently licensed by their heads. So in an early phase, children do not project AgrP. The child must then determine the properties of the target agreement system in order to either project or not project AgrSP. Therefore these properties have to be easily accessible, especially the property which makes an agreement system rich enough to allow an empty specifier.

In a slightly different account, Phillips (1995) offers a non-merger approach to the phenomenon and challenges the validity of some of the data. His idea is that optional root infinitives are not due to lack or optionality of structure, i.e. a lack of grammatical knowledge, but to a performance problem, namely the difficulty of accessing morphological knowledge. In other words, the cost of producing the correct inflectional suffix is still too high for the child to always add the inflection. Therefore "root infinitives are fully represented finite clauses in which (morphological) merger of the verb with inflection has been delayed" (Phillips 1995: 325). This gives (40a) as an analysis.

(40) a.

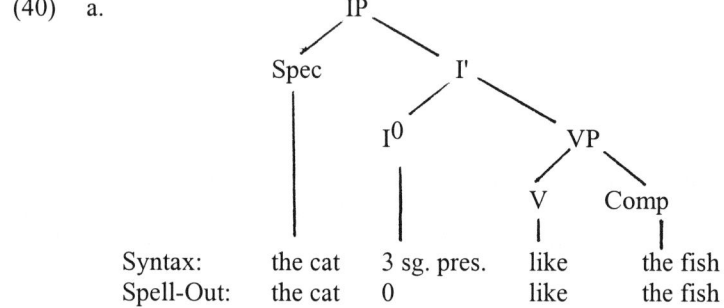

	Syntax:	the cat	3 sg. pres.	like	the fish
	Spell-Out:	the cat	0	like	the fish

For French, we would have the Spell-Out (40b). This already points to the problems because it seems odd to claim that a 0-morpheme has been added to arrive at the *er*-infinitive.

(40) b. Spell-Out: le chat   0   aimer   le poisson

Phillips' idea finds support in the fact that most errors in the use of inflectional morphology are errors of omission, not substitution. The same ideas and arguments have been proposed for L2-acquisition of adolescents and adults (Prevost and White 2000) and also for a young L2-learner (Belletti and Hamann 2000).

They do not seem to hold for first language acquisition as there are regularities in the use of child infinitives that cannot be predicted by a morphological spell-out difficult. One is the fact that the most convincing counterevidence to Boser et al. (1992)'s null-aux analysis carries over to (40). As Haegeman (1996b) points out, nothing in Boser et al.'s analysis prohibits the occurrence of subject clitics with optional infinitives. The same holds for (40): there is a position availabe for the clitic, the clitic is licensed by the presence of inflection and it is not the case that clitics need a morphologically filled host (chapter 2). So clitics can well attach to non-overt inflectional heads, and there is no reason why children should not produce *il aimer le poisson* in parallel to *le chat aimer le poisson.* The availabe data show that clitics are practically unattested in optional infinitives, see Pierce (1989) and section 7 of chapter 2.

The other data problem concerns the placement of finite verbs in V2-languages. Even if the systematic occurrence of finite verbs in Dutch, German and French Wh-questions or in topicalization structures is due to the passage of the verb through I (as Phillips suggests), there remain all the declaratives with subjects in first positions. Here Phillips has to assume that these do not involve the passage of the verb through I to C because there are many infinitives in such declarative structures. On the other hand 90% of the finite verbs occur in V2 position. If the difference between a finite and a non-finite child declarative is the application of morphological merge only, then there is no explanation for correct verb placement. In fact, a well discussed phase of L2-Acquisition of German shows that infinitives (chosen due to problems with the verbal paradigm) are consistently placed in V2 position (see Klein and Perdue 1997).

For these reasons, I think that the non-merger analysis of root infinitives does not capture the empirical facts, but I will repeatedly come back to the data discussed in Phillips (1995) because they are meticulously presented and can be evaluated from different points of view.

CHAPTER 8

EMPIRICAL DATA AND THE EVALUATION OF APPROACHES

1. AREAS OF INVESTIGATION

In this chapter the two most influential approaches to root infinitives and null subjects, namely the truncation and the missing tense hypothesis, will be evaluated in the light of acquisition data. Especially new data from Danish and French will be decisive. The three observations which any theory of root infinitives and null subjects has to deal with and which I want to examine from an empirical point of view are the asymmetry in 0-subject use in finite and non-finite constructions, the asymmetry in null subject use with auxiliaries and main verbs, and the close developmental parallel of root infinitives and null subjects. Data on these areas will be discussed in sections 3, 4, and 5 of this chapter. Moreover, there is another observation which any theory will have to account for and this is the fact that children acquiring a true pro-drop language like Catalan, Italian or Spanish do not go through a pronounced root infinitive stage. This will be discussed in section 6.

It is clear that the missing tense theory which was designed to account for exactly the asymmetry in subject omission in finite and non-finite constructions can deal with such an empirical observation in a straightforward way, whereas truncation will have to offer an explanation. As to the asymmetry in null subject use in auxiliary and main verb constructions, the missing tense hypothesis can handle this directly under standard assumptions about auxiliaries as base inserted in the tense node, whereas the truncation approach cannot offer a straightforward account but has to resort to licensing conditions of the auxiliary which presuppose the presence of the CP. Things become more interesting, however, when we consider the more recent observation about a close developmental parallel for the use of optional infinitives and finite null subjects. Here, missing tense and underspecification accounts cannot give an explanation, while it follows naturally from truncation.

It has been pointed out above that a PRO analysis of null subjects (i.e. a missing tense analysis) predicts their proliferation in infinitives, but has to introduce a different null subject to explain subject omission in finite child utterances. This second null subject has been carelessly dubbed a topic-drop subject. In some cases it may belong to the target language (if the language has topic-drop), in other cases it is an option constrained to the child use which must later disappear. We have already argued that for these reasons it makes more sense to speak of a diary-drop subject in child speech. Most languages have the diary register so that it could be argued that only the felicity conditions have to be acquired in order for the phenomenon to vanish from child speech. Proponents of a tense omission or underspecification account are reluctant to speak of a diary-drop subject because Haegeman (1996a,b,c) analyses adult diary null subjects as occurring in truncated structures and the use of truncation is avoided where possible. A truncation approach needs to postulate only one kind of null subject that can occur in different positions according to the locus of truncation. So a close developmental parallel is predicted even for finite null subjects and infinitives in so far as both exist only as long as the child can truncate freely.

One could also claim that the infinitival null subject is PRO, but the finite null subject is the diary null subject based on truncation. Then the same close developmental parallel can be expected. This would mean, however, that truncation is not a free option but is restricted to truncation of CP - otherwise we would have two types of null subjects in infinitives just as for free truncation. This idea is not to be rejected off-hand because it captures the many facts about CP-trouble which have been discussed in the literature (see Clahsen, Kursawe and Penke 1996, Penner 1994b, 1998), without implying that the same kind of problems should be observable for the IP or lower projections. It leaves us with the idea of missing tense combined with truncation of CP which is not very satisfactory and cannot directly account for a developmental parallel - unless missing tense can also be reduced to "CP-trouble". We will develop this idea further in a later section. Note here, that when adopting this speculative approach, we do not expect a developmental parallel of infinitives and finite null subjects if the finite null subject is a topic-drop subject because topic-drop does not rely on the absence, but on the presence of the CP. We predict the parallel only if the finite null subject is a diary null subject.

The aim of this section is not only an evaluation of the theoretical approaches, however. It also aims for a comprehensive presentation of much recent cross-linguistic research and for a broader empirical basis. The addition of new data to the few corpora we have of French, and the new results we obtain for a hitherto only sparsely investigated language like Danish will give a better basis for our discussion.

2. DANISH AND FRENCH GRAMMAR

2.1. Inflection

Both Danish and French are interesting from our point of view because they mark the infinitive morphologically so that it cannot be confused with a stem form. Danish is even more revealing than French with respect to finiteness marking for the following reason. In French, the finite forms of main verbs occurring in child speech are predominantly singular at an early age and therefore do not have an overt phonological marking. The three singular finite forms could thus also be analyzed as (non-finite) stem forms. Danish does not allow this interpretation because even if it does not have agreement, the language marks finiteness with the *-er* ending in the present tense, distinguishing it from the bare stem, and this ending occurs form early on.

Verb inflection in Danish is traditionally described as in (1), but see Plunkett and Strömqvist (1990) for more details.

(1)   stem form: køb-,   imperative: køb   buy
      infinitive: køb-e
      present tense: køb-er
      past tense: køb-de.

The Danish infinitive is thus clearly distinct from the stem form and also distinct from the tensed form. It can be debated whether the *-er* inflection really marks tense or should be better described as marking just finiteness, as in the reanalysis suggested by Wexler (2000). Finiteness usually comprises tense and agreement marking because in most languages these two markings cannot be separated. But Danish clearly does not mark agreement (person, number), so in this case tense marking and finiteness marking coincide. We will therefore neither follow Wexler (2000) nor Hoekstra and Hyams (1996) who consider the *-er* marking as an eroded number marking, we treat verbs marked in *-er* as carrying tense. This will be discussed in more detail in section 6.

French shows the following paradigm for a verb taking the *-er* infinitive, where it has to be remembered that orthography and phonological realization are far apart. We indicate this by bracketing phonologically non-overt forms or using computerized phonetic symbols (see chapter 2):

(2) stem form: aim-   imperative: aim(e)   love
     infinitive: aim-er

     present tense: past tense (imparfaît):

                sg   pl   sg   pl
     1st   aim(e)   aim-ons   aim-ais [E] aim-ions
     2nd   aim(es)   aim-ez   aim-ais [E] aim-iez
     3rd   aim(e)   aim(ent)   aim-ait [E] aim-aient [E]

2.2. Verb Placement

Danish belongs to the Mainland Scandinavian languages which are all very similar in structure. It is a Germanic language which has the V2 phenomenon: in main clauses the finite verb is always in second position following the subject or a topicalized consitutent (object or adverb).

(3) a. Helge har købt bogen
        Helge has bought the book
     b. Bogen har Helge købt
        the book has Helge bought
     c. Nu har Helge købt bogen.
        now has Helge bought the book

We assume that the finite verb has moved to the complementizer system, because this contains features (finiteness or tense) which are verb-related (see Platzack and Holmberg 1989, Vikner 1991,1995). In Danish, main clause negation follows the inflected verb as in (4a), but the finite verb occurs after the negation in subordinate clauses as in (4b). This is taken to indicate that in the main clause, the verb is indeed in the complementizer system, but in the subordinate clause this position is occupied by the complementizer and the verb must stay to the right of negation. Because negation marks the upper boundary of the verb phrase, this also indicates that in a Danish subordinate clause the verb is not in any of the positions which are in principle available in the inflectional projection, so Danish lacks V-to-I movement. See Plunkett and Strömqvist (1990) for a discussion of the basic phenomenon of verb placement in Scandinavian and Vikner (1991) for a fuller discussion.

(4)   a. Helge har ikke købt bogen
       Helge has not bought the book
   b. Johan siger at Helge ikke har købt bogen.
       Johan says that H. not has bought the book

For child language these facts of verb placement are interesting in so far as a consistent placement of the finite verb to the left of negation in main clauses and of non-finite verbs to the right of negation is a decisive indication that the child knows the syntactic consequences of the morphological marking on the verb.

French is a Romance language which is SVO like Danish, but lost the V2 property during the middle ages, (5a,b,c). There is a phenomenon called left dislocation which is reminiscent of but different from V2 (5d,e). So French does not have V-to-C movement, but it has V-to-I movement as Pollock (1989) has shown. Because of the lack of V-to-C movement, V-to-I movement is visible in negated main clauses, see (6a,b).

(5)   a. Hier, Jean a rencontré Pierre.   (SVO)
       yesterday, J. has met P.
   b. *Hier a Jean rencontré Pierre
       yesterday has J. met P.
   c. *Pierre a Jean rencontré
       Pierre has Jean met
   d. À Pierre, Jean a raconté une histoire
       to Pierre, Jean has told a story
   e. Moi, je ne veux pas le voir   left dislocation
       Me, I (ne) want not him see
       'me, I don't want to see him'

(6)   a. Jean admet de ne pas l'aimer
           Jean admits of (ne) not him love
           'Jean admits not to like him'
       b. Jean ne admet pas de l'aimer
           Jean (ne) admits not of him to love
           'Jean doesn't admit to like him'

Danish and French are not pro-drop languages, which can be seen easily from the unacceptability of (7a),(7b) and (8a), (8b).

(7)   a. ??? har ikke købt bogen
               has not bought the book
       b. * Johan siger at _ ikke har købt bogen.
           Johan says that not has bought the book

(8)   a. ??? _ a pas acheté le livre
           ??? _ has not bought the book
       b. *Jean dit que _ a pas acheté le livre
           Jean says that _ has not bought the book
       c. _ faut pas rever
           (one) must not dream

For French (8a) may be admissible, not as topic-drop but as diary-drop, and there are certain examples with the verb *falloir* as in (8c) where the expletive may be dropped in colloquial language so that it is certainly not topic-drop, but at most diary-drop. (7a) may be marginally possible because topic-drop or diary-drop in Danish is not totally excluded on some stylistic levels and drop from the first position of the sentence is better than drop from other positions as shown in (9c). Moreover, subject drop as in (7a) seems worse than object drop in certain fixed phrases as in (9a) or (9b).

(9) a. ?(Det) kender jeg ikke
        (that) know I not
        'I don't know that'
    b. ?(Det) tror jeg (ikke)
        (that) believe I (not)
        'I don't believe that

c. Jeg kender *(der) ikke
I know (that) not
'I don't know that'

Acceptability judgments on these phrases are hard to obtain because speakers tend to reject them as stylistically very colloquial. On the other hand there could be a bias for acceptance because they are possible in diary contexts - and therefore qualify as possible in the language.

Table 33: Distribution of null subjects in adults interacting with the child

language	child/age	overt initial s.	null initial s.	% null initial s
Dutch	Thomas/2;3	150	4	2.5
	Hein/2;4	202	16	7.3
	Niek/2;8	40	10	20
German	Elisa3;3	45	5	10
Danish	Anne/1;8/1;9	62	0	0
	Anne/2;7	130	2	1.5
	Anne/5;10	222	2	0.8
	Anne total	414	4	0.9
	Jens/1;6	168	1	0.6
	Jens/2;4	126	2	1.5
	Jens/6;1	180	2	1.1
	Jens total	474	5	1.0
French	see Rasetti	2150	11	0.5

As it is a question of linguistic debate at the moment whether Danish has topic-drop or not, and certain theories predict that it should have the construction just like Dutch, German or Swedish, the actual use of topic-drop by Danish adults in some of the child recordings was investigated (see also Hamann and Plunkett 1998). The same type of data analysis with the same type of speech sample (an adult's conversation with a child) is available for French (Rasetti 1996), which unequivocally does not have topic-drop, and for Dutch (Haegeman 1996c), where topic-drop is a common colloquial construction. I add the data from the adult speaker in one of the files from the German child Elisa, where we also expect topic-drop and do indeed find it in this speech sample. A comparison with the actual occurrence of topic-drop in the same sort of speech sample to a non-topic-drop language like French and topic-drop languages like Dutch and German should at least give a strong indication as to the existence or non-existence of the construction in Danish. As it turns out, Danish sides with French not with Dutch or German, so that we can conclude that the construction is certainly not predominant in the child's input and probably not even included in the grammar of colloquial Danish. Table 33 presents the figures for adult subject drop in Danish, Dutch and French, where the Danish counts were made for 5 native speakers of Danish in the Jens and the Anne corpus in recordings before the manifestation of child subject drop, at the peak of the phenomenon and for the last recording at an age where the child did no longer drop subjects. The counts show that initial null subjects occur very rarely in adult speech and that there is no variation in input. Haegeman counted the adult null subjects in the first recording of the respective corpora and Rasetti counted the adult null subject utterances of six French adults in Daniel 1, Daniel 5, Nathalie 7, Augustin 2 (age of 2;1) and Augustin 9 (age of 2;9).

So we can establish that Danish is not a pro-drop nor a topic-drop language. Nonetheless, the phenomenon of child subject drop was very marked as figures 6a,b showed. For the occurrence of root infinitives in Danish we refer to figures 8a and 8b, both graphs showing a very clear profile.

3. THE FINITE/NON-FINITE ASYMMETRY IN DANISH AND OTHER LANGUAGES

Let us now turn to the first observation about the distribution of null subjects and illustrate it in detail with Danish: subject drop is more likely in infinitives than in finite constructions - in a language which marks the infinitive morphologically.

It emerges quite clearly that in infinitives both Danish children omit subjects more often than they use overt subjects. At the peak of infinitive use, subjects are omitted between 40% and 80% from infinitives by Anne, and the same holds for Jens as can be seen from figures 10a,b.

Comparing the development of infinitive and missing subject use in Danish, as done in figures 11a,b, shows a remarkable similarity for both children: Infinitives and missing subjects appear together, reach their maxima at the same time, and go into a steep decline at the same time. We could therefore suppose that it is the occurrence of missing subjects in infinitives which makes up the bulk of the phenomenon.

EMPIRICAL DATA 221

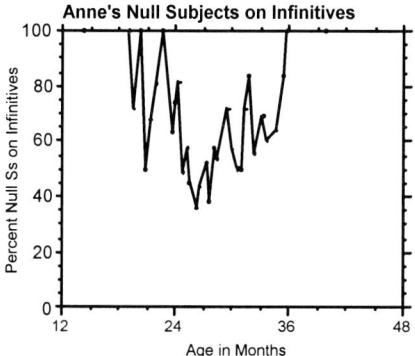

Figure 10a: Anne's Null Subjects on Infinitives
from Hamann and Plunkett 1998

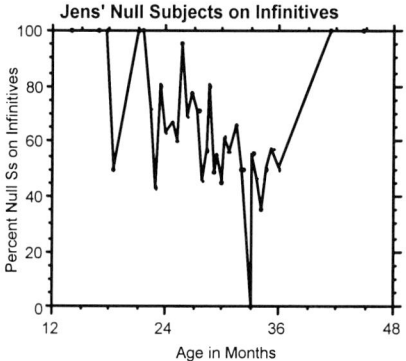

Figure 10b: Jens' Null Subjects on Infinitives
from Hamann and Plunkett 1998

Indeed this high occurrence of null subjects on infinitives is the observation which lies at the bottom of the PRO hypothesis for null subjects as proposed by Wexler (1994). Cross-linguistic data show that English behaves somewhat differently from languages which mark the infinitive morphologically. Phillips (1995) suggests that English does not conform to the generalization that null subjects are the preferred subject of infinitives.

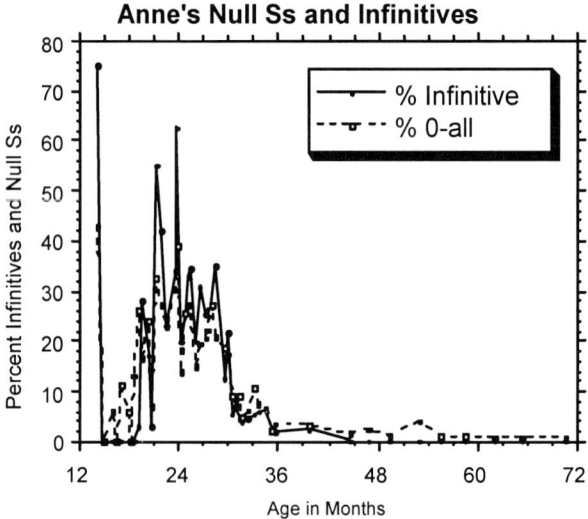

Figure 11a: Anne's Null Subjects and Infinitives
from Hamann and Plunkett 1998

If figures 11a,b show the very close developmental similarity of null subjects and infinitives in child speech, table 34 shows the occurrence of null subjects in finite and non-finite structures respectively. Rasetti (1996) collected part of the data in table 34 from the literature doing a recount on the results of Pierce (1989) for French, but leaving aside utterances with past participles (see also chapter 10) and utterances which arguably contain a pre-syntactic device, not a subject clitic. I add the results on Danish as emerging from the analysis of the two Danish children Anne and Jens during the manifestation of the null subject phenomenon in their speech (see also

Hamann and Plunkett 1997, 1998). The same time frame was chosen for both children to make comparison easier. This lead to a flattening of Anne's finite average because her null-subject period indeed does not extend to her 3rd birthday. But we leave the figures as they are and refer to figures 12a,b for more details on the development of finite null subjects. I also add the results on the French child Augustin as presented in Hamann, Rizzi and Frauenfelder (1995, 1996) and refined in Rasetti (1996, 2000).

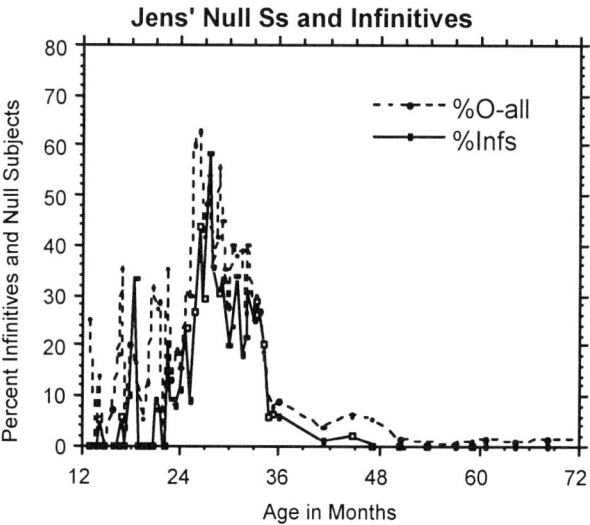

Figure 11b: Jens' Null Subjects and Infinitives
from Hamann and Plunkett 1998

Table 34: Cross-linguistic distribution of null subjects in finite and infinitive/non-finite structures

	0-s finite	%	0-s non-finite	%	Total
Danish			infinitives		
(Hamann and Plunkett 1997)					
Anne (1;8 -3;0)	366:3379	10.8	394:667	59.1	4046
Jens (1;8 - 3;0)	742:3173	23.4	539:937	57.5	4110
Dutch			infinitives		
(Kraemer 1993, Haegeman 1996a)					
Thomas	165:596	27.7	246:267	92.1	863
Hein	1199:3768	31.8	615:721	85.3	4489
English (Phillips 1995)			non-finite		
Adam	34:113	30.1	47:242	19.4	355
Eve	8:86	9.3	17:155	11.0	241
Faroese (Jonas 1995)			non-finite		
O.	8:52	15.4	67:161	41.6	213
Flemish (Kraemer 1993)			non-finite		
Maarten	23:92	25.0	89:100	96.6	867
French			infinitives		
(Rasetti 1996, Hamann et al. 96)					
Daniel	191:408	46.8	189:227	83.3	635
Nathalie	92:303	30.4	52:69	75.4	372
Philippe	322:1397	23.0	225:246	91.5	1643
Augustin	157:586	26.8	66:70	94.3	656
German			non-finite		
(Behrens 1993, Kraemer 1993)					
Simone	781:3699	21.1	2199:2477	88.8	6176
Andreas	34:263	12.9	69:101	68.3	364
Hebrew			non-finite		
(Rhee and Wexler 1995)					
26 children, non-adult 0-s	52:779	32.3	85:88	96.6	867

As was pointed out in the preceding discussion, the missing tense hypothesis with the assumption of the PRO null subject in infinitives can easily explain the asymmetry documented in table 34. PRO is the natural null subject in infinitives and can occur whenever an infinitive is used. The residue of finite null subjects was considered to be due to another kind of null subject, notably topic-drop (Bromberg and Wexler 1995). Only with new data (see section 4) this explanation was changed as outlined in chapter 7.

Truncation can also easily explain the asymmetry because in infinitives there is the special child null subject, i.e. the null constant or copy in the topmost position, plus whatever null subject is licensed in adult grammar. As PRO is always licensed by infinitives in adult speech, the occurrence of PRO null subjects in child speech is to be expected. In finite constructions, however, only the child null subject can surface.

Therefore the observed asymmetry in subject drop from finite and non-finite structures cannot decide in favor of one or the other theory. The next step is to investigate subject omission in finite constructions in more detail.

4. THE DEVELOPMENTAL SIMILARITY OF INFINITIVE USE AND FINITE SUBJECT OMISSION

It is problematic for the missing tense hypothesis, but not for truncation, that even in non topic-drop languages null subjects do occur with finite verbs not only to a residual but to a quite noticeable degree as figures 12a,b,c,d show.

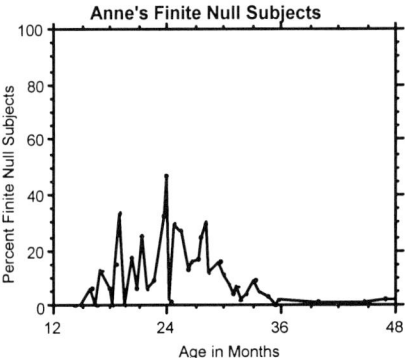

Figure 12a: Danish - Anne's Finite Null Subjects
from Hamann and Plunkett 1998

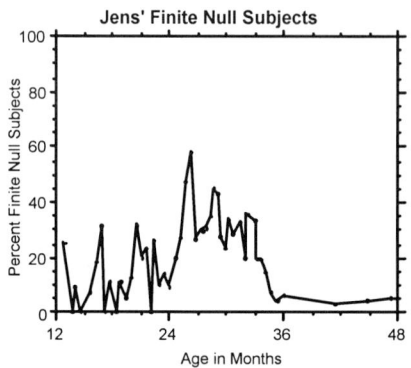

Figure 12b: Danish-Jens' Finite Null Subjects
from Hamann and Plunkett 1998

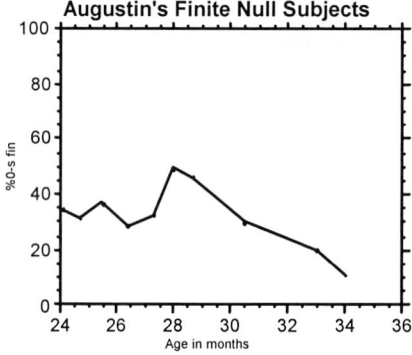

Figure 12c: French-Augustin's Finite Null Subjects

Though the occurrence of null subjects in finite constructions could be explained for French within a missing tense hypothesis by assuming that the so-called finite form is in fact a stem form as Wexler (1998) suggests, this cannot explain finite null subjects in Danish because finiteness is explicitly marked in that language, as was argued in section 2. We will return to the reanalyis of Danish morphology given in Wexler (2000) in ection 7 and then also discuss the French data again.

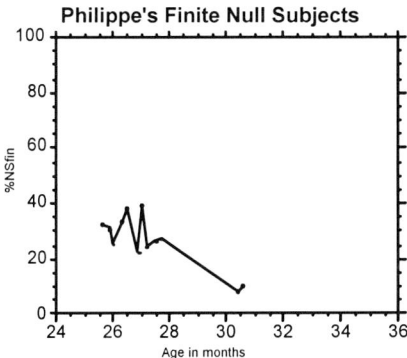

Figure 12d: French-Philippe's Finite Null Subjects

Figures 13a,b show that the bulk of subject omission in Danish is not made up of omissions in infinitives. At the peak of subject omission, both Danish children drop subjects from finite contexts almost as often as from infinitives: from 24 months Anne has an equal or even greater number of finite missing subjects. Jens has more missing subjects in finite contexts throughout this phase. Given the greater number of finite utterances, this makes up an occurrence of about 20% missing subjects in finite contexts between 1;6 and 2;6 in Anne's speech and an occurrence of 30% missing subjects in finite contexts between 2;0 and 2;8 months for Jens as figures 12 a,b show.

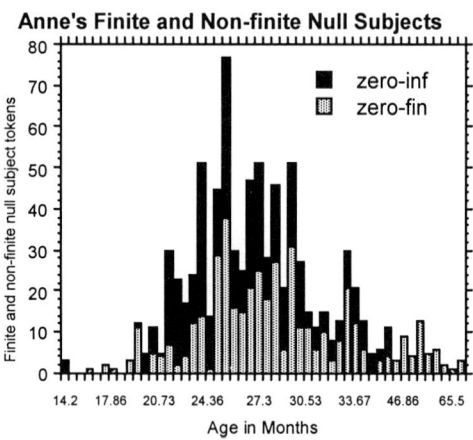

Figure 13a: Anne's Finite and Non-finite Null Subject Tokens
from Hamann and Plunkett 1998

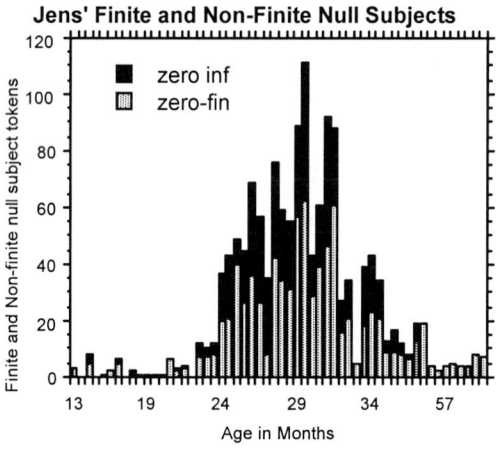

Figure 13b: Jens' Finite and Non-Finite Null subject Tokens
from Hamann and Plunkett 1998

Even more remarkable than such a substantial occurrence of missing subjects in finite contexts, is the fact that the use of bare infinitives and the omission of subjects in finite contexts show a parallel development as can be seen from figures 14a,b. In particular, we observe that the peak of the phenomenon and the sharp decrease in the use of both options occurs at the same time - and this is true for the speech of both children. Moreover, Hamann and Plunkett (1998) show that these two developmental curves are strongly correlated.

This result is fully compatible with the truncation approach, even if the graphs for both phenomena are not "close together" at each of the given data points. The developmental curves are still significantly similar. Moreover, the truncation approach does not predict that the occurrences of finite null subjects is necessarily high when the occurrence of infinitives is high, it just predicts that the option to produce a root infinitive exists at the same time at which a finite null subject may be dropped because both depend on the possibility of truncating the structure. Once this possibility is lost, both options will disappear. That both graphs reach their maxima at approximately the same time, mirrors the fact that the option of truncation is chosen more often at that time. Haegeman (1996a) was the first to point out this developmental similarity and its significance for the existence of an underlying grammatical mechanism for both constructions. She presented results on Dutch child language which show in essence the same similarity of finite null subjects and root infinitives in development over time, but she did not have the broadness of the data base so that the effect was less obvious in her data. The same is true for French as Rasetti (1996) showed the similarity of development for Daniel, Nathalie, Philippe and Augustin.

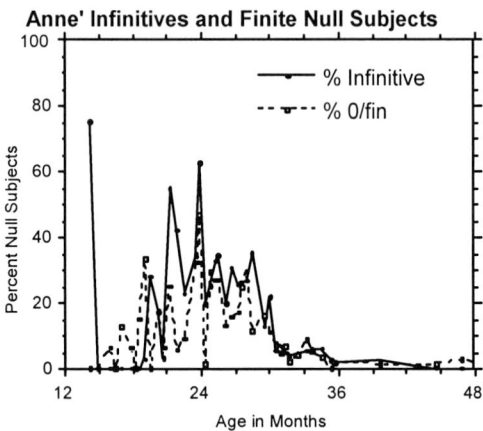

Figure 14a: Anne's Infinitives and Finite Null Subjects
from Hamann and Plunkett 1998

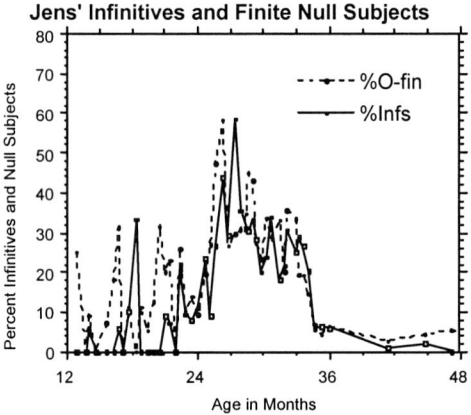

Figure 14b: Jens' Infinitives and Finite Null Subjects
from Hamann and Plunkett 1998

Using Rasetti (1996)'s data tables, we reproduce the graphs for Augustin and Philippe, with an age-measure for the x-axis, not the integer measure of file number, in order to make them comparable to our graphs on Danish. It emerges from figures 15a,b that the similarity is not as marked as for Danish, presumably because the rate of infinitive usage is much lower in French than in Danish, but for Phillippe both phenomena peak at approximately the same time and go on the decline together, while the data for Augustin show a persistence of subject omission in finite constructions even after the decline of the use of root infinitives. His overall use of root infinitives is very low (ca. 10%), however, so that conclusions are hard to draw.

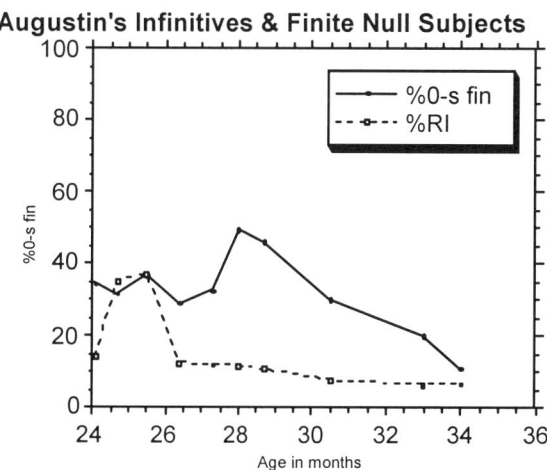

Figure 15a: Augustin's Infinitives and Finite Null Subjects

On the strength of the very clear developmental similarity of finite null subjects and infinitives in Danish, it appears that any theory that postulates two different types of null subjects for the finite and the infinitival environment is weaker in predictive power than a theory which explains both types of null subjects together with the occurrence of infinitives from the same underlying assumptions. In particular, it is not plausible that Danish or French finite null subjects are topic-drop.

The phenomenon shown in figures 14a,b for Danish was first published in Hamann and Plunkett (1997, 1998). Wexler (2000) calls this finding a "puzzle" and suggests the morphological reanalysis of Danish discussed in chapter 7, section 3.3 and in section 7 in this chapter. His solution is that so called finite verbs with the *–er* marking still lack the tense feature and thus allow null subjects. Before we come back to this suggestion and test it in particular environments like past tense forms and fronted Wh-questions, we will concentrate on another asymmetry observed in the literature, the asymmetry concerning auxiliaries and main verbs.

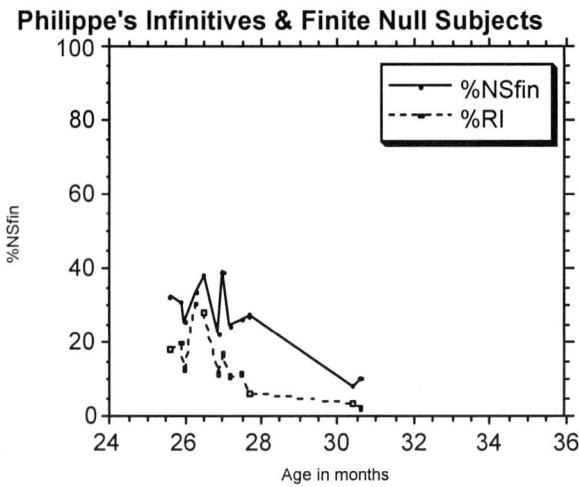

Figure 15b: Philippe's Infinitives and Finite Null Subjects

5. THE AUXILIARY/MAIN VERB ASYMMETRY IN DANISH AND OTHER LANGUAGES

When Plunkett and Strömqvist (1991) first drew attention to the asymmetry of subject omission in copula and main verb constructions in Scandinavian languages, they claimed (following Bowerman 1973) that this effect was due to the slow acquisition of subjecthood. They argued that the argument structure of a main verb is lexicalized and so more implicit information about the subject is available. Therefore, subject omission is more likely with lexical main verbs than with auxiliaries, which lack a theta grid. Their observation was corroborated for English. Valian (1991) showed that subjects of modals are dropped much less frequently (5%) than subjects of lexical verbs (11%), Sano and Hyams (1994) found a 30% difference between auxiliaries and lexical main verbs for Adam and Eve, and Schütze and Wexler (1996a) document a 12% difference for Naomi.

Apart from the explanation given in the developmental account of Plunkett and Strömqvist (1991), there is the missing tense or the underspecification hypothesis, which were designed to capture exactly this asymmetry (see chapter 7, specifically 3.1. and 3.4). These grammatical approaches make use of the fact that English Aux is base generated in Tense and always carries tense, whereas main verbs in child language are underspecified with respect to tense and do not necessarily raise (Sano and Hyams 1994, Schütze and Wexler 1996a,b). The truncation approach cannot easily explain the asymmetry, unless with special assumptions as to the nature of auxiliaries and modals.

There is another observational generalization underlying the missing tense account of the auxiliary/main verb asymmetry: Auxiliaries (and copulas) very rarely occur in the infinitive in child speech. Therefore, it can be argued, the asymmetry is quite natural as only main verbs occur in the infinitive and only infinitives (without a tense feature) license null subjects. From this perspective it seems interesting to extend the investigation to finite main verbs and examine whether the asymmetry persists. Actually, verb raising languages like French (V-to-I) or Danish (V-to-C) are predicted to show no such asymmetry because the finite verb and the copula/auxiliary occupy the same high position which necessarily includes tense in adult language.

For child language we have to make sure, therefore, that French or Danish children raise finite verbs. We know that this is the case from the facts of verb placement and negation as reported in Pierce (1992) or Verrips and Weissenborn (1989) for French, and Plunkett and Strömqvist (1990) for Danish. The latter authors report a very stable distribution: Anne always places the finite verb before negation and the infinitive after the negation, Jens always places the infinitive after the negation and has some very rare exceptions to the regular pattern of negation following the finite verb. One of the exceptions Plunkett and Strömqvist (1990) quote is (10).

(10)   Det ikke er munden.   Jens, 22.28
           that not is mouth-the
           'that is not the mouth'

A fresh analysis of all the occurrences of negation in the Jens-corpus shows that in the 333 occurrences of finite negations in the relevant period (from 1;8 to 3;8) only 15 have the finite verb following the negation. Some of these are probably constituent negation and some are topicalizations of *ikke*, which is possible in Danish (Vikner, p.c).Thus we have at most about 4% non-adult performance, probably much less. We therefore have pretty solid evidence that Danish children move the finite verb across negation to a higher position in the clause. Unfortunately, the evidence from negation is available only from approximately the second year of age for these two children: Jens starts using syntactic negation at the age of 1;9 and Anne uses syntactic negation productively from 2;0 onwards. We thus do not have any hard evidence for verb movement in the early phase of null subject use for Anne, but we can be reasonably sure that verb movement is firmly acquired when the phenomenon is at its peak. So we can assume that finite main verbs and auxiliaries occupy the same position in child Danish. We nevertheless find an asymmetry in subject omission as shown in table 35.

Table 35: Null subject use on copulas and finite main verbs

	Anne, 1;7,4-2;11,23		Jens, 1;6,26-3;0,1	
	copulas	finite main verbs	copulas	finite main verbs
overt subject	1333	967	1037	1177
null subject	73	232	153	490
total	1406	1199	1190	1667
percent null subjects	5.2	19.3	12.8	29.4

Hamann and Plunkett (1998) compared copula/auxiliary constructions and finite main verb structures in order to check the above prediction. Modals which can be auxiliaries and main verbs in Danish were considered separately and excluded here. Danish *have,* like English *have,* German *haben,* and French *avoir* can function as an auxiliary or a main verb. During the relevant time, both children used it exclusively as a main verb. Therefore *har* was counted with the finite main verbs.

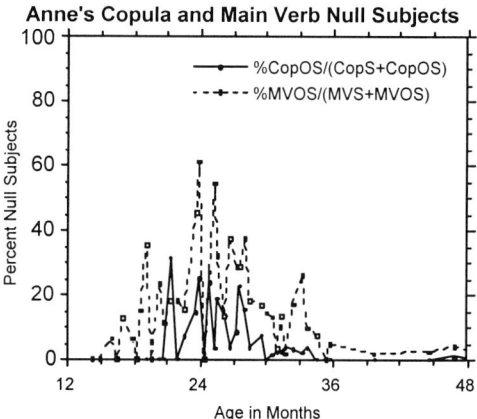

Figure 16a: Anne's Null Subjects on Copula and Main Verb
from Hamann and Plunkett 1998

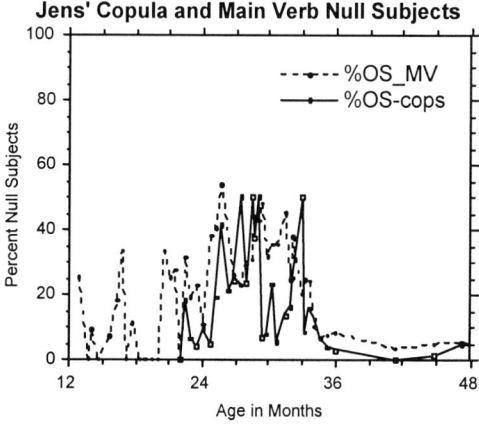

Figure 16b: Jens' Null Subjects on Copulas and Main Verbs
from Hamann and Plunkett 1998

As we can see from figures 16a,b and from table 36, which shows only the null subject period, there is a significant asymmetry for Jens and Anne. Let us now compare the effect of asymmetry in Danish, French and English in order to see how the argument about the different or similar positions of auxiliary and main verb in different languages has to be evaluated.

An overview of cross linguistic data as discussed by Sano and Hyams (1994), Schütze and Wexler (1996b) for English, Rasetti (1996) based on Lightbown for French with a new count on Augustin (Hamann, Rizzi and Frauenfelder 1995, 1996) is given in table 36, though there is a general problem with the smallness of the samples for French and English. The interesting fact is that there may be variation between subjects, and some children (Augustin) even drop more subjects from auxiliaries than from finite lexical verbs. In any case, we observe an asymmetry in all three languages.

Table 36: Cross-linguistic distribution of null subjects with respect to verb form

	% 0-s/finite lexical verbs	% 0-s/copulas
Jens	29.4	12.8
Anne	19.3	5.2
Danish total	25.2	8.7
Augustin	22.2	34.1
Daniel	52.8	13.6
Nathalie	31.4	19.2
French total	34.2	25.9
Naomi	12	3
Eve*	26	0
Adam*	41	11.4

* infinitives are included in the main verb count

It is interesting to note that even if we find a striking asymmetry, subject omission from auxiliary constructions is possible. If we do not just consider the overall occurrences of null subjects in auxiliary constructions over the whole period of time but make a detailed analysis of each recording, we find that the Danish children show rates of subject omissions which clearly are not performance errors. Anne has 31% subject omission with copulas at the age of 21.3 months (here days are recalculated as proportions of a month to give a decimal figure), 25% at 23.9 months, 24% at 24.8 months and 23% at 27.6 months. Jens has 41% null subjects in copula constructions at 25.7 months, 24% at 26.8 months, 23% at 28 months, 37% at 28.7 months, and

50% at 28.5, 29.1 and 33 months. These high rates make it unlikely that it is indeed the missing tense feature which is responsible for the licensing of null subjects in child language: the tense feature is present in such constructions and yet the subject can be omitted.

Note that we can be sure that the finite verb has left the VP and is presumably in the same position as the auxiliary if it has raised across negation. If the child has raised the finite main verb across negation while at the same time omitting the subject, we can assume that no confusion as to the finite status of the verb is responsible for subject omission. Such examples exist for Danish from early on. For Jens we find early utterances where an auxiliary, a finite main verb or a modal has raised across negation. For Anne we find only one example of a finite main verb with a missing subject and clear evidence of raising across negation, but many modals in main verb function which occur in the same construction. The following list is exhaustive for main verbs (13), but not for auxiliaries/copulas (11) or modals (12). The examples are not frequent, of course, because negation is not used very often and a combination of three factors had to be found: negation, subject omission and the use of a main verb. But this is a case where the occurrence of very few examples is decisive.

(11)   er ikke synd   Jens 2;1 (cop)
        is not pity
        '(it) is not a pity'

(12) a. skal ikke sidder der   Jens 2;2 (modal)
        shall not sit there
        's/he shall not sit there'
    b. kan ikke sige noget   Jens 2;4 (modal)
        can not say anything
        '(I) can't say anything'

(13) a. gider ikke   Jens 1;9 (mv, finite)
        like not
        '(I) don't like it'
    b. gider ikke   Jens 1;10 (mv, finite)
    c. sidder ikke   Jens 2;1 (mv, finite)
        sit not
        's/he isn't sitting'

238 CHAPTER 8

        d. synger ikke   Jens   2;4   (mv, finite)
            sings not
            's/he sings not'
        e. kører ikke rundt nu   Jens   2;5   (mv, finite)
            drives not around now
            '(it) doesn't drive around now'
        f. græder ikke dernede   Jens   2;8   (mv, finite)
            cries not down there
            'he doesn't cry down there'
        g. gider ikke den   Jens   2;8   (mv, finite)
            like not that
            '(I) don't like that'
        h. gider ikke   Jens   2;9   (mv, finite)
            like not
            '(I) don't like (it)'
        i. duer ikke   Jens   2;10   (mv, finite)
            is good not
            '(it) is no good'
        j. kommer ikke noget   Jens   2;10   (mv, finite)
            comes not something
            '(there) doesn't come anything'

(14)   a. må ikke   Anne   2;0   (modal, mv)
            may not
        b. kan ikke se   Anne   2;0   (modal)
            can not see

(15)   a. duer ikke   Anne   2;0   (mv, finite)
            '(it) is no good'
        b. duer ikke   Anne   2;1   (mv, finite)
        c. gider ikke   Anne   2;1   (mv, finite)
            '(I) don't like (it), I don't feel like it'
        d. duer ikke   Anne   2;2   (mv, finite)
        e. falder ikke   Anne   2;11   (mv, finite)
        f. fall(s) not
            '(I, you, he etc.) doesn't fall'

The examples from the French child Augustin given in (16) are not as convincing. They either involve the verb *falloir,* where subject drop is possible in adult French, or they involve the combination *(je) sais* 'I know' where the adult pronunciation is [ZE] and it is not clear whether the child has dropped the subject or made the phonological assimilation. For Philippe the examples in (17) are clearer and show that finite main verbs, auxiliaries, and modals are uniformly raised across *pas* and still occur without a subject.

(16) a. [tE pa esine] (?)sais pas dessiner   Aug   2;3,10   mv
        know not draw
        '(I) can't draw'
     b. [tE pa]   (?)sais pas   Aug   2;4,1   mv
        know not
        '(I)don't know'
     c. faut pas mettre comme ça   Aug   2;9   mv
        must not put like that
        'one must not put it like that'

(17) a. trouve pas   Phil 2;2,3   mv
        find not
        '(I) don't find it'
     b. marche pas   Phil 2;2,3   mv
        works not
        '(it) doesn't work'
     c. reconnais pas?   Phil 2;2,10   mv
        recognize not
        'don't (you) recognize (it)?
     d. donne pas des bleues   Phil 2;2,10   mv
        gives not bruises
        '(it) doesn't make bruises'
     e. baille pas   Phil 2;2,26   mv
        yawn not
        'I'm not yawning'

(18) a. non, a pas le hoquet   Phil 2;3,14 mv/aux
        no, has not the hiccup
        'no, (he) doesn't have the hiccups'
     b. a pas fait la bouche du monsieur   Phil 2;7   aux
        has not made the mouth of the gentleman
        '(s/he has not made (drawn) the gentleman's mouth'

(19)   est pas mort   Phil   2;1,6.   cop
       'is not dead'
       's/he is not dead'

(20)   veux pas   Phil   2;3,7   mod
       want not
       '(I) don't want to/it'

Considering the fact that French is definitely not a topic-drop language, it has to be noted, that subject drop in auxiliary structures can be as high as 34% and is on the average about 25%. The only way to explain this in an account which assumes that auxiliaries always activate the Agr and Tense position would be to claim that the French child has not yet classified auxiliaries as [+agr]. But if we do that, there is no reason why the same should not be true for other languages and the whole structure of underlying assumptions of the missing (or underspecified) tense account would be in doubt. Also, there is evidence that a misclassification of auxiliaries is not at the bottom of the problem. Though it is the case that the French child Augustin for a long time only uses the forms 'est' and 'a' without using the other inflectional forms of the auxiliaries in the singular, there is evidence that even after some of these distinctions (*ai* for the first person singular of *avoir,*) and even after a plural form is acquired, this plural auxiliary can still occur without a subject. The same is true for Philippe, who has the *a/ai* distinction and the plural *sont* much earlier than Augustin, see (21).

(21)   a. [i] sont ou les...les ciseaux?
           they are where the...the scissors
           where are the scissors'
           sont là.   Aug   2;9,2
           are there
           'there they are'
       b. sont pas tous   Phil   2;3,14
           are not all
           'these are not all'

In any case, the fact that Danish has the greatest asymmetry but has the unambiguously finite verb in the same position as the auxiliary (or modal) makes one consider with caution those accounts which explain the asymmetry with lack or presence of tense depending on the respective positions of these verb types.

So we return briefly to a discussion of two other possibilities. One account, which comes close to what Plunkett and Strömqvist (1991) had in mind, is to look for a generalization in terms of theta-grids. Auxiliaries don't have a theta grid and require a subject only in the sense that the whole predication requires it, whereas main verbs assign specific thematic roles to their subjects. Unfortunately, this idea cannot explain the fact that subject omission, regardless of verb type, is restricted to initial position and occurs only rarely in finite Wh-questions (see Bromberg and Wexler 1995, Roeper and Rohrbacher 2000). This latter finding could be corroborated in Danish and will be discussed in more detail in chapter 9. So, even if the argument structure of the verb plays a crucial role, there must be something else which blocks or licenses subject omission. The fact that subject omission in general is not possible in finite Wh-questions clearly involves some structural constraint and poses a problem also for the developmental account which assumed that subjecthood is acquired gradually (see also Bowerman 1973). And even if there is a certain plausibility to the semantic side of this account, it is hard to explain that children master the syntactic reflex of subjecthood, namely subject-verb agreement from early on (see Poeppel and Wexler 1993 for German, Guasti 1992,1993 for Italian).

The Plunkett and Strömqvist account resembles the missing tense account in so far as it assumes that auxiliaries are something special. Whereas it is stated that auxiliaries always carry tense and this is true also for English modals, modals are different in Danish in that they do occur in the infinitive. Let us therefore follow a recent suggestion of Rizzi (1995b) and assume that auxiliaries and also the copula need to be licensed from some higher position, presumably from the Finiteness position in the Split CP system for independent reasons. So the occurrence of an auxiliary would activate the CP to satisfy this licensing condition. As a consequence null subjects cannot occur unless certain by-passing conditions are fulfilled (see chapter 9).

The data, though showing an uncontestable asymmetry, thus do not decide pro or contra a current theory. Even though it seems difficult for truncation to explain such an asymmetry, an explanation is available if certain assumptions about the licensing of auxiliaries turn out to be well motivated for independent reasons. On the other hand, the existence of this asymmetry across verb raising and verb lowering languages as well as the rather high rate of subject drop from auxiliaries in French and in some recordings of the Danish children seems to be rather problematic for the missing tense hypothesis.

6. Pro-DROP AND OPTIONAL INFINITIVES

The last observation which has to be accounted for is the fact that optional infinitives are not universal. Guasti (1992), Sano and Hyams (1994), Phillips (1995), Hoekstra and Hyams (1996), and Schoenenberger et al. (1996) discuss the fact that optional infinitives in pro-drop languages are rare and - if they exist at all - only occur during a very brief period of time. Trying to group the data (see table 37), we find that in Swedish, Danish, Dutch and German rather high rates of optional infinitives occur at certain periods in the children's development, that in French moderate rates have been found, and that in Italian, Spanish and Catalan the rates are very low.

Table 37: Cross linguistic occurrence of optional root infinitives

Danish child	age	%OI	Swedish child	age	%OI	German child	age	%OI
A	1;7	2.9	F	1;8-1;10	12	S	1;10	61
	1;8	17.1		1;11-2;0	38		1;11	73
	1;9	54		2;1-2;3	21		2;1	53
	1;10	22.6					2;2	40
	1;11	62.5	E	1;8-1;10	61		2;4	17
	2;0	25.2		1;11-2;1	33	(Weissenborn)		
	2;1	34.4	(Platzack)					
	2;2	30.8				A	2;1	17
	2;3	26.3				(Poeppel and Wexler)		
	2;4	35						
	2;5	12.6						
	2;6	5.3						
J	1;5-1;10	6.9						
	1;11-2;2	21.5						
	2;3	58						
	2;4-2;6	29.3						
	2;7-2;10	22.2						
	2;11-3;8	3.8						

Dutch child	age	%OI	French child	age	%OI
H			D	1;8.-1;10	37.5
	2;4-2;7	24		1;11.	13.2
	2;8-2;9	14.5			
	3;0-3;1	5	N	1;9.-1;11	14
				2;0	40
T	2;3-2;4	50.5		2;1-2;2	25.5
	2;5-2;6	24		2;3	4.5
	2;7-2;9	13.3			
	2;10-2;11	6	P	2;1-2;2,3	16.3
				2;2,10-2;2,26	29
N	2;8-2;11	69		2;3,0-2;3,14	12.2
	3;0-3;2	27.3		2;3,21-2;6,20	3.8
	3;4-3;10	4.7			
			A	2;0	14
(Haegeman 1996b)				2;0,23-2;1,15	35.5
				2;2-2;4	11.2
				2;6-2;9	6.6
			J	1;7	10.3
				1;8-2;0	0
			(Rasetti 1996)		

Italian child	age	%OI	Catalan child ages	OI	Spanish child age	OI
D	1;10	3	4 children		2 children	
	1;11-2;0	0	1;9-2;5,		1;8	12
	2;1	1	1;9-2;6,		2;6	5
			1;9-2;6		from Phillips (1995)	
M	1;8	7	1;10-2;6	5 OIs		
	1;9	22	(Torrens 1995)			
	1;11	16				
	2;1	4				
	2;3	0				
	(Guasti 1992)					

The cross-linguistic data show that optional infinitives are indeed a phenomenon in Germanic languages which lasts for several months, whereas it is short-lived in French (3 to 4 weeks in Philippe's and Augustin's speech and at most two months for Daniel and Nathalie) and occurs very early in Italian and Spanish and only to a low percentage. It is remarkable on the one hand that the French child Jean has the same sort of profile that is documented for Italian children and that on the other hand Cipriani et al. (1993) report a higher occurrence of optional infinitives in Italian SLI children than in normally developing children. This seems to argue for the existence of such a phase, however short, even in Italian.

For the explanation of these data, there are three basic ideas. Rizzi (1994) follows the arguments of Belletti (1990) and Guasti (1992) about the placement of infinitives with respect to certain negative adverbs (Rizzi 1994:386)

(22) a. non leggere   più   il libro
        not read (inf) (più)   the book
        'not to read the book'
     b. *non più leggere   il libro
         not (più) read (inf)   the book

and suggests that Italian infinitives are raised higher than Germanic or French infinitives and are in fact as high as AgrSP. This is so because Rizzi assumes strong AgrS features both for the tensed and the untensed form of Italian verbs. It poses a slight problem if we consider the possibility of a short-lived existence of root infinitives. But in this case it could be assumed that the child first considers the AgrS feature as weak on the untensed form and does not raise the infinitive. This can be expected if the child starts out with a default grammar which assumes weak features throughout as Platzack (1996) suggests. Such a phase cannot last long in the Italian case, however, given the open evidence of infinitive raising.

Another explanation is offered by Hoekstra and Hyams (1996), who suggest that only those languages which do not have person, but only number distinctions in their paradigm, show a root infinitive phase. As in Hyams (1996), the overall aim is to give parallel explanations for DP and IP underspecifications - and number is common to both. Now, Dutch and English do not have person distinctions and have the root infinitive phase. The infinitive phase can be explained for French by the fact mentioned before: children at first only use singular forms which do not show a person distinction. For German, the facts are slightly more complicated, and Hoekstra and Hyams argue that the third person marking is in fact a number, not a person distinction, while it is a well known fact of German acquisition research (Clahsen 1991, Duffield 1993) that the use of root infinitives decreases drastically once the second person marking is acquired by the child. In this system, languages which have person marking (Italian, Spanish, Catalan) will not show a root infinitive phase and neither will languages which have only tense distinctions, but neither number nor person distinctions like Japanese. In fact, Sano (1995) reports that root infinitives do not exist in Japanese child language. It seems to me that - just as for the null subject account of Jaeggli and Safir (1989) - the problem lies in the Scandinavian languages which show tense distinctions in their verbal paradigm, but neither person nor number. They have a marked infinitive phase, however, as table 37 above and the discussion in chapter 6 show. Hoekstra and Hyams (1996) in their footnote 5 argue that the *-er/ar* ending is not a tense marking but the erosion of a former person and number agreement. Though they present an argument about the passive construction which may indicate that these endings do not necessarily encode present tense, there is nothing to suggest that the supposed 'erosion' only effected person but not number and that *-er* "instantiates Number even though it does not express a number distinction".

The argument about the passive is constructed as follows. The passive *-s* in Norwegian combines with the past *-t,* but the so-called present *-er* does not show up in the present passive: *jeg valger* 'I choose', *jeg valges* 'I am chosen', *jeg valgte* 'I chose', *jeg valgtes* 'I was chosen'. One has to be careful with this argument, however.[1] First, not all verbs with the *-s* passive show a *-t* in the past. The verb *snakke* (talk) has the *-s* passive *snakkes* and the past tense *snakket*, but there is no past-passive *snakkets*. Some dialects have *snakkte-s,* but not all. So it is probably a phonological reduction rule which sometimes removes the *-t,* but not always, and a similar rule could well be responsible for the absence of *-r*. Second, it is more likely that the *-s* of the passive combines with the participle, not the tensed verb. Then one could say that the past tense participle happens to coincide with the past tense verb, but that the present tense participle is not morphologically marked. Moreover, the plural *-r* marking for nouns, clearly has nothing to do with the *-r* in the verbal paradigm, it marks singular and plural. The conclusion is that there are no convincing morphological arguments for the assumption that Scandinavian *-er, -ar* is eroded number agreement. In fact, native speakers of Scandinavian languages do not have any intuitions supporting this argument, but clearly prefer the assumption that this suffix marks tense. So the Scandinavian languages remain a problem for the interesting account proposed by Hoekstra and Hyams (1996).

The UCC account of Wexler (1998, 2000) was designed to explain the auxiliary/main verb asymmetry as was pointed out in chapter 7. We repeat some of the features of this account here. In his missing [agr] or missing [tns] account of optional infinitives Wexler points out that the occurrence of nominative subjects with infinitives argues against the assumption that subjects raise for case reasons. Instead, AgrS contains a D-feature which has to be checked by a DP. For null subject languages, the AgrSP does not contain the same sort of D-feature because it is itself a D. This captures the old intuition that the agreement system of null subject languages is pronominal. He then asks what forces optional infinitives in some languages, but not in others, and points to the difficulties children have with specificity and to the fact that determiners are often omitted. With the additional assumption of the UCC (see also Borer and Wexler 1987), it follows that optional infinitives will surface in those languages which have an AgrSP with a [-interpretable] D-feature: [-interpretable] D erases after checking with [DP] in a finite TP and the derivation would crash because a [-interpretable] D-feature in AgrSP cannot be checked and subsequently deleted. But if Tense is deleted, an optional infinitive surfaces and the DP can check the D-feature of AgrSP. Alternatively, the child could delete Agr not Tense and would also get a convergent derivation. In a null subject language, the UCC and the assumption that D is [+interpretable] will not lead to a crash of the derivation because there is nothing in AgrSP to be checked and deleted. So deletion of Tense is not needed to save checking of AgrSP, and therefore optional infinitives do not occur. The problem for this account is that optional infinitives do occur for some Italian children, if only for a brief time, and that they do occur in the speech of Italian SLI children. If SLI is in general an extended optional infinitive phase as Rice and Wexler (1996) suggest, then the dilemma is obvious. It is the more pronounced as Wexler (1998)'s account of the pro-drop/no optional infinitives correlation relies practically exclusively on assumptions about child grammar which should all hold for the SLI child. If the reason for the non-occurrence of root infinitives is sought in specific properties of the particular language, then there are more possibilities to account for a delay in the recognition of these properties. This will be pursued in chapters 11 and 12, where I discuss the tenses from a semantic point of view.

The truncation account, though very simple and not initially designed to account for the asymmetries in subject omission in infinitives and finite verbs, in auxiliaries and main verbs or the non-occurrence of infinitives in pro-drop languages, thus deals with these empirical facts with language specific assumptions. Other accounts have to add assumptions specific to the acquisition mechanism and do not seem to be quite so successful. Truncation also has the advantage of accounting for subject omission in finite and non-finite structures in a unified way. Before we decide for a version of truncation, perhaps a modification as suggested by Haegeman (1996c) in a Split CP framework, there are some remaining problems to discuss.

7. FINITE NULL SUBJECTS AND MORPHOLOGICAL REANALYSES IN THE UCC ACCOUNT

When matching the UCC account against these data, the main problem crystallized around the finding that the development of infinitives and finite null subjects is strongly correlated in Danish (see Hamann and Plunkett 1998). This clearly showed that null subjects occurring in finite constructions cannot plausibly be analyzed as topic-drop. Extending this reasoning to French finite null subjects require that both French and Danish verb morphology are given an analysis such that the finite null subjects are PRO and are licensed by the absence of the tense feature. For both, French and Danish, the same proposition is therefore made (see Wexler 1997, 1998 for French and Wexler 2000 for Danish): the endings that are normally analyzed as fully finite, only have a sort of general agreement feature, but are unmarked with respect to Tns. For French, there is a certain plausibility to this idea as the finite forms occurring in the early phases are mostly singular and hence lack any overt morphological marking. They could thus be treated as stem forms and as such may not raise.

It has been repeatedly observed in the preceding chapters and explicitly in section 5 of this chapter that there is overt evidence that children raise these forms across negation and still omit subjects. So these forms are definitely not treated as unraised stem forms in French. In Danish it is not likely that the *–er* forms can be treated as stems, they clearly have some morphological marking. With the reanalysis it could be argued that given the morphological difference to infinitives and the presence of an agreement feature postulated for both French and Danish, children raise these forms as far as the AgrSP. They would not be bothered with the TnsP because this has been erased by the UCC and ATOM. If this is the case, however, the occurrence of such forms on the left of negation does not prove anything about the acquisition of finiteness anymore and even less about the acquisition of the syntactic consequences of finiteness. A form, which is clearly not fully finite, which is classified as a manifestation of ATOM and therefore would surface as an infinitive in English, would presumably be raised to a position appropriate only to fully finite forms.

Putting these unwanted consequences aside, the morphological reanalysis and the UCC can explain the correlation of finite null subjects and infinitives. In Danish, the child can have the adult specification [+agr, +tns] which gives adult *køb-er*, the child with the UCC and ATOM could alternatively specify [-agr, +tns] which surfaces as *køb-e* or [+agr,-tns] which according to these assumptions would surface as *køb-er*. The latter would license null subjects. The [-agr, +tns] and [+agr, -tns] forms would be lost with the UCC and ATOM and thus infinitives and finite null subjects would disappear at the same time.

One clear prediction of the theory is of course that forms which are marked as [+tns] do not allow null subjects. Such forms are the auxiliaries/copulas and the past tense forms. It has been shown that the rate of occurrence of null subjects on copulas is not so low as to be a performance error neither in French nor in Danish. It is 34.1% on average for Augustin and as high as 50% in some recordings of Jens.

As to past tense forms, these do not occur very frequently in the early phase when null subjects proliferate. Nevertheless a search and count was made of the occurrence of past tense forms in the period when null subjects occurred. For Jens null subjects occurred to more than 10% from 20 to 34.7 months (sessions 16-46), and for Anne from 18 to 30 months (sessions 20-40), henceforth the 'crucial periods' for Jens and Anne.

In his crucial period, Jens has 28 past tense forms with subjects and 14 past tense forms without subjects. This gives a percentage of 33% subject omission in contexts with the tense feature. Note that among the first three occurrences of past tense forms, two are without a subject (22.5-24.1 months). An extension of the period up to the time when the rate of subject drop was about 5%, gives the following. There are 95 past tense forms, 18 without a subject. This still amounts to an average rate of subject omission of 18.9% in past tense forms.

For Anne we find a similar picture, but as in all phenomena, the occurrence of subject omission on past tense forms is more restricted for her. In her crucial period, she has 33 past tense forms, 13 with subject omission. This gives a rate of subject omission on past tense forms of 39.4%. Her past tense null subjects all occur between 27-30 months (sessions 35-40), with a peak of 71% at 28 months. Here she produces 12 past tense forms with 10 null subjects. Extending the period for Anne adds many more productions of past tense forms, but no more null subjects. In the period from 18 to 35.4 months, when she still has about 5% null subjects, gives 108 past tense forms, and the 13 past tense null subjects occurring in the crucial period. This gives a rate of 12.0% subject drop on average in her null subject period.

The evidence from an investigation of subject omission in past tense forms in Danish thus shows rather conclusively that such subject drop is licensed and occurs to a rather high rate during a certain time. It is in fact even higher than the average occurrence of subject omission in finite constructions in the crucial period., which is 25.3% for Jens and 18.7% for Anne. Table 38 gives a summary of these data.

Table 38: Jens and Anne: null subjects on finite verbs, on past tense forms, and copulas

	Jens (20-34.7months)		Anne (18-30 months)	
finite verbs	2870		1589	
0-s on finite verbs	725	(25.3%)	297	(18.7%)
past tense forms	42		33	
0-s on past tense forms	14	(33%)	13	(39.4%)
copulas	1147		725	
0-s on copulas	156	(13.6%)	62	(8.5%)

As there are only very restricted data on past tense forms, it is fortunate that there is another area where the UCC approach together with the morphological reanalysis of Danish or French makes very different predictions from the truncation approach. If we consider fronted finite Wh questions, then the truncation approach predicts that null subjects should not occur or be rare in such contexts, whereas there is nothing in the proposal suggested by Wexler (2000) to constrain the occurrence of null subjects in such contexts. We will therefore consider French and Danish Wh questions in more detail in chapter 9.

CHAPTER 9

WH-QUESTIONS : INFINITIVES, NULL SUBJECTS AND THE PROBLEM OF INTERPRETATION

1. OVERVIEW

1.1. Predictions

In the present chapter we investigate the occurrence of root infinitives and child null subjects in Wh-questions. The crucial predictions from the ATOM model and from truncation are the following. ATOM predicts the occurrence of infinitives and null subjects in fronted Wh questions and, due to the morphological analysis of French or Danish also predicts null subjects in finite fronted Wh questions. Moreover, if a language has a fronted and an in-situ structure for Wh-questions, ATOM predicts no differences in these two structures as to the licensing of infinitives or null subjects. Truncation, on the other hand, predicts that languages with a clear distinction of finite verbal forms and infinitives will not show infinitives in fronted Wh-questions, and clearly prohibits the occurrence of child null subjects in finite fronted Wh-questions. As to the predictions on in-situ questions, there are some things to be considered before clear statements can be derived in a truncation framework.

In particular, we have to consider what sort of material forces a projection so that truncation is no longer possible. In its original form, truncation assumes that a projection can be truncated only if there is no material which has to be accommodated. Hence, it follows that if there is material that needs to be placed, then the projection cannot be truncated. I want to ask in particular what kind of material prohibits truncation.

An obvious answer is that overt morphological material will force the presence of a projection and not allow truncation. This is the case of fronted Wh as Rizzi (1992) originally argues: the presence of the fronted Wh-operator forces the projection of CP, hence all the lower projections must be present, hence neither root infinitives nor null subjects can occur. This is clearly an empirical question and will be investigated in this chapter.

The crucial question is, however, if the converse also holds. In other words: Is truncation possible whenever there is no overt morphological material? This means in particular, that non-overt material would not block truncation. The answer can be affirmative only if we do not assume that the child is communicating, i.e. must be pairing utterances and meanings. If we assume that the child assigns meanings to her/his utterances, then a phrase that is allowed by the child's grammar must necessarily arrive at the level of LF, the interpretative level. In other words, the derivation should crash if the principle of Full Interpretation is not met. We therefore have to reckon with the requirements of LF and conclude that a projection cannot be truncated if it must accommodate material at LF. This is relevant for the predictions made by the truncation hypothesis concerning French Wh-in-situ.

Though it will be argued that some interpretative material is recoverable from discourse and then need not be present at LF in the child grammar, this is not the case for scope marking processes. Thus a question, unless it is an echo-question, will always need an operator in the topmost position in order to mark the whole phrase as the scope of the question. In many languages this is overtly marked in the syntax by the fact that the Wh-operator is the first element of the structure. For the less obvious case of Wh-in-situ, the standard analysis is that the Wh-operator moves covertly at LF. In a language like French, which has fronted Wh but also Wh-in-situ, we should therefore be able to test the question whether covert LF material can be truncated. The predictions are indeed very straightforward. If covert material does not count and can be truncated, then we predict the occurrence of infinitives and null subjects in children's Wh-in-situ questions, but not in fronted Wh-questions. This was the prediction made by Crisma (1992).

If we assume, however, that both types of questions need a scope marking question operator even in child grammar, then "Avoid Structure" cannot apply without crashing the derivation. It follows that neither question form involves truncation. Under this assumption we do not expect to find infinitives nor null subjects in either fronted or in-situ questions in French. If differences are observed in these two types of questions, the explanation cannot be found in truncated structures.

In the following I give an overview of the data from English (section 1.2) and German (section 1.3.) as discussed in the literature, then focus on a new analysis of the Danish data (1.4) and finally investigate French more closely, especially with respect to possible differences of the two major question types (section 1.5. and section 2).

1.2. Wh-questions in Early English

The evidence from English on the occurrence of infinitives in (fronted) Wh-questions is rather controversial. Valian (1991) found 9 null subjects in 552 Wh-questions across 21 English children and Rizzi (1992) found only 12 null subjects for Eve (1;6-2;4) in 191 Wh-questions. This makes for low percentages of 1.6% and 6.3% respectively. However, Radford (1996b) quotes Klima and Bellugi (1966), Plunkett (1992) and Vainikka (1994) for examples of null subjects in questions with overt Wh-words and provides the following figures from Hill (1983): 39% (11/28) of the Wh-questions of a child called Claire were null subject phrases. Similar figures are presented by Bromberg and Wexler (1995), who also report the substantial occurrence of infinitives in Wh-questions. As the occurrence of null subjects with infinitival forms can always be PRO, which is admitted by truncation in its more recent formulations, the above figures about null subjects are not decisive.

A study that meticulously separates finite and non-finite forms and investigates these with respect to null subjects is Roeper and Rohrbacher (2000), who give a table of pronoun use and null subjects in finite and non-finite Wh-questions. We can deduce the following: of 327 Wh-questions in the Adam corpus 115 had a null subject and 204 were non-finite, i.e. 35% of all Wh-questions contained a null subject, 62,4% of all Wh-questions were non-finite (including present and perfect participles in the count of non-finite forms). However, only 6 of 113 Wh questions with an inflected verb also contained a null subject, i.e. 4.6%, whereas there were 49% null subjects (99 of 204) in questions containing uninflected material.

This asymmetry is very sharp and follows from a truncation account as well as from ATOM. As to the occurrence of infinitives in English Wh questions, these are problematic for truncation only if they are genuine infinitives. As the language under investigation is English, lack of inflection and infinitives are hard to distinguish. Other languages, namely German, Danish, and French therefore give more decisive data.

4.5. Wh-questions in Early German

Neither Weissenborn (1990) nor Tracy (1994) report the occurrence of infinitives or null subjects in early German Wh-questions. The study of Clahsen, Kursawe and Penke (1996) investigates 9 German children with an age range of 1;7-3;0 in a first stage. In this stage, the children produce constituent questions with and without a Wh-element. If the Wh-element is present, it is fronted. There are 709 fronted Wh-questions, and 99% of these are finite. The same holds for the constituent questions with no Wh-element: 98% of 241 such questions are finite. So infinitives do not occur in constituent questions. As to null subjects only 4% of the fronted Wh-questions contain a null subject in contrast to 18% null subjects occurring in the questions without a Wh-element, showing a 14% difference that is statistically significant.

The basic facts emerging from this study are that infinitives do not occur in either type of German early constituent question, whereas null subjects are prohibited only after an overt fronted Wh-element. Unfortunately, the study does not give figures for the use of infinitives and null subjects in declaratives. However, if the children are representative for normal German development, infinitives can be considered to occur at around 50% for the younger and at around 10% for the older children (see table 37) whereas null subjects in finite constructions are expected to 20% (see table 34).

1.4. Wh-Questions in Early Danish

1.4.1. Background

For this new analysis of question use I consider the two children Jens and Anne described in chapters 6 and 8 (see also Hamann and Plunkett 1998 and Plunkett and Strömqvist 1990). It has been shown that the null subject periods of these two children coincide with their production of infinitives. The figures 6a,b, 8a,b, and 11a,b show that these periods last from 18-36 months for Anne and from about 20-47.3 months for Jens, when their use of null subjects has dropped below the 5% mark. For the purpose of the present study, the crucial periods have been slightly redefined in order to ensure a high rate of subject omission overall to compare with the rate of subject omission in Wh-questions. We consider the periods where overall subject omission is over or close to 10%. This gives us the 'crucial periods' of 18-30 months for Anne and 20-34.7 months for Jens.

In order to have a measure of comparison, the rates of null subjects on finite verbal utterances, on finite main verbs and on copulas were recalculated for these periods. Note that in Danish modals are like main verbs, and indeed subject omission is high on modals. There are 261 modals in this period for Anne and 76 show subject omission (29.1%). There are 323 modals in this period for Jens and 130 show subject drop (40.2%). Adding the modals to the count of finite main verbs (which was not done for figures 16a,b and table 35 in chapter 8), gives table 39 which is only minimally different from the previous counts.

Table 39: Null subject use overall in finite verbal utterances for Anne and Jens
(modified periods and counting method)

	Jens (20-34.7 months)		Anne (18-30 months)	
finite verbs	2870		1589	
0-s on finite verbs	725	(25.3%)	297	(18.7)
finite main verbs/mod with s	1254		660	
finite main verbs/mod with 0-s	635	(33.6%)	261	(28.3%)
copulas with s	991		663	
copulas with 0-s	156	(13.6)	62	(8.5%)

1.4.2. Constituent Questions

The occurrence of the question words *hvad* (what), *hvem* (who), *hvordan* (how), *hvornår* (when), *hvor* (where), *hvor laenge* (how long*)*, *hvilk-en, -et, -e* (which), *hvorfor* (why) were extracted with the help of CLAN from the tier of the child (see MacWhinney 1990). Non-initial occurrences were not considered, subordinate interrogatives were treated separately. *Hvornår* was not found by the program due to an error in the input spelling, no other search was instigated for this form because it was not considered that occurrences of 'when' would be found massively in the period under consideration. Only 'what', 'who', 'where' and 'why' were found in this period.

Anne's and Jens' Questions. In the 18-30 months period, Anne has only *hvad*, *hvem* and *hvor*-questions. There are 9 fronted *hvem*-questions, all of which are subject questions, contain a copula and are finite. They are thus relevant for the count on infinitives, but irrelevant for a subject count. There are 107 fronted *hvad*-questions, 105 are subject questions, 2 are object questions. Both object questions involve finite main verbs and have subjects. As to *hvor*, there are 80 occurrences of finite *hvor*-questions, and 6 of these show subject omission. 78 of these *hvor* questions are a copula construction, only 2 are main verb constructions. One finite main verb question is without a subject, 5 of the copula constructions show subject omission. There are also 3 *hvor*-questions in the infinitive and 2 of these show subject omission. In sum, for subject counts we find 82 relevant finite questions in the period under consideration, 6 of which contain a null subject (7.3%).

In the 20-34.7 period, Jens has only *hvad*, *hvem*, *hvor* and *hvorfor*-questions. There are 20 *hvem* questions which are all subject questions, 1 of these contains an infinitive. *Hvorfor* occurs mostly in its bare form or without a verb, but there is 1 finite (copula) construction, which contains a subject. There are 109 occurrences of *hvor* with a finite construction. 9 of these show subject omission. Of these, there are 88 copula constructions, 1 with a null subject, and 21 main verb constructions, 8 with a null subject. 5 of these main verb constructions with a null subject occur inside of about 10 minutes in one file. There are also 12 occurrences of infinitives in *hvor* questions, 3 with a null subject. There are many subject *hvad*-questions from early on, most of them involve the almost formulaic: *hvad er det*? 'What is that?'. However, there are also 84 object *hvad*-questions in this period all involving a finite main verb. 12 of these show subject drop. In sum, we find 194 finite questions relevant for subject counts, with 20 occurrences of subject omission. Of these finite forms, 105 are main verb constructions and 19 of these have a null subject.

Null Subjects in Danish Constituent Questions. Table 40 sums up the findings on null subjects in Wh-questions for Anne and Jens. This table shows the occurrence of null subjects in finite utterances that are not Wh-questions and the occurrence of null subjects in finite fronted Wh-questions. We aim for a comparison of Wh-questions and declaratives, which is better able to highlight a possible asymmetry than a comparison of finite Wh-questions and finite constructions overall as available so far. For procedural reasons we have to subsume under the label 'pseudo-declarative' true declaratives and yes-no questions. Note that the expectation of null subject occurrence in yes-no questions patterns with that for declaratives (Crisma 1992, Hamann 2000a, and section 2.4 of this chapter) so that such a treatment will not confuse trends. For the count on Wh-questions, subject questions were excluded. The remaining questions are called 'relevant Wh-questions' in table 40. We find roughly a 15% difference in subject drop which is compatible with the prediction of an asymmetry due to the presence of the Wh-element in initial position. In order to avoid that this result is biased by the fact that copula constructions are the prevalent question structures and subject drop occurs less in copula constructions, a more detailed analysis as to null subjects occurring with main verbs and copulas is given in addition to the overall figures. We see that for Jens an 18% difference in subject drop is found across main verb questions and copula questions, and for Anne, surprisingly, we find a difference of about 6% for copulas and cannot say much about similarity or difference for main verbs due to their rare occurrence. Preliminary statistical tests showed, that the asymmetry is significant for Jens for both main-verb and copula constructions, and significant for both children taken together in all the constructions under consideration, whereas it is not significant for Anne. It seems unlikely that the asymmetry found in Jens is due to a difference inherent in copula and main verb constructions. It is more probable that we are dealing with an asymmetry due to a structural property common to both types of structures. Note in particular, that ATOM with the reanalysis of verbal morphology as suggested in Wexler (2000) does not predict an asymmetry and especially does not predict the same kind of asymmetry for main verbs and copulas. In the ATOM model finite main verbs of the Danish paradigm may be [–TNS], copulas are always [+TNS]. So copulas should not take null subjects regardless of structure and main verbs should allow null subjects regardless of structure. So the data from Jens are problematic for this account.

On the other hand, only one child, Jens, has a clear difference in 'pseudo-declarative' copular constructions and in Wh-questions with copulas, whereas the figures for Anne are equivocal. Therefore, due to the prevalence of copular constructions in questions, too clear a conclusion is not possible. A more detailed statistical analysis will give more indications (see Hamann and Rizzi in preparation).

Table 40: Overview of null subject occurrences in finite 'pseudo-declaratives' and in finite fronted Wh-questions for Jens and Anne in their 'crucial periods'

	Jens (20-34.7 months)	Anne (18-30 months)	total
% 0-s in finite 'pseudo-declaratives'	28.5	21.3	26.0
relevant finite Wh-questions	194	82	276
cases of 0-s	20	6	26
% of 0-s in rel. finite Wh	10.3	7.3	9.4
% 0-s in finite main verb 'pseudo-declaratives	36.8	28.6	34.0
relevant finite m-v Wh	105	4	109
0-s in m-v Wh questions	19	1	20
% of 0-s in m-v Wh	18.1	25	18.3
% 0-s in 'pseudo-declaratives' with copulas	18.1	12.2	16.0
relevant copula Wh questions	89	78	167
0-s in copula Wh	1	5	6
% 0-s in copula Wh	1.1	6.5	3.5

Infinitives. As to infinitives, in the crucial period Anne has 3 infinitives in 201 questions with finite verbs, which makes up 1.5%. It has to be noted that though there is one infinitive with a main verb out of 11 occurrences of main verbs, we also have one copula in the infinitive (vaere). There is one null subject on these infinitives.

Jens produces 17 infinitives in overall 367 questions, which gives 4.6%. 8 infinitives are with main verbs, 9 infinitives are the copula form *vaere*. 8 of the infinitives do not occur in subject questions, 2 of these contain a null subject.

Though the first impression is that the non-occurrence of infinitives is again due to the overwhelming presence of copula constructions, this does not seem to be quite true. Jens produces as much (or more) infinitives on copulas as on main verbs in his questions.

1.4.3. Summary

In Danish, the prevalence of copula constructions makes a final judgement very difficult. However, we have shown in chapter 8 that null subjects do occur on copulas to surprisingly high percentages in certain files, and we see here that even infinitives are possible in such constructions. So the fact that we have only very few infinitives in questions remains to be explained and might well be due to the presence of the Wh-element. For null subjects we have the same picture. Though the conclusion cannot be too strong due to between subject variation, the data on Jens and on both children taken together indicate an asymmetry of null subject occurrence in 'pseudo-declaratives' and null subject occurrence in questions. This asymmetry seems to be present for constructions with finite main verbs and with copulas.

1.5. Wh-questions in Early French

The outstanding fact about French fronted Wh-questions is that they do not show infinitives and that there is a very sharp asymmetry as to the occurrence of null subjects in the post Wh-context and in declaratives. Crisma (1992) pointed out that there were no infinitives in Philippe's Wh-questions (2;1-2;3), even if he produces 36.8% infinitives in declaratives from 2;1 to 2;2 months and 15.2% infinitives from 2;2-2;3 months. As to null subjects, Crisma found 1 null subject in 104 Wh-questions in these two periods, whereas Philippe produces 406 null subjects in 1002 declarative constructions at the same time. This asymmetry was corroborated by the results of Levow (1995) who studied Gregoire (1;9-2;3) Daniel (1;8-1;11) and Nathalie (1;9-2;3) and found no infinitives in the 39 Wh-questions produced by these children. During the periods under investigation, Daniel has 32.6% RIs overall, Nathalie has 19.7%, and Gregoire has 26%. As to null subjects, there were only 2 (5%), both from Grègoire, whereas there were 55% null subjects in declaratives on average for the three children. See section 2 for more detailed data. The data from the first two children from the Genevan Corpus, Augustin and Marie, confirm this clear trend (see also Hamann 2000a and section 2 of this chapter). In the 11 fronted Wh-questions these children produce, there is no infinitive. There are 3 null subjects, all occurring with the Wh-element 'pourquoi'. As this element has special properties, these null subjects may be licensed by a by-passing mechanism as discussed in Haegeman (2000). Tables and details will be given in section 2 of this chapter when I compare the production of question types. We can conclude, however, that in French, infinitives do not occur in Wh-questions, and that null subjects in finite fronted Wh-questions are very rare. This leads to a clear asymmetry, as infinitives and null subjects occur freely in declaratives.

The asymmetry concerning the very restricted occurrence of null subjects in post Wh-contexts with finite verbal forms cannot be explained by ATOM and the assumption that French finite verbal forms lack a tense specification in child language. It rather corroborates a truncation approach to infinitives and child null subjects.

As mentioned earlier, a study of the two major forms of French questions, fronted Wh and Wh-in-situ, can also verify predictions made by ATOM or truncation in a direct way. Before we procede to this empirical investigation, it is important to keep in mind that especially the study of Wh-in-situ will in addition address the question raised in section 1.1. of this chapter about what activates a projection and blocks truncation.

Let us recapitulate that truncation admits two possibilities for the analysis of Wh-in-situ in children. If only overt material activates a projection, in-situ questions may be truncated structures and so null subjects are expected. Jumping the gun and taking some of the results for granted already, this could be supported by the data found for Augustin, who, unlike Philippe, does produce Wh-in-situ and has 23% null subjects in his Wh-in-situ questions. He does not have infinitives (not even in his main verb Wh-in-situ questions) however, so that a simple truncation analysis does not seem to be appropriate. Another argument against a straightforward truncation analysis in the Wh-in-situ case is the fact that Philippe has only fronted Wh in the phase where his use of root infinitives is at its peak. If Wh-in-situ is a truncated structure in child grammar and Philippe is still in the truncation phase, there is no reason why he should not use this option.

So the second possibility is that both constructions, fronted Wh and Wh-in-situ, activate the same projections for reasons of interpretation, especially for reasons of scope marking. This leaves the problem of explaining syntactic differences as, for example, the occurrence of null subjects in Augustin's Wh-in-situ questions.

One explanation of this phenomenon is to assume that overt and covert movement are sufficiently different, the latter being less constrained than the former. Indeed, certain syntactic phenomena have led to the assumption that covert movement is not constrained by the ECP or subjacency:

(1) a.   Who reads the books that who writes
    b.   *who do you read books that e writes

This assumption has always been controversial. In a minimalist framework, the problem is not amenable to such an assumption anyway because with the disappearance of surface structure, level-dependent movement constraints cannot be formulated. Moreover, it is empirically wrong that LF movement is not constrained. Reinhart (1991) shows that in comparative and elliptical constructions the correlates move and adjoin at LF constrained by subjacency. It follows that differences cannot be explained by assuming two kinds of movement which obey different constraints.

Another possibility is to assume the involvement of two different scope marking question operators. This is the idea I want to pursue in the following investigation (see also Hamann 2000a and Hamann in press). As it turns out, the data from French child language provide some good arguments for the involvement of two different operators accounting for certain differences in occurrence. These differences are thus due to the different nature of the operators, not to the truncation option (which might have been supposed to apply in one case but not the other). We can therefore maintain our assumption that truncation does not apply whenever interpretation requires more structure.

Ultimately, this leads to the question of what can be truncated in the child grammar without violating interpretative requirements. The conclusion will be that only interpretative material which is also available in a default model can be truncated. As deictic anchorage is always available, this provides the default model, which then regulates tense, pronouns, definite DPs and factive presuppositions. (See also Avrutin 1999 for similar proposals formulated in the file card semantics proposed by Heim 1982). This confronts us with the interface problem in a very acute form. There are two possible ways to treat this.

We could assume that there is a projection hosting operators that bind those constituents which need discourse identification. If this is the projection which is the root of the clause in adult language and if we call it LinkP, we can reformulate Rizzi (1992)'s axiom as (2):

(2)   LinkP = root.

It would be this axiom which is not yet operative in child language and thus leads to the general truncation option.

We could also simplify the proposal and take it back to the original observation that children have 'CP-trouble'. For this purpose it is necessary to identify the syntactic trouble in the CP that leads to exactly the observed problems in the interface. Such an identification can be achieved in so far as marking of "old" or "discourse-given" information, a classical topic-property located in the CP, may be lacking and would directly imply the observed problems. We will elaborate the second proposal in chapter 11.

2. FRENCH CONSTITUENT QUESTIONS: FRONTED WH AND WH-IN-SITU

2.1. Theoretical Background

A question with a fronted Wh-pronoun (3a) has the representation (4a). For the question (3b), the Wh-word, though in situ on the surface, also needs to have wide scope in order to achieve the correct reading.

(3) a.   qui   as-tu   vu?
         who   have-you seen
    b.   tu as vu qui?
         you have seen who

(4) a.   CP[qui$_i$ C'[as IP [tu VP[vu e$_i$]]]].

The standard answer to this problem is to assign representation (4a) not only to (3a) but also to (3b). The difference of (3a) and (3b) is explained by assuming covert LF movement for (3b) while in (3a) the question word has moved overtly at SS. This outlines the movement approach to scope marking which can be described as the overt or covert application of QR. This approach originates from Chomsky (1976) and has been developed by others, notably by Huang (1982) for Chinese Wh-in-situ constructions.

A competing analysis goes back to Baker (1970), who suggested that every question contains an abstract Q-morpheme. This captures the old intuition that an interrogative pronoun contains an abstract question morpheme (the *w* or *wh*-part) and the basic existential pronoun 'someone'. In

Baker's approach, in-situ Wh-constituents are bound directly by Q as shown in (4b):

(4) b. [Q_i $_{IP}$[tu [as $_{VP}$[vu qui$_i$]]]]

The label of the first bracket is irrelevant as long as the quantifier c-commands the Wh-constituent. So Q could be in CP as suggested by Baker (1970), or adjoined to IP. The idea that scope assignment does not necessarily involve movement has since been elaborated by Williams (1986) and by Pesetski (1987). The latter maintains that D-linked in-situ questions in English cannot be derived by movement, but are best treated with direct binding by a Q-operator which acts as unselective binder in the sense of Heim (1982). Though this account was proposed only for *which NP* questions, there is reason to believe that it is a more general scope marking procedure and could thus be evoked for general in-situ questions, as discussed in Reinhart (1995). Developing these arguments Reinhart (1995,1997) suggests that this type of scope marking is best captured by existential binding of a choice function, not by unselective binding. Her basic arguments are that the mechanism of unselective binding incorrectly predicts that intervening quantifiers block wide scope readings of the Wh-operator, which does not apply to an analysis involving a choice function. For a further discussion of the advantages and disadvantages of a choice function analysis, for definitions and for details of the analysis, I refer the reader to Reinhart (1997), Stechow (1999), Mathieu (to appear) and Hamann (2000a and in press), but will in the following adopt this analysis for Wh-in-situ. What is important here is the fact that for marking question scope in Wh-in-situ a general procedure is available which does not involve silent movement of the Wh-element.

So the following alternative approaches are obtained. For fronted Wh, scope marking takes place overtly by the Wh-operator. But for Wh-in-situ there are two possibilities: covert Wh-movement or a procedure involving a choice function bound by an existential operator.

2.2. The Data From Child French

In the light of the theoretical discussion and the questions formulated in section 1, let us now investigate the data from child French, which provides the test case for the use of both question types. The data we present show the question production of three French speaking children, Philippe (2;1,19 -

2;7,18) from Leveillé (Childes) as analysed by Crisma (1992), Augustin (2;0,1 - 2;9,30), a child taped and analyzed in Geneva and introduced in chapter 2, and Marie (1;8,26 - 2;3,3), who also was recorded in the framework of the Interfaculty Project in Geneva and whose data have recently become available.

Table 41: Development of Root Infinitives (RI), Null Subjects (NS), Fronted Wh (Fr-Wh) and Wh-in-situ (Wh-i-s) questions for Philippe, Augustin and Marie

			%RI (overall)	%NS (overall)	Fr-Wh	Wh-i-s
Phil	T1	2.1.19-2.2.17	21.8	38.6	35	0
	T2	2.2.26-2.3.21	8.6	33.2	78	1
	T3	2.6.13-2.7.18	1.6	9.8	118	81
Aug	T1	2.0.2-2.4.22	17.5	49.3	1	27
	T2	2.6.16-2.9.30	6.1	26.1	7	59
Marie	T1	1.8.26-2.3.3.	17.9	40.2	3	27

For Philippe, we adopt the periods defined by Crisma (1992): T1 is 2;1,19-2;2,17, T2 is 2;2,26-2;3,21 and T3 is 2;6,13-2;7,18. We introduce a similar devision in periods for Augustin, for whom the time spans are longer: T1 is 2;0,2-2;4,22 and T2 is 2;6,16.-2;9,30. Marie's production cannot be developmentally divided into phases, so we call the time span from 18.8.26 to 2.3.3 her T1.

We see in table 41 that Wh-in-situ is used by French children, but that there is variation in the development of Wh–questions. Whereas Philippe starts with fronted Wh and has Wh- in-situ only in T3 at the age of 2.6, Augustin starts with Wh-in-situ, and shows fronted Wh from the age of 2.6. Marie also starts with Wh-in-situ and has her first fronted Wh at the age of 2.1.28, when she produces the routine inversion *qu'est-ce que c'est* (2 times). At the same age she uses the first fronted Wh-question without inversion as shown in (5).

(5)   où il est canard?   Marie 2;1,28.
      where he is duck

Though two of the children start with Wh-in-situ and other French children who have recently been tested in that area also seem to prefer Wh-in-situ (see Hulk and Zuckermann 2000 and Plunkett 1999), we cannot speak of a "general" economy strategy avoiding overt movement: The data provided by Philippe are too sharp to allow such a general conclusion. Note also that the children start with one Wh-strategy and then, at approximately the same point in development, begin to use both question forms. The existence of these markedly different acquisition routes is a strong indication for the existence of two different interrogative processes. Moreover, the fact that the asymmetry in question use seen in Philippe and Augustin is most marked at a time when both children are undoubtedly in the root infinitive phase, argues against a truncation analysis of Wh-in-situ.

2.2.1. Root Infinitives and Question Types

Table 42: Finite and non-finite Wh-questions

	Phil		Aug		Mar	
	Fr –Wh	Wh-i-s	Fr - Wh	Wh-i-s	Fr –Wh	Wh-i-s
FIN	231	82	8	86	3	27
INF	0	0	0	0	0	0

We now investigate the two properties described above, the occurrence of root infinitives and null subjects depending on the type of question produced. As to root infinitives, table 42 shows that neither question form occurs with root infinitives. For Philippe, this may not be conclusive as Phillips (1995) argues. Philippe has mostly auxiliaries in his questions, not main verbs, and for auxiliaries it is well known that they do not occur as root infinitives.

In the light of Phillips (1995)'s criticism, we reinvestigate Philippe in more detail. Philippe's Wh-questions contain almost exclusively auxiliaries, and so root infinitives seem to be a priori excluded. Phillips makes a new count of the Philippe corpus using the following criteria for exclusion of an utterance:

1) multiple repetition of the same utterance
2) repetitions of all or a large part of the preceding adult utterance
3) common routines like *c'est* and *il y a*

Following these criteria, he arrives at the tables 43 and 44. Note that for Phillips, an auxiliary infinitive is the morphological infinitive (*être* or *avoir*), whereas for Sano and Hyams (1994) and Schütze and Wexler (1996a) an auxiliary counts as non-finite if it is missing.

Table 43: Distribution of root infinitives in Philippe's auxiliaries
(Phillips 1995)

Phil 2;1-2;3	finite Aux	inf.Aux
declaratives	166	0
Wh-questions	63	0

Table 44: Distribution of root infinitives in Philippe's main verbs
(Phillips 1995)

Phil 2;1-2;3	finite V	infin. V
declaratives	444	182
Wh-questions	1	0

A close look at the tables 43 and 44 in comparison to table 41 reveals the following astonishing fact: of Crisma's original 807 finite verbs and 195 nonfinite verbs in declaratives about 610 finite verbs pass the test of non-repetition and about 182 non-repetition verbs survive as infinitives in declaratives. We have thus 1002 original verbs of which 792 survive the new criteria. So only about 20% are eliminated. But the same criteria cut the question population in half: of 114 Wh-questions only 64 survive the repetition test and of the main verbs only one survives. This seems to call for a deeper investigation.

First, though it is clear that *c'est ça* and some other forms are a routine, this does not seem to justify the exclusion of every occurence of *c'est*, which can be considered as part of the clitic paradigm, the other forms of which Philippe certainly uses: *il est, elle est, on est*. Moreover, the exclusion of this form will obliterate the very interesting development of Philippe's *que'est-ce que c'est* questions which for a time are rendered as *que c'est ça*. The same problem surfaces in the occurrence of (6) because *où il est, où elle est* occur at the same time. Therefore, many of these forms should be included.

(6) où c'est dehors   Phillipe 2;3,14
     where it is outside
     'where is it outside'

Second, there is the problem of what counts as an auxiliary. In German, English, Danish and also French auxiliary *haben, have, avoir* should be distinguished from the main verb indicating possession. It seems to be the case, however, that all occurrences of *avoir* have been excluded by Phillips from the count. On the other hand, all occurrences of *aller* seem to have been counted in, though some clearly are periphrastic and could be counted as auxiliaries.[1]

Third and most important, the criterion of exclusion if the child question contains large chunks of a foregoing adult or child utterance is certainly too restrictive. Full repetitions must be excluded, especially if the question word is taken up from the adult utterance, but this criterion should not be applied if the child is forming a question with the material of the adult sentence or foregoing child utterances. We are investigating question formation, so this creative act of transforming an adult or child foregoing declarative into a question should be one of the most interesting sources for our observations. Consider (7) in this light:

(7) PHI: va monter au pied   go go-up on foot   Phil 2;3,0
     PHI: enlever son pneu   take off its wheel
     PHI: enlever son pneu   take off its wheel
     MAD: pourquoi?   why
     PHI: oh. a plus pneu la voiture
                                     oh, has no more wheel the car
     PHI: pourquoi j'enleve le pneu?
                                     why I take off the wheel?

The point here is that the child has taken up the question word from the adult, thus taking over an important cue. But then he changes his own declarative infinitive into a finite utterance to form the question! This seems to indicate strongly that infinitives are not allowed in questions in the child grammar, and excluding such examples from the count just misses the point.

In any case, this discussion has shown why it is possible that the question population in Phillips (1995) is only about half of what Crisma (1992) discusses. Of course, Crisma did not include run-of-the-mill repetitions. She might have considered some of the above examples involving vocabulary chunks or *c'est* as productive questions, however, which in some cases makes more sense than excluding them from the count. A count of all of Philippe's Wh-questions which are not repetitions of a question involving the same question word and counting only *comment, pourquoi,* spontaneous *que c'est ça, qui, quel(le), quoi, où* without considering the many occurrences of non-adult *qu'est ce* which might be attempted repetitions, brings us to a count of 96 Wh-questions in T1 and T2, which cuts the question population to a similar degree as the declaratives. Because of the minimal difference, we do not set up our own count, but repeat Crisma's table as table 45.

Table 45: The development of question formation concerning null subjects and root infinitives for Philippe
(from Crisma 1992: 117 and 119)

T1	Tot	%null sub	%RI
declarative	491	41.9	36.8
wh-question	35	2.8 (1)	0
yes-no question	28	25.0	14.3
T2			
declarative	511	39.3	15.2
wh-question	79	0	0
yes-no question	29	13.8	3.4
T3			
declarative	611	13.2	2.4
wh-question	199	0.5 (1)	0
yes-no question	100	7.0	0

It is true, however, that 99% of the examples involve auxiliaries so that the very clear result on the non-occurrence of root infinitives is not really conclusive. But let us point out that even the strict application of Philipps' criteria and his tables 43 and 44, do not allow the conclusion he draws:

> "English subject wh-questions and colloquial French wh-questions on the other hand do not require verb movement to C, and as a result, the verbs behave just as they would in a declarative, and therefore allow root infinitives." (Phillips 1995:346, my emphasis)

For Augustin, however, 23 of his 98 Wh-questions have a main verb, 20 of these are non-repetitive, and none occurs in the infinitive. There is a low rate of root infinitives at this time in development, however. Fortunately, Marie gives corroboration of the data on Augustin: 6 of her 30 Wh-questions have a main verb (*faire, aller, avoir*), 4 of these occur at 2.1.28 where she has 20% root infinitives. Table 46 and table 47 provide a file by file analysis of Augustin's and Marie's development in question production, also showing their null subject use.

Table 46: Occurrence of Wh, root infinitives and null subjects in the Augustin-corpus

Age	% 0-s	% RI	Wh tot	% RI	Wh-fr	% 0-s	Wh i-s	0-s	% 0-s	inv
2;0,2	46.9	14.3	0	0	0	0	0	0	0	0
2;0,23	60.9	39.1	0	0	0	0	0	0	0	0
2;1,15	46.6	46.1	0	0	0	0	0	0	0	0
2;2,13	36.4	13.6	3	0	1	0	2	0	0	0
2;3,10	30.3	12.2	0	0	0	0	0	0	0	0
2;4,1	54.7	9.4	12	0	0	0	12	6	50	0
2;4,22	47.8	17.4	16	0	0	0	16	8	50	
2;6,16	37.0	7.0	46	0	4	75 (3)	42	9	21.4	1
2;9,2	24.8	5.7	8	0	1	0	7	0	0	1
2;9,30	14.3	6.0	12	0	2	0	10	0	0	1
Total		10.8	97	0	8	37.5	89	23	25.8	

Table 47: Occurrence of Wh, root infinitives and null subjects in the Marie-corpus

Age	% 0-s	% RI	Wh tot	% RI	Wh-fr	% 0-s	Wh i-s	0-s	% 0-s	iv
1;8,26	51%	23%	4	0	0	0	4	0	0	0
1;9,3	31%	22%	8	0	0	0	8	0	0	0
1;9,10	49%	20%	(1)							
1;10,1	30%	12%	0	0	0	0	0	0	0	0
1;11,5	34%	8%	1	0	0	0	1	0	0	0
2;0,9	46%	13%	0	0	0	0	0	0	0	0
2;1,7	46%	18%	1	0	0	0	1	0	0	0
2;1,28	33%	19%	11	0	3	0	8	1	12.5	2
2;33,3	52%	23%	5	0	0	0	5	1	20	0

We deduce that none of the three children uses an infinitive in either question form. This finding is corroborated by other children's data as stated in section 1.4. So far not one infinitive has been documented in a French Wh-question, see Levow (1995) and Weissenborn (1991).

2.2.2. Null Subjects and Question Types

As to null subjects, we see from table 48 (which groups the information on null subjects also available from tables 45, 46, and 47 in a more concise form) that Wh-in-situ allows null subjects whereas fronted Wh does not. For Augustin this result is particularly clear as he has the same percentage of null subjects in his Wh-in-situ questions (23 of 86 or 27%) as in his overall finite constructions (27%, see Hamann 2000a and Rasetti 2000). Marie also has null subjects in her in-situ questions (2 of 27 or 7.4%), but not as many as in her overall finite utterances (22.1%, see Rasetti 1996). For Philippe, the analysis is inconclusive once again, as he has only one null subject in his in-situ-questions, but this occurs in T3 when his use of null subjects in finite declaratives has gone down to 13% (see Crisma 1992 and Rasetti 1996). Note that we do not need to separate auxiliaries and main verbs for the count on null subjects as we have established in chapter 8 that subject drop from copula constructions is rather high in French, especially for Augustin.

Table 48: Null Subjects (NS) and Overt Subjects (OS) in Fronted Wh and Wh-in-situ, Philippe, Marie and Augustin

	Phil		Aug		Mar	
	Fr-Wh	Wh-i-s	Fr-Wh	Wh-i-s	Fr-Wh	Wh-i-s
NS	1	1	3	23	0	2
OS	230	81	5	63	3	25

Levow's data on null subjects corroborate this finding as was pointed out in section 1.4. of this chapter. Table 49 shows the data in detail, grouped in the same way as Crisma's analysis of Philippe. Note that only one child produces null subjects in fronted Wh and that in one of his questions, there is considerable confusion as to question formation. In (8b) Grégoire fronts the interrogative pronoun *quoi-* 'what', which is restricted to in-situ position.

(8) a. Où est?   Grégoire
        where is
    b. quoi fait?   Grégoire
        what does(3rd)

Table 49: Percentage of null subject utterances by child in Wh-questions, Yes-No questions, and declaratives
(from Levow 1995:293)

Child	Type	NS	Overt S	Total	%NS
Gregoire	declarative	156	240	396	39.4
Gregoire	Wh-qu	2	12	14	14.2
Gregoire	yes-no qu	16	14	30	53.3
Daniel	declarative	457	207	664	68.8
Daniel	Wh-qu	0	23	23	0
Daniel	yes-no qu	0	1	1	0
Nathalie	declarative	166	186	352	47.2
Nathalie	wh-qu	0	2	2	0
Nathalie	yes-no qu	2	1	3	66.6
total	declarative	779	633	1412	55.2
total	wh-qu	2	37	39	5.1
total	yes-no	18	16	34	52.9

As to the preferred question types used by Philippe and Augustin, during T1 and T2, (9a) is the typical question for Philippe, whereas it is (9b) for Augustin throughout the whole period of observation.

(9) a. où il est?   Phil 2;1,19
        where he is
    b. est où?   Aug   2;6,16
        is where

In T3 (2;6,13-2;7,18) Philippe has less than 10 genuine Wh-in-situ questions with main verbs as in (10a-c), while the Wh-in-situ constituent is often part of a PP as in (11a-c).

(10) a. elle ecrit quoi   Philippe T3
      she writes what
      'what does she write?'
   b. elle fait quoi alors
      she does what then
      'what does she do then?'
   c. elles sont où
      they are where
      'where are they'

(11) a. ça va dans quoi
      that goes in what
      'where does that fit in'
   b. avec quoi il joue   du tambour
      with what he plays of drummer
      'He plays the drummer with what?'
   c. pour aller où   elle est parti
      for to go where she is gone
      'For where to go has she left?'

So Philippe's use of Wh-in-situ even in T3 seems to be rather limited in productivity: though we now find 40.7% Wh-in-situ, about 90% of these are of the form *"c'est quoi"* which is the in-situ variant of *"qu'est-ce que c'est"*.

Fronted Wh-questions in these children's production do not allow null subjects except for four cases all involving *pourquoi*. This can be explained by the special status of *pourquoi* as discussed in Rizzi (1990b). There it is maintained that *pourquoi* does not undergo movement but is base generated in the Comp system. The reasons for this assumption are that *pourquoi* does not occur in French in-situ questions and does not license stylistic inversion as shown in (12a,b,c).

(12) a. Pourquoi tu   verse   de l'eau?
      why   you   pour   of the water
      'why do you pour water?'
   b. *Tu verse de   l'eau   pourquoi?
      you pour of   the water why
   c. *Pourquoi part-Jean?
      why   leaves-John
      'Why does John leave'

2.3. The Licensing of Null Subjects in Wh-in-situ

As not one question is non-finite, an analysis of null subjects depending on (straightforward) underspecified tense can be excluded. If we assume ATOM with the particular analysis of finite verb forms as lacking the tense specification, then null subjects would be licensed but should also occur in fronted Wh questions. Note also that the majority of null subject cases involves an auxiliary, especially for Augustin, see (9b). This is interesting in itself, and might suggest that in French child language, the null subject is of a different type than in the English case where null subjects with copulas are rare (see Hyams and Sano 1994, and Schütze and Wexler 1996b). The first possibility which comes to mind is that, while the English null subject is PRO as suggested by the above authors, in child French the null subject is *pro*. Then one could make the further assumption that it is verbal inflection which licenses this *pro* because the French child is confronted with a richer agreement system than the English child. This implies that *pro* should be possible in (9a). We have to ask therefore, if (9a) is an exception, or the rule for Philippe.

As it turns out, (9a) is typical, and none of Philippe's Wh-questions involves inversion or the periphrastic *est-ce-que* form till a very late time. This has to be understood in the following way. Periphrastic *est-ce que* does not occur in any other question form than in the frozen *qu'est-ce que c'est*. But even though this form does occur, it is extremely rare till T3. There are 3 occurrences in the first two files, but then the non-adult *qu'es-ce c'est* is used and, even more revealing, the form *que c'est ça* interspersed with some *qu'es-ce c'est ça* appears predominantly till the end of T2. It seems reasonable to assume that Philippe analyses what has been transcribed as *qu'es-ce* and which is phonetically [kEs] as one question word, so that 99% of his questions in T1 and T2 have the order "Wh subject-clitic AUX". Only in T3 there are 46 cases, which could be analyzed as inversion and all involve *qu'est-ce que c'est*. In T3 Philippe also uses main verbs in fronted Wh-questions, there are 30 lexical main verbs, 1 occurrence of main verb *avoir*, 1 of *falloir* and 3 cases of periphrastic *aller* None of these occur with a null subject, none with a root infinitive. Even in T3 we find only non-inverted questions, apart from the form *qu'est-ce que c'est* as discussed above. (13a-e) show some of Philippe's main verb fronted Wh-questions in T3.

(13) a. où on le met
where one him put
'where should we put him'
b. où elle va maman
where she goes mama
'where does mama go?'
c. où ils travaillent maintenant
where they work now
'where do they work now?'
d. comment ça roule
how that rolls
'how does that roll?'
e. comment on fait pour l'ouvrir
how one does for him-open
'what does one do to open it/him'

Therefore, the order of "subject-clitic + verb/auxiliary" is the same for Philippe and Augustin in the relevant phase. As the local licensing and identification configuration are exactly the same (14), this makes it extremely unlikely that the null subject in the in-situ case (9b) is licensed by agreement, but agreement could not license a null clitic in (9a).

(14)

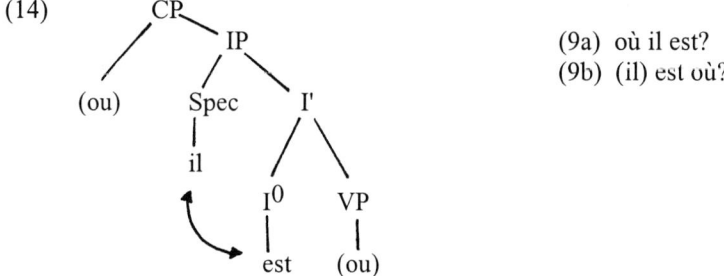

(9a) où il est?
(9b) (il) est où?

Another possibility is that non-inverted French child questions are clefts, a hypothesis which has been used to assign analysis (15b) to the English example (15a). Then Philippe's (9a) would in fact be (16a) and the non-occurrence of null subjects in this type of question would follow because null subjects are not found in subordinate clauses in child language.

(15) a. Where dis goes?   Adam 2;8
 b. Where (is it that) this goes.

(16) a. Où (est-ce qu') il est?
 where (is it that) he goes
 b. Où c'est qu' il est?   Cleft for (9a)
 where it is that he is

There are several counter arguments against this idea. First, it still needs to be explained why null subjects do not occur in subordinate clauses which is rather surprising under the assumption that agreement licenses null subjects. Second, it is doubtful whether French *est-ce que* can be analysed as a cleft. The cleft for (9a) is (16b), not (16a). Moreover, in Yes-No questions *est-ce que* cannot be a cleft, as focalization is not possible. It is thus rather unlikely that French finite null subjects are licensed by agreement.

Summing up the licensing options for null subjects in Wh-in-situ, we have excluded licensing of PRO through an underspecified tense head and licensing of *pro* by agreement. Hence, it seems to be the privileged initial position which makes omission possible in (9b), but not in (9a). So a topic-drop or diary-drop analysis for child null subjects which goes together with the possibility of truncation seems more appropriate.

2.4. The Problem (Again)

This brings us back to our original question. As mentioned in section 1.4. of this chapter, Crisma (1992) argued that null subjects are expected in Wh-in-situ because the CP level is not activated, can be truncated and thus the empty category is in topmost position and can survive. But if truncation were possible, then the child might decide to truncate even lower than IP level so that we would expect occurrences of RIs like *aller où* which have not been attested. Predictions are hard to make, however, because for Augustin we have 12 Wh-in-situ questions at a time when there are 9.4 % root infinitives (2;4,1), 16 Wh-in-situ questions when we have 17.4% infinitives (2;4,22), and 42 Wh-in-situ questions when there are 7% infinitives (2;6,16).

The other big problem for Crisma's idea is the assumption that the child is uttering meaningful sentences and the derivation must arrive at an LF representation. If the derivation involves silent movement of the Wh-constituent, then CP must be activated at LF for Wh-in-situ and a difference to fronted Wh is not expected. Indeed Crisma uses exactly this line of argumentation to explain why Philippe has Wh-in-situ so late: he avoids the SS/LF contradiction arising from truncating CP at SS but needing CP at LF. This explanation cannot be applied to Augustin or any of the other Wh-in-situ children discussed in the literature. They would be confronted with the same contradiction and do not seem to care. Let us therefore conclude that Crisma's explanation is not needed in any case because the 'delay of Wh-in-situ' does not exist.[2] So we have a genuine problem for the truncation analysis. The CP must be projected at LF in both cases. We are faced with the apparent dilemma that null subjects are possible in one case, but not the other.

As briefly indicated in section 1, a possible solution is the following idea: If Wh-in-situ does not involve a silent Wh-operator, but something more like an existential operator, then the difference can be explained by the difference of the features concerned. In a split CP analysis as suggested by Rizzi (1997), and given mechanisms of by-passing as worked out by Haegeman (2000) for examples like (17), the empty category could raise higher than the binder thus exempting the ECP. Such a mechanism could by-pass an existential operator, but could never by-pass a Wh-operator.

(17) a. Sur une voiture monte encore   Philippe 2;3,
         on   a   car   climb again
         '(I) climb on a car again'

One argument for the idea of a non-movement analysis comes from the observation that practically the only fronted Wh-element which allows null subjects is *pourquoi*. As *pourquoi* is base inserted and has not moved, it is natural to assume the same for the scope assigning operator in Wh-in-situ. Another argument is the fact that null subjects occur freely in Yes-No questions. This can be seen in tables 45 and 49 for French and has also been shown for German. Hamann (1996b) found 20% null subjects in the Yes-No questions of two German 3-year olds (see chapter 10). Note also that German fronted Wh questions pattern with French fronted Wh in neither allowing infinitives nor null subjects and that early German constituent questions without a Wh-element pattern with French in-situ: they allow null subjects to 18% but no infinitives (see Clahsen, Kursawe and Penke 1996). These data are summed up in table 50.

Table 50: Occurrence of infinitives and null subjects in specific question types

	French			German		
	fronted Wh	Wh-in-situ	Yes-no	fronted Wh	no Wh	yes-no
RI	-	-	-	-	-	-
NS	-	+	+	-	+	+
		22%	32%		18%	20%

In the current line of argumentation I suggest that the operator marking scope and question force in yes-no questions is an unmarked operator, different in feature content from the genuine Wh-operator and can probably be assimilated to the Wh-in-situ operator.

3. TOWARDS A SOLUTION

3.1. The By-passing Mechanism

Haegeman (1997) assumes that child null subjects are the same as diary null subjects, which she analyses as a null constant licensed by an anaphoric operator or by its occurrence in the topmost sentence position. So (18) should be ruled out by the ECP.

(18)   avant   nc veux   chocolat   Nath. 2.2
       before   want   chocolat

In order for the empty category to escape the ECP, by-pass the adjunct, and arrive in top-most position, Haegeman (1997) makes the following assumptions: The top-most projection of a Split CP is truncated; topic adjuncts are not adjoined, but have their own projections; Agr- projections can be generated above projections with a contentful functional head. It is the Agr-projection above the topic projection that serves as escape hatch for the empty category.

3.2. The Ingredients

Let us assemble these ingredients. As has also been discussed in chapter 7, Rizzi (1997) has argued that the Comp System serves as an interface between the propositional content and the superordinate structure, which leads to a split into a ForceP and a FinP. As topic-comment relations have to be sandwiched in between, we arrive at a system as outlined in (19).

(19)   Force > Topic > Focus > Topic > Finite > IP.

From the existence of argument/non-argument asymmetries with respect to subject extractions, Culicover (1991) and Rizzi (1997) have argued for independent topic projections. If one assumes that preposed adverbs are adjoined to TopP, whereas arguments occupy SpecTopP, and that every contentful functional head activates its own dominating agreement projection, then (18) can be modeled on subject extractions across adjuncts. For more details, I refer the reader to Rizzi (1997), Haegeman (1997, 2000), and Hamann (2000a).

3.3. Child and Diary Null Subjects

The analysis of (18) is given in (20): the Force projection is truncated, an agreement phrase dominating the topic phrase is available, and the empty category can move to the specifier of this AgrP. It thus escapes the c-commanding adverb; moreover, the empty category is licensed because it can check the agreement features of the topic head which have not yet been checked. As there is truncation of the ForceP, the top-most layer is missing, and the empty category is now again in a licit position.

(18)   Avant nc veut chocolat

(20)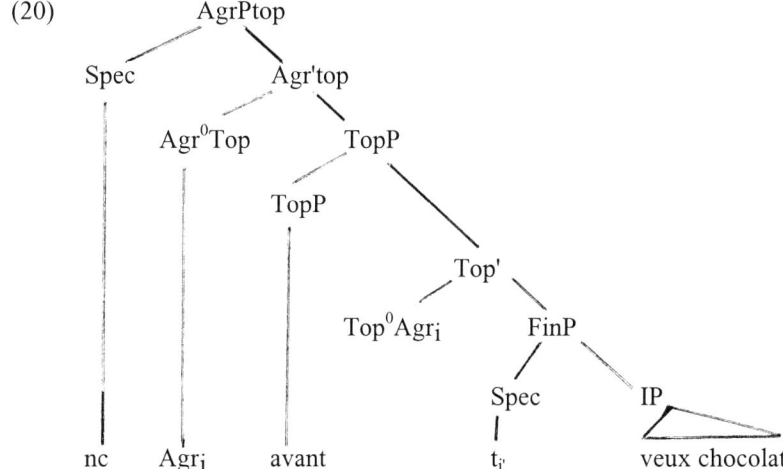

3.4. Null Subjects and WH

3.4.1. Fronted Wh

It is now clear how the Wh-problem will be solved. Fronted Wh will be treated in parallel to the argument case where subjects cannot be extracted; Wh-in-situ will be treated like the adjunct case. For fronted Wh, the question constituent is assumed to occupy the specifier of the FocusP in the Split CP system. It is here that the Wh-Criterion is satisfied or the interrogative feature is checked, i.e. the Wh-constituent occupies SpecFocP and checks its Wh-features against the Wh-features present in the Foc head. This exhausts the agreement option, and no by-passing is possible in fronted Wh as shown in (21). For an account of how feature checking is possible or how the Wh-criterion can be satisfied in French non-inverted questions, I refer to the idea of dynamic agreement as developed in Rizzi (1991).

(21)

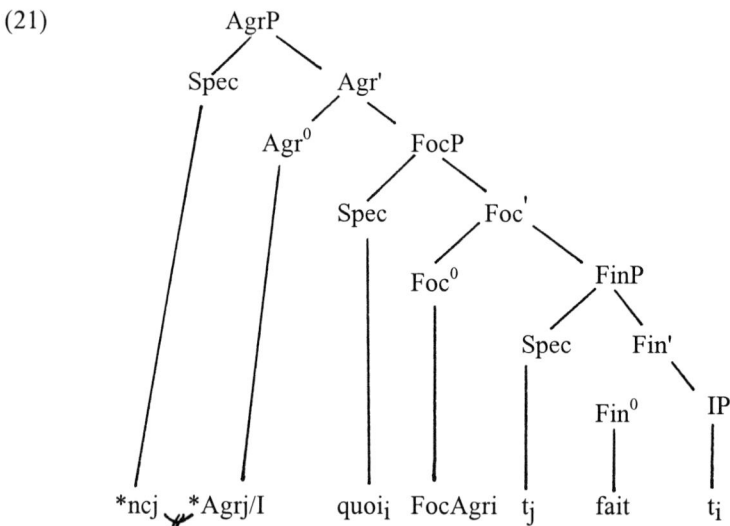

3.5.2. Wh-in-situ Questions

In parallel to (21), I suggest the analysis (22b) for (22a). Crucially, in SpecFocP there is no silent Wh-operator that has to check the interrogative feature and must also check its other features (+/-human, case etc.). The operator binding a choice function is different from the usual interrogative operator binding an individual variable, though both are ultimately represented as the existential operator. The point is that overt movement of the Wh-pronoun moves the whole lexeme, which includes the N-restriction in the usual analysis of indefinites. The choice function analysis leaves the N-restriction in place, and no feature checking motivated by the features of the restriction has to take place. In an approach using the Wh-Criterion, this operator would not even have to check for the Wh-feature, as the criterion does not apply to Wh-words in argument position. (For convenience and readability, I only indicate the presence of the choice function by the index f on the question word and then bind it by the operator Q_f. See Hamann 2000a or Hamann in press for details).

(22) a. fais quoi?   Marie 2;3,3
do what
'what do I/you do ?'

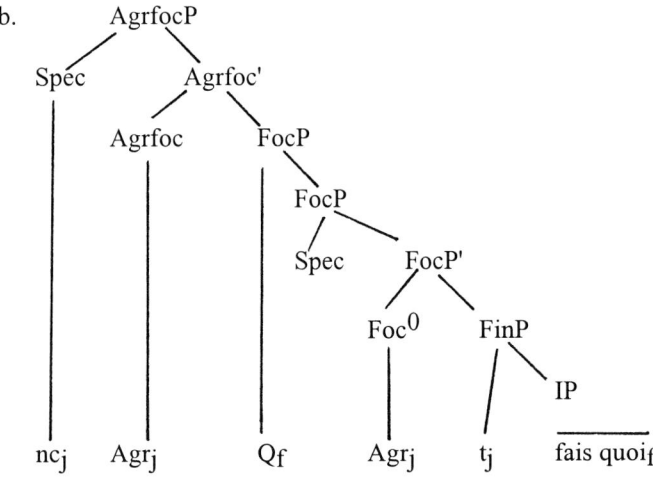

4. SUMMARY

In this chapter I have investigated early constituent questions in several languages. The focus was on the occurrence of child infinitives and null subjects especially in fronted Wh-questions. The basic finding is that though in English questions infinitives may occur, there is clear evidence that these are rare in constituent questions in German, Danish, and French. We attribute this finding to the peculiarities of English inflection and the fact that the other three languages under investigation all distinguish the infinitive morphologically from the stem. The findings for German, Danish and French are compatible with a truncation type analysis, whereas ATOM has no easy explanation for these results.

Another basic finding is that null subjects do not occur (or occur only rarely) in fronted Wh in German, Danish, and French. If we investigate only finite fronted Wh questions, this holds even for English. It is this finding in particular that makes an ATOM approach to null subjects very unlikely, even with the modifications suggested for the analysis of early verbal morphology in French and Danish. Recall that this modification implies that finite forms are in fact disguised non-finite forms so that there is nothing in this approach which could constrain the occurrence of null subjects on finite verbal forms in constituent questions.

From the investigation of French, another central fact emerges. Contrary to some earlier results (Crisma 1992), we find two different routes to the full acquisition of Wh-questions in French: a) fronted Wh or b) Wh-in-situ (see also Roeper and Weissenborn 1990, Plunkett 1999, and Zuckermann and Hulk 2000). Moreover we find that Wh-in-situ is 'in between' declaratives and fronted Wh in not allowing root infinitives, but allowing null subjects. This property is found also in Yes-No questions in French and German as well as in early German constituent questions without Wh-elements.

This finding is unproblematic for truncation in its simple form where it is assumed that only morphological material activates a projection. In this model, Wh-in-situ and early German Wh-questions without a Wh-element can be analyzed as truncated structures. This assumption would also predict infinitives in these structures, however, and these do not occur. It was therefore argued that covert interpretative material, especially scope marking constituents, activate a projection and Wh-in-situ does not represent a truncated structure for the child. This left the problem of the occurrence of null subjects in these structures.

To explain why WH-in-situ occurs with null subjects, but fronted WH never does, the following ingredients were needed. First, a movement analysis for both types of questions had to be excluded. Instead quantification over a choice function was employed for Wh-in-situ. Second, it had to be assumed that preposed topics and focus constituents are not simply IP adjoined but create full projections with substantial heads. Third, substantial functional heads carry agreement and project a dominating Agreement Phrase. Fourth, adverbial topics and the existential quantifier (without any N-restriction) do not exhaust the agreement features in the respective head so that the features are free to be checked in the dominating AgrFP. Last, ForceP must be truncated so that there is no higher position from which the empty category could be c-commanded.

In this sense, the analysis of null subjects in Wh-in-situ still depends on truncation. Note further that the by-passing mechanism is not an ad-hoc invention for Wh-in-situ constructions. It is modeled on subject extractions across adjuncts and may be operative for null subjects in a limited number of other constructions as for preposed adverbials and auxiliaries. Note also that only ForceP is truncated, so root infinitives are not expected in either type of Wh-question.

CHAPTER 10

OTHER AREAS OF INVESTIGATION: NEGATION AND LATE ARGUMENT DROP

1. INTRODUCTION

From the investigation of infinitives and null subjects in Wh-questions and from the results presented in Chapter 8, it emerges that the truncation approach as well as the ATOM approach must assume two kinds of null subjects in order to explain the fullness of the data. Rizzi (2000) considers the child null subject occurring in the specifier of the root as the primary source of the null subject phenomenon in child language but admits the occurrence of PRO null subjects in infinitival structures because these are always licensed by UG. The first assumption explains the results of the previous chapter and the occurrence of null subjects in finite and non-finite environments, the latter explains the higher rate of null subjects in infinitival structures. The ATOM approach has always suggested that in addition to the PRO null subject licensed by [–TNS] infinitives, null subjects occurring in finite structures may be topic-drop (see Bromberg and Wexler 1995). This conjecture was motivated precisely by the observation that null subjects do practically not occur in finite Wh-questions in English. It was the correlation of the developmental curve of infinitives and null subjects in finite structures as shown for Danish by Hamann and Plunkett (1997, 1998) that made a topic-drop approach to finite null subjects unlikely. However, only a topic-drop approach can take care of the data distribution in Wh-questions in languages like Danish, German and French. So in the ATOM approach, it is assumed that topic-drop still plays a role – even if (in this approach) the bulk of finite null subjects in Danish is explained by their 'disguised' non-finite nature.[1] However, if we admit topic-drop as a possibility for an initial finite null subject (especially in topic-drop languages like German), there remains the rarity of infinitives in Wh-questions which needs another, unrelated explanation.

In view of these problems it is interesting to discuss two areas which may confirm or disconfirm the findings on Wh and the idea that several factors may intervene in the phenomenon of finite null subjects. These areas are negation and the occurrence of late argument drop in German child language. The first was discussed in detail in Hamann (1996a and 2000b), the latter has been given some scope in Hamann (1992, 1994, 1995, and 1996b). Because details of analysis and implications on linguistic theory have been given in these articles, I will be brief on both subjects in this chapter though some theory is necessary to evaluate the data.

2. NEGATION AND INFINITIVES

2.1. The NegP and the Neg-Criterion

Based on Pollock (1989), Zanuttini (1997) and Haegeman (1995a) it has generally been accepted that the clause structure contains a functional projection NegP. In French this functional projection is headed by *ne* where *ne* has to co-occur with another negative constituent:

(1) a.   Jean ne viendra *(pas).
         Jean ne come(fut) not
         'John does not come'
    b.   Jean ne viendra *(jamais).
         J.ean ne come (fut) (n)ever
         'Jean does never come'
    c.   Jean ne parlera *(a personne).
         Jean ne speak(fut) to anybody
         'Jean does not speak to anybody'

For French it has been observed that there is a dependency relation between the negative head and negative constituents. First, the head requires the presence of another negative XP (see (1a,b,c)), and second, there are ECP effects as in (2a,b).

(2) a. Je n'exige que tu voies personne
        I ne insist that you see nobody
        'I insist that you do not see anybody'
    b. Je n'exige que personne vienne (*personne* has narrow sope)
        I ne insist that nobody come
        'I insist that nobody come'

In (2b) the negative element *ne* has moved to the higher clause, but its trace in the lower clause must be licensed by the presence of *personne* so that only a narrow scope reading is possible.

In parallel to Wh-questions (see Rizzi 1991), this dependency has been explained by a well formedness condition at LF (see Haegeman and Zanuttini 1991 and Haegeman 1995a). This well formedness condition which determines the distribution of negative elements is formulated as the Neg-Criterion.

(3) **Neg-Criterion**
     i. A NEG-Operator must be in a Spec-head configuration with an X^0 [NEG].
     ii. An X^0 [NEG] must be in a spec-head configuration with a NEG-operator.

For the purposes of this chapter, we will assume that in parallel to French *pas*, German *nicht* is a specifier in adult and child language and occupies the specifier position of the NegP. See Hamann (2000b) for the discussion of different assumptions as to the status of *nicht* in adult and child language.

2.2. Truncated Structures

Given the presence of a NegP in the clause and the fact that NegP selects TP, the truncation approach predicts that negation, similar to fronted Wh-questions, should not occur with infinitives at all. The presence of negation, i.e. morphological material in the NegP implies the activation of this and of all lower projections.

With a tree as in (4) assumed universal by Belletti (1990), it then follows that as soon as a projection higher than TP is involved, the tense morpheme necessarily has to be bound, so infinitives cannot occur.

(4)
```
CP
 \
  AgrsP
   \
    NegP
     \
      TP
       \
        AgroP
         \
          VP
```

Though the order of projections presented in (4) applies to Romance languages and to French in particular, it has been suggested that the position of the NegP is subject to parameterization. For German and other V2-languages, it has been argued that the NegP is below TP (see Grewendorf 1990, Haegeman 1991 and 1995a). This, together with the fact that German has an imperative or admonition use of negative infinitives, predicts that infinitives can occur in negative constructions in child language. The child will hear *nicht weinen, nicht anfassen, nicht hinauslehnen, nicht loslassen, nicht springen* etc. a hundred times a day and will certainly imitate this construction and probably overgeneralize it to other uses. There is also the possibility that the occurrence of these forms and of frequent constituent negations in German leads the child to analyze the negative particle as an adverb (see Hoekstra and Jordens 1994 for Dutch). This would also admit the use of infinitives with negation.

With a clause structure as given in (4) for French, there should not be infinitives in negative child structures, whereas we expect German children to produce a certain amount of infinitives in negative environments. The data confirm this prediction as will be briefly demonstrate with material from Hamann (1996a and 2000b).

2.3. Negation and Non-finite Utterances in French

Beginning with the data from French as discussed in the literature and shown in tables 51 and 52, we are faced with rather high numbers of infinitives in negation.

Table 51: The distribution of non-finite structures in verbal utterances in French
(from Pierce 1989)

all verbal utterances			negative verbal utterances		
total	-Fin	+Fin	total	-Fin	+Fin
2035	694(33,8%)	1359	275	79(28,7%)	196

all verbal utterances			negative verbal utterances		
- 50 cases of negative infinitives in Nathalie's first file:					
total	-Fin	+Fin	total	-Fin	+Fin
2035	694(34,1%)	1359	225	29(12,9%)	196

(Nathalie 21-27, Philippe 25-30, Daniel 20-23 months)

The data of table 51 are taken from Pierce (1989). They include infinitives and participles, and the same holds for the data in Table 52. At first glance, in the Pierce count the percentage of non-finite structures in negative utterances and in positive utterances seems to be of equal importance and is too high to be compatible with the truncation theory and the NegP-above-TP order as normally assumed for French. There are a number of problems, however, with the counting procedure, especially with regard to the first file of Nathalie, and it has been concluded that this file should be discarded for the purpose of these counts (see Rizzi 1994 and Hamann 2000b). We are left with 29 cases, or 12,9% of non-finite structures in negative verbal utterances as the lower part of table 51 shows.

The same magnitude of percentage for non-finite negative structures, namely 16,1%, was found across 6 French children ranging in age from 1;8 - 3;3 by Verrips and Weissenborn (1989). Unfortunately, no figures for the use of positive infinitives are included, so that there is no way of telling how many optional infinitives are used in all. Still, this figure seems to argue against Rizzi's truncation theory, as there is little doubt about the high position of NegP in French.

290   CHAPTER 10

Table 52: The distribution of <u>non-finite</u> structures in verbal utterances in French
(from Verrips and Weissenborn 1989)

all verbal utterances			negative verbal utterances		
total	-Fin	+Fin	total	-Fin	+Fin
-	-	-	984	158(16,1%)	826(83,9%)

Fabienne 1;8-3;3 (equal spacing of files),
Loic 2;5-2;11(equal spacing of files)
Benjamin 2;0 -2;9 (heavy concentration of files at 2;3-2;6-2;7)
Philippe 2;1-2;8 (equal spacing)
Florence 2;2-2;10 (concentration at 2;6 and 2;7)
Romain 2;4-3;0 (concentration at 2;10)

There is one problem, however, which makes these figures, though indicative for verb movement and the use of non-finite structures, not at all conclusive for the predictions of truncation. Both, Pierce (1989) and Verrips and Weissenborn (1989), include participles in their count, which makes perfect sense for their purpose. It is not useful for ours in so far as participles and infinitives occupy different positions in the tree and are differently specified with respect to aspect or even tense. This has consequences for their interplay with the tense projection. According to Zeller (1994) and his syntactic treatment of tense, the participle is itself a tense head. This assumption is quite natural if we consider that in many languages participles come as present and past participles. In any case, the assumption implies that if the auxiliary of a compound tense is missing, the participle activates its own tense projection. It follows that bare participles should not always be counted with the infinitives: they may not be carrying agreement, but they may be carrying tense. With respect to the counting of participles, the many problems and ambiguities from the point of view of linguistic theory and especially from the point of view of interpretation, lead Friedemann (1992) to decide in the opposite way from Pierce (1992) and Levow (1995): he does not include participles and considers only infinitives. This decision was adhered to in the counts on Augustin especially in view of the considerations about compound tenses mentioned above. The count of Friedemann (1992) presented here in tables 53a and 53b, shows that without bare participles, the cases of negation with 'untensed' forms practically vanish: Friedemann's figures indeed point to the correctness of economy driven truncation approaches.

Table 53a: The distribution of non-finite structures in verbal utterances in French
(Friedemann 1992)

all verbal utterances			negative verbal utterances		
total	-Fin	+Fin	total	-Fin	+Fin
?	?	?	137	16(11,7%)	121

Table 53b: Distribution of infinitives in verbal utterances

	negative verbal utterances		
	total	Inf	+Fin
	127	6 (4,7%)	121

(Philippe 2;1-2;3, Gregoire 1;11-2;3 – bare participles are not included)

We now find only a very low number of infinitives in negative structures, which is reminiscent of the data on Wh and corroborates the truncation approach. The Augustin corpus confirms these findings as emerges from table 54. (Tables giving the numbers for each recording are provided in Hamann 2000b). Clearly, Augustin does not use infinitives with negation.

Table 54: Distribution of infinitives in verbal utterances in French
(from Hamann 2000b)

	all verbal utterances			negative verbal utterances		
File	Total	Fin	Inf	Total	Fin	Inf
01-07	373	295	78	17	16	1
		79.1%	20.9%		94.1%	5.9%
08-10	391	367	24	47	47	0
		93.9%	6.1%		100%	
Total	764	662	102	64	63	1
		86.6%	13.4%		98.4%	1.6%

(Augustin 2;0-2;4 and Augustin 2;6-2;10)

2.4. Negation and Non-finite Utterances in V2-languages

The expectations for German, which has a low NegP, is that we find a substantial percentage of negative infinitives. Let us again start with a check on the data as known from the literature. Tables 55 and 56 present data from Tracy (1991) and Verrips and Weissenborn (1989).

Table 55: Distribution of infinitives in negated verbal utterances in German
(from Tracy 1991)

	total	Infinitive	Finite
Julia 2;1-2;6	10	1	9
Stephanie 1;8-2;2,2	27	7(25%)	20(75%)

Table 56: Distribution of non-finite structures in negated verbal utterances in German
(from Verrips and Weissenborn 1989)

child/ages	total	Non-finite	Finite	files
Lukas (1;10-2;1)	34	5(14,7%)	29(85,3%)	(8 files, 5 from 2;1)
Simone (1;10-2;2)	185	15(8,1%)	170(91,9%)	(19 files)
Bo, files 9-18 (2;1-2;6)	123	7(5,7%)	116(94,3%)	(10 files, 3 at 2;2., 3 at 2;3)
Benjamin (1;9-3;0)	16	3(18,7%)	13(81,3%)	(9 files spaced a month, 2;5 missing)

As in some of the children the phenomenon of infinitives in negative utterances manifests itself at more than 10%, it certainly has to be dealt with. However, the data as drawn from the literature are not conclusive, as they do not allow a comparison with the use of infinitives in positive utterances at the same time. Thus it might well be the case that the low figure for Simone and Bo is simply the result of the fact that the children have passed out of the optional infinitive stage at some point of data taking. Moreover, just as for French, the count of Verrips and Weissenborn (1989) for German includes participles, so that the percentages are not conclusive for the problem at hand.

Three German corpora from the Childes Data base have been checked carefully for negative infinitives and positive infinitives. One subject is Katrin (1;5), whose data were collected by Wagner. The second is Julia (1;11-2;5), collected by Clahsen. The third is Andreas (again collected by Wagner) for whom it has been established by Poeppel and Wexler (1993) that he is definitely in the optional infinitive stage.

Table 56 shows that Katrin uses 42% infinitives in her positive verbal utterances, but not one single negative infinitive, and Julia (1;11-2;3) uses infinitives to 52% in her positive verbal utterances, and to 20% in her negative verbal utterances. So far we would have to say that infinitives are much rarer in negation than in positive utterances, and that the analysis of only 12 cases of verbal negation for Katrin and only 25 cases for Julia cannot be statistically convincing. Andreas (2;1), however, provides us with 56 cases of verbal negation, and shows an equal distribution of infinitives in positive and negative utterances (about 25% in both). On the face of the data, we seem to get some individual variation as was observed for French by Levow (1995), but also an indication that negative infinitives are quite common in German child language. Let us keep in mind that these analyses are based on the same counting method as for Augustin, considering only infinitives not participles. So table 57 for German reveals a marked difference to French.

Though the data from Katrin and Julia are not conclusive, the cases of negative root infinitives in Andreas lead to the assumption, that here is a phenomenon to be accounted for. The same seems to emerge for Julia at the ages of 2;4 and 2;5 (see Hamann 2000b for a file by file analyses). Thus, either the German NegP is lower than TP, or German children treat *nicht* as an adverb, or both.

Table 57: Distribution of infinitives in verbal utterances in German
(from Hamann 2000)

	Katrin 1;5			Andreas 2;1		
	total	Inf	+Fin	total	Inf	+Fin
all verbal utts	415	167 40%	248 60%	785	218 28%	567 72%
pos verbal utts	403	167 42%	236 58%	729	204 28%	525 72%
neg verbal utts	12	0	12	56	14 25%	42 75%
	Julia 1;11-2;5					
all verbal utt	193	93 48,2%	100 51,8%			
pos verbal utt	170	88 51,8%	82 48,2%			
neg verbal utt	25	5 20%	20 80%			

Data from Schaner-Wolles (1994) as shown in table 58 of two children speaking Austrian German corroborate the conclusion. Her data on negation are fully compatible with those in table 57 because participles were not counted. In her data, however, infinitives in negation occur to a much higher percentage than in the overall distribution of verbal utterances. This might be due to the fact that the figures for the occurrence of infinitives in all utterances are drawn from her tables on verb placement and thus do not include two-word verb-final utterances which are ambiguous as to a V2 or V-final position.

Table 58: Distribution of infinitives in verbal utterances in Austrian German
(from Schaner-Wolles 1994)

	Nico 2;2-2;9			Hannes 2;4-2;6		
	total	Inf	+Fin	total	Inf	+Fin
all utt	849	96 11,3%	753 88,7%	151	37 24,5%	114 75,5%
neg utt	146	34 23,3%	112 76,7%	23	10 43,5%	13 56,5%

Therefore, on the evidence of these German data, we seem to be safe in concluding that the German NegP, or even the Germanic NegP, is low or *nicht* is an adverb. Confirmation of this conclusion comes from Dutch data as analyzed by Haegeman (1996b) and shown in table 59. In the Hein corpus, Haegeman counts 635 cases of negative verbal utterances in all, of which 38 are in the infinitive. Under modification of her calculation in order to adapt the figures to the format of the above tables, we find that 6% of verbal negative utterances in the Hein corpus occur in the infinitive. This, though admittedly a lower number than the one for German, is nonetheless taken by Haegeman to strengthen her other convincing arguments for a low NegP. This is corroborated by the fact that in the first phase, where infinitives are used in about 20% of all utterances, the percentage of negative infinitives is 9,3%. For a more detailed data analysis see Haegeman (1996b).

Table 46: Distribution of infinitives in verbal utterances in Dutch
(from Haegeman 1996b)

Hein 2;4-2;8	total	Inf	+Fin
all utt.	2326	484	1842
positive utt.	2008	455 22,6%	1553 77,4%
negative utt.	318	29 9,3%	289 90,7%

Given that the position of the NegP is parameterized differently in French and in the Germanic V2 languages, it can be concluded that the cross-linguistic data of children's negative utterances are compatible with those found for Wh-questions. Whenever the presence of material in a higher projection prohibits the truncation of the TP, infinitives do occur only rarely. With respect to negation there is not only the parameterization of the position of the NegP to complicate the picture, but an adverb analysis of the negative particle cannot be excluded and appears to be likely in some cases. So considerable individual variation is to be expected (see Lewov 1995).

3. LATE ARGUMENT DROP

3.1. More Than One Type of Null Subject

We have discussed the early child null subject and its relation to the occurrence of root infinitives. The observation that finite null subjects typically occur in the specifier of the root (as shown by the data on Wh-questions and on negation) is not only exploited by the truncation approach, but also by Bromberg and Wexler (1995), who suggest that finite null subjects are topic-drop. For languages that have adult topic-drop, both these approaches predict that the child null subject will have a natural continuation in the adult construction. So the expectation for German (and Dutch) is that the percentages of use may level off to the percentage of adult subject drop, but that a (finite) null subject, whether an early child null subject, a late child null subject or an adult null subject, always conforms to the structural constraint of occurring in initial position.

This is not the case, however, as was first pointed out in Hamann (1992) where I discussed the occurrence of post-verbal null subjects in the speech of two German 3-year olds. Subsequent research (Duffield 1993, Hamann 1994, 1995, 1996b, Bol 1996, Haegeman 1995b and Haegeman 1996c,d) showed that the phenomenon indeed exists in German in a certain late period of development, but that it may also exists in Dutch and French. In these languages the phenomenon was observed even in the early phase, but to a lower degree than in German. Especially Hamann (1996b) used this observation as well as the completely different behavior of object-drop at the same time to argue against a general topic-drop analysis of child null subjects as proposed by de Haan and Tuijnman (1988). I argued that there are two null subject constructions in the target grammar and that the German agreement paradigm has certain properties that can mislead for a time.

Following Hamann (1996b) very closely, the essential arguments are the following. First, object-drop does not parallel subject-drop in German child language. Additionally, children use post-verbal referential empty subjects in declaratives in this phase, a construction that is not admitted under topic-drop. Last, post-verbal empty subjects and initial empty subjects finally drop under a 5% level while the figures for object-drop remain more or less constant. Thus the intuition about a relationship of subject-drop and the development of the inflectional system cannot be ignored even for topic-drop languages like German.

In any case, the problem of empty subjects is more complicated for German than it has so far appeared. Adult German does not only have the possibility of topic-drop but also has an empty expletive in subordinate clauses. So the child has to acquire both these structures and licensing mechanisms and the phase of late empty subjects can be seen as an interface between the early phase and the target. An analysis is proposed which allows more than one strategy in this phase: while there is the child null subject and adult topic-drop, there is also a competing strategy of licensing null subjects in government configurations. The latter is necessary for licensing empty expletives in any case, but is extended by the child to license post-verbal referential subjects. This is possible within the bounds of UG because German inflection is not rich in the Italian sense but rich enough in the sense defined by Roberts (1992) or Rohrbacher (1994) and discussed by Hamann (1996b). The strategy is abandoned when the child realizes that the incorporation of agreement features does not change the German Comp-head, which provides the V2 position, into an agreement head. This realization is triggered when the Comp-system has become obligatory and the child encounters expletive subjects in the specifier of the relevant Comp-projection.

Thus the properties of this phase indeed depend partly on the properties of the agreement system. For that reason it was predicted that the phenomenon of post-verbal subjects can only be observed after the manifestation of agreement. For German, this prediction has been borne out by the data discussed in Duffield (1993) so that the analysis gains in substance.

Before we enter into a discussion of the data, we need some facts about German. Chapter 7 already introduced the basic facts about German grammar, but we need to add some details.

3.2. More German Grammar

When we examine the German agreement paradigm, we observe that German is not morphologically uniform as discussed already in chapter 6. The agreement paradigm for the verb *gehen* 'walk' is shown in (5).

(5)
	Sg.	Pl.
1st	geh (e)	gehen
2nd	gehst	geht
3rd	geht	gehen

with the infinitive *gehen* and the imperative *geh*.

On the basis of the occurrence of a stem-form in the imperative and also in the first person singular in colloquial language, German is morphologically mixed. So one could adopt Clahsen's (1991) argumentation for null subjects in German child language: The German child first analyses agreement as rich and uniform, once the child grasps the mixed nature of the agreement system, s/he stops licensing referential null subjects. However, s/he then could never learn to license expletive null subjects because morphologically mixed languages do not allow empty subjects of any sort (Jaeggli and Safir 1989).

Since German is not morphologically uniform, the occurrence of expletive *pro* in (6a,b) needs a different explanation. In the spirit of Rizzi (1986a), where languages are parameterized with respect to which head can license *pro*, Tomaselli (1990) postulates that C^0 is such a licensing head in German. I discuss older work here, so I use the C^0-locution, but the reader will have to keep in mind that we are actually talking about Fin^0 as introduced in chapter 7 for the V2-position.

(6) a. Mir   wurde *pro* geholfen
        me(dat) was   helped
        'I was helped'
    b. ...daß *pro* getanzt wurde.
        ...that   danced was
        'that there was dancing'
    c. Es/ * pro wurde t getanzt
        it   was   danced
        'there was dancing'

As there are no number/person features in C^0, only expletive *pro* can survive. This argument carries over to FinP if Fin^0 contains only a V-feature or only a tense feature, but no agreement features. An argument in favor of licensing *pro* only in government configurations is (6c). An expletive *pro* should be possible in (6c) if licensing took place under spec-head agreement. So, following Tomaselli (1990) and using old terminology, we formulate (7).

(7)   In German, C^0 licenses *pro* under government.

Exploiting the diachronic facts of Old French and following Roberts (1992) closely, I further argued in Hamann (1996b) that even fairly rich verbal morphology can license referential null subjects under government. The assumption is that government is a more direct relation than spec-head agreement and thus even an impoverished, but still fairly rich agreement system can transfer its features under government. In the case of licensing under agreement, Agr^0 must be functionally rich in order to allow feature transfer and thus recovery.

Clearly, we must distinguish two kinds of "richness" of Agr^0. One has been called "formal morphological uniformity" for which it suffices that there is a slot provided for inflection, i.e. an ending for each person though not all have to be different and some might be empty. This would also be the case of modern German. We will call such an inflectional system fairly rich. "Functional richness", on the other hand, leads to the marking of Agr^0 as [+pronominal] and requires that at least 5 of the 6 endings are different as in Italian. We will call this a rich inflectional system. The idea of formal richness clearly needs refinement and details are given in Roberts (1992). Rohrbacher (1994) also introduces a distinction among the morphologically mixed languages, grouping fairly rich inflectional systems on one side and poor systems on the other. He does not set the criterion with the plural as Roberts does, but with the existence of distinct endings for the 2nd person singular and the first person plural.

If we apply these notions to German, we conclude in the first place that German has a formally uniform or fairly rich inflection. In the second place, we get our argument that it must indeed be a complementizer head, not Agr^0 which licenses expletive *pro* in the above examples. If the licensing head were Agr^0 (incorporated to C^0 or Fin^0), referential null subjects should be identified under government. This means that in "XP V S" structures, we should expect that the post-verbal subject may be referential *pro*. As post-verbal null subjects do not occur in adult language, it must be C^0/Fin^0 which is the licensing head.

This more complicated notion of morphological richness has a direct impact on acquisition in that the German child cannot discover straightaway that Agr^0 is not rich enough to license a referential null subject. German Agr^0 is fairly rich and content recovery should be possible given licensing under government. If children use this option of licensing, the prediction is that they will have referential null subjects in post-verbal position. Unless there is a misclassification of the agreement paradigm, they should not license referential null subjects in preverbal position because German Agr^0 is only fairly rich, not pronominal, and cannot identify *pro* under spec-head agreement. The normal child null subjects thus cannot be explained by this mechanism. Post-verbal null subjects are predicted, however, and should disappear when the child discovers that even if the agreement features have risen to C^0/Fin^0, the licenser is not the incorporated head Agr^0 but the host.

3.3. Ambiguous Input and Null Subjects in German Child Language

In the light of the above discussion, German subject topic-drop is highly ambiguous input because it suggests licensing under spec-head agreement and identification by Agr^0, just as in Italian. This would lead the child to assume a functionally rich agreement for German with the consequence of null subjects in subordinate clauses, which are perfectly possible in Italian, but ungrammatical in German. If children misclassify in this way, they will have null subjects in subordinate clauses.

To complicate matters, the second person singular pronoun can be dropped from other positions than the specifier of the root as (8) shows. This may lead the child to favor the Italian type analysis and disfavor the topic-drop possibility before the nature of the constraint is discovered.

(8) a. Was hast ec gekauft?
what have (2) bought
'what have (you) bought'
b. Hast ec das gekauft?
have (2) that bought
'have (you) bought that'
c. (?)Ich weiß, daß ec das gekauft hast.
I know that that bought have (2)
'I know that (you) have bought that'

d. Gestern hast ec   das gekauft.
    yesterday have (2) that bought
    'yesterday, (you) have bought that

The discussion of the diverse German null subject phenomena, will have shown that it is not easy for the child to determine what counts as evidence for the relevant parameter - and it is by no means evident what this parameter must encompass. In any case, the child seems to be faced with data that allow more than one analysis. So it is not surprising that the process of distinguishing topic-drop from the licensing of expletive *pro* and the relegation of the second-person phenomena to the periphery or a different register of language cannot be achieved by the recognition of one specific trigger. This complexity also explains the diverse findings and analyses proposed for null subjects in child German and it might be reason enough for the lingering of the phenomenon.

It has also emerged that apart from the child null subject at an early phase, there may be an agreement driven phenomenon in child German which interferes with the topic-drop strategy of adult German. For this reason, 2 children who were no longer in the root infinitive phase were studied as to the properties of their null subjects in Hamann (1996b). The focus was on the positional properties of null subjects and on a comparison of object- and subject-drop, both of which are crucial for a topic-drop analysis.

3.4. Method

The two children investigated were Elisa and Christoph communicating with each other in weekly or fortnightly play-sessions. During the 3 months of the investigation, they produced 4956 utterances, not including repetitions or short answers like *ja, nein* etc. The children were observed for a period of three months, Elisa from age 3;1 to age 3;4 and Christoph from age 3;4 to age 3;7. The first six recordings show enough linguistic homogeneity to have been analyzed as one period. The same holds for recordings 9, 10 and 11. Recordings 7 and 8 are only one day apart and so have been analyzed together, but separated from the two other groups for control reasons. Recordings 11 and 12 are almost a month apart, so 12 has been analyzed separately. We obtain four periods as shown in table 60.

Table 60: Periods and ages of the two German children, Elisa and Christoph

	Elisa		Christoph	
period	age span	total of utterances	age span	total of utterances
P1	3;1,5-3;2,9	1185	3;3,28-3;5,2	522
P2	3;2,23-3;2,24	605	3;5,16	231
P3	3;2,29-3;3,20	1296	3;5,22-3;6,13	592
P4	3;4,13	507	3;7,6	81

Both children are fairly advanced in their development. They do not use optional infinitives any longer, have 86-99% correct agreement, use V2 consistently with finite verbs, have correct verb-placement with respect to negation, produce subordinate clauses with lexical complementizers, and also use past tense forms. For more details on the children and examples of typical productions see Hamann (1996b).

3.5. Results

The data confirm the margin of 10-20% null subjects many researchers have found for the age under discussion It is also quite clear from the data that objects are dropped quite frequently in this late phase. Thus at first glance there is corroboration of what Weverink (1989) and de Haan and Truijman (1988) found for Dutch, and Weissenborn (1990, 1991) claims for German: not only subjects, but also objects are dropped. Therefore an analysis of empty arguments as topic-drop seems plausible. A closer look at the overall data for empty subjects and empty objects shows, however, that things are not as simple as such an assumption suggests.

If topic-drop is the overall strategy, there are phenomena in child language which do not conform to adult topic-drop, as the examples of post-verbal empty subjects show. As it could be the case that children use topic-drop inappropriately or generalized, all occurrences of empty subjects and empty objects were counted for the first overview. This means that empty subjects were counted in preverbal, i.e. sentence initial position, but also post-verbally, in embedded clauses and in questions. Obligatory empty subjects were not counted, i.e. imperatives, imperative infinitives, and subject questions were not included. Immediate repetitions were not counted, but identical utterances separated by time and context were included in the count.

A similar procedure was used for empty objects. They were counted in the context of complement taking verbs in sentence initial position but also in in-situ constructions which cannot be adult-construed as intransitive. Whenever a verb had two readings, i.e. a transitive and an intransitive reading or could easily be constructed with an intransitive meaning, the missing object was not included in the count nor was the context counted as transitive. Obligatory contexts for empty objects were excluded from the count, specifically object questions and object relatives. As both children are out of the phase where they use infinitives as declaratives, the number of utterances against which the number of null-arguments was matched included only finite constructions.

Figures 17a and 17b show the development of null subjects in comparison to null objects in the periods P1, P2, P3, and P4. The vertical bars marking the data points represent the statistical error.

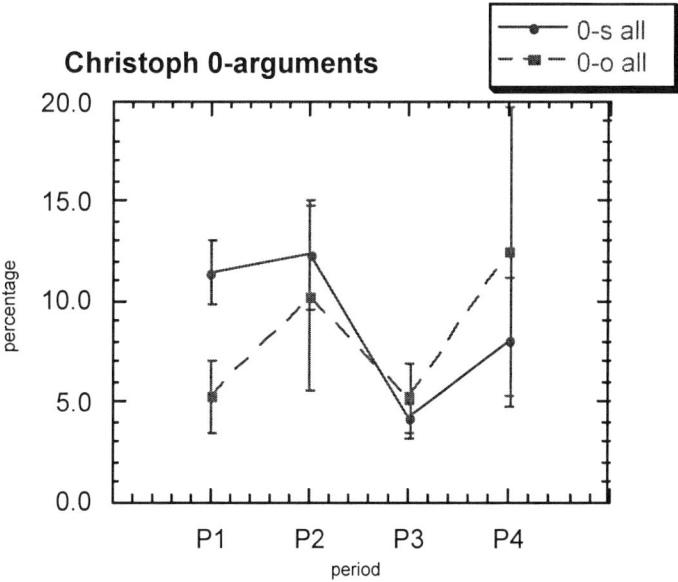

Figure 17a: Christoph's null arguments overall

It emerges that, over the whole period of obervation, German children drop objects to about the same percentage as subjects, showing a symmetry. If we compare this to the acquisition of general argument drop in Chinese, we note that according to Wang et al. (1992), Chinese children drop objects to about 22% and subjects about twice as much. Even if a comparison is difficult to make because the Chinese children investigated by Wang and colleagues are younger than the two German children, the fact remains that the picture is different. Moreover, we note a rather interesting phenomenon for the younger German child and to a certain degree even for the older one: Figures 17a and 17b show that the graphs cross each other, i.e. subject-drop starts out higher than object-drop but finally is lower than object-drop. Subject-drop even is a decreasing function in the whole interval of observation in figure 17b whereas object-drop is not.

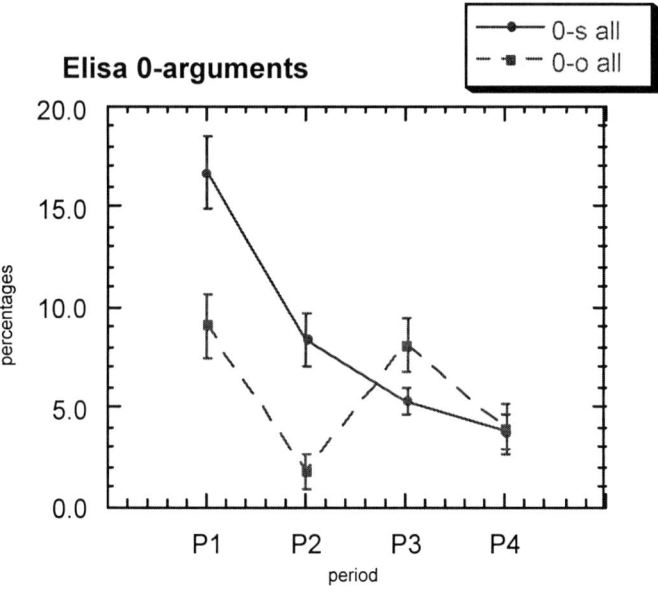

Figure 17b: Elisa's null arguments overall

Cases of post-verbal and embedded null subjects as well as in situ null objects had been included in this count on the assumption that they might be explained as generalized topic-drop along the Chinese lines. This cannot be born out, however by a close look at object-drop. Though there are cases of objects dropped in-situ, these are much rarer than objects dropped from sentence initial position. In Christoph's speech we find a range of 1.3-5% dropped objects from the in-situ position compared to a range of 28.5-50% object-drop from initial position. The same contrast is found for Elisa, who has 0.5-2.3% object-drop in-situ compared to 13-42% object-drop in initial position. We deduce that objects are indeed rarely dropped in situ, but quite frequently from topic position. Moreover, objects are not dropped from embedded clauses. Christoph drops neither subjects nor objects from his 103 embedded clauses with frequent transitive contexts. Elisa drops 13 subjects, but only one object from her 306 embedded clauses, where transitive contexts occur normally. Thus we have only one dropped object in overall 409 embedded clauses. The same holds for Wh-questions. From a total of 163 Wh-questions not one object is dropped, though transitive contexts occur at a normal rate. Therefore it can be claimed that the children do not follow a generalized topic-drop strategy.

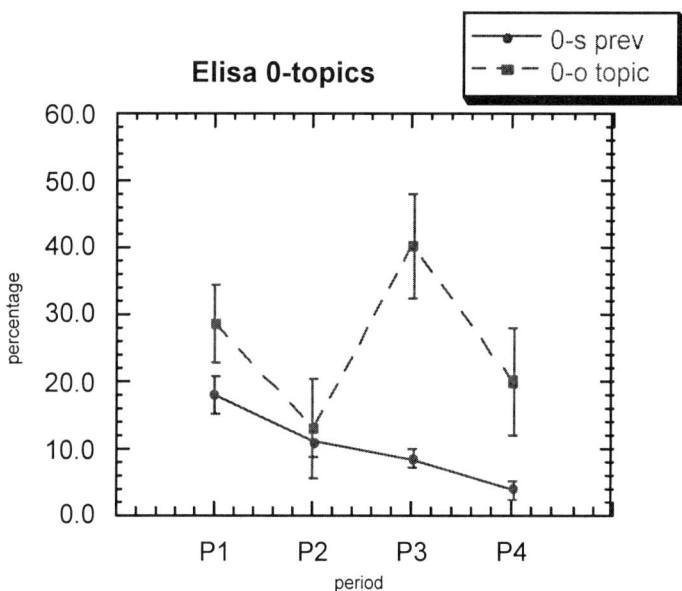

Figure 18: Elisa's null topics

In a next step, object-drop from initial position was taken as a sort of prototypical topic-drop and compared to subject drop in initial position. The aim was to see whether both show the same or a different development. It could be shown that especially for the younger child there is a clear difference.

Figure 18 shows a strong decrease from 18% to 4% in Elisa's null subject data, which is nowhere mirrored in the null object data. Given the statistical error for object drop, it can be argued that, contrary to subject drop, there is no development for this phenomenon. Therefore it can be concluded that Elisa's null subject development cannot be explained by assuming topic-drop as the only licensing mechanism. It also emerges that the acquisition of pragmatic principles could not be responsible for the decrease of subject-drop without equally influencing the use of object-drop. For more details and the data on Christoph see Hamann (1996b).

The remarkable observation made by Hamann (1992, 1994 and 1996b) was that both children use post-verbal null subjects as shown in the examples (9a-d). These are not restricted to the second person use allowed in adult grammar.

(9) a.   Das muß/1 ec zusammenbauen   Ch 3;4,5
         that must/1 put together
         'I must put that together'
   b.   Ganz viele hab/1 hier   E 3;1,12
         very many have here
         '(I) have quite a lot here'
   c.   Nachher kanns/2 weggehen   E 3;1,29
         afterwards can away go
         ' afterwards (you) can go away
   d.   Dann klingelt/3(expl)   E 3;1,12
         then rings
         'then (it) rings'

A further examination of the environments in which null subjects occur, revealed the percentages given in table 61 for the two children. For graphs on these phenomena see Hamann 1996b.

Table 61: Types of null-subjects in percentages of all null-subjects

null-subjects	Elisa	Christoph
preverbal	58,0%	82,9%
postverbal	17,0%	11,4%
yes-no qu	17,5%	5,7%
subord-cl	5,3%	0
Wh-qu	1,4%	0

Particularly the occurrence of post-verbal null subjects and of null subjects in yes-no-questions is predicted in an analysis allowing not only topic-drop but identification of post-verbal *pro* by fairly rich agreement in government configurations. In view of the previous analysis of Wh-questions given in chapter 9, it now remains a puzzling fact that null subjects (if licensed under government) are so rare in Wh-questions. Following Müller and Sternefeld (1993), Hamann (1996b) suggested that the children already have a split CP, that in a Wh-question the verb has therefore moved higher and, due to intervening structure, cannot license a null subject in Spec AgrSP. This explanation can be adapted to the more sophisticated Split CP discussed in chapter 7.

It was argued that there are two distinct licensing strategies at this age: adult topic-drop (perhaps some remnants of the child null subject) and licensing under agreement. As the use of null subjects continues to decrease, however, the children obviously grow out of this misanalysis of German agreement. What has to be learned is the fact that even with incorporated agreement features, German C^0/Fin^0 cannot identify referential null subjects.

How this may happen was shown with the help of data from Simone as discussed by Verrips and Weissenborn (1992) and Duffield (1993). Duffield (1993) shows that post-verbal empty subjects are practically not found up to a certain age, are then manifest to 15-23%, and vanish again. As it happens, the increase in the use of post-verbal empty subjects from 3.1 % in file 7 to 23.3% in file 8 occurs at exactly the same time at which Clahsen and Penke (1992) and Duffield (1993) fix the acquisition of agreement for Simone. It vanishes a month after the time for which they fix the acquisition of CP. The crucial fact for the story given in Hamann (1996b) is that Clahsen (1991) and also Duffield (1993) determine the acquisition of agreement with the help of the acquisition of the second person singular ending *-st*. Once *-st* is acquired, Clahsen (1991) argues, agreement is acquired. This means that the appearance of post-verbal empty subjects co-occurs with the manifestation of this ending in Simone's speech. Thus it is likely that it is this ending which is significant for the classification of the German agreement paradigm as fairly rich. This is compatible with Rohrbacher's (1994) analysis of fairly rich agreement and also ties in with a proposal of Hoekstra and Hyams (1996) concerning the division of agreement systems in systems marking only number and systems marking person and number. They quote the above results in connection with their idea that once the *-st* ending is acquired in German, the child treats the system as more Italian-like because now a person distinction is available.

But whatever triggers the appearance of post-verbal null subjects, it has to do with agreement. As to 'delearning', it was proposed in Hamann (1996b), that it is the occurrence of the expletive and of atonic pronouns in Spec CP/FinP main clauses but not in subordinates which finally tells the child that C^0 is not an agreement head. This is the more plausible as a temporal coincidence of the disappearance of post-verbal empty subjects and the acquisition of *es* can be documented in the data.

Another prerequisite for arriving at the right conclusion is the obligatoriness of CP (ForceP) in the sense that truncation is no longer possible. Only if this is the case, the child must necessarily conclude that sentence initial *es* or an unstressed inanimate pronoun is indeed occupying SpecFinP and not SpecAgrSP.

It can be stipulated that post-verbal null subjects are excluded when expletives and CP are present. So post-verbal null subjects will vanish in a German child's speech whenever both of these are acquired, and whichever is acquired last, will herald their disappearance. Duffield's (1993) results for Simone can be neatly explained with this stipulation: once CP is obligatory, the post-verbal empty subject phenomenon vanishes - provided there is evidence about the nature of the CP projection in the use of *es*. This seems to be the case. A look at Duffield's tables shows that between file 9 and file 10 the use of the pronoun *es* jumps from 5.8% to 34.5% and between file 11 and file 12 the use of empty post-verbal subjects drops from 15.8 % to 7.9%. Thus obligatoriness of CP (CP is acquired in file 10 by Duffield's criteria) and acquisition of *es* take place at about the same time for Simone, and there is an immediate subsequent drop in post-verbal empty subjects. A similar relation of the appearance of *es* and the disappearance of post-verbal null subjects was found for Elisa and Christoph as discussed in Hamann (1996b) with *es* appearing later than the CP. At the same time, these two children start to use atonic pronouns (*er sie, es*) more frequently whereas they preferred tonic pronouns (*der, die ,das*) before.

Summing up, the data from Christoph and Elisa and the data available in the literature show that German children pass through a phase of post-verbal empty subjects which is explained by the nature of the fairly rich agreement system and which ends with the full recognition of the properties of the German SpecCP position and the discovery of the distribution of lexical and empty expletives and of personal pronouns. Finally the child knows that German C^0/Fin^0 is a licenser but not an agreement head and stops identifying referential *pro* in government configurations.

Looking for confirmation of this analysis suggests an investigation of cross-linguistic data which was begun by Hamann (1996b) with respect to Dutch and French data available from the literature (Schaeffer 1990, Bol 1996, Haegeman 1996b,c). Dutch is very much like German because it has an inflectional system with three different endings and it also has the expletive null subject in subordinate clauses. An important difference between Dutch and German in the inflectional system is the fact that Dutch marks the second person singular like the third person. French does not have a second person singular ending either and behaves differently with respect to non-referential *pro*. The prediction therefore is that Dutch and French should not show the phenomenon of post-verbal null subjects. The Dutch and French data discussed in Hamann (1996b) indicate that post-verbal null subjects in these languages also exist, though at an earlier age and to a lesser degree. The data from Bol (1996) seem to confirm the idea that it is the second person inflectional ending which is crucial for the child to assume a fully rich agreement system for a time: German children encounter this ending and have a considerable percentage of post-verbal null subjects in a late phase, Dutch children do not encounter this evidence, do not have many post-verbal null subjects in the root infinitive phase and have no post-verbal subjects once out of this phase. The data from Haegeman (1996c, 2000) point to an approach where post-verbal null subjects in the root infinitive phase are possible cross-linguistically but depend on a different explanation and so are in fact a different phenomenon from the late post-verbal subjects discussed above.

Another test case for the involvement of fairly rich agreement and an initial misclassification are the Mainland Scandinavian languages, which, under classical analyses, do not show agreement and certainly do not have a second person marking. The prediction is therefore that (late) post-verbal null subjects should not occur. Unfortunately, declarative environments could not be investigated so far, whereas the rarity of null subjects in Wh-questions is shown in chapter 9. The available data thus do not disconfirm the hypothesis outlined above.

4. SUMMARY

The most important facts about the data on late empty arguments are that German three- year-olds show a quantitative and qualitative difference in object- and subject-drop. We find a steady decrease in subject-drop which is not found in object-drop, and we find the occurrence of post-verbal empty subjects which is not matched by the occurrence of in situ objects. We conclude that at this age topic-drop cannot explain finite null subjects. While empty objects are dropped topics throughout the period of observation, empty subjects are licensed by two strategies also needed in the adult grammar. They are partly dropped topics, partly referential *pro* identified in government configurations. The occurrence of expletives in the specifier of the Comp projection in contrast with their non-occurrence in subordinate clauses serves as the trigger for reclassifying the Comp-head. This trigger can become operative only after the Comp projection has become obligatory.

Apart from the evidence provided in section 3 for the existence of several types of null subjects in the language of three year olds the main conclusion is another one. The data discussed in section 3 of this chapter as well as the data of section 2 and chapter 9 point to the important role of the CP in the acquisition sequence. Once the CP is fully obligatory and may no longer be truncated, the child has a practically adult system on the syntactic level but also, it appears, on the level of discourse anchorage. This is only to be expected because, as was argued before, the CP mediates between certain (anaphoric) elements of an utterance and the preceding discourse.

So it is not surprising that the disappearance of post-verbal null subjects may also be related to another major shift in the development of the child. The change from tonic to atonic pronouns observed for Elisa and Christoph described in Hamann (1996b) is indicative of a change in identification of reference and can be interpreted as one of the outward manifestations of a general shift from deictic or situational anchoring to establishing reference via a reference point given by context. Such a shift will influence the acquisition of tense as well as the possible identification mechanisms of empty arguments. This issue will be crucial for the following chapter and the suggestion made there about the nature of apparent interface problems.

CHAPTER 11

DISCOURSE ANCHORAGE AND THE CP

1. DISCOURSE ANCHORAGE AND CHILD GRAMMAR

We have shown that children have trouble identifying the reference of pronouns in Principle B environments, and that there is a strong tendency to use infinitives and null subjects in a certain phase. The latter two phenomena can be linked to problems with the identification of referents in the given linguistic discourse, the first, though also connected to problems with proper reference assignment, is slightly more complicated as has emerged from chapter 5. A connection between the occurrence of infinitives, null subjects and problems with anchorage has been pointed out in work by Roeper (1992), who adds children's problems with factivity to the above anchoring problems, but also by Hamann (1992), Haegeman (1996b), Hyams (1996) and Wexler (1996). Hamann (1992) observed that German children at the age of three still prefer the use of strong/demonstrative pronouns over the use of personal pronouns, a fact we alluded to in section 3 of the last chapter. So there also is a difficulty with assigning reference to pronouns in an early phase, which is different from, albeit related to, the later difficulty with Principle B. It was speculated in Hamann (1992) that the non-use of personal pronouns and the frequent use of null subjects is tied to the fact that in adult grammar a discourse antecedent is needed for identification, but that this procedure is not yet available and probably not needed by the child.

In the meantime, the meticulous coding for previous mention of a subject in discourse carried out in the "Projekt Barnesprog" (see Plunkett 1985) made it possible to verify this speculation. The two Danish corpora described in chapter 8 were coded for the children's subject use, overt or omitted, concomitantly with a coding for previous mention of this subject or its referent in the discourse. The expectation was that the child would be more likely to drop the subject if it had previously been mentioned in discourse.

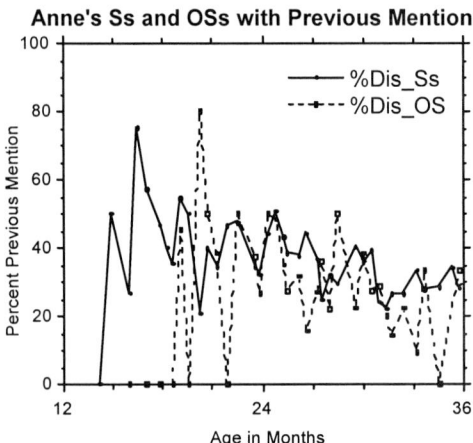

Figure 19a: Anne's subjects and null subjects with previous mention in discourse[1]

The surprising result of Hamann and Plunkett (1997, 1998)'s study is that no such correlation of subject omission and previous mention in the discourse exists. Figures 19a and 19b both show that, if anything, the converse is true. The graphs depict the percentage of how often omitted subjects and (overt) subjects had been mentioned in previous discourse. It emerges that overt subjects have generally been mentioned more often than omitted subjects and that we find an oscillation that suggests random anchorage. See Hamann and Plunkett (1998) for statistical corroboration of these observations.

In order to verify that this is due to the lack of proper discourse anchorage, the previous mention of 3rd person subject pronouns was studied in the same way. Figure 20a and 20b show that 3rd person pronouns, which should receive reference by identification with a salient discourse individual, are not properly anchored either. Only from the age of 36 months, the likelihood of previous mention of a third person pronoun is about 40%. Only *han* 'he', *hun* 'she', *de* 'they' were included in this analysis. The pronoun *det* 'it, that' can function as an expletive and as a demonstrative and was excluded.

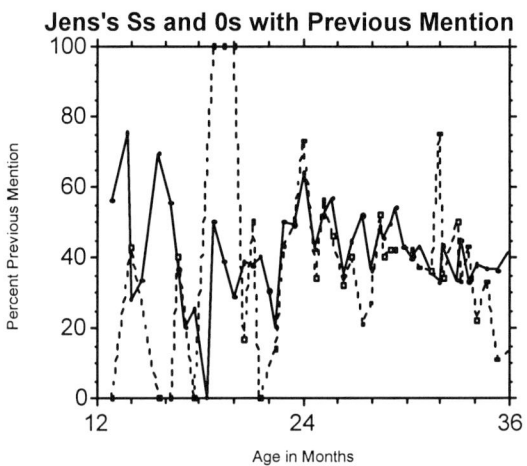

Figure 19b: Jens' subjects and null subjects with previous mention in discourse

So we now have strong empirical support for the conclusion that discourse anchorage is random in the phase where subjects are omitted and infinitives are used. This clearly suggests an approach where these phenomena are not just temporally concomitant with the lack of discourse anchorage but are related in a principled way. Indeed, many analyses intend to establish a link between the observed grammatical phenomena and lack of discourse anchorage.

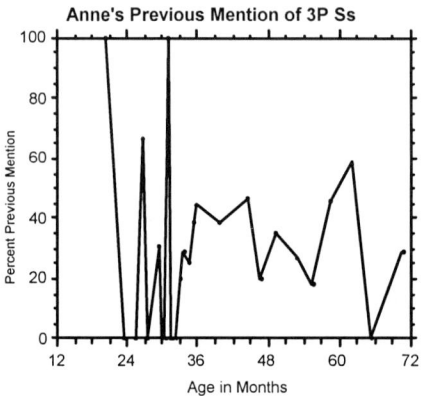

Figure 20a: Anne's previous mention of 3rd person singular pronouns

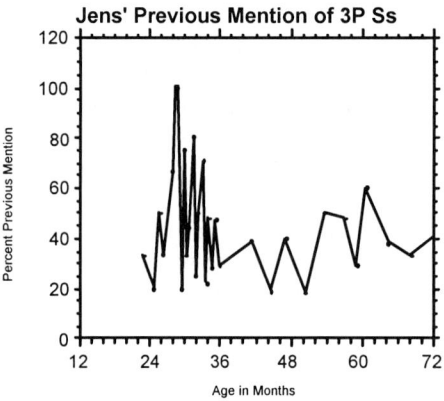

Figure 20b: Jens' previous mention of 3rd person singular pronouns

Hamann (1992:32), referring to Partee (1973), predicted that if the problems with pronouns are in part due to the "child's infelicitous anchoring procedures", then similar problems should surface in the use of tense.

Following Enç (1987) and Guéron and Hoekstra (1992, 1995), a close connection to the use of tense has been assumed in work by Hyams (1996) and Haegeman (1996b). Haegeman (1996b) sees "CP as context anchor" and points out that with the notorious context dependence of Reichenbachian reference time and its location in Comp (Guéron and Hoekstra 1992, 1995), with the coding of illocutionary force in CP (Wh) and with CP the locus of topic and focus, C^0 indeed becomes "the anchoring point of the clause in the context" (Haegeman 1996b:275). Haegeman speculates that the maturation of tense and its anchoring to C^0 (anchoring in the syntactic sense of Enç) would then lead to maturation of CP.

Haegeman (1996b,c) argues in a truncation framework, where the empty category in initial position is identified through discourse. Another possible path to take is to assume the underspecification of certain categories, as suggested by Hyams (1996), Schütze and Wexler (1996b) or Hoekstra and Hyams (1996), discussed here in chapter 7. Hyams (1996) explicitly introduces anaphoric operators for the identification of tense and definite DPs and argues that the child has a default interpretation which can do without these operators. The problem is referred to the breakdown of Grodzinski and Reinhardt (1993)'s coreference rule, discussed in chapter 3. It is assumed that in the presence of a default interpretation, it is possible for the child not to identify the discourse referent of the tense variable, the definite description, or the pronoun by binding it to the operator. Much the same is true for the approach outlined in Schütze and Wexler (1996b). Here too, direct access to the discourse context in the sense of a default interpretation is assumed for the identification of a null subject, which in their approach is PRO. They have to assume crucially that this PRO can be controlled directly from discourse. A third possibility is to assume that "child utterances lack reference though they have meaning" (Roeper 1992:1) and then investigate the areas where such lack of reference will play a role. Roeper (1992) suggests that these areas are DPs, tense, and factive clauses. More recently, Avrutin (1999) has treated the problem of assigning reference to pronouns, to definite DPs and to tense as problems of the syntax-discourse interface. He gives a discourse-based account of root infinitives using discourse semantics (see Heim 1982). In its basic assumptions if not in the details of the formal treatment, this analysis resembles the account developed in Hamann (1987, 1991, 1997), and used in Hamann et al. (1997 and 2001) for explaining certain phenomena in the speech of German children with specific language impairment (SLI). This latter analysis which uses standard truth-theoretical tools is adopted here.

All these accounts have to explain how the problem of discourse anchorage is overcome in the developmental sequence, and here we have two basic possibilities. Hyams (1996) directly refers to an interface rule and assumes that this rule will mature. Wexler (1996) pursues essentially the same line of thought in suggesting that it is 'grounding' which matters and that it is the interface that matures. This does not necessarily appeal to language independent, general cognitive development because the interface is viewed as part of the language module. As the interface crucially determines interpretative possibilities and these may decide about the crash of a derivation, maturation of the interface will induce changes in the set of possible derivations and thus syntactic changes.

But there is a radically different approach, as Roeper (1992) points out. He claims that with the development of functional categories the utterance can be linguistically linked to context so that direct reference can develop. Indeed data from SLI children show (Penner 1998, van der Lely and Stollwerck 1997, Rice and Wexler 1996 and Hamann et al. 1998) that though these children's cognitive development is that of their peers at age six (or older), their language development seems to be frozen in the phase we have been describing. Syntactic problems that are all related to the CP projection persist in these children's speech. German children with SLI, have no adult Wh-questions, no subordinations with complementizers, no object topicalization and crucially they very often leave finite verbs in sentence final position (see Hamann et. al. 1998). Because of these results from SLI, we can conclude that it is not the knowledge base which grows nor cognitive operations on the knowledge base which mature. It seems more reasonable to assume that it is indeed syntax that matures. I want to argue below that maturation or development crucially involves one functional layer, the CP system, the system which has already been identified as having interface functions.

All the above approaches share three crucial assumptions: First, the grammatical 'problems' are connected to problems of referring or anchoring to discourse, also called D-linking. Second, in a certain phase there is direct access to a default interpretation, circumventing the adult grammatical coding for identification through discourse. Third, at a certain point full specifications become available or, alternatively, the CP projection becomes obligatory.

2. ANCHORING FROM A SEMANTIC POINT OF VIEW

2.1. Similarities of Pronouns and Tense

In the previous discussion I have often referred to anchoring to discourse or to discourse identification, and it has always been tacitly assumed that this is the task of the interface and also, on the syntactic side, of the CP. Let us now study the semantic side of anchoring and, as a first step, make precise what is the similarity of pronouns and tense with respect to this problem. In this brief chapter I cannot properly introduce formal semantics, but I hope that the main points become clear nevertheless. For introductory material or precisions on the formalizations I can only refer to the references quoted in the text or to Partee, ter Meulen and Wall (1990).

Let us briefly recapitulate what we know from acquisition research. It is well established that children between the ages of 2 and 3 years make a distinction between finite and non-finite verbs and have mastered the syntactic consequences, particularly verb raising (cf. Pierce 1989, Poeppel and Wexler 1993, Weissenborn 1990). This implies that children of that age have IP or at least agreement. The problems we have discussed in the preceding chapters centered on the early availability (truncation or underspecification) of the CP system and the general consensus that maturation is involved.[2]

One possibility of capturing this is to assume that the principle 'Avoid Structure' slowly loses out to other requirements, first acknowledging thematic selection, then morphological selection and finally selection by discourse. As the matrix CP is the only projection selected by discourse, this gives the desired result (cf. Rizzi 1995a, and Rizzi 2000). This idea is especially attractive in the light of the discussion in chapter 9, where we argued that items which are indispensable for interpretation cannot be truncated, and therefore 'Avoid Structure' cannot overrule requirements of interpretation. It was also argued that whenever a default interpretation is available, the requirements of discourse identification can be overruled by the child and truncation is possible. This concerns especially ForceP but probably also other parts of the CP system.

In the following, the parallel in the semantics of pronouns and tense will be exploited in order to define more precisely what exactly it is that has to be anchored and what we mean by the locution 'anchorage'. It will turn out that it must be indeed anchorage to the context of utterance in the sense of Buehler (1934) or Fillmore (1971) which is not available in the first phases of language acquisition.

Since Frege, we are aware of the two sides of the meaning of an expression (**Sinn** and **Gedanken**). In Kaplan (1977)'s formulation, the sentence *I run* always has the same **character,** a function which will assign a proposition to this sentence in a certain situation. In different situations, however, it will have different **content** depending on who is uttering the sentence, i.e. it will express different propositions. The interpretation of some expressions, e.g. pronouns, always depends on the situation of utterance, others are less variant (e.g. *run*). So we need two steps to assign a truth-value to *she runs*.[3] First, we need to identify the situation of utterance and the female person referred to by *she* in this situation. We can then check whether this person indeed runs at the time at which the sentence is being evaluated. So we minimally need a formal system where expressions are interpreted at two indices, one specifying the time of utterance, the second specifying the time of evaluation. Then we can give the information content of *she runs* roughly as follows:

(1) *she runs* is the function f from times into temporal intensions such that for any time i, f(i) is the temporal intension p such that for any time j: p(j)=1 iff the person which the speaker refers to by *she* at i is running at j.

The relation between tenses and pronouns has been first pointed out by Partee (1973). The same article also points to a definite use of tense which is clearly related to the use of definite DPs - both require the presupposition of the existence of a unique entity (a time interval in the case of tense) to which the tense or the definite DP is anaphorically anchored or D-linked. The crucial example which argues against a Priorean treatment of tense as an unrestricted existential quantifier is (2).

(2) John didn't switch off the stove

In (2) a specific occasion before speech time known to speaker and hearer provides the time at which *John not switch off the stove* has to be evaluated. Whatever a treatment of tense assumes - and they all need the time of utterance and the time of evaluation - it will have to accommodate such a definite time. This can be achieved by introducing a third temporal parameter which has either been identified with Reichenbach's reference time (RT) (see Reichenbach 1947, Partee 1984, Nerbonne 1986, Hamann 1989, Klein 1994) or with Bäuerle (1979)'s frame time (Stechow 1995a, Zeller 1994). It can also be done by introducing a dummy frame-adverb, a phonologically empty *then* into tensed sentences. Frame-setting adverbs like *today, yesterday, at six o'clock* shift the reference or frame time parameter in the former approach and simply replace the dummy in the latter.

(3)   Today Vashek always barked

For the interpretation of (3) the scope relations have to be captured with *always* in the scope of the past tense and *today* as frame-setter scoping over the tense because otherwise we get empty quantification. A semantics of tense as proposed by Stechow (1995b) takes account of these facts. The corresponding syntax of tense proposed there uses the well-established projections TP and AspP to accommodate temporal material and places the reference time in the specifier of the TP. These scope relations can also be treated in a more specialized syntax as proposed by Zeller (1994), who elaborates the suggestions of Stowell (1993). For Zeller, frame time or reference time is in the specifier position of the ZP, which is the temporal argument of the TP. The head of this ZP is occupied by tense morphology while its complement is a quantificational phrase where frequency adverbs and quantifiers like *once, always, three times* can be accommodated. The semantics and syntax proposed by Stechow will be introduced in section 2.2 because it is simpler and allows to treat the problems we are interested in.

If a semantic treatment is chosen where the frame parameter is a temporal index, we will find formulations like "the frame time has to be determined by context" (Stechow 1995a) or "In their anaphoric use, tense morphemes refer to a reference point independently provided by discourse" (Hinrichs 1986). If we choose to spell out this parameter as dummy *then (then** in Stechow 1991 and temporal PRO in Zeller 1994) it will have roughly the semantics given in (4). So we obtain the semantics (6) for sentence (5).

(4)   *then**   is the function g from times into temporal intensions such that for any time i, g(i) is the temporal intension p such that for any j, p(k) =1 where k is that subinterval of j which the speaker refers to with *then** at the utterance time i.

(5)   John ran

(6)   *then** (PAST(John (run)) is the function g from times to temporal intensions such that g(i) is the temporal intension p

such that for any j, p(j) =1 iff John is running at j, and j is the maximal interval before utterance time i and contained in k, where k is the interval which the speaker refers to with *then** at the utterance time i.

The difficulty in the use of pronouns and tense is now apparent. In both (1) and (6) we find the formulation "which the speaker refers to with x at i". The problem thus consists of applying the character of an utterance to the context of utterance. If children have difficulty with this, it could have manifold reasons, one of which could be the notorious problems involved in awareness of the consciousness of others known as 'Theory of Mind".

2.2. Elaborating the Syntax and Semantics of Tense

It follows from the brief discussion in section 2.1 that tenses have a reference time which, in the absence of temporal adverbs, needs to be identified in discourse like a pronoun as Partee (1973, 1984) was the first to point out. Stowell (1993) and Guéron and Hoekstra (1992, 1995) have further developed the idea that tenses are like pronouns. In these treatments tenses, like pronouns, are co-indexed or counterindexed with the tense operator and a sort of polarity item approach guarantees that the right combinations survive. This approach may lead to an elegant syntactic system, but it is rather hard to arrive at a model theoretic implementation as Stechow (1995a) points out.[4] We will therefore use a more orthodox semantics as suggested in Stechow (1995a) especially as it lends itself to a straightforward syntactic representation.

In his by now classical treatment of tense, Reichenbach (1947) assumes three tense arguments: event time, speech time, reference time. In agreement with most authors (see Enç 1987, Hamann 1987, Guéron and Hoekstra 1992, Stowell 1993, Klein 1994, Stechow 1995a), we adopt these three tense arguments. Following Abusch (1993), Stowell (1993), Heim (1994) and Zeller (1994), we distinguish morphological and semantic tense: morphological tenses are T-heads, semantic tenses are arguments and occur in specifier positions. In my earlier work on tense, I assumed that the temporal relations expressed by the tenses make a direct contribution to the truth conditions. This leads to some problems for the conditions under which tensed sentences can come out as false. A treatment of temporal relations as presuppositions as Heim (1994) and Stechow (1995a) suggest, solves these problems.

Intuitively, we want to say that "*John left* is true in a world w_0 at a time t_2, if *John leave* is true at t_2 and it is presupposed about t_2, that $t_2 < t_0$ (where t_0 is the designated time, normally the speech time)". We write this as (7).

(7)   SS: John left
        LF: $PAST_{2(0)}$ John left
       Interpretation: *leave (John) (t_2: $t_2 < t_0$) (w_0)*

We now need definitions for the semantics of the present and the past tense, given in 8(a) and 8(b) respectively, where 'o' signifies overlap of the intervals and '<' signifies precedence.

(8) a. $PRES_{i(0)}$ translates as $(t_i; t_i \text{ o } t_0)$
     b. $PAST_{i(0)}$ translates as $(t_i; t_i < t_0)$

We write 'Past' for the past tense morpheme in the head position of the TP, and $PAST_{2(0)}$ for the past tense argument, which occupies the specifier position of the TP. This argument is not the event time but the reference time and can be identified by a temporal adverb. In order to arrive at an interpretation as in (7), the TP part of our LF must roughly look like (9), where the utterance situation w_0 also provides the speech time index in the PAST argument. (9) is an extension of Stechow (1995b)'s original tree in so far as the root of the structure is CP, not AgrP as in Stechow, and the evaluation index w_0 therefore is an index on CP.

So far we have not introduced any argument which might correspond to event time. In order to capture the interplay of aspectual information (morphological or lexical), event time and reference time, which will describe the difference in (10a,b), we stipulate that event times are denoted by aspect variables. So we adopt Klein (1994)'s theory, which defines tense as the relation between speech time and reference time and aspect as the relation between reference time and event time. Event time therefore is an argument occurring in the specifier of the Aspect Phrase.

(9)

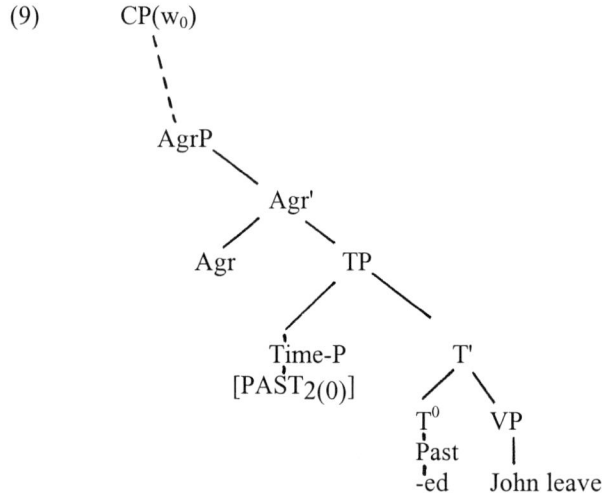

(10) a. John came home yesterday
 b. John was home yesterday

To capture the interplay shown in (10a,b), the aspects 'perfective' and 'imperfective' have to be interpreted so that the event time of a perfective verb phrase (lexically or morphologically marked as perfective) is fully contained in the reference time, and the event time of an imperfective verb phrase fully contains the reference time. Again, the temporal relations of including or being included in another interval are introduced as presuppositions about the relevant time argument t_j, and we obtain (11a,b) as formal definitions.

(11) a. Perfective $PERF_{i(j)}$ translates to $t_i; t_i \subset t_j$
 b. Imperfective $IMPERF_{i(j)}$ translates to $t_i; t_i \supset t_j$

The examples (12a-d) show that certain adverbs identify or narrow down reference times. The point of (12d) is that in English the reference time of the perfect tense corresponds to speech time so that a true past adverbial will lead to a contradiction. Therefore (12d), where the event is undoubtedly in the past, shows that certain adverbials indeed identify reference time, not event time.

(12) a. John came at five o'clock
      b. John came yesterday
      c. Yesterday John came
      d. *John has come at five 0'clock

Let us now try to give a full derivation for the interpretation of (12b) and (12c). There are two more details to note, before we can formalize this sentence. For reasons of scope, the adverb has to be higher than the tense for both sentences, and the interpretation we want is (13c), which we derive stepwise from (13a). Because of the interplay of frame adverbs like 'today' with the past tense and with frequency adverbs, Stechow (1995a) argues for an operator MAX (P, t_i) which, in the case of P being PAST, roughly speaking determines the maximal time t which is before speech time and is contained in the time interval t_i. In the case of 'yesterday' this is the whole of the day before speech time, in fact, it is the interval denoted by 'yesterday'.

(13) a. yesterday λ_1[MAX(PAST$_2$,1) λ_3 $\exists_4$[PERF 4(3) [John came]]]

      b. $\lambda t_1[\lambda t_3 \exists t_4$[come(John) ($w_0$) ($t_4$; t_4 t_3)] (MAX(t_2; t_2 <
                                                                        t_0,t_1))] (yesterday)

      c. $\exists t_4$[come (John) (w_0)(t_4; t_4 MAX(t_2; t_2 < t_0, yesterday))]

For this reading we have the LF in (14) which I adapt from Stechow (1995b). I cannot go into the details of the notation and the λ-calculus here,[5] so it must suffice to say that in the step from (13a) to (13b) we have applied the definitions (7a), (10a) and have then written the adverb *yesterday* as an argument of the function created by the λ-expression λ_1[....]. In the next step we apply λ-conversion in replacing all the variables which have the right index, i.e. the index 1, by the term *yesterday*. This and the application of the definition of MAX to PAST and 'yesterday' and the repeated application of the conversion operation to all the other λ-expressions gets us to (13c) and an interpretation. We indicate this replacement of indices in the λ-expressions by the appropriate terms in the tree (14) by drawing a sort of mnemonic arrow line into the derivation. In this example, the presence of the adverb identifies the reference time because the time span referred to by the adverb becomes the value of the RT-variable which is subsequently put into the appropriate relation with ET.

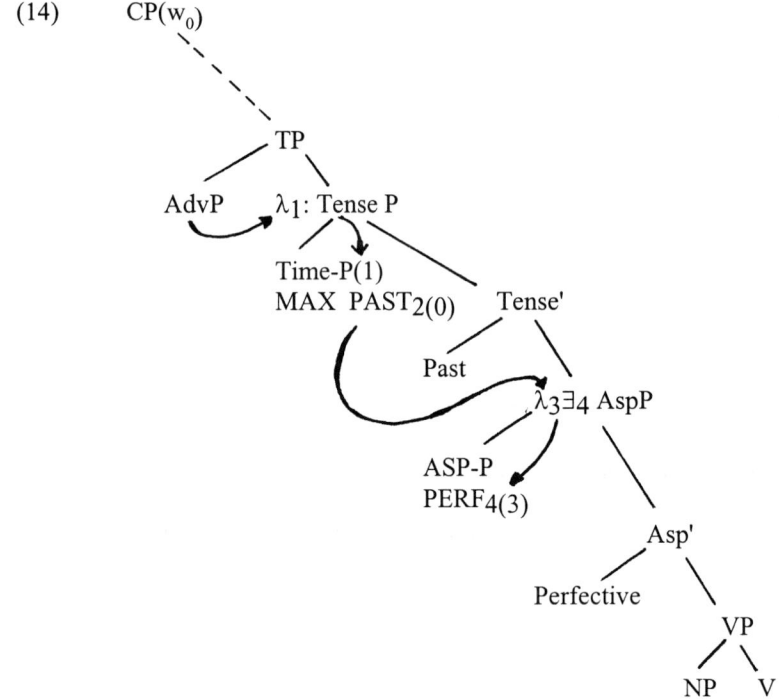

(14)

In order to get at the syntactic essentials, we can strip the tree in (14) of all the interpretative apparatus. We need to mark the following facts: the reference time occupies SpecTP (or the specifier of a special Time Phrase - ZP) and the event time occupies SpecAspP. So we simplify (14) to (15).

(15)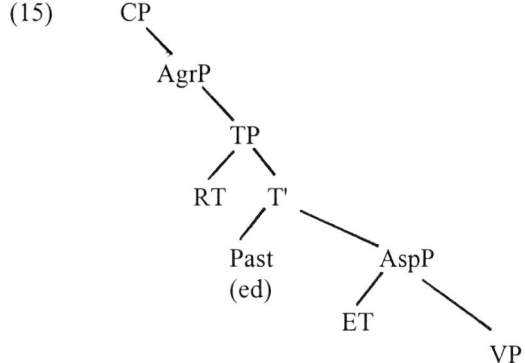

We have obscured one important difference between RT and ET by this simplification. The event time is always bound by the existential operator, the reference time is bound by the higher lambda-operator. In the absence of an adverb, however, the variable cannot be "identified" in the sense that we cannot perform the substitution from step (13b) to (13c). It has already been said that the presence of an adverb "identifies" the time variable in the TP (see the λ-conversion of 13b). So we now find the situation that an empty category is licensed (bound by the lambda operator) but not identified. If there is no adverb, we have an unidentified empty argument in SpecTP. This could be a variable as we have assumed in (14) for this purpose, but it could also be a temporal PRO as Stowell (1993) and Zeller (1994) argue. In any case, this empty category has to be identified from higher up. If we do not want to use a dummy *then* as suggested by Stechow (1991), identification will be achieved through a salient time in discourse mediated by a discourse operator in CP.

This can be achieved without assuming any additional syntactic apparatus, if we take the terminology suggested in Klein (1994) seriously. Klein (1994) does not use the term Reference Time introduced by Reichenbach. Because this time is usually given or known from previous discourse, he calls this temporal argument Topic Time instead. So in the above case we are dealing with a silent topic. We only have to apply Huang (1984)'s analysis for topic drop, modify it so that it fits a Split CP analysis, and restrict it in a suitable way to variables denoting times. This can be done if we postulate that we always have a projection for topic times which may be occupied by an empty operator or by an overt adverb. We obtain a tree like (16). Note that marking a constituent as a topic or as bound to the topic position will mark it as old information. This will amount to identifying it with some salient time argument in the given discourse, or - in the terms of Huang (1984) - to identifying the operator in the discourse. The semantics of this operator will be roughly: "at that time" or "at the time when...".

We may then assume that overt adverbs raise to SpecTopT at LF in those cases where there is no reference time specified in the context. If, however, this is the case and the reference time is already bound by a topic operator which itself is already identified in discourse, then the adverb will modify another time, presumably the event time.

(16)

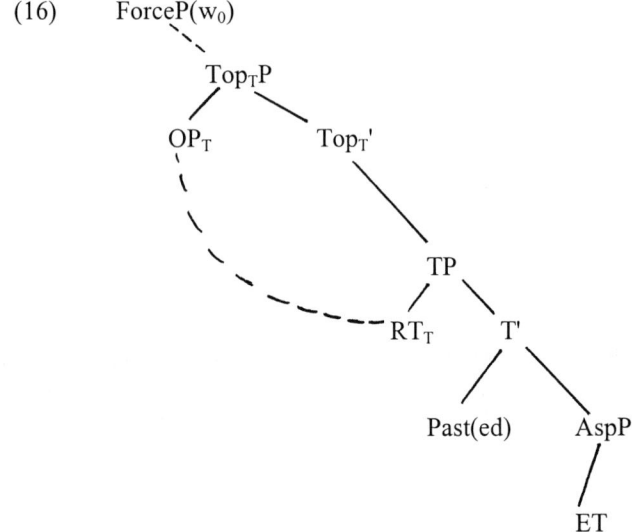

So even if there is no need to postulate a tense operator in the CP from the semantic point of view - the interpretation or model is well able to assign a truth value directly to (14) - the traditional (syntactic) way of handling discourse identification through an operator in the specifier of a CP projection suggests that the CP is needed to give an interpretation to tense. Note that all the necessary temporal arguments are present in the representation and are all found in the TP projection and its complements. This is not true for speech time, which was not coded as an argument occupying a syntactic position but which was given in the form of the utterance index. This seems reasonable as any utterance, and be it just the utterance of the sound 'uh', can establish the time of utterance without recourse to any syntactic property of this utterance, whereas it does not make sense to try and identify a reference or event time for such an utterance. Therefore, even if tenses semantically have three arguments, only two of these are coded in the syntax, which corresponds to the fact that only two have morphological reflexes (tense morphology and aspect morphology). In a sense, the suggested treatment combines the approaches of Enç (1987) and Guéron and Hoekstra (1995). The former claims that it is speech time that must be located in the CP and provides the anchoring point, the latter argue for reference time in the CP. We have linked reference time to the CP via the operator, and speech time is included in the world index of the CP.

2.3. Implications for Child Language

These considerations lead to several conclusions with respect to child language. First, the child could simply not have TP, and so not have the reference time, and thus produce utterances which lack anchorage on the time line. This is essentially the approach Wexler (1992,1994) suggests. Second, the child can have the full IP (AgrP and TP) structure and still produce infelicitous temporal utterances if the anchoring is not guaranteed because there is 'CP-trouble'. Third, a model which assumes the 'here and now' as interpretative indices and identifies the reference time with the 'now' will always be available. Fourth, in parallel to child (diary) null subjects, random identification of the temporal empty category in the 'here and now' or with whatever the speaker has in mind is possible as long as this 'CP-trouble' persists.

If one assumes a simple lack of TP, this cannot directly account for the difficulties with other categories. In order to capture all of these, one could assume that the child does not recognize the necessity to anchor certain arguments in discourse. One of the consequences of this assumption would be that the reference point could be missing without any consequences for interpretation. This implies that some cognitive development or maturation suddenly leads to anchorage, or it has to be claimed that it is the interface as part of the language faculty which matures. This will then trigger the maturation of TP because now a place for the reference time argument is needed.

The assumption of the maturation of general cognitive abilities becomes doubtful when examined in the light of what is known about SLI children's development. It was Rice and Wexler (1996) who created the term 'Extented

Optional Infinitive Phase' for SLI children's grammar. This means that children, who are cognitively well past the decisive development, are still producing temporally unanchored utterances. Moreover, in an experiment inspired by the above view of tense, Hamann et al. (1997) and (2001) showed that German children with SLI have 'CP-trouble' and, at the same time, are incapable of interpreting past perfect sentences which notoriously require the recuperation of a reference time from discourse. This seems to show rather conclusively that it is not general cognitive maturation that leads to systematic discourse anchorage. Especially the result on German SLI points to the crucial involvement of the CP in the anchoring process.

Let us therefore assume the availability of the TP system, but some sort of CP-trouble which is responsible for the failure of anchorage. We then obtain the following situation. If morphological tense marking occurs that requires a specific presupposition, this presupposition can only be verified in the speech situation, not in discourse. This allows infinitives as default forms, it clearly allows the present. It predicts that past tense is rare, can occur only when the full CP is projected, or if an adverb is present. If an adverb is present, the discourse is not needed for the verification of the presupposition and a correctly tensed form is expected - if the temporal meaning of the adverb is clear for the child. On the other hand, we do not expect a root infinitive with an ongoing interpretation in the presence of a reference time adverb. This seems to be true for German children with SLI as Hamann et al. (1997 and 2001) have shown. It is also true for normally developing children in so far as the few temporal adverbs used by the (German) children on the Childes data base never occur with root infinitives. It also receives corroboration by the observation that German children go through a phase where finite verb forms, especially those used in a narrative, are mostly accompanied by a 'dummy' *da* This dummy will introduce some reference time the speaker has in mind without necessarily identifying this reference time with a special interval on the time line. Since, in the absence of adverbs, only one interpretation is available, tense morphology does not contribute to the distinction of interpretations and is in this sense itself without interpretation (see Wexler 1994). So the default form, i.e. the infinitive, will be used side by side with the present tense. Uses of infinitives with different time reference have been reported by Behrens (1993) and Fantuzzi (1995).

More such data come from an experiment with two-year olds by Schuetze and Wexler (2000). They elicited main verb descriptions of unambiguous past events in contrast to habitual events where the simple present is used in English. The striking result was that infinitives surface in past or present contexts, but that tensed verb forms were always used in the appropriate contexts. We can explain such uses of the infinitive in the present framework if the CP is truncated and tenses remain unanchored. Note that nothing prohibits a truncation of the TP as well, so that we also obtain the usual explanation for the occurrence of infinitives. The correct use of tense morphology in the appropriate contexts indicates that children at that age differentiate past and present, as Schuetze and Wexler point out, and correctly analyze verbal endings in English as tense morphology. The result can be explained in a truncation approach, however, when we consider that elicitation always includes the lead-in and this contained a reference time setting adverb in the above experiment. As the child has just parsed this lead-in and this includes assigning a CP and identifying the reference time with the time span given by the adverb, it is probable that sometimes the child will keep the CP and reference time activated for its own production. In this case, correct tense use is expected. The other possibility always is that 'Avoid Structure' will take over for the child and an infinitive will surface. This is indeed what we find in spontaneous speech. Finite forms marked as past tense are very rare in the phase where the anchoring problem is evident. The data from Danish on past tense use as reported in figure 21 and on pronoun anchorage as shown in figures 20a,b demonstrate that the use of past tense morphology comes in at the time when discourse anchorage with pronouns becomes more reliable. This is predicted by the account given here.

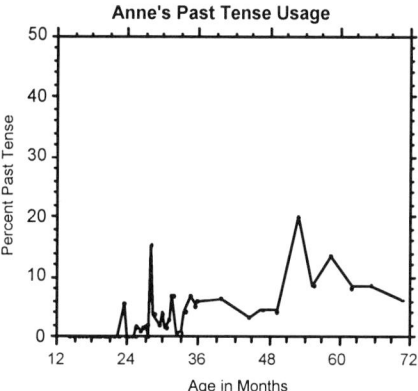

Figure 21: Anne's percent past tense usage

3. CONCLUSION AND OUTLOOK

In giving a full standard semantics of tense, we could identified the CP as the locus of the anchoring problem for tense in a precise way. Pursuing the idea about a temporal topic feature, we could suppose that other anaphoric elements are linked to discourse also via an appropriate topic feature. We could then ask whether the problem lies in the truncation option or in the underspecification of topic features. Assuming such an underspecification would again lead to the question of how the full specification can be acquired. Will it be some cognitive leap that makes the child distinguish old and new information or will the grammatical feature matrix mature? So it seems that the truncation approach is better suited to deal with the syntactic phenomena we have observed and the obvious problems with discourse anchorage which occur at the same time. It supplies the tool for linking the syntactic with the discourse problems in a natural manner. It also suggests that the obligatoriness of the CP does not simply mature, but that it is the principle of 'Categorial Uniformity' (see chapter 7) which finally achieves an adult balance with 'Avoid Structure'.

CHAPTER 12

CHILD LANGUAGE: FROM SYNTAX TO DISCOURSE

1. LOOKING BACK

In this cross-linguistic investigation of early child language, I started with data on the acquisition of pronominal clitics and the binding principles, I presented data on subject omission and infinitive use, and passed on to data about the early use of negation and Wh-questions. If this extensive compilation and juxtaposition of results from the literature and of new results from new or hitherto not fully analyzed corpora proves relevant for future research, one aim of this work has been attained. From the theoretical point of view, many issues were discussed, as for example the status of clitics in French, the assignment of nominative case by agreement or by tense, the parameterization of the order of functional projections, and the underlying LF-representations of different question constructions. These are areas, where child data can contribute to linguistic knowledge and may be decisive for the choice of one theoretical analysis over another.

The investigation of the properties of Romance pronominal clitics showed a delay in the acquisition of complement clitics which was explained by adopting the typology for pronominals suggested by Cardinaletti and Starke (2000). In their system, complement clitics are more deficient than subject clitics. So they are more marked and therefore more difficult to acquire or, being more deficient, they are more susceptible to 'Avoid Structure'.

Though Romance children have to surmount this difficulty inherent in the syntactic structure of clitic pronouns and so may be later in the production of complement pronouns, they are able to assign correct reference to complement pronouns in binding configurations from about their third birthday. In two experiments on binding in French, it was shown that the most likely explanation of the remaining difficulty with binding in embedded contexts is the overextension of guise creation. This cannot apply in a simple clause as Romance clitic pronouns are generally not deictic. Clitic pronouns are therefore strongly anaphoric and take their guise directly from the identifying DP and therefore overextended guise creation in a simple situation is excluded. The scenario sketched in chapter 11 ties in with the fact that from about the third birthday pronouns in simple contexts are interpreted correctly. From that time onwards, null subjects and root infinitives are no longer observed, subordinate clauses are produced with a complementizer and so there is ample evidence that the CP is obligatory. Therefore identification of the clitic pronoun by its discourse antecedent is possible and interacts with the child's knowledge of Principle B. Only in the special embedded context described in chapter 5, guise creation is possible for clitics and vindicates Heim (1993)'s interpretation of accidental coreference. Even if systematic guise creation by young children may indicate a reluctance to search for the proper discourse antecedent, the rules which constrain guise creation are pragmatic. Thus it is not surprising that even if discourse anchorage and guise creation both touch the syntax-discourse interface, mastery of the latter rules may be delayed with respect to the simpler requirements of discourse anchorage and it may show language specific patterns. We have argued that discourse anchorage is driven from within syntax, guise creation seems truly pragmatic as it is guided by felicity conditions, and their acquisition is notoriously problematic. See Thornton and Wexler (1999) for a similar view. So even if a fully developed syntactic clause structure determines the proper use of anaphoric expressions in discourse, there is another component of the language faculty that must develop in order for utterances to be used felicitously. We thus take the binding problems as pragmatic problems which may be rooted in the early difficulty with discourse anchorage because guise creation provides a tool for avoiding just such anchorage. In the course of development other pragmatic problems like the proper interpretation of discourse, restricted world knowledge, and the acquisition of felicity conditions become intervening factors. Their persistence into the sixth year of life contrasts with the manifestation of mastery in many syntactic areas by the third birthday. The relative earliness of discourse anchorage can therefore be taken as another indicator that it is indeed syntax and not pragmatics which drives its mastery.

In the chapters 6-10, we dealt with the phenomena of child null subjects and root infinitives. The focus was on a study of the relation of these two phenomena and on the models which account for the data. These are especially tense based models as inspired by Wexler (1992, 1994) and economy based models as inspired by Rizzi (1992, 1994). Data from the literature and from my own research on German, French and Danish were matched with the models. Without going into the details of the discussion here, I want to remind the reader that the crucial evidence involves the fact that there are more null subjects on infinitives than on finite verbs (except in English), that null subjects on finite verbs are quite frequent, however, and that their development correlates with the development of infinitives. Especially the latter point indicates that an economy based model like truncation fares better in explaining these data than tense based models. Some of the remaining chapters dealt with various possibilities to explain this correlation in a tense based model focusing on the evidence provided in the structural environments of past constructions, in Wh-questions and negation. The accumulated evidence, though not totally conclusive on all points, indicates that an approach which restricts child null subjects to the specifier of the root is compatible with the overall data, whereas there remain problem areas for tense based accounts.

Passing beyond a descriptive analysis of the data and their relevance for the respective models, I argued in chapter 11 that the child use of root infinitives and null subjects is best explained by problems with the projection that provides the syntactic side of the syntax-discourse interface, the CP. It emerged that the current theories of acquisition all assume that certain problems with tense are at the bottom of the use of optional root infinitives. I argue that an account involving the truncation of the CP has the additional merit of providing a natural explanation of the concomitant failure of discourse anchorage. That such CP-trouble is at the bottom of the anchoring problems and so at the bottom of many of the phenomena of child speech has been assumed in several recent approaches. In the last speculative chapter, the semantic side of these anchoring problems was investigated and related to the idea that the CP is the anchoring point of the phrase. It emerges that anchoring becomes available and many of the characteristic phenomena of the early phase vanish when the full properties of the CP are acquired, or when the CP has become obligatory. In this sense, the child steps from syntax to discourse.

2. REMAINING PROBLEMS

A question which has to be answered is why the requirements of interpretation do not force the projection of the CP or of the relevant topic projection in the case of tense marking. It was argued in chapter 9 for Wh-in-situ that the requirements of interpretation force projection if a scope marking operator has to be placed for interpretative purposes. So why does the same not apply in the case of tense?

In chapter 9 there is an indication of what the answer must be. It was argued that only material which cannot be interpreted by a default mechanism is necessarily projected for reasons of interpretation. So projections need not be activated and can be truncated if their interpretative contribution can be exhausted by a default. In declaratives such a default is always given in the utterance situation. Hence infinitives and present are easily explained and past tense will be rare as the existence of the default will lead the child to truncate and use an infinitive. Early, rare past tense occurrences can still be explained if the child has truncated. The interpretation in the default situation allows an aspectual reading in this case which may be indistinguishable from the true past "tense" reading.

As the CP is optional in the truncation approach, one might expect more past tense occurrences, and more anchored pronouns, however. This may indeed be a problem for the hypothesis sketched above. It is likely, however, that ForceP and TopP are never projected in this early phase precisely because the available default interpretations (for declaratives) allows 'Avoid Structure' to dispense with them. In this case, the interdependence of interpretation and syntax would be very important for early language development.

There is another interesting empirical problem, concerning the universality of the anchoring failure. If there is a general anchoring failure which is due to truncation of a CP projection, then we expect that the effects are universally observable in child language. In chapter 8 we had deduced from table 37 that optional infinitives in child language are not a universal phenomenon, but depend on certain language specific properties. Let me state first that even in Italian some root infinitives occur. As to their rarity this may well be a function of the morphology of a language. Let us assume that in Italian, infinitives raise as high as TP as has been argued by Belletti (1990) and by Rizzi (1994). This implies that they carry some temporal presupposition. Therefore they are not the easiest way out of the dilemma of anchoring failure. Moreover, they cannot be chosen as the default morphology in the absence of tense distinctions.

There is one other problem that may indicate that the relation of discourse anchorage and the truncation option should not be too close. It has generally been claimed that omission of articles, especially of the definite article, is closely related to the general failure of discourse anchorage because it requires anaphoric identification (see Hyams 1996, Hoekstra and Hyams 1996 and Avrutin 1999). So it is only natural to assume that one cause is responsible for both phenomena as is done in the work by the above authors.

New findings on two French SLI children indicate, however, that there may be a dissociation of these two phenomena (see Arabatzi et al. in preparation). If it turns out that the grammatical development of SLI children is deviant from normal development, this result may be without consequence for the present argumentation. Under the assumption of delayed but parallel development it is very revealing. As it turns out, the study of determiner use of one normal French child as conducted by Arabatzi et al. (in preparation) for comparison shows that the development of determiner omission and of root infinitives does not pattern in totally parallel fashion. So there may be a genuine problem. The relation of the failure of discourse anchorage and the use of root infinitives I have outlined in chapter 11 predicts that once projections have been truncated down to and including the TP discourse anchorage is no longer possible and so article omission is expected with infinitives. However, in my approach it is possible that the TP is present and so a finite construction is possible in the present tense with a default interpretation anchored in the speech situation. The linking projection may still be truncated. So article omission could occur in finite contexts and a fully parallel development is not expected. Clearly more data are needed to decide on this crucial issue.

3. CONCLUSION

This work has collected data showing the detailed syntactic knowledge of small monolingual children learning their native language. Areas of difficulties were investigated with special care and it was concluded that the syntactic system is not at fault in general. It is functioning well - under a number of constraints, however, that may obscure the underlying knowledge.

An existing, truncation based, model was extended to encompass not only the areas of syntactic difficulties but also the general difficulty with discourse anchorage. In view of data from normal development and from the language development of children with SLI it was argued that the anchoring problems are related to the optionality of the CP. So I conclude that without a proper syntax, the child cannot develop proper discourse relations. Moreover, I have argued that it is not just 'interface' conditions which are involved and which are not properly mastered. In the case of discourse anchorage, I hope to have shown that it is the syntactic side of this interface which drives the development. Other problems of child language may well be determined by the pragmatic side of these interface conditions as it is the case for the apparent trouble with the binding principles, which is in fact trouble with the felicitous creation of guises. In so far as felicitous use is involved, it is an interesting question whether the correct use of phrases in discourse is regulated by interface rules, i.e. language particular rules alone or whether we must reckon with general, cognitive development and learning strategies. The nature of the overall problem strongly indicates that both are involved, perhaps to different degrees depending on the specific requirements.

Only detailed empirical data, especially meticulous timing of fine grained phenomena in relation to other phenomena for normally developing children, a comparison to children with SLI, but also data on the acquisition of a second language, can decide about some of the above predictions and speculative solutions. In particular, such data will distinguish between the areas of language acquisition which are independent from general cognitive development, and the areas where linguistic and cognitive development as well as the development of world knowledge are closely interwoven. So even if I have provided data which can settle some of the debates in acquisition research and can serve as a basis of comparison, I have raised just as many new questions for further research.

NOTES

CHAPTER 2

[1] Kaiser (1994) refers to utterances like (i) and (ii) and claims that these do not mark any special pragmatic function (emphasis) in Colloquial French.

(i) Jean il mange
John he eats
(ii) Lui il mange
him he eats

[2] See Jaeggli (1982) for a different argument.

[3] The notation of age is "year;month,day". The conventions of transcription which were applied to the Augustin-corpus were also used in the transcriptions of the German children Christoph and Elisa. Moreover, the counting procedures (no repetitions, no incomplete utterances, no 'yes' or 'no' answers etc.) are the same throughout this work. Apart from my own transcriptions for Christoph and Elisa, the Augustin-corpus transcribed under my supervision, and the Danish corpora of Anne and Jens, which were made available to me in their entirety by Kim Plunkett, I have used other corpora transcribed in the Interfaculty project in Geneva (cf. the Marie-corpus), the Childes data base (see McWhinney and Snow 1990), especially the Clahsen (1982), Wagner (1985) and Wijnen (1994) corpora for German and Dutch, and the Leveillé corpus for French. Other data are from the literature as specified. Phonetic transcriptions are sometimes indicated in angled brackets, [ ]. For these transcriptions the SAM-PA symbols as described in Wells (1989) are used. The data analysis of the Childes corpora and the corpora available in Geneva were made with the standard UNIX tools. Other corpora were analysed by hand.

[4] Note that apposition is only possible with strong pronouns *Er, der Topf, ist weg* , whereas repetition of the subject in a dislocated structure is only possible with weak pronouns **Er kommt gleich, Peter*. Interestingly enough, the last sentence becomes possible if the name is made into a normal definite description: *Er kommt gleich, der Peter*.

[5] See Cardinaletti and Starke (1995, 2000) concerning a similar assumption with respect to binding.

[6] Participles are not treated on a par with infinitives because they occupy a different, a higher, position in the tree. In some recent treatments of tense (see Zeller 1994) they are even analysed as tense heads. So if child infinitives are basically characterized by a lack of tense, they cannot be assimilated to participles. See also chapter 10 for more arguments.

CHAPTER 4

[1] See also the discussion on the role of the case feature for referentiality in Chomsky (1981), Reinhart and Reuland (1993), and Philip and Coopmans (1996b).

[2] See also Cardinaletti and Starke (1995) and Baauw, Escobar and Philip (1997).

[3] See Cardinaletti and Starke (2000) for a different account, where the clitic lacks a case feature and must undergo a movement process to be associated with a functional case feature. It must be in a local relationship to some Agr in order to constitute functional case through incorporation. In both accounts movement must take place in order to check certain features.

[4] See Belletti (1999) for a fuller discussion.

[5] See Haverkort (1993) for a similar assumption.

[6] For Cardinaletti and Starke (2000) the clitic must move to the Agr projection in order to consitute functional case. See also footnote 3.

[7] If this result on the referentiality of clitics seems counterintuitive, it is because clitics always attach to something else. Why would they do this unless they are in incomplete? This incompleteness could be due to case as suggested in footnote 1 and in the Cardinaletti and Starke approach. We cannot pursue this argument any further here, but suggest that a definition of referential completeness or independence might include a structural part, requiring that the item in question is not structurally impoverished. The effects of such an addition have not been fully evaluated and may prove to have very undesirable consequences.

CHAPTER 5

[1] I thank William Philip for preparing the statistics and the description of the experiment.

[2] Personal communication by Sergio Baauw, who could accept the Spanish versions of the setnences (18), (19) and (29) of Chapter 4 on the 07/04/97 at the Edinburgh GALA conference. Recently, his judgment has changed.

[3] This objection does not hold against Coopmans and Philip (1995)'s original proposal about underspecification of case.

[4] In the system of Cardinaletti and Starke (1995), chance performance on Romance strong pronouns would follow from their generalization that accidental coreference is possible (only) with strong pronouns.

CHAPTER 6

¹ See table 4 for Augustin's verbal development

² See Cipriani et al. (1993), corpora available on Childes.

³ Recently, the EPP proposed in Chomsky (1982) has been challenged in accounts which assume that the specifier position of a projection may remain radically empty, if the head of the projection is rich enough in feature content to give life to the projection. Such accounts would assume that missing subjects in adult language occur if IP has no specifier position. Compare Speas (1994) for an approach to null arguments, Brandner (1993) for an analysis of expletives, and Roeper and Rohrbacher (2000) for an application to child language.

⁴ See Wexler (1996) for a discussion of some of these learnability questions.

⁵ That the Comp system is missing in an early phase of language acquisition has been claimed for German by Meisel (1990), Clahsen (1991) and Meisel and Müller (1992), for English by Lebeaux (1988), Kazman (1990), and Radford (1990), for French by Pierce (1989, 1992), and for Bernese Swiss German by Penner (1990a,b, 1994). With the exception of Radford (1990), these authors mostly assume that the IP (or some functional projection above VP) is available from early on so that this approach has been termed 'Weak Continuity' approach. Poeppel and Wexler (1993), Deprez and Pierce (1994), and Hyams (1996), on the other hand, argue for the availability of the full tree of functional projections from early on, and call this assumption the 'Full Competence Hypothesis'.

⁶ Weissenborn (1990) claims that about 5% null subjects occur in adult German as well as in adult French. This is the result of the evaluation of many spoken French and German texts done in the course of the Language Acquisition Project conducted at the Max Planck Institute of Psycholinguistics in Nijmegen (Weissenborn, personal communication). Table 32 in chapter 8 shows, however, that in French, subject drop is much lower (under 1%), whereas in German subject drop is about 10%. Even if that is so, the above reasoning has to be taken with a grain of salt. It is always possible that the child's pragmatic intentions are different from the adult's or that there is a gradual shift towards the same kind of communicational situations and aims. In that case, such a development would only be natural

CHAPTER 7

¹ See Clahsen, Kursawe and Penke (1996), Roeper and Weissenborn (1991) for German, and Roeper and Rohrbacher (2000) for the existence of such a root-effect for finite null subjects in English.

² Compare Zwart (1993) for an approach which assumes a head-first IP for Dutch and German, and Kayne (1994) for the view that all projections are head- first. Especially for German there are problems with these accounts (see Büring and Hartmann 1994) so that for the present moment there is no reason to adopt them. Compare also the results of Penner,

Schoenenberger and Weissenborn (1994) with respect to the non-occurrence of V_{inf} O orders in early child German.

³ In reintroducing the operator, we may be making the wrong choice, however, because Cardinaletti (1990)'s arguments still hold. Moreover, it is not difficult to write a discourse semantics which identifies an nc via a salient discourse element, whereas this could be problematic for an operator. The choice of an nc therefore seems to be preferable.

⁴ The problem with the German data and numbers (not the Dutch) is the fact that in some varieties of German - and also in the variety of Elisa's mother - the strong pronoun *das* can be used as a quasi-argument (*das regnet schon wieder*). Such a strong pronoun in initial position could be dropped under a normal topic-drop analysis.

⁵ Wexler (1992) focussed on the **optionality** of child infinitives, whereas Rizzi (1992) discusses them as **root** infinitives because of their constrained distribution. I will use both terms throughout, ' optional infinitive' and 'root infinitive', without meaning to imply that an 'optional infinitive' has to be analysed as in Wexler's framework and a 'root infinitive' as in a truncation approach.

⁶ See Hoekstra and Hyams (1996) for an argument that the *-er* ending is an abstract number marking, and therefore is agreement, not tense. This does not seem to hold under closer examination, however, as I show in chapter 8, section 6.

⁷ See Clahsen, Eisenbeiss and Penke (1996) for a different approach, and Schaeffer (1997) and Avrutin (1999) for a formulation of discourse rules.

⁸ See Clahsen, Eisenbeiss and Penke (1996), who link the DP and the AgrSP in a grammatical approach, Schaeffer (1997) for a clearly pragmatic solution of the anchoring problem, and Avrutin (1999) for an approach using discourse semantics.

CHAPTER 8

¹ I am grateful to Arild Hestvik (personal communication May 1997) for providing the essential arguments against the 'eroded number' analysis and for the traditional 'tense' analysis of the *-er/-ar* ending in Scandinavian.

CHAPTER 9

¹ The lack of a distinction of main verb and auxiliary uses of *avoir* and other verbs may be problematic. In Germanic languages the equivalent forms to possessive *have* do occur as root infinitives as the often quoted (i) proves.

(i)   Torst'n das haben
        Torsten that have

In fact, some of the German files availabe on Childes revealed a rather frequent occurrence of infinitival possessive *haben*. Daniel (Clahsen, Childes) at the age of 2;10,14 uses 4 possessive forms of *haben*, 2 of which are infinitives. At the age of 3;3,21 he produces 6 possessive forms one of which is an infinitive. Daniel's twin Mathias at the age of 2;9,7 produces 6 possessive uses of *haben*, 3 of which are infinitives. Julia at the age of 2;2,21 has all three of her possessive *haben* in the infinitive, at the age of 2;3,21 she uses one such *haben* in the infinitive, at the age of 2;4,21 she produces 6 possessive forms of *haben* of which 2 are infinitives, and at the age of 2;5,28 she uses 7 possessive *haben* of which 3 are infinitives. In fact, all of Julia's uses of *haben* are possessive uses. Mathias uses *haben* as an auxiliary at the age of 2;11,14 for the first time and Daniel has auxialiary *haben* at the age of 3;1,21. It has to be noted that Daniel and Mathias despite their age are still in the root infinitive phase (cf. Clahsen 1991). The relevant examples of infinitival possessive *haben* for these three children are (ii), (iii), (iv), whereas their first auxiliary uses are shown in (v):

(ii)   ich schaufel haben   Dan 2;10,14
       I shovel have
       ich schaufel diese haben   "
       I shovel this have
       ich das haben   Dan 3;3,21
       I that have

(iii) i nur haben   Mat 2;9,7
       I only have
       habn
       have
       haben # nein
       have, no

(iv)   das haben   Jul 2;2,21
       that have
       das haben (not an immediate repetition)
       that have
       da haben auch   Jul 2;3,21
       there have also
       da du haben   Jul 2;4,21
       there you have
       das haben
       that have
       ich haben   Jul 2;5,28
       I have(inf)
       Julia das haben
       Julia that have
       Julia das auch haben
       Julia that also have

(v) na # ich hab nitten ab   Dan 3;1,21
     na, I have cut off
     jetz ich hab fertig schaff   Mat 2;11,14
     now I have ready managed
     'now I have all managed'
     ich hab sehn
     I have seen

Interestingly enough, for none of the three children an occurrence of the infinitive *sein* was found, neither as copula nor as auxiliary. One of the examples from Andreas and one Danish example from Anne and 6 from Jens, however, involve the infinitival copula *be* :

(vi) der ikke være   Anne
      it   not be.

For Philippe, an inclusion of the copula in the count as a main verb would include almost all occurences of *où* -questions which would raise the count of main verb questions to over forty. Evidently this is not the case in Phillip's count, so he cannot have included the copula use of *être*. Possessive use of *avoir* did not occur in Philippe's questions, but sometimes we have existential *avoir* as in (vii). Inclusion of this construction in the count of main verb questions would again raise the numbers.

(vii) qui y a dehors   Philippe 2;3,14
       who there has outside
       'who is there outside?'

Existential *avoir* was excluded by Phillips on the grounds that it is a frozen form. It does also occur as *il y avait* in Philippe's speech, but only as a repetition.

So it emerges that Phillips (1995) counted all occurrences of forms of *avoir* or *être* as auxiliaries (discarding *c'est* and *y a*) and did not make a distinction according to their function in the sentence. In the same manner, occurrences of the verb *aller* seem to have been counted as main verbs regardless of their function. When Phillips discusses a prototypic repetition example, namely (viii), he speaks of a main-verb example which supports the above inference regarding his counting procedures with respect to auxiliaries.

(viii) avec quoi elle va chercher mamie   Philippe 2;2,3
        with what she goes seek mamie
        'with what will she pick up grandma?'

CHAPTER 10

[1]   Speculatively, it could be suggested that the child cannot adhere to the UCC in fronted Wh-questions because the Wh-criterion forces verb movement in multiple steps (see Philip 1995). This argument is dubious because the UCC only concerns the D-feature, not the wh-feature, but it could prohibit a [–TNS] specification for verbal forms in Wh-questions and so exclude infinitives and PRO null subjects. Topic-drop null subjects would also be excluded in this environment hence the rarity of null subjects finite Wh-questions.

CHAPTER 11

[1] I thank Kim Plunkett for his help in preparing the data for these figures

[2] Note that Penner (1994b, 1998) offers an alternative to a maturational account in assuming that parameters which are not globally set can be delayed. So his account for CP-trouble is such a delay in the setting of the V2-parameter.

[3] We are abstracting away from the notorious difficulty of giving a semantics for the English Simple Present. The semantics given in (1) is probably capturing the English Present Progressive, but this is not relevant for the discussion.

[4] See Stechow (1995a) for a full critique of Enç (1987) and Stowell (1993).

[5] The syntax of the λ-operator:
Whenever x is a variable of type a and α is a wellformed expression of type b then [λx α] is a wellformed expression of type <a,b>.

The interpretation of the λ-operator:
Whenever x is of type a, α is of type b, and I is an interpretation with I=(M,β) then λx α is satisfied in I iff there is a function f: D_a -> D_b such that for any object k in D_a, f(k) is the denotation of α in M,β[k/x].

λx α (k) $\Leftrightarrow$ α[k/x], where k is any appropriate term and α[k/x] is the result of substituting k for all occurrences of x in α.

REFERENCES

Abusch, D. (1993). "Sequence of Tense Revisited: Two Semantic Accounts of Tense in Intensional Contexts". Ms. University of Stuttgart. [Appeared as : Sequence of Tense and Temporal De Re. *Linguistics and Philosophy* 20, 1-50]
Aldridge, M. (ed) (1996). *Child Language*. Clevedon: Multilingual Matters.
Aldridge, M., R.D. Borsley, and S. Clack (1995). "The Acquisition of Welsh Clause Structure". In D. MacLaughlin and S. McEwen (eds). *BUCLD 19*, 37-47.
Allwood, J. (ed) (1990). *Gothenburg Papers in Theoretical Linguistics 59*, University of Gothenburg, Gothenburg, Sweden.
Almong, J., J. Perry, and H. Wettstein (eds) (1979): *Themes from Kaplan*. Oxford, New York: Oxford University Press.
Arabatzi, M., L. Baranzini, L. Chillier, S. Cronel-Ohayon, S. Dubé, J. Franck,U. Frauenfelder, C. Hamann, L. Rizzi, M. Starke, P. Zesiger (in preparation): "On the Dissociation of the Nominal and the Verbal Functional Domains in French Language Impairment". Alternate paper at BUCLD 26, November 2001.
Avrutin, S. (1994). *Psycholinguistic Investigations in the Theory of Reference*. Ph.D. dissertation, MIT.
Avrutin, S. (1999). *Development of the Syntax-Discourse Interface*. Dordrecht: Kluwer.
Avrutin, S. and K. Wexler (1992). "Development of Principle B in Russian: Coindexation at LF and Coreference", *Language Acquisition* 2, 259-306.
Baauw, S. (2000). *Grammatical Features and the Acquisition of Reference. A Comparative Study of Dutch and Spanish*. Doctoral dissertation, Utrecht University.
Baauw, S., L. Escobar and W. Philip (1997). "A Delay of Principle B-Effect in Spanish Speaking Children: The Role of Lexical Feature Acquisition", in A. Sorace, C. Heycock and R. Shillock (eds): *GALA* 1997, Edinburgh, 16-21.
Babyonyshev, M. (1993). "Acquisition of the Russian Case System". In C. Phillips (ed). *MITWPL 19*, 1-43.
Baker, C. L. (1970). "Notes on the Description of English Questions. The Role of an Abstract Question Morpheme", *Foundations of Language* 6, 107-219.
Bäuerle, R. (1979). *Temporale Deixis, temporale Frage*. Tübingen:Niemeyer.
Beckman, J. (ed) (1995). *Proceedings of the North East Linguistic Society 1995. NELS 25*, GLSA, University of Massachussetts.
Behrens, H. (1993). *Temporal Reference in German Child Language*. Doctoral Dissertation, University of Amsterdam.
Belletti, A. (1990). *Generalized Verb Movement*. Turin: Rosenberg and Sellier,.
Belletti, A. (1993). "Case Checking and Clitic Placement: Three Issues on (Italian/Romance) Clitics", *Geneva Generative Papers* 1(2), 101-118.
Belletti, A. (1999). "Italian/Romance Clitics: Structure and Derivation". In H.van Riemsdijk (ed): 543-579.

Belletti, A. and C. Hamann (2000). "Ca on fait pas! On the L2-Acquisition of French by Two Young Children with Different Source Languages". In C. Howell, S. Fish and T. Keith-Lucas (eds). *BUCLD* 24, 116-127.

Belletti, A. and L. Rizzi (eds) (1996): *Parameters and Functional Heads*. Oxford: Oxford University Press.

Berman, S, J.W. Choe and J. McDonough (1986). *Proceedings of the North East Linguistic Society 1986. NELS 16*. GLSA, University of Massachussetts.

Berwick, R. (1982). *Locality Principles and the Acquisition of Syntactic Knowledge*. Ph.D. thesis, MIT.

Bickerton, D. (1984). "The Language Bioprogram Hypothesis", *Behavioral and Brain Sciences*, Vol 7, 173-221.

Blevins, J. and J. Carter (eds) (1988). *Proceedings of the North East Linguistics Society, NELS 18*, GLSA, University of Massachussetts.

Bloom, L. (1970). *Language Development: Form and Function in Emerging Grammars*. Cambridge, Mass. : MIT Press.

Bloom, P. (1990). "Subjectless Sentences in Child Language". *Linguistic Inquiry* 21, 491-504.

Bol, G. W. (1996). "Optional Subjects in Dutch Child Language". In Ch. Koster and F. Wijnen (eds).GALA, 125-134.

Borer, H. (1984). *Parametric Syntax*. Dordrecht: Foris.

Borer, H. and K. Wexler (1987). "The Maturation of Syntax." In T. Roeper and E. Williams (eds), 123-172.

Boser. K., B. Lust, L. Santelmann, J. Whitman (1992). "The Syntax of CP and V2 in Early German. The Strong Continuity Hypothesis". In K. Broderick (ed). *NELS 22*, 51-65.

Bottari, P., P. Cipriani & A. M. Chilosi (1992). "Proto-syntactic Devices in the Acquisition of Italian Free Morphology", *Geneva Generative Papers*, 0(1-2), 85-101.

Bottari, P., P. Cipriani, and A. M. Chilosi (2000). "Dissociations in the Acquisition of Clitic Pronouns by Dysphasic Children: a Case Study from Italian". In S. Powers and C. Hamann (eds)., 237-278.

Bowerman, M. (1973). *Early Syntactic Development*. Cambridge: CUP.

Brandner, E. (1993). "The Projection of Categories and the Nature of Agreement". In G. Fanselow (ed), 73-121.

Broca, P. (1865). "Sur le siège de la faculté du langage articulé". *Bulletin de la Société d'Anthropologie* 6, 337-393.

Borderick, K. (ed) (1992): *Proceedings of the North East Linguistics Society. NELS 22*, GLSA, University of Massachussetts.

Bromberg, H.S. and K. Wexler (1995). "Null Subjects in Wh-Questions". In C. Schütze, J. Ganger, and K. Boihier (eds). *MITWPL 26*, 221-248.

Bühler, K. (1934). *Sprachtheorie. Die Darstellungsfunktion der Sprache*. Jena.

Büring, D. and K. Hartmann (1994): "Der Kayne war ihr Schicksal". Paper presented at *Generative Grammatik im Süden*, Tübingen, May 1994.

Cardinaletti, A. (1990). "Subject/Object Asymmetries in German Null-topic Constructions and the Status of Spec CP". In J. Mascaro and M. Nespor (eds), 75-84.

Cardinaletti, A. and M.T. Guasti (eds.) (1995). *Syntax and Semantics 28. Small Clauses*. New York: Academic Press.

Cardinaletti, A & M. Starke (1995). "The Tripartition of Pronouns and Its Acquisition: Principle B Puzzles are Ambiguity Problems". In J. Beckman (ed). *NELS 25*, 1-12.

Cardinaletti, A. & M. Starke (2000). "An Overview of the Grammar of Clitics". In S. Powers and C. Hamann (eds), 165-186.

REFERENCES

Chien, Y.-C. and K. Wexler (1990). "Children's Knowledge of Locality Conditions in Binding as Evidence for the Modularity of Syntax and Pragmatics". *Language Acquisition* 1, 225-295.
Chomsky, C. (1969). *The Acquisition of Syntax in Children from 5 to 10*. Cambridge, Mass: MIT Press.
Chomsky, N. (1959). "A review of Skinner's Verbal Behavior". *Language* 35, 26-58.
Chomsky, N. (1965). *Aspects of the Theory of Syntax*. Cambridge, Mass: MIT Press.
Chomsky, N. (1976). "Conditions on Rules of Grammar", *Linguistic Analysis*, vol 2., no.4. Reprinted in N. Chomsky: *Essays on Form and Interpretation*. Amsterdam: North Holland, 1977.
Chomsky, N. (1981). *Lectures on Government and Binding*. Dordrecht: Foris.
Chomsky, N. (1982). *Some Concepts and Consequences of the Theory of Government and Binding*. MIT Press, Cambridge, Mass.
Chomsky, N. (1986). *Knowledge of Language: Its Nature, Origin, and Use*. Praeger, New York.
Chomsky, N. (1993). "A Minimalist Program for Linguistic Theory". In K. Hale and S. Keyser (eds).
Chomsky, N. (1995): *The Minimalist Program*. Cambridge, Mass: MIT Press.
Chomsky, N. and H. Lasnik (1993). "Principles and Parameters". In J. Jacobs, A. von Stechow, W. Sternefeld, and T. Vennemann (eds)., 506-569.
Cipriani, P., A.M Chilosi, P. Bottari, and L. Pfanner (1993). *L'acquisizione della morfosintassi in italiano: Fassi e processi*. Padua: UniPress.
Clahsen, H. (1982). *Spracherwerb in der Kindheit*. Tübingen: Narr.
Clahsen, H. (1986). "Verb Inflections in German Child Language: Acquisition of Agreement Markings and the Functions they Encode". *Linguistics* 24, 79-122.
Clahsen, H. (1988). "Kritische Phasen der Grammatikentwicklung". *Zeitschrift für Sprachwissenschaft* 7, 3-31.
Clahsen, H. (1991). "Constraints on Parameter Setting". *Language Acquisition* 1, 361-391.
Clahsen, H. (ed) (1996): *Generative Perspectives on Language Acquisition*. Amsterdam, Philadelphia: Benjamins'.
Clahsen, H. and M. Penke (1992). "The Acquisition of Agreement Morphology and its Syntactic Consequences: New Evidence on German Child Language From the Simone Corpus". In J. Meisel (ed), 181-224.
Clahsen, H., S. Eisenbeiss and M. Penke (1996). "Lexical Learning in Early Syntactic Development". In H. Clahsen (ed), 129-160.
Clahsen, H., Kursawe and M. Penke (1996): "Introducing CP". In Ch. Koster and F. Wijnen (eds). *GALA*, 5-22.
Clark, E. (1985). "The Acquisition of Romance with Special Reference to French". In D. Slobin (ed), 687-782.
Clark, R. (1992). "The Selection of Syntactic Knowledge". *Language Acquisition* 2. 83-149.
Cooper, R. (1986). "Tense and Discourse Location in Situation Semantics". *Linguistics and Philosophy* 9, 17-36.
Coopmans, P. and W. Philip (1995): "The Role of Lexical Feature Acquisition in the Development of Pronominal Anaphora", paper presented at *Child Language Seminar*, Bristol, April 1995.
Crain, S. and C. McKee (1986). "Acquisition of Structural Restrictions on Anaphora". In S. Berman, J.W. Choe, and J. McDonough (eds). *NELS 16*, 94-110.
Crain, S. and R. Thornton (1990). "Levels of Representation in Child Grammar", Paper presented at the *13th Annual Colloquium of the International Society for Linguistics*, Cambridge, England.

REFERENCES

Crisma, P. (1992). "On the Acquisition of Wh in French". *Geneva Generative Papers* 0(1-2), 115-112.
Crysmann, B. and N. Müller (2000). "On the Non-parallelism in the Acquisition of Reflexive and Non-reflexive Object Clitics". In S. Powers and C. Hamann (eds, 207-236.
Culicover (1991). "Topicalization, Inversion and Complementizers in English". In D. Delfitto, M. Everaert, A. Evers, and F. Stuurman (eds), 1-45.
Davidson, D. and G. Harman (eds) (1972). *Semantics of Natural Language*. Dordrecht: Reidel.
de Haan, G.J. and K. Tuijnman (1988). "Missing Subjects and Objects in Child Grammar". In P. Jordens and J. Lallemans (eds), 101-121.
Delfitto, D., M. Everaert, A. Evers, and F. Stuurman (eds) (1991). *Going Romance and Beyond*. OTS Working Papers, University of Utrecht.
Deprez, V. and A. Pierce (1990). "A Crosslinguistic Study of Negation in Early Syntactic Development". Paper presented at the 15th *Boston University Conference on Language Development*.
Deprez, V. and A. Pierce (1994). "Crosslinguistic Evidence for Functional Projections in Early Grammar". In T. Hoekstra and B. Schwartz (eds), 57-84.
Duffield, N. (1993). "Roots and Rogues: Null-Subjects in German Child Language". Ms., McGill University.
Eimas, P., E.R Siqueland, P.W., Jusczyk, and J. Vigorito (1971). "Speech Perception in Infants". *Science* 171, 303-306.
Eisenbeiß, S. (1994). "Kasus und Wortstellung im deutschen Mittelfeld". Ms., *Lexlern-Projekt*, University of Düsseldorf.
Eisenbeiß, S. and M. Penke (1996). "Children Checking Checking Theory: A Comparison of Case-filter and Feature Checking Approaches". Paper given at WCHSALT, OTS, Utrecht University.
Elman, G., E. Bates, M.H. Johnson, A. Karmiloff-Smith, D. Parisi, and K. Plunkett (1996). *Rethinking Innateness*. Cambridge, Mass.: MIT Press.
Enç, M. (1987). "Anchoring Conditions for Tense". *Linguistic Inquiry* 18, 633-657.
Fanselow, G. (ed) (1993). *The Parametrization of Universal Grammar*. Linguistik Aktuell, Vol 8, Amsterdam: Benjamins'.
Fantuzzi, Ch. (1996). "The Acquisition of Tense and Temporal Reference". In A. Stringfellow, D. Cahana-Amitay, E. Hughes, and A. Zukowski (eds). *BUCLD 20*, 201-212.
Fiengo, R. and R. May (1994): "Syntactic Identity and Semantic Homophony". Ms., CUNY and University of California, Irvine.
Fillmore, Ch. (1971). *Santa Cruz Lectures on Deixis*. Also in: *Indiana University Linguistics Club*, Bloomington, 1975.
Fodor, J.A. (1983). *The Modularity of Mind*. Cambridge, Mass.: MIT Press.
Frazier, L. and J. de Villiers (eds) (1990). *Language Processing and Language Acquistion*. Dordrecht: Kluwer.
Friedemann, M.A. (1992): "The Underlying Position of External Arguments in French". *Geneva Generative Papers* 0(1-2), 123-144.
Friedemann, M.A. (1995): *Sujets syntaxiques; positions, inversions et pro*. Doctoral dissertation, University of Geneva.
Friedemann, M.A. and L. Rizzi (eds) (2000). *The Acquisition of Syntax*. London: Longman.
Galloway, T. and M. Simons (eds) (1995). *Proceedings of SALT V*.
Gawlizek-Maiwald, I., R. Tracy, and A. Fritzenschaft (1992). "Language Acquisition and Competing Linguistic Representations". In J. Meisel (ed), 139-180.
Gerken, L.A. (1994). "Young Children's Representation of Prosodic Phonology: Evidence from English Speakers' Weak Syllable Omission". *Journal of Memory and Language* 33, 19-38.

REFERENCES

Gerken, L.A., B. Landay, and R.E. Remez (1990). Function Morphemes in Young Children's Speech Perception and Production. *Developmental Psychology* 25, 204-216.
Gibson, E. and K. Wexler (1994). "Triggers". *Linguistic Inquiry* 25, 407-454.
Gloor, C., M.-C. Lachat, and M. Maini (1996). *Etude de l'Utilitsation des Teneurs de Place et des Catégories Fonctionelles par un Enfant Francophone*. Recherche de deuxième cycle de Psychologie, University of Geneva.
Gonzàlez, M. (ed) (1994). *Proceedings of the North East Linguistics Society 1995. NELS 24*. GLSA, University of Massachussetts.
Greenhill,A., M. Hughes, H. Littlefiueld, and H. Walsh (eds) (1998). *Proceedings of the22nd Boston University Conference on Language Development. BUCLD 22*. Somerville, Mass: Cascadilla Press.
Grewendorf, G. (1989). *Ergativity in German*. Dordrecht: Foris.
Grewendorf, G. (1990). "Verb-Bewegung und Negation im Deutschen". *Groninger Arbeiten zur germanistischen Linguistik* 30, 57-125.
Grimshaw, J. and S. Rosen (1990). "Knowledge and Obedience: The Developmental Status of the Binding Theory". *Linguistic Inquiry 21*, 187-222.
Grodzinsky, Y. and T. Reinhart (1993). "The Innateness of Binding and Coreference". *Linguistic Inquiry* 24, 69-102.
Groenendijk, J., T. Janssen and M. Stokhof (ed*). Formal Methods in the Study of Language*. Mathematical Centre Tract 135, Amsterdam.
Gruber, J. (1967). "Topicalization in Child Language", *Foundations of Language* 3, 37-65.
Guasti, M.T. (1992). "Verb Syntax in Italian Child Grammar". *Geneva Generative Papers* 0(1-2), 145-162.
Guasti, M.T. (1993/4). Verb Syntax in Italian Child Grammar". *Language Acquisition* 3, 1-40.
Guéron, J. and T. Hoekstra (1992). "Chaînes temporelles et phrases réduites". In H.G. Obernauer and A. Zribi-Hertz (eds), 69-91.
Guéron, J. and T. Hoekstra (1995). "The Temporal Interpretation of Predication". In A. Cardinaletti and M.T. Guasti (eds), 77-108.
Haegeman, L. (1990). "Non-overt Subjects in Diary Contexts". In J. Mascaro and M. Nespor (eds), 167-186.
Haegeman, L. (1991). "Negative Concord, Negative Heads". In D. Delfitto, M Everaert, A. Evers, and F. Stuurman (eds). *OTS Working Papers*., 47-81.
Haegeman, L. (1993). "Object Clitics in West Flemish and the Identification of A/A' ". *Geneva Generative Papers* 2(1), 1-30.
Haegeman, L. (1995a): *The Syntax of Negation*. CUP, Cambridge.
Haegeman, L. (1995b): "Register Variation and Grammatical Theory. Null Subjects in Non prodrop Languages". Ms., University of Geneva. To appear in *Journal of English Language and Linguistics*.
Haegeman, L. (1996a). "Root Infinitives and Initial Null Subjects in Early Dutch". In Ch. Koster and F. Wijnen (eds). *GALA*, 239-250.
Haegeman, L. (1996b). "Root Infinitives, Clitics and Truncated Structures". In H. Clahsen (ed), 271-308.
Haegeman, L. (1996c). "Verb Second, the Split CP, and Null Subjects in Early Dutch Finite Clauses". *Geneva Generative Papers* 4(2), 133-175.
Haegeman, L. (1996d). "Null Subjects and Null Objects (I+II)". Lecture handout, University of Geneva, May 1996.
Haegeman, L. (1996e). "Truncation, Root Infinitives and the Landing Site of Clitics: A Comparison of Dutch and French". Lecture handout, University of Geneva, May 1996.

REFERENCES

Haegeman, L. (ed) (1997). *Elements of Grammar. A Handbook of Generative Syntax*. Dordrecht: Kluwer.

Haegeman, L. (2000). "Adult Null Subjects in Non-pro-Drop Languages". In M.-A. Friedemann and L. Rizzi (eds), 129-169.

Haegeman, L. and R. Zanuttini (1991). "Negative Heads and the Neg Criterion". *The Linguistic Review* 8, 233-251.

Hale, K.L. and S.J. Keyser (eds) (1993). *The View from Building 20: Essays in Linguistics in Honour of Sylvain Bromberger*. Cambridge, Mass.: MIT Press.

Halle, M. and A. Marantz (1993). "Distributed Morphology and the Pieces of Inflection". In K. Hale and S.J. Keyser (eds), 111-167.

Hamann, C. (1987). "The Awesome Seeds of Reference Time". In A. Schopf (ed). 27-69.

Hamann, C. (1989). "English Temporal Clauses in a Reference Frame Model". In. A. Schopf (ed), 31-154.

Hamann, C. (1991). "Semantics and Pragmatics - The Case of Temporal Conjunctions". *Linguistische Berichte* 136, 403-437.

Hamann, C. (1992). "Late Empty Subjects in German Child Language", *Technical Reports in Formal and Computational Linguistics* No. 4., University of Geneva.

Hamann, C. (1994). "Null Arguments in German Child Language". *Geneva Generative Papers* 2(2), 62-90.

Hamann, C. (1995). "Null Arguments in German Child Language". In D. MacLaughlin and S. McEwen (eds). *BUCLD 19*, 240-254.

Hamann, C. (1996a). "Negation and Truncated Structures". In M. Aldridge (ed). 72-83.

Hamann, C. (1996b). "Null Arguments in German Child Language". *Language Acquisition* 5, 155-208.

Hamann, C. (1996c). "Wh-in situ, to Move or Not to Move". *Geneva Generative Papers* 4(1), 34-47.

Hamann, C. (1997). *From Syntax to Discourse. Children's Use of Pronominal Clitics, Null Subjects, Infinitives and Operators*. Habilitation thesis, University of Tübingen.

Hamann, C. (2000a). "The Acquisition of Constituent Questions and the Requirements of Interpretation". In M.A. Firedemann and L. Rizzi (eds), 170-201.

Hamann, C. (2000b). "Negation, Infinitives and Heads". In S. Powers and C. Hamann (eds), 423-478.

Hamann, C. (in press): The Acquisition of French Wh Revisited. In N. Scott (ed). *Proceedings of the Liverpool Questions Conference*, November 1998. Liverpool: Liverpool University Press.

Hamann, C., S. Cronel-Ohayon, S. Dubé, U. Frauenfelder, L. Rizzi, M. Starke, and P. Zesiger (in press): "Aspects of Grammatical Development in Young French children with SLI". *Developmental Science*.

Hamann, C., O. Kowalski, and W. Philip (1997). "The French 'Delay of Principle B' Effect". In E. Hughes, M. Hughes, and A. Greenhill (eds). *BUCLD 21*, 205-219.

Hamann, C., K. Lindner and Z. Penner (2001). "Tense, Reference Time and Language Impairment in German Children." In. C. Fery and W. Sternefeld (eds), 182-213.

Hamann, C., Z. Penner and K. Lindner (1997). "German Impaired Grammar: 'Reference Time' Disorders as Indications for a Syntax-Discourse Interface Problem." *Geneva Generative Papers* 5(2), 21-42.

Hamann, C., Z. Penner and K. Lindner (1998). "German Impaired Grammar: The Clause Structure Revisted." *Language Acquisition* 7, 193-246.

Hamann, C. and K. Plunkett (1997). "Subject Omission in Child Danish". In E. Hughes, M. Hughes, and A. Greenhill (eds). *BUCLD 21*, 220-231.

REFERENCES

Hamann, C. and K. Plunkett (1998). "Subjectless Sentences in Child Danish". *Cognition* 69, 35-72.

Hamann, C., L. Rizzi, and U. Frauenfelder (1995). "On the Acquisition of the Pronominal System in French". In C. Jakubowicz (ed). *Recherches Linguistiques de Vincennes*, No 24, 83-101.

Hamann, C., L. Rizzi, and U. Frauenfelder (1996). "The Acquisition of Subject and Object Clitics in French". In H. Clahsen (ed), 309-334.

Harris, M. (1985). "Word Order in Contemporary French: a Functional View". *Working Papers in Functional Grammar* 1, 1-16.

Haverkort, M. (1993). *Clitics and Parametrization: Case Studies in the Interaction of Head Movement Phenomena*. Doctoral dissertation, Tilburg University.

Haverkort, M. and J. Weissenborn (1991). "Clitic and Affix Interaction in Early Romance". Paper presented at the *16th Boston University Conference on Language Development, BUCLD 16*.

Heim, I. (1982). *The Semantics of Definite and Indefinite Noun Phrases*. Ph.D. dissertation, University of Massachusetts, Amherst. Published 1989 by Garland.

Heim, I. (1993). "Anaphora and Semantic Interpretation". *SfS-Report-07-93*, University of Tübingen.

Heim, I. (1994). "Comments on Abusch's Theory of Tense". Ms., MIT.

Hestvik, A. (1990). *LF-Movement of Pronouns and the Computation of Binding Domains*. Ph.D dissertation, Brandeis University.

Hestvik, A. and W. Philip (1997). "Chain Condition Errors and Lexical Feature Acquisition in Norwegian Children". Paper presented at *GALA*, Edinburgh, 1997.

Higginbotham, J. (1983). "Logical Form, Binding, and Nominals". *Linguistic Inquiry* 14, 395-420.

Hill, J.A.C. (1983). "A Computational Model of Language Acquisition in the Two-Year-Old". *Indiana University Linguistics Club*, Bloomington.

Hoehle, B. and J. Weissenborn (1998). "Sensitivity to Closed Class Elements in Preverbal Children". In A. Greenhill, M. Hughes, H. Littlefiueld, and H. Walsh (eds). *BUCLD* 22, 348-349.

Hoekstra, T. and N. Hyams (1996). "Missing Heads in Child Language". In Ch. Koster and F. Wijnen (eds). GALA, 251-260.

Hoekstra, T. and P. Jordens (1991, 1994). "From Adjunct to Head". Paper presented at GLOW, 1991. Also in T. Hoekstra and B. Schwartz (eds), 119-149.

Hoekstra, T. and B. Schwartz (eds) (1994). *Language Acquisition Studies in Generative Grammar*. Amsterdam: Benjamins'.

Hornstein, N. and D. Lightfoot (eds) (1994). *Verb Movement*. Cambridge: CUP.

Howell, C. S. Fish and T. Keith-Lucas (eds) (2000). *Proceedings of the 24th Boston University Conference on Language Development*. Somervill, Mass.: Cascadilla Press.

Huang, J. (1982). *Logical Relations in Chinese and the Theory of Grammar*. Ph.D dissertation, MIT.

Huang, J. (1984). "On the Distribution and Reference of Empty Pronouns". *Linguistic Inquiry* 15, 531-574.

Huebner, T. and C. Ferguson (eds) (1991): *Crosscurrents in Second Language Acquisition and Linguistic Theories*. Benjamins', Amsterdam.

Hughes,E., M. Hughes, and A. Greenhill(eds) (1997). *Proceedings of the 21st Boston University Conference on Language Development. BUCLD 21*, Somerville, Mass.: Cascadilla Press.

Hulk, A. (1997). "The Acquisition of Object Pronouns by a Dutch/French Bilingual Child". In A. Sorace, C. Heycock and R. Shillcock (eds). GALA, 521-526.

REFERENCES

Hulk, A. and S. Zuckermann (2000). "The Interaction between Input and Economy: Acquiring Optionality in French Wh-Questions". In S. C. Howell, S. Fish and T. Keith-Lucas (eds). *BUCLD 24*, 438-449.
Hyams, N. (1983). *The Acquisition of Parametrized Grammars*. Ph.D. dissertation, CUNY.
Hyams, N. (1986). *Language Acquisition and the Theory of Parameters*. Dordrecht: Reidel.
Hyams, N. (1987). "The Theory of Parameters and Syntactic Development", in T. Roeper and E. Williams (eds)., 1-22.
Hyams, N. (1989). "The Null-Subject Parameter in Language Acquisition". In O. Jaeggli and K. Safir (eds), 215-238.
Hyams, N. (1991): "The Genesis of Functional Categories". Ms., UCLA.
Hyams, N. (1996). "The Underspecification of Functional Categories in Early Grammar". In H. Clahsen (ed), 91-128.
Hyams, N. and K. Wexler (1991): "On the Grammatical Basis for Null Subjects in Child Language". *Linguistic Inquiry* 24, 241-159.
Jacobs, J., A. von Stechow, W. Sternefeld, and T. Vennemann (eds) (1993): *Syntax: An International Handbook of Contemporary Research*. Berlin: Mouton - de Gruyter.
Jacobs, R. and P. Rosenbaum (eds) (1970): *Readings in English Transformational Grammar*. Waltham, Mass.: Ginn.
Jaeggli, O. (1982). *Topics in Romance Syntax*. Dordrecht: Foris.
Jaeggli, O. and C. Silva-Corvalan (eds.) (1986): *Studies in Romance Linguistics*. Dordrecht: Foris.
Jaeggli, O. and N. Hyams (1988). "Morphological Uniformity and the Setting of the Null Subject Parameter". In J. Blevins and J. Carter (eds). *NELS 18*, 238-253.
Jaeggli, O. and K. Safir (1989). "The Null Subject Parameter and Parametric Theory".In Jaeggli and Safir (eds), 1-44.
Jaeggli, O. and K. Safir (eds) (1989). *The Null Subject Parameter*. Dordrecht: Kluwer.
Jakubowicz, C. (1989). "Linguistic Theory and Language Acquisition Facts: Reformulation, Maturation or Invariance of Binding Principles". Paper presented at *Knowledge and Language*, Groningen, May 1989.
Jakubowicz, C., N. Müller, O.-K. Kang, B. Riemer, and C. Rigaut (1996). "On the Acquisition of the Pronominal System in French and German". In A. Stringfellow et al. (eds). *BUCLD 20*, 374-385.
Jakubowicz, C., N. Müller, B. Riemer, and C. Rigaut (1997). "The Case of Subject and Object Omission in French and German", in E. Hughes, M. Hughes, and A. Greenhill (eds). *BUCLD 21*, 331-342.
Jakubowicz, C., L. Nash, C. Rigaut, Ch.L. Gérard (1998). "Determiners and Clitic Pronouns in French-Speaking Children with SLI". *Language Acquisition* 7, 113-160.
Jakubowicz,C., L. Nash, and K. Wexler (eds) (in press). *Essays on Syntax, Morphology and Phonology in SLI*. Cambridge, Mass.: MIT Press.
Jonas, D. (1995). "On the Acquisition of Verb Syntax in Faroese". In C. Schütze, J. Granger, and K. Broihier (eds). *MITWPL 26*, 265-280.
Jordens, P. and J. Lallemans (eds) (1988). *Language Development*. Dordrecht: Foris.
Juszyk, P. (1997). *The Discovery of Spoken Language*. Cambridge, Mass.: MIT Press.
Kaiser, G. (1992). *Die klitischen Personalpronomina im Französischen und Portugiesischen. Eine synchronische und diachronische Analyse (=Editionen der Ibero-americana*, Reihe III,4). Frankfurt a.M: Vervuert.
Kaiser, G. (1994). "More about INFL-ection and Agreement: the Acquisition of Clitic Pronouns in French". In J. Meisel (ed), 131-160.

REFERENCES

Kamp, H. (1981). "A Theory of Truth and Semantic Representation". In J. Groenendijk, T. Janssen and M. Stokhof (ed), 277-32.
Kaplan, D. (1977). "Demonstratives". In J. Almong, J. Perry, and H. Wettstein (eds) (1979).
Kapur, S. and R. Clark (2000). "The Automatic Identification and Classification of Clitic Pronouns". In S. Powers and C. Hamann (eds), 299-318.
Kasher, A. (ed) (1991). *The Chomskyan Turn.* Oxford: Blackwell.
Kayne, R. (1975). *French Syntax.* Cambridge, Mass.: MIT Press.
Kayne, R. (1983). *Connectedness and Binary Branching.* Dordrecht: Foris.
Kayne, R. (1994). *The Antisymmetry of Syntax.* Cambridge, Mass.: MIT Press.
Kazman, R. (1990): "The Acquisition of Functional Categories and the Lexicon. A Psychologically Plausible Model". Ms., Carnegie-Mellon University, Pittsburgh.
Klein, W. (1994). *Time in Language.* London: Routledge.
Klein, W. and C. Perdue (1997). "The Basic Variety (Or Couldn't natural languages be much simpler.*)" Second Language Research* 13, 4, 301-347.
Klima, E.S. and U. Bellugi (1966). "Syntactic Regularities in the Speech of Children". In J. Lyons and R. Wales (eds), 183-207.
Koopman, H. and D. Sportiche (1991). "The Position of Subjects". *Lingua* 85. 211-258.
Koster, J. (1978). *Locality Principles in Syntax.* Dordrecht: Foris.
Koster, Ch. and F. Wijnen (eds) (1996). *Proceedings of the 1995 Groningen Assembly on Language Aquisition*, GALA.
Kraemer, I. (1993). "The Licensing of Subjects in Early Child Language". In Phillips (ed). *MITWPL 19*, 197-212.
Kusumoto, K. (ed) (1996). *Proceedings of the North East Linguistics Society 1996. NELS 26*, GLSA, University of Massachussetts.
Lakoff, G. (1972). "Linguistics and Natural Logic". In D. Davidson and G. Harman (eds), 545-665.
Lasnik, H. (1989). *Essays on Anaphora.* Dordrecht: Kluwer.
Lasnik, H. and T. Stowell (1991). "Weakest Cross-over". *Linguistic Inquiry* 22, 678-720.
Lebeaux, D. (1988). *Language Acquisition and the Form of the Grammar.* Ph.D. dissertation, University of Massachusetts.
LeBlanc, D. (1995). "An Activation Model for Parameter Setting', *Amsterdam Series of Child Language Development, ASCLD* 4, 81-106.
Lenneberg, E. (1967). *The Biological Foundations of Language.* New York: John Wiley and Sons.
Levow, G.-A. (1995). "Tense and Subject Position in Interrogatives and Negatives in Child French: Evidence For and Against Truncated Structures". In C. Schütze, J. Ganger, and K. Boihier (eds). *MITWPL 26*, 281-304.
Leyat, J. and K. Micalizzi (1998). *Reconnaissance des Pronoms.* Recherche de deuxième cycle de Psychologie. University of Geneva.
Lightbown, P.(1977). *Constituency and Variation in the Acquisition of French.* Ph.D. dissertation, Columbia University.
Lightfoot, D. (1989): "The Child's Trigger Experience: Degree-0 Learnability", *Behavioral and Brain Sciences* 12, 321-375.
Lyons, J. and R. Wales (eds) (1966): *Psycholinguistic Papers.* Edinburgh University Press, Edinburgh.
Manzini, R. and K. Wexler (1987). "Parameters, Binding Theory, and Learnability". *Linguistic Inquiry* 18, 413-444.
MacLaughlin, D. and S. McEwen (eds) (1995). *Proceedings of the 19th Boston University Conference on Language Development. BUCLD 19.* Somerville, Mass.: CascadillaPress

MacWhinney, B. (1991). *The Childes Project: Tools for Analysing Talk*. Hillsdale, NJ: Lawrence Erlbaum. See also the new edition.

MacWhinney, B. and C. Snow (1990). "The Child Language Data Exchange System: an Update". *Journal of Child Language* 17, 457-472.

Marcus, G., S.Pinker, M. Ullman, M. Hollander, T John Rosen and Fei Xu (1992). "Overregularization in Language Acquisition", *Monographs of the Society for Research in Child Development* 57/4, Serial No. 228.

Mascaro, J. and M. Nespor (eds) (1990): *Grammar in Progress*. Dordrecht: Foris.

Mathieu, E. (in press). "French Wh-in-situ and Intervention Effects". In N. Scott (ed). *Proceedings of the Liverpool Question Conference*, November 1998. Liverpool: Liverpool University Press.

McCawley, J.D. (1981). *Everything that Linguists Have Always Wanted to Know about Logic (but were afraid to ask)*. Oxford: Blackwell.

McClellan, J.L. and D.E. Rumelhart and the PDP Research Group (eds) (1986): *Parallel Distributed Processing: Explorations in the Microstructure of Cognition. Volume 2: Psychological and Biological Models*. Bradford Books. Cambridge Mass.: MIT Press.

McKee, C. (1992). "A Comparison of Pronouns and Anaphors in Italian and English Acquisition". *Language Acquisition* 2, 21-54.

Mehler, J. and E. Dupouy (1990). *Naître humain*. Editions Odile Jacob, Paris.

Meisel, J. (1990). "INFL-ection: Subjects and Subject-Verb Agreement in Early Child Language". In J. Meisel (ed), 237-298.

Meisel, J. (ed) (1990). *Two First Languages. Early Grammatical Development in Bilingual Children*. Dordrecht: Foris.

Meisel, J. (ed) (1992): *The Acquisition of Verb Placement. Functional Categories and V2 Phenomena in Language Acquisition*. Dordrecht: Kluwer.

Meisel, J. (ed) (1994). *Bilingual First Language Acquisition. French and German Grammatical Development*. Amsterdam: Benjamins'.

Meisel, J. and M-J. Ezeizabarrena (1996). "Subject-Verb and Object-Verb Agreement in Early Basque". in H. Clahsen (ed), 201-241.

Meisel, J. and N. Müller (1992). "Finiteness and Verb Placement in Early Child Grammars: Evidence from Simultaneous Acquisition of French and German Bilinguals". In J. Meisel (ed), 109-138.

Miller, M. (1979): *The Logic of Language Development in Early Childhood*.Springer Verlag, Berlin.

Montague, R. (1974): "The Proper Treatment of Quantification", in R. Thomason (ed). 247-270.

Müller, N. (1994). "Parameters Cannot be Reset, Evidence from the Development of Comp". In J. Meisel (ed), 235-269.

Müller, G. and W. Sternefeld (1993): "Improper Movement and Unambiguous Binding". *Linguistic Inquiry* 24, 461-507.

Nakisa, R., K. Plunkett and U. Hahn (1996). "A Cross-Linguistic Comparison of Single and Dual-Route Models of Inflectional Morphology". Ms., University of Oxford.

Nerbonne, J. (1986). "Reference Time and Time in Narration". *Linguistics and Philosophy* 9, 83-95.

Obernauer, H.G. and A. Zribi-Hertz (eds) (1992): *Structure de la phrase et théorie du liage*. Presses Universitaires de Vincennes, Vincennes.

Partee, B. (1973). "Some Structural Analogies between Tenses and Pronouns". *Journal of Philosophy* 70, 603-609.

Partee, B. (1984). "Nominal and Temporal Anaphora", *Linguistics and Philosophy* 7, 234-286.

Partee, B., A. terMeulen, and R. Wall (1990). *Mathematical Methods in Linguistics.* Dordrecht: Kluwer.
Penner, Z. (1990a): "The Acquisition of the Syntax of Bernese Swiss German, the Role of Functional Elements in Restructering Early Grammar", paper presented at the 15*th Annual Boston University Conference on Language Development, BUCLD 15.*
Penner, Z. (1990b): "On the Acquisition of Verb-Placement and Verb Projection Raising in Bernese Swiss German". In M. Rothweiler (ed), 166-189.
Penner, Z. (1992). "The Ban on Parameter Resetting, Default Mechanisms, and the Acquisition of V2 in Bernese Swiss German". In J. Meisel (ed), 245-283.
Penner, Z. (1994a). "Asking Questions without CPs". In T. Hoekstra and B. Schwartz (eds), 177-214.
Penner, Z. (1994b). *Ordered Parameter Setting in First Language Acquisition. The Role of Syntactic Bootstrapping and the Triggering Hierarchy in Determining the Developmental Sequence in Early Grammar.* Habilitation thesis, University of Berne.
Penner, Z. (1998): "Learning-Theoretical Perspectives on Language Disorders in Childhood. Developmental Dysphasia in Swiss German". Fachgruppe Sprachwissenschaft der Universität Konstanz, *Arbeitspapier 89.* (Linguistic Working Papers 89, University of Konstanz), 110-187.
Penner, Z., M. Schoenenberger, and J. Weissenborn (1994). "The Acquisition of Object Placement in Early German and Swiss German". *Linguistics in Potsdam* 1, 93-108.
Penner, Z., R. Tracy, and J. Weissenborn (2000): "Scrambling in Early Developmental Stages in Standard and Swiss German". In S. Powers and C. Hamann (eds), 127-164.
Pesetski, D. (1987). "Wh-in-situ: Movement and Unselective Binding". In E. Reuland and A. terMeulen (eds)., 98-129.
Philip, W. and P. Coopmans (1996a). "The Double Dutch 'Delay of Principle B Effect'". In Stringfellow, A., D. Cahana-Amitay, E. Hughes, and A. Zukowski (eds). *BUCLD 20*, 576-587.
Philip, W. and P. Coopmans (1996b). "The Role of Referentiality in the Acquisition of Pronominal Anaphora". In K. Kusumoto (ed). *NELS 26*, 241-256.
Phillips, C. (ed) (1993). *Papers on Case and Agreement II, MITWPL 19.*
Phillips, C. (1995). "Syntax at Age Two: Cross Linguistic Differences". In C. Schütze, J. Ganger, and K. Boihier (eds). *MITWPL 26*, 325-382.
Pierce, A. (1989). *On the Emergence of Syntax: a Cross-linguistic Study.* Ph.D. dissertation, MIT.
Pierce, A. (1992). *Language Acquisition and Syntactic Theory.* Dordrecht:Kluwer.
Pinker, S. (1994). *The Language Instinct.* Penguin, London.
Pinker, S. and A. Prince (1988). "On Language and Connectionism: Analysis of a Parallel Distributed Processing Model of Acquisition". *Cognition* 28, 73-193.
Piaget, J. (1955). *The Language and Tought of the Child.* Meridian Books.
Platzack, Ch. (1990). "A Grammar Without Functional Categories: A Syntactic Study of Early Swedish Child Language". *Nordic Journal of Linguistics* 13, 107-126.
Platzack, Ch. (1996). "The Initial Hypothesis of Syntax: A Minimalist Perspective on Language Acquisition and Attrition". In H. Clahsen (ed), 369-414.
Platzack, Ch. and A. Holmberg (1989). "The Role of AGR and Finiteness", in *Working Papers in Scandinavian Syntax,* vol. 43, 51-76.
Plunkett, B. (1992). "Continuity and the Landing Site for Wh-movement". In *Bangor Research Papers in Linguistics* 4, 53-77.
Plunkett, B. (1999). "Targetting Complex Structure in French questions." In A. Greenhill, H. Littlefield and C. Tano (eds). *BUCLD 23*, 764-775.

Plunkett, K. (1985). "Projekt Barnesprog", *Nordisk Psykologi* 38, 14-26.
Plunkett, K. and V. Marchman (1993). "From Rote Learning to System Building", *Cognition* 38, 43-102.
Plunkett, K. and S. Strömqvist (1990). "The Acquisition of Scandinavian Languages". In J. Allwood (ed). *GPTL 59*. Also in Slobin (ed).
Plunkett, K. and S. Strömqvist (1991). "The Acquisition of Subject in Danish and Swedish". Paper presented at the *16th Boston University Conference on Language Development, BUCLD 16*.
Poeppel, D. and K. Wexler (1993). "The Full Competence Hypothesis of Clause Structure in Early German". *Language* 69, 1-33.
Pollock, J.Y. (1989). "Verb Movement, Universal Grammar and the Structure of IP". *Linguistic Inquiry* 20. 365-424.
Postal, P. (1974). *On Raising*. Cambridge, Mass.: MIT Press.
Powers, S. (1995). "The Acquisition of Pronouns in Dutch and English". In D. MacLaughlin and S. McEwen (eds). *BUCLD 19*, 439-450.
Powers, S. and C. Hamann (eds) (2000). *The Acquisition of Scrambling and Cliticization*. Dordrecht: Kluwer.
Prévost, P. and L. White (2000). "Accounting for Morphological Variation in Second Langague Acquisition: Truncation or Missing Inflection?" In M.-A. Friedemann and L. Rizzi (eds), 202-235.
Radford, A. (1988): " Small Children's Small Clauses", *Transactions of the Philological Society*, Vol. 86, No. 1, 1-43.
Radford, A. (1990). *Syntactic Theory and the Acquisition of English Syntax*. Oxford: Blackwell.
Radford, A. (1996a). "The Nature of Children's Initial Clauses", in M. Aldridge (ed), 112-148.
Radford, A. (1996b): "Towards a Structure Building Model of Acquisition". In H. Clahsen (ed), 43-90.
Radford, A. (1997). *Syntax. A Minimalist Introduction*. Cambridge: Cambridge University Press.
Rasetti, L. (1995): *La distribution du sujet nul dans la grammaire enfantine du français*. Mémoire de licence, University of Geneva.
Rasetti, L. (1996). "Null Subjects and Root Infinitives in the Child Grammar of French". *Geneva Generative Papers* 4(2), 120-132.
Rasetti, L. (2000): "Null subjects and Root Infinitives in the Child Grammar of French." In M.-A. Friedemann and L. Rizzi (eds), 236-268.
Reichenbach (1947). *The Elements of Symbolic Logic*. New York: Free Press.
Reinhart, T. (1983). *Anaphora and Semantic Interpretation*. London: Croom Helm.
Reinhart, T. (1991). "Elliptic conjunctions: Non quantificational LF". In A. Kasher (ed).
Reinhart, T. (1995). "Interface Strategies", *OTS Working Papers*, University of Utrecht.
Reinhart, T. (1997). "Quantifier Scope: How Labor is Divided between QR and Chice Functions". *Linguistics and Philosophy* 20 (4), 335-397.
Reinhart, T. and E. Reuland (1993). "Reflexivity". *Linguistic Inquiry* 24, 675-720.
Reis, M. and I. Rosengren (1991). "What Do Imperatives Tell Us about Wh-movement?" *Natural Language and Linguistic Theory* 10, 97-118.
Reuland, E. and A. terMeulen (eds) (1987). *The Representation of (In)definites*. Cambridge, Mass.: MIT Press.
Rice and Wexler (1996). "A Phenotype of Specific Language Impairment: Extended Optional Infinitives". In A. Stringfellow et al. (eds). *BUCLD 20*, 610-621.
Rizzi, L. (1982). *Issues in Italian Syntax*. Dordrecht: Foris.
Rizzi, L. (1986a). "Null Objects and the Theory of pro". *Linguistic Inquiry* 17, 501-557.

Rizzi, L. (1986b). "On the Status of Subject Clitics in Romance". In O. Jaeggli and C. Silva-Corvalan (eds), 391-419.
Rizzi, L. (1990a). "Speculations on Verb Second". In J. Mascaro and M. Nespor, (eds), 375-386.
Rizzi, L. (1990b). *Relativized Minimality*. Cambridge, Mass.: MIT Press.
Rizzi, L. (1991). "Residual Verb Second and the Wh-criterion", *Technical Reports on Formal and Computational Linguistics* No. 2, Geneva University. Appeared in A. Belletti and L. Rizzi (eds), 371-393.
Rizzi, L. (1992). "Early Null Subjects and Root Null Subjects". *Geneva Generative Papers*, 0(1-2). 102-115. Appeared in T. Hoekstra and B. Schwartz (eds), 151-177.
Rizzi, L. (1993). "A Parameter Approach to Comparative Syntax: Properties of the Pronominal System". *English Linguistics* 10, 1-27.
Rizzi, L. (1994). "Some Notes on Linguistic Theory and Language Development: the Case of Root Infinitives". *Language Acquisition* 3, 371-393.
Rizzi, L. (1995a). "Early Null Subjects and Economy of Representation". Plenary talk presented at the *Groningen Assembly on Language Acquisition, GALA*.
Rizzi, L. (1995b). "A Note on Do-Support". Ms., University of Geneva.
Rizzi, L. (1997). "The Fine Structure of the Left Periphery". In L. Haegeman (ed), 281-337.
Rizzi, L. (1998). "Remarks on Early Null Subjects". In A. Greenhill, M. Hughes, H. Littlefield, and H. Walsh (eds). BUCLD 22, 14-37.
Rizzi, L. (2000). "Remarks on Early Null Subjects". In M.A. Friedemann and L. Rizzi (eds), 269-292.
Roberge, Y. (1990). *The Syntactic Recoverability of Null Arguments*. Kingston and Montreal: McGill-Queen's University Press.
Roberts, I. (1992). *Verbs and Diachronic Syntax*. Dordrecht: Kluwer.
Roeper, T. (1992). "Reflections on Reference in Language Acquisition". Ms., University of Massachussetts.
Roeper, T. and B. Rohrbacher (2000). "Null Subjects in Early Child English and the Theory of Economy of Projection". In S. Powers and C. Hamann (eds), 345-396.
Roeper, T. and J. Weissenborn (1990). "How to Make Parameters Work: Comments on Valian". In L. Frazier and Jill de Villiers (eds), 147-162.
Roeper, T. and E. Williams (eds) (1987). *Parameter Setting*. Dordrecht: Reidel.
Rohrbacher, B. (1994). *The Germanic VO Languages and the Full Paradigm: A Theory of V to I Raising*. Ph.D. dissertation, University of Massachussetts, Amherst.
Ross, J.R. (1970). "On Declarative Sentences", in R. Jacobs and P. Rosenbaum (eds). 222-272.
Ross, J.R. (1982). "Pronoun Deleting Processes in German", paper presented at the *Annual Meeting of the Linguistic Society of America*, San Diego, California.
Rothweiler, M. (ed) (1990). *Spracherwerb und Grammatik. Linguistische Untersuchungen zum Erwerb von Syntax und Morphologie. Linguistische Berichte*, Sonderheft 3, Westdeutscher Verlag, Opladen.
Rumelhart, D.E. and J.L. McClellan (1986). "On Learning the Past Tense in English". In McClellan and Rumelhart (eds).
Sano, T. (1995). *Roots in Language Acquisition: A Comparative Study of Japanese and European Languages*. Ph.D. dissertation, UCLA.
Sano, T. and N. Hyams (1994). "Agreement, Finiteness and the Development of Null Arguments". In M. Gonzàlez (ed). *NELS 24*, 543-558
Santelman, L. (1995a). *The Acquisition of Verb Second Grammar in Child Swedish: Continuity of Universal Grammar in Wh-questions, Topicalization and Verb Raising*. Ph.D. dissertation, Cornell University.

REFERENCES

Santelman, L. (1995b). "Topicalization, CP and Licensing in the Acquisition of Swedish", in D. MacLaughlin and S. McEwen (eds). *BUCLD 19*, 499-510.

Santelman, L. (1996). "Subject Initial V2 as IP: Evidence from Subject/Non-subject Asymmetries in the Acquisition of V2 in Mainland Scandinavian", paper presented at *WCHTSALT*, OTS, June 1996.

Schaeffer, J. (1990). *The Syntax of the Subject in Child Language: Italian Compared to Dutch.* Master's thesis. University of Utrecht.

Schaeffer, J. (1997). "Object Scrambling, Object (-clitic) Placement and Nominal Specificity in Dutch Child Language". In E. Hughes, M. Hughes, and A. Greenhill (eds). *BUCLD 21*, 527-537.

Schaner-Wolles, Ch. (1994). "The Acquisition of Negation". Paper presented at GLOW, Vienna, April 1994.

Schoenenberger, M., A. Pierce, K. Wexler, and F. Wijnen (1996). "Accounts of Root Infinitives and the Interpretation of Root Infinitives". *Geneva Generative Papers* 3(2)., 47-71.

Schopf, A. (ed) (1987). *Essays on Tensing in English.* Vol 1. Tübingen: Niemeyer.

Schopf, A. (ed) (1989). *Essays on Tensing in English.* Vol 2. Tübingen: Niemeyer.

Schütze, C. (1995). "Children's Subject Case Errors: Evidence for Case-related Functional Projections". In *Proceedings of FLSM VI*, Vol. 1, 155-166.

Schütze,C., J. Ganger, and K. Boihier (eds) (1995). *Papers on Language Processing and Acquisition. MITWPL 26.*

Schütze, C. and K. Wexler (1996a). "Subject Case Licensing and English Root Infinitives". In A. Stringfellow et al. (eds). *BUCLD 20*, 670-681.

Schütze, C. and K. Wexler (1996b). "What Case Aquisition Data Have to Say about the Components of INFL". Paper presented at *WCHTSALT*, OTS, Utrecht University, June 1996.

Shlonsky, U. (1992). "The Representation of Agreement in Comp". *Geneva Generative Papers* 0(0), 39-52.

Sigurjónsdóttir, S. and P. Coopmans (1996). "The Acquisition of Anaphoric Relations in Dutch", *Amsterdam Series on Child Language Development, ASCLD* 5. Instituut Algemene Taalwetenschap 68, Amsterdam.

Slobin, D. (ed) (1985). *The Cross-linguistic Study of Language Acquisition.* Hillsdale, New Jersey: Erlbaum Press.

Solan, L. (1983). *Pronominal Reference: Child Language and the Theory of Grammar.* Dordrecht: Reidel.

Sorace, A., C. Heycock and R. Shillock (1997). *Proceedings of the GALA 1997 Conference on Language Acquisition*, Edinburgh: HCRC.

Speas, P. (1994). "Null Arguments in a Theory of Economy of Projection". *University of Massachussetts Occasional Papers in Linguistics* 17, 179-209.

Sportiche, A. (1992). "Clitic Constructions". Paper presented at the GLOW Conference, Lisbon.

Stowell, T. (1993): "Syntax of Tense". Ms., MIT.

Stringfellow, A., D. Cahana-Amitay, E. Hughes, and A. Zukowski (eds) (1996): *Proceedings of the 20th Boston University Conference on Language Development. BUCLD 20*, Cascadilla Press, Somerville, Mass.

Taraldsen, K.T. (1978). "On the NIC, Vacuous Application and the That-Trace Filter". *Indiana University Linguistics Club*, Bloomington.

Thomason, R. (1974). *Formal Philosophy. Selected Papers of Richard Montague.* New Haven: Yale University Press.

Torrens, V. and K. Wexler (2000). "The Acquisition of Clitic Doubling in Spanish". In S. Powers and C. Hamann (eds), 279-298.

REFERENCES

Thornton, R. (1990). *Adventures in Long-distance Moving: The Acquisition of Complex Wh-Questions*. Ph.D. dissertation, University of Connecticut.
Thronton, R. and K. Wexler (1999). *Principle B, VP Ellipsis, and Interpreation in Child Grammar*. Cambridge, Mass.: MIT Press.
Tomaselli, A. (1990). "COMP as a licensing head". In J. Mascaro and M. Nespor (eds), 433-445.
Tracy, R. (1991). *Sprachliche Strukturentwicklung*. Tübingen: Narr.
Tracy, R. (1994). "Raising Questions: Formal and Functional Aspects of the Acquisition of Wh-questions in German". In R. Tracy and E. Lattney (eds), 1-34.
Tracy, R. and E. Lattney (eds) (1994). *How Tolerant is Universal Grammar? Essays on Language Learnability and Language Variation*. Tübingen: Niemeyer.
Vainikka, A. (1994). "Case in the Development of English Syntax". *Language Acquisition* 3, 257-325.
Valian, V. (1990). "Logical and Psychological Constraints on the Acquisition of Syntax". In L. Frazier and J. de Villiers (eds), 119-146.
Valian, V. (1991). "Syntactic Subjects in the Early Speech of American and Italian Children". *Cognition* 40, 21-81.
van der Lely, H. and L. Stollwerck (1997). "Binding Theory and Specifically Language Impaired Children". *Cognition 62*, 245-290..
van Riemsdijk, H. (ed): *Clitics in the Languages of Europe*. Berlin: Mouton - de Gruyter.
Verrips, M. and J. Weissenborn (with R. Berman) (1989). "Negation as a Window to the Structure of Early Child Language". Ms., Max-Planck-Institute of Psycholinguistics, Nijmegen.
Verrips, M. and J. Weissenborn (1992): "Routes to Verb Placement in German and French", in J. Meisel (ed), 283-333.
Vikner, S. (1991). *Verb Movement and the Licensing of NP-Positions in the Germanic Languages*. Doctoral dissertation, University of Geneva.
Vikner, S. (1995). *Verb Movement and Expletive Subjects in the Germanic Languages*. Oxford: Oxford University Press.
v. Stechow, A. (1991). "Intensionale Semantik - eingeführt anhand der Temporalität". *SFB-Report*, University of Konstanz.
v. Stechow, A.(1995a): "On the Proper Treatment of Tense". In T. Galloway and M. Simons (eds), 362-386.
v. Stechow, A. (1995b). "Tenses and the Time Arguments in Extensional Contexts", paper presented at the University of Geneva, November 1995.
v. Stechow, A. (1999). "Some Remarks on Choice Functions and LF Movement". Ms., University of Tübingen.
v. Stechow, A. and W. Sternfeld (1988). *Bausteine syntaktischen Wissens*. Opladen: Westdeutscher Verlag.
Wagner, K. (1985). "How Much Do Children Say in a Day?". *Journal of Child Language* 12, 475-487.
Wang, Qi and D. Lillo-Martin, C. T. Best, and A. Levitt (1992). "Null Subject vs. Null Object: Some Evidence from the Acquisition of Chinese and English". *Language Acquisition* 2, 221-254.
Weissenborn, J. (1988). "The Acquisition of Clitic Object Pronouns and Word Order in French: Syntax or Morphology?". Paper presented at the *3rd International Morphology Meeting*, Krems, July 1988.
Weissenborn, J. (1990). "Functional Categories and Verb Movement: the Acquisition of German Syntax Reconsidered". In M. Rothweiler (ed), 166-189.

Weissenborn, J. (1991). "Null Subjects in Early Grammars". in J. Weissenborn, H. Goodluck, and T. Roeper (eds), 269-299.
Weissenborn, J., H. Goodluck, and T. Roeper (eds) (1991). *Theoretical Issues in Language Acquisition*. Hillsdale, NJ: Lawrence Erlbaum.
Weissenborn, J., T. Roeper, and J. deVilliers (1996). "Superiority. Syntax or Semantics?" Paper presented at WCHTSALT, OTS, Utrecht University.
Wells, J.C. (1989). "Computer-Coded Phonemic Notation of Individual Languages of the European Community". *Journal of the International Phonetic Association* 19, 31-54.
Werker, J.F. and R.C. Tees (1983). "Developmental Changes across Childhood in the Perception of Non-Native Speech Sounds". *Canadian Journal of Psychology* 37. 278-286.
Weverink, M. (1989). *The Subject in Relation to Inflection in Child Language*. Master's thesis, University of Utrecht.
Wexler, K. (1992). "Optional Infinitives, Head Movement and the Economy of Derivations in Child Grammar". *MIT Occasional Papers # 45*.
Wexler, K.(1994). "Optional Infinitives, Head Movement and the Economy of Derivations in Child Grammar". In N. Hornstein and D. Lightfoot (eds), 305-350.
Wexler, K. (1996). "Maturation and Growth of Grammar". Ms., MIT. To appear in W.C. Ritchie and T.K. Bathia (eds). *Handbook of Language Acquisition*.
Wexler, K. (1997). "Explanatory Models of Language Acquisition". Plenary talk presented at *GALA*, Edinburgh, 1997.
Wexler, K. (1998). "Very Early Parameter Setting and the Unique Checking Constraint: a New Explanation of the Optional Infinitive Stage". *Lingua* 106, 23-79.
Wexler, K. (2000). "Three Problems in the Theory of the Optional Infinitive Stage: Stage/Individual Predicates, Eventive Verbs, and Finite Null Subjects". In R. Billerey et al. (eds). *Proceedings of WCCFL 19*. Somerville, Mass.: Cascadilla Press, 101-114.
Wexler, K. (in press)." The Unique Checking Constraint as the Explanation of Clitic Omission in SLI and Normal Development". In C. Jakubowicz, L. Nash, and K. Wexler (eds).
Wexler, K. and Y-C. Chien (1985). "The Development of Lexical Anaphors and Pronouns". *Papers and Reports on Child Language Development (PRCLD)*, Stanford University, 138-149.
White, L. (1996): "Clitics in L2-French". In H. Clahsen (ed), 335-368.
Wijnen, F. (1994). "Incremental Acquisition of Phrase Structure: a Longitudinal Analysis of Verb Placement in Dutch Child Language". Ms., University of Groningen.
Williams, E. (1986). "A Reassignment of the Functions of LF". *Linguistic Inquiry* 17, 265-299.
Wode, H. (1977). "Four Early Stages in the Development of LI Negation", *Journal of Child Language* 4, 87-102..
Zanuttini, R. (1997). *Negation and Clausal Structure: A Comparative Study of Romance Languages*. New York, Oxford: Oxford University Press.
Zeller, J. (1994). *Die Syntax des Tempus*. Opladen: Westdeutscher Verlag.
Zribi-Hertz, A. (1994). "Les clitiques nominatifs du français". *Cahiers de Recherche en Linguistique*, Département des sciences du langage, Université de Paris 8.
Zwart, J.W. (1993). *Dutch Syntax*. Doctoral dissertation, University of Groningen.

INDEX

A-bound, 72f
A-chain, 53, 82, 92, 96f
A-movement, 53
A'-position, 54
accidental coreference, see coreference
acquisition, 1, 149
    instantaneous, 5
act-out-task, 109
adjunct, 278, 281
adverb,
    temporal, 321
Agr, 164, 277, 299
AgrOP, 96
AgrSP, 180f, 210
agreement, 58, 177, 180, 200, 202f, 210, 274f, 282, 297, 307f, 331
    fairly rich, 299f, 307, 309
    rich, 151, 164, 210, 298
    spec-head, 164
    subject-verb, 202, 204
    systems. 160
anaphor, 21, 65f, 72, 74
anaphoric marker, 91
    strong, 91
anchor, 179, 198, 207, 315
anchorage, 311f, 317, 327
    deictic, 261, 310
anchored, 178
anchoring, 17, 68, 150, 310, 330
antecedent, 66

quantified, 109, 127f,
anti-subject orientation, 128f
argument, 92
    chain, see A-chain
    drop, 286, 310
    position, 92
    quasi-, 192f,
argument/non-argument asymmetry, 278
aspect, 321
    variable, 321
ATOM, 205, 247, 251-257, 260, 273, 285
Austrian, 294
auxiliary, 206, 208f, 213, 232-248, 265, 267f, 270, 273
    null, 177
    missing AUX see missing
Avoid Structure, 100, 196, 252, 317, 329, 331, 334

base generation, 94, 98
binding, 65
    Condition, 88
    error, 110
    domain, 111
    unselective, 263
binding principles, 16, 22f, 92, 331
    standard, 66, 67, 72, 87, 145
binding theory, 18, 150
by-passing, 260, 276f, 282

c- command, 66, 72
case
    assignment, 161
    default, 201
    feature, 71, 82, 93
    nominative, 331
    structural, 82
    system, 53, 86
Catalan, 242f,
Categorial Uniformity, 179f, 195f 330,
category,
    empty, 160, 181f, 185, 207, 277f, 280, 282
    functional 53, 56, 61f, 163, 180, 316
Chain-Condition, 71, 82-85, 98, 126, 128, 132
chain formation, 143
character, 318
child infinitive, see infinitive
child null subject, see subject
Chinese, 304
choice function, 263, 280, 282
cleft, 274f,
clitic, 61, 65, 70, 100, 102, 130, 211
    at LF, 129
    climbing, 143
    complement, 36ff, 41, 331
    doubling, 22, 98f,
    object, 21f, 25, 31, 34-39, 42f, 47, 51f, 59, 94
    paradigm, 91
    parameter, see parameter
    placement, 23
    position, 24, 44, 181
    pronoun, 16, 65, 91, 332
    pronominal, 17, 18, 23,114, 145, 331
    reflexive, 114
    subject, 25f, 31, 33, 36ff, 42f, 47, 51f, 55f, 58f, 61, 180f,
cliticization, 25, 59
    site, 60, 62
co-argument, 81, 128f,
co-determination, 89f,
Co-index, 73
co-indexation, 66, 79, 128
co-indexed, 65, 72
co-linking, 88
complement, 9
complement clitics, see clitic
Condition B, 83,
constituent question, see question
content, 318
contra-indexation, 128
contra-indexed, 65, 75, 79f
copula, 234ff, 241, 248f, 255, 257f,
copy, 181
coreference, 68, 72, 78, 94, 98,
    accidental , 69, 71, 75f,
    90, 98, 100, 102, 106f, 127-147, 332
    rule, 71, 76, 78ff, 85, 129, 145, 208, 315
coreferential, 68
CP, 12,18, 57, 178ff, 182, 186, 194, 196,213, 275f, 299, 308, 310, 316, 328ff, 332f
    trouble, 214, 262, 327, 333
Creolization, 5
crucial period, 254f
ça, 45ff, 61

D-feature, 205, 246
D-linking, 127, 263, 316
Danish, 153, 158, 168f, 171, 182,

204, 213-242, 251, 253ff, 281, 311, 329
declarative,
  root, 179f, 195
default, 261, 317, 334
delay of principle B, 16, 21f, 65, 68, 79, 90, 110
delay of object clitics, 22, 36, 38-43, 62
determiner, 55f, 335
diary
  drop, 156, 168, 181f, 191-194, 214, 217, 275
discourse, 183, 194, 196, 198f, 207, 252, 262, 311f, 315, 327f,
  anchorage, 130, 144, 147, 313, 316, 332f, 335
  identification, 261, 317, 326f
  semantics, 315
distributional constraint, 45
domain,
  nominal, 208
  temporal, 208
DP, 207, 315, 318, 332
dummy *then*, 319, 325
Dutch, 85f, 96, 111, 132, 167, 180, 187, 193, 201, 229, 242ff, 295f, 309

ECM, see Exceptional Case Marking
Economy of Projection, 201
ECP, see Empty Category Principle
ECR, see Exceptional Co-indexing Rule
elicited production, 109
empty category, see category
Empty Category Principle, 261, 276f, 286
emtpy object, see object

empty subject, see subject
English, 10, 16, 69, 110, 132, 158, 203, 236, 244, 253, 281,
entropy, 8
est-ce que, 273
event time, see time
Exceptional Case Marking, 70, 81, 96, 98, 112, 143, 145
Exceptional Co-indexing Rule, 89, 107, 126, 145
explanatory adequacy, 5
expletive, 161f, 192f, 209
Extended Guise Creation, see guise
extended optional infinitives, 246
extentional, 77

Faroese, 201
feature,
  weak, 244
field of vision, 134
filter, 72
finiteness, 187,
finite, 253f,
finite context, 227
finite construction, 225
finite form, 173, 282
finite null subject, see subject
finite verb(s), 11, 55, 197, 216, 233, 317
finite utterance, 213f,
FinP, 187, 278
FocP, see FocusP
FocusP, 187, 279,
Force, 190
  illocutionary, 187
ForceP, 187, 191, 193, 278, 281, 317, 334
frame time, see time
free inversion, 26

French, 11f, 21-63, 65, 69, 96, 109, 125, 132-145, 157f, 168f, 180, 193ff, 204, 213-247, 251ff, 259 261-264, 273, 276, 281, 288, 291, 296, 309, 331
   Colloquial, 26
   Old, 299
   Standard, 26
Full Competence, 178
Full Continuity, 177
functional category, see category
functional projection, see projection
functional structure, see structure

German, 10, 12f, 146f, 158, 167ff, 171, 180-187, 193, 201, 203, 242-245, 253f, 276, 281, 288, 292f, 296, 299f, 310
Germanic, 146, 244
grounding, 79, 130
guise, 77f, 89, 90, 105ff, 126, 130-134, 141-145, 336
   creation, 142f, 146, 332
   Extended Guise Creation, 131f, 146f
   Lower Subject Guise, 144, 147

head, 9
head movement, see movement
Head-Movement-Constraint, 95

I-to-V, 197
identification, 161, 165, 182
identified, 198
imperfective, 322
index, 73, 208, 318
   inner, 88
indexing, 72
indexation, 66, 73

inflected verb, see verb
inflection, 11, 160, 215, 273, 297
   fairly rich, 299
inflectional system, 206
infinitive, 11, 13f, 30, 51, 59f, 149ff, 168, 170-175, 177f, 181f, 195-200, 207, 211, 215, 225, 227, 233, 244, 248, 253-259, 270, 281, 288f, 291f, 311, 328, 334
   child, 15, 177, 200
   optional, 15, 150, 202, 204, 214, 242
   root, 15, 23, 48ff, 52f, 56, 58f, 61, 150, 179-182, 196, 206, 208, 213, 244f, 251f, 265, 268, 275, 296, 331ff
input, 113
   context-setting, 113
   target, 114
   visual, 113
intentional, 77f
interface, 16, 150, 195f, 208, 261, 277, 310, 316f, 332f, 336
interface condition, 17
interpretation, 260, 334
   Full, 252
   modal, 198
interpretative level, 252
inversion, 273
   free inversion, see free
IP, 12, 18, 177ff, 182f, 194
Italian, 69, 110, 132, 158, 242ff, 334

Japanese, 245

L2-acquisition, 210
lambda-calculus, 323
   operator, see operator
learnability, 8f, 162

lexical properties, 71
    of clitics, 71
    of pronouns, 71
LF, see Logical Form
LF clitic, see clitic
licensing, 161, 182, 198
    head, 298
linking, 88
LinkP, 261,
Logical Form, 72, 75, 87, 194f, 197f, 252, 275f, 321, 331
Lower Subject Guise, see guise

maturation, 8, 9, 68, 149, 195, 316, 327
missing Aux, 57
missing tense, see tense
MLU, 156
modal, 255
model theoretic semantics, 73
morphological reanalysis, 248f,
morphical uniformity, 164f, 298
    formal, 299
movement, 54
    covert, 262
    head, 53, 197
    overt, 262
    verb, 54

N-restriction, 280
negation, 12,18, 216f, 233f, 237, 285-296, 331, 333,
negative evidence, 8
negative infinitive, 288f, 291ff
negative structure, 291
negative utterance, 291f
Neg-Criterion, 287
NegP, 181, 286, 288, 296
non-finite, 213, 253, 317

non-merger, 209
Norwegian, 128
null constant, 181
null object, see object
null subject, see subject
null topic, see topic
number, 177, 216, 244f, 299

object, 185
    clitics, see clitics
    drop, 294-297, 304ff, 310
    empty, 303
    lexical, 35, 39
    missing, 35, 39
    omission, 35, 39, 186
    pronominal, 92
old information, 101
operator, 79, 181, 252, 261, 277, 280, 315, 326, 334
    discourse, 325
    existential, 276
    lambda (λ), 73, 325
    temporal, 207
    tense, 207, 320
    Wh, see Wh
optional infinitive, see infinitive
optionality, 57, 179

parameter, 9, 14, 53, 61, 150, 161
    clitic, 9, 23, 47
    head-complement, 9
    pro-drop, 9, 14, 28, 162
    verb-raising, 9, 11, 12
parameter (re)setting, 7, 149, 162
participle, 289f,
    bare, 49
    past, 30
past tense, see tense
perfective, 322

performance, 210
person, 245, 299
phi-feature, 71, 82, 93, 96
phoneme perception, 3
picture-matching task, 109f
place-holder, 55f
pourquoi, 272, 276
poverty of stimulus, 1, 5, 66f
pragmatic problems, 68, 70
pragmatic rule, 68
pragmatics, 69
previous mention, 312
principle(s), 6, 7, 53, 66
Principle A, 66f, 74
Principle B, 16, 66, 68, 72, 208
Principle C, 66, 68
Principle P, 78f
principles and parameters, 6, 7, 8
pro, 161, 185, 299, 309
   expletive, 298f, 301, 309
   referential, 310
pro-drop, 149f, 150, 156, 160, 167, 174, 205, 220, 242,
pro-drop parameter, see parameter
PRO, 162, 198ff, 206f, 214, 222, 247, 273, 285, 315
processing, 68f, 80
   capacity, 69
   limitation, 69
pro-form, 32f, 48
projection, 18
   functional, 57, 177ff, 331
pronominal 61
pronominal clitics, see clitic
pronominal system, 21
pronoun(s), 5, 14, 16
   Germanic, 69, 93
   strong, 91, 100, 126, 132, 147,
   weak, 60f, 93, 100, 102, 130,

146f,
   zap, 166
Q-morpheme, 262
Q-operator, 262
QR, see Quantifier Raising
quantification, 68
quantified expression, 68
quantified NP, 79
quantifier, 27
   floating, 60
Quantifier Raising, 73, 87, 262
quantifying in, 74
quasi-argument, see argument
qu'est-ce que, 273
question, 255f, 258, 26, 267,
   constituent, 281
   root, 163, 180, 182
   Yes-No, 276, 282

range, 100
range restriction, 100, 104f, 107, 130
recovery, 164, 181f,
   content, 300
reference, 311
   of pronouns, 21f
   temporal, 207
   time, see time
referent, 73, 145
referential, 71, 83
   index, 100
referential properties of pronouns, 16, 65, 147
referentiality, 71, 83, 92, 94, 97, 104
   feature, 93, 96, 126, 130
referring expression, 65
reflexive, 36, 84
   clitic, see clitic
   interpreted, 81f
   marked, 81f

Reflexivity, 81, 83, 85, 126, 128
    framework, 80, 145
Relevance Maxime, 146
rich agreement, see agreement
richness
    of inflection, 160
Romance, 11, 16, 65, 69, 132
root declarative, see declarative
root infinitive, see infinitive
root/non-root asymmetry, 185f, 191
root question, see question
routine, 265f,
Rule of Interpretation, 89
Russian, 201

salience, 75
salient, 165
Scandinavian, 204, 245, 309
scope, 252, 260f, 263, 276f, 282, 319, 323, 334
screening condition, 115
SLI, see Specific Language Impairment
SOV, 10, 151
Spanish, 127, 242ff,
Specific Language Impairment, 315f, 327f, 335f
specifier, 9
spec-head agreement, see agreement
speech time, see time
Spell-Out, 75,
Split CP, 186f, 277
stem form, 215, 247
structural ambiguity, 71, 142, 144
Structural Economy, 179, 195
structural deficiency, 100, 104, 130, 147
structure,
    functional, 178

Structure Building Model, 182,
structured meaning, 77, 89, 107
subject, 185
    clitic (see clitic)
    drop, 153, 174f, 257, 297, 301, 304, 306, 310
    empty, 298
    expletive, 297, 308ff,
    extraction, 278, 281,
    finite null, 200, 214, 248, 296, 332
    missing, 56
    null, 14f, 56, 151, 158, 165, 174f, 177f, 180, 182, 186, 181, 185, 191-204, 206, 213, 220, 251-259, 270-276, 281, 285, 302, 311, 332f
    omission, 149, 157, 227, 232, 248f, 254, 256, 331
    overt, 200, 220
    post-verbal (empty) null, 297, 300, 302, 304, 306f, 308,
    post-verbal referential, 297
    referential null, 299
subject-verb-agreement, see agreement
Subset Principle, 195
SVO, 10, 151, 217
Swedish, 242,

temporal reference, see reference
tense, 57f, 177, 209, 315, 321, 330, 331, 333
    missing, 213f, 225, 233
    morphological, 320
    past, 248f, 321, 334
    semantic, 320
Tense, Tns, 197, 199, 202ff
tense chain, 207

tense semantics, 319
  syntax of, 319
TP, 177, 180, 193, 198, 329, 335
theory of mind, 134, 141
theta-grid, 241
time
  of evaluation, 318
  event, 198, 320f, 325f,
  frame, 318f
  reference, 198, 208f, 315, 318-326
  speech, 208, 320, 326
  topic, 325
  of utterance, 318
topic, 186, 261, 277
  criterion, 190
  drop, 156, 166f, 181-186, 192ff, 200, 214, 218f, 220, 225, 231, 247, 275, 285f, 296f, 300ff, 304, 310
  null, 159, 165
  projection, 278
  time, see time
topicalization, 189
TopP, 187, 334
trace, 181
trigger, 8, 149, 162
triggering, 149
  problem, 162, 196
truncation, 53, 57, 59f, 175, 177, 179, 181f, 194ff, 202, 213f, 225, 229, 233, 247, 251ff, 260, 265, 278, 285, 289f, 315, 330, 333, 335
truth-theoretic semantics, 315
truth-value, 318
truth-value judgement task, 133
two-word-stage, 153, 156

UCC, see Unique Checking Constraint
UG, see Universal Grammar
underspecification, 214, 233
  of tense, 58, 206
underspecified, 273
unindexed, 76
Unique Checking Constraint, 43, 62, 177, 205f, 246-249
Uinversal Grammar, 7, 8, 9, 14, 53, 65, 67, 149, 285, 297,
universality, 66
utterance
  situation, 334
  verbal, 31, 153

V2, 12, 151, 165, 183, 187, 189, 205, 211, 216
V-to-I, 151, 217
V-to-C, 217
variable, 73
  assignment, 74
  free, 74, 87
verb,
  finite, see finite
  inflected, 170
  main, 233, 237-239, 253, 257, 268, 270
verb-movement, see movement
verb placement, 233
verb-raising, 317
VP, 12, 18, 183, 237,
VP-ellipsis, 67

Wh-Criterion, 187, 189, 279f,
Wh-constituent, 187
Wh-element, 260
Wh-feature, 279
Wh-in-situ, 194, 251f, 260, 262-282

334
Wh-operator, 180, 189f, 252, 263, 276f, 280,
Wh-question, 167, 175, 180f, 186, 241, 249, 251-259, 264-270, 331, 333
  finite fronted, (257f), 281
  fronted, 186, 251f, 260ff, 270-282, 285, 287, 307,
Wh-word, 194

Yes-No question, see question

STUDIES IN THEORETICAL PSYCHOLINGUISTICS

1. L. Solan: *Pronominal Reference.* Child Language and the Theory of Grammar. 1983 ISBN 90-277-1495-9
2. B. Lust (ed.): *Studies in the Acquisition of Anaphora.* Volume I: Defining the Constraints. 1986 ISBN 90-277-2121-1; Pb 90-277-2122-X
3. N. M. Hyams: *Language Acquisition and the Theory of Parameters.* 1986 ISBN 90-277-2218-8; Pb 90-277-2219-6
4. T. Roeper and E. Williams (eds.): *Parameter Setting.* 1987 ISBN 90-277-2315-X; Pb 90-277-2316-8
5. S. Flynn: *A Parameter-Setting Model of L2 Acquisition.* Experimental Studies in Anaphora. 1987 ISBN 90-277-2374-5; Pb 90-277-2375-3
6. B. Lust (ed.): *Studies in the Acquisition of Anaphora.* Volume II: Applying the Constraints. 1987 ISBN 1-55608-022-0; Pb 1-55608-023-9
7. G. N. Carlson and M. K. Tanenhaus (eds.): *Linguistic Structure in Language Processing.* 1989 ISBN 1-55608-074-3; Pb 1-55608-075-1
8. S. Flynn and W. O'Neil (eds.): *Linguistic Theory in Second Language Acquisition.* 1988 ISBN 1-55608-084-0; Pb 1-55608-085-9
9. R. J. Matthews and W. Demopoulos (eds.): *Learnability and Linguistic Theory.* 1989 ISBN 0-7923-0247-8; Pb 0-7923-0558-2
10. L. Frazier and J. de Villiers (eds.): *Language Processing and Language Acquisition.* 1990 ISBN 0-7923-0659-7; Pb 0-7923-0660-0
11. J.A. Padilla: *On the Definition of Binding Domains in Spanish.* Evidence from Child Language. 1990 ISBN 0-7923-0744-5
12. M. de Vincenzi: *Syntactic Parsing Strategies in Italian.* The Minimal Chain Principle. 1991 ISBN 0-7923-1274-0; Pb 0-7923-1275-9
13. D.C. Lillo-Martin: *Universal Grammar and American Sign Language.* Setting the Null Argument Parameters. 1991 ISBN 0-7923-1419-0
14. A.E. Pierce: *Language Acquisition and Syntactic Theory.* A Comparative Analysis of French and English Child Grammars. 1992 ISBN 0-7923-1553-7
15. H. Goodluck and M. Rochemont (eds.): *Island Constraints.* Theory, Acquisition and Processing. 1992 ISBN 0-7923-1689-4
16. J.M. Meisel (ed.): *The Acquisition of Verb Placement.* Functional Categories and V2 Phenomena in Language Acquisition. 1992 ISBN 0-7923-1906-0
17. E.C. Klein: *Toward Second Language Acquisition.* A Study of Null-Prep. 1993 ISBN 0-7923-2463-3

STUDIES IN THEORETICAL PSYCHOLINGUISTICS

18. J.L. Packard: *A Linguistic Investigation of Aphasic Chinese Speech.* 1993
     ISBN 0-7923-2466-8
19. J. Archibald: *Language Learnability and L2 Phonology:* The Acquisition of Metrical Parameters. 1993 ISBN 0-7923-2486-2
20. M.W. Crocker: *Computational Psycholinguistics.* An Interdisciplinary Approach to the Study of Language. 1996   ISBN 0-7923-3802-2; Pb 0-7923-3806-5
21. J.D. Fodor and F. Ferreira (eds.): *Reanalysis in Sentence Processing.* 1998
     ISBN 0-7923-5099-5
22. L. Frazier: *On Sentence Interpretation.* 1999   ISBN 0-7923-5508-3
23. S. Avrutin: *Development of the Syntax-Discourse Interface.* 1999
     ISBN 0-7923-5936-4
24. B. Hemforth and L. Konieczny (eds.): *German Sentence Processing.* 2000
     ISBN 0-7923-6104-0
25. M. De Vincenzi and V. Lombardo (eds.): *Cross-linguistic Perspectives on Language Processing.* 2000   ISBN 0-7923-6146-6
26. S.M. Powers and C. Hamann (eds.): *The Acquisition of Scrambling and Cliticization.* 2000   ISBN 0-7923-6249-7
27. M. Schönenberger: *Embedded V-to-C in child grammar: The acquisition of verb placement in Swiss German.* 2001   ISBN 0-7923-7086-4
28. M. Walsh Dickey: *The Processing of Tense.* Psycholinguistic Studies on the Interpretation of Tense and Temporal Relations. 2001
     ISBN 1-4020-0184-3; Pb 1-4020-0185-1
29. C. Hamann: *From Syntax to Discourse.* Pronominal Clitics, Null Subjects and Infinitives in Child Language. 2002
     ISBN 1-4020-0439-7; Pb 1-4020-0440-0

KLUWER ACADEMIC PUBLISHERS – DORDRECHT / BOSTON / LONDON

OHIO UNIVERSITY LIBRARY

Please return this book as soon as you have finished with it. In order to avoid a fine it must be returned by the latest date stamped below. All books are subject to recall after two weeks or immediately if needed for reserve.

CF